T0361143

Harwood Fundamentals of Pure and Applied Economics

# ENVIRONMENTAL AND NATURAL RESOURCE ECONOMICS

# FUNDAMENTALS OF PURE AND APPLIED ECONOMICS

## EDITORS IN CHIEF

J. LESOURNE, Conservatoire National des Arts et Métiers, Paris, France

H. SONNENSCHEIN, University of Pennsylvania, Philadelphia, PA, USA

## ADVISORY BOARD

K. ARROW, Stanford, CA, USA
W. BAUMOL, Princeton, NJ, USA
W. A. LEWIS, Princeton, NJ, USA
S. TSURU, Tokyo, Japan

---

## ENVIRONMENTAL AND NATURAL RESOURCE ECONOMICS

# ENVIRONMENTAL AND NATURAL RESOURCE ECONOMICS

Non-Renewable Resources Extraction Programs and Markets

*John M Hartwick*

Models of the Oil Market

*Jacques Crémer and Djavad Salehi-Isfahani*

Long-Term Control of Exhaustible Resources

*Pierre Lasserre*

First published in 1989, 1991 and 1991 by
Harwood Academic Publishers GmbH

Reprinted in 2001 by
Routledge
2 Park Square, Milton Park, Abingdon, Oxon, OX14 4RN

Transferred to Digital Printing 2007

*Routledge is an imprint of the Taylor & Francis Group*

The publishers have made every effort to contact authors/copyright holders
of the works reprinted in *Harwood Fundamentals of Pure & Applied Economics*.
This has not been possible in every case, however, and we would welcome
correspondence from those individuals/companies we have been unable to
trace.

These reprints are taken from original copies of each book. in many cases
the condition of these originals is not perfect. the publisher has gone to
great lengths to ensure the quality of these reprints, but wishes to point
out that certain characteristics of the original copies will, of necessity, be
apparent in reprints thereof.

*British Library Cataloguing in Publication Data*
A CIP catalogue record for this book
is available from the British Library

Environmental and Natural Resource Economics
ISBN 0-415-26951-2
Harwood Fundamentals of Pure & Applied Economics
ISBN 0-415-26907-5

# NON-RENEWABLE RESOURCES EXTRACTION PROGRAMS AND MARKETS

JOHN M HARTWICK

# Non-renewable Resources Extraction Programs and Markets

John M. Hartwick
*Queen's University, Kingston,
Ontario, Canada*

A volume in the Natural Resources and Environmental
Economics Section

edited by

C. Henry
*Ecole Polytechnique,
Paris, France*

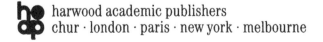 harwood academic publishers
chur · london · paris · new york · melbourne

© 1989 by Harwood Academic Publishers GmbH
Poststrasse 22, 7000 Chur, Switzerland
All rights reserved

Harwood Academic Publishers

Post Office Box 197
London WC2E 9PX
England

58, rue Lhomond
75005 Paris
France

Post Office Box 786
Cooper Station
New York, NY 10276
United States of America

Private Bag 8
Camberwell, Victoria 3124
Australia

---

**Library of Congress Cataloging-in-Publication Data**

Hartwick, John M.
  Non-renewable resources: extraction programs and markets/John
M. Hartwick.
    p. cm.—(Fundamentals of pure and applied economics; v. 33.
Natural resources and environmental economics section)
    Bibliography: p.
    Includes index.
    ISBN 3-7186-4896-2
    1. Nonrenewable natural resources.  I. Title.  II. Series:
Fundamentals of pure and applied economics; v. 33.  III. Series:
Fundamentals of pure and applied economics. Natural resources
and environmental economics section.
HC59.H35593   1989
333.7—dc 19                                                    88-27285
                                                                    CIP

---

# CONTENTS

# Introduction to the Series

Drawing on a personal network, an economist can still relatively easily stay well-informed in the narrow field in which he works, but to keep up with the development of economics as a whole is a much more formidable challenge. Economists are confronted with difficulties associated with the rapid development of their discipline. There is a risk of "balkanization" in economics, which may not be favorable to its development.

*Fundamentals of Pure and Applied Economics* has been created to meet this problem. The discipline of economics has been subdivided into sections (listed inside). These sections include short books, each surveying the state of the art in a given area.

Each book starts with the basic elements and goes as far as the most advanced results. Each should be useful to professors needing material for lectures, to graduate students looking for a global view of a particular subject, to professional economists wishing to keep up with the development of their science, and to researchers seeking convenient information on questions that incidentally appear in their work.

Each book is thus a presentation of the state of the art in a particular field rather than a step-by-step analysis of the development of the literature. Each is a high-level presentation but accessible to anyone with a solid background in economics, whether engaged in business, government, international organizations, teaching, or research in related fields.

Three aspects of *Fundamentals of Pure and Applied Economics* should be emphasized:

—First, the project covers the whole field of economics, not only theoretical or mathematical economics.

—Second, the project is open-ended and the number of books is not predetermined. If new and interesting areas appear, they erate additional books.

—Last, all the books making up each section will later be grouped to constitute one or several volumes of an Encyclopedia of Economics.

The editors of the sections are outstanding economists who have selected as authors for the series some of the finest specialists in the world.

*J. Lesourne*                                                                          *H. Sonnenschein*

# Preface and Acknowledgements

This monograph surveys the state of knowledge of the economics of exhaustible resources, primarily in the theoretical realm. The material formed the base of a ten week course in economics and I have benefitted from comments of many students. Numerous friends have offered very helpful comments on research in exhaustible resources over more than a dozen years. This volume reflects the fruitful collaboration I have enjoyed with David Yeung and exchanges with Robin Lindsey. My special thanks to them. Robin Broadway and Peter Townley provided guidance in matters of taxation of exhaustible resources. Claude Henry offered good editorial suggestions and Angie Street word-processed this manuscript in a busy schedule of tasks. Perry Sadorsky prepared the index. Thanks to them, also.

John M. Hartwick
*Queen's University*
*Kingston, Ontario*

# Non-renewable Resources Extraction Programs and Markets

JOHN M. HARTWICK

*Queen's University, Kingston, Ontario, Canada*

## 1. INTRODUCTION

This survey of theoretical investigations into what economic "forces" determine the rate of using up of stocks of exhaustible resources and the rate of discovery of new stocks relies on a few key ideas in economics. In other words what follows are variations on a few standard themes. This arises because we make much use of the paradigm of decision makers optimizing over time. Conditions characterizing optimal solutions of intertemporal optimizing have become fairly well known, certainly since the 1960's. Much of what we discuss deals with decision makers optimizing in relatively easily delineated environments. Complications abound when the environment being dealt with involves subtle strategic interactions with competitors, a dynamic game theoretic environment. We touch on such environments when we discuss oligopoly and exploration but for the most part deal with simpler environments in which strategic interactions among extractors are not complicated. The key ideas we make use of are zero profit arbitrage conditions across time periods. These are basic optimality conditions for intertemporal profit maximization. Resource stock owners cannot expect to make more or less profit over time than agents who tie up the same capital in other investment opportunities of a similar risk class. Unfortunately tests of whether the data support these basic conditions are not conclusive. Data are difficult to obtain in a form which makes a test straightforward. Actual markets are rife with many forms of uncertainty which enter into the zero profit intertemporal arbitrage conditions in complicated ways. We introduce many of these uncertainties into our modeling but only one at a time, in a

1

serial not simultaneous approach. We do not report on the varied
attempts that have been made to test whether actual extraction
paths appear to be generated by some of the less elaborate
intertemporal optimization procedures ascribed to representative
decision makers. Despite progress to date in this area, more
statifactory results can be expected in the near future.[1]

We do then "generate" extraction paths for a variety of cases.
Though somewhat distant from observed extraction paths, we
suggest that those we generate shed light on how actual extraction
paths emerge. The analysis segments quite naturally into extraction
paths for competitive firms, paths for monopoly and oligopoly,
exploration, taxation, and economic growth with exhaustible resources. The competitive case lends itself to a diagrammatic
introduction and we shall pursue this course. There are actually
sixteen cases of interest which we indicate below.

| | passive backstop | | active backstop | |
|---|---|---|---|---|
| firm | homogen stock | certainty uncertain | homogen stock | certainty uncertain |
| | heterog stock | certainty uncertain | heterog | certainty uncertain |
| industry | homogen stock | certainty uncertain | homogen stock | certainty uncertain |
| | heterog | certainty uncertain | heterog | certainty uncertain |

The backstop is a supply which comes on stream as a substitute for
the resource being depleted. For example energy produced from oil
may be produced from fusion reactors in the future. Fusion power is
the backstop technology in this case and oil is the exhaustible

---

[1] Some recent papers on resource rent estimation for extraction programs or paths
are Heal and Barrow [38], Smith [81], Slade [80], Devarajan and Fisher [16], Stollery
[92], Halvarsen and Smith [32], Farrow [26], Miller and Upton [66].

resource. The owners of the backstop might try to influence the speed of extraction from the resource stock. In this case we would consider the backstop to be *active*. There is an implicit game between resource stock owners and backstop technolgoy developers. There is in addition a natural separation of the analysis into that for resource extracting firms, each firm examined in isolation, and resource extracting industries, comprising many firms. The case of extraction of homogeneous stocks of ore is a special case of that for heterogeneous stocks, the later involving rents arising from the quality differences, that is differential or Ricardian rent. Finally the analysis cleaves fairly naturally into that involving certainty of parameters of stock characteristics, cost, and demand and uncertainty in these parameters.

Let us review what we report on in detail concerning the extracting firm with a known homogeneous stock of say oil to deplete. We suppose extraction costs increase at each date if more is extracted and that extraction costs on the marginal ton rise with more extracted. The path which maximizes the present value of profits or surplus is characterized by $p - mc(t + 1)$ equalling $(1 + r)[p - mc(t)]$ on the marginal ton extracted between successive periods where $p$ is price for a ton extracted, $r$ is the interest rate and $mc(t)$ is the cost of extracting the marginal ton at period $t$. This zero profit intertemporal arbitrage condition or $r\%$ rule is illustrated in Figure 1.

The vertical distance $p - mc$ is referred to as dynamic or Hotelling rent per ton per period. The area *abc* in Figure 1 is a quasi-rent accruing to the extracting firm. The $r\%$ rule on rent per ton rising is a rule related to the marginal ton extracted in a period. For the deposit or stock as a whole an optimal extraction program satisfies the basic intertemporal arbitrage condition.

(Current Profit) + (Current "Depletion")

$$= r \cdot \text{(Price of the Deposit)}.$$

where Current "Depletion" is economic depreciation or the decline in the selling price of the deposit because $q(t)$ is currently removed from it. In Figure 1, current "depletion" turns out to be the negative of the rectangle of Hotelling rent (area $[p - mc(q(t))]q(t)$) and current profit is Hotelling rent plus the triangle *abc* of quasi-rent. Thus period by period quasi-rent equals $r$ multiplied by

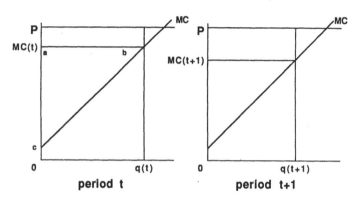

FIGURE 1  $p - MC$ grows at rate $r\%$. $q(t)$ and $q(t+1)$, quantities extracted, are governed by the zero arbitrage or $r\%$ rule: $p - MC(t + 1) = (1 + r)[p - MC(t)]$.

the selling price of the deposit, this latter declining over time because the stock is being run down or depleted.

Suppose the firm faces an uncertain price $p$ for output in the future. Then $p$ in Figure 1 can be viewed as the mean or average price. We observe below that if $p$ is random or future price is uncertain, the present value of the firm's profits are higher than if the mean price was observed for certain in the future. This is paradoxical of course since it indicates that on average a firm will make more money if future price is uncertain than if the future price is known for sure. This same paradoxical behavioral is observed if extraction costs are uncertain ($c$ in Figure 1 a random variable) or if the future value of the interest rate is uncertain. We demonstrate these results below and discuss them. The analysis of stock size uncertainty is slightly different because the rate at which a firm extracts affects how much "uncertainty" remains. We investigate this issue below.

The case of the competitive industry with many small price taking firms, each with say a stock of one homogeneous ton can be illustrated in a two period diagram like Figure 1. For an industry demand schedule with some negative slope, output price will rise as less quantity is extracted and brought to market. Across periods the owner of the marginal ton extracted will be indifferent between selling his or her marginal ton in period $t$ or period $t + 1$ if

$p(t+1) - mc(t+1) = (1+r)[p(t) - mc(t)]$. This yields the rule, rent on the marginal ton rises at a rate of $r\%$ for the case of homogeneous stocks. Suppose each ton of ore extracted has a different amount of salable mineral and $c_i$ is the cost of extracting the material and processing it to yield one ton (ton $i$) of salable mineral. We are then in a world of heterogeneous quality of stock. The same logic must hold for the owner of the marginal ton of mineral sold across consecutive periods as we observed above, but now the marginal ton required different processing than say any other ton. If the $i$th ton with processing costs $c_i$ is the marginal ton extracted in period $t$, its owner must observe

$$p(t+1) - c_i = (1+r)[p(t) - c_i]$$

or rise in price across consecutive periods must be such that discounted profit per ton from selling next period (i.e. $t+1$) is the same as rent or profit per ton gleaned by extracting in this period (i.e., period $t$). We illustrate in Figure 2.

In Figure 2, each ton is distinct so that the marginal ton extracted in period $t$ is almost the same as the "most marginal" ton extracted

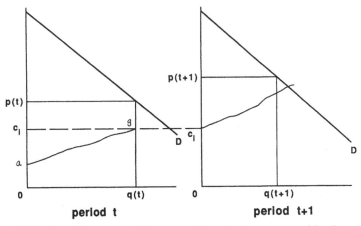

FIGURE 2  Quantities extracted for consecutive periods are governed by the zero profit arbitrage condition $[p(t) - c_i](1+r) = p(t+1) - c_i$ when quality per ton declines. Area $ac_ig$ is labelled differential or Ricardian rent and is ascribable to differences in quality of ore. Area $[p(t) - c_i]q(t)$ is Hotelling rent or dynamic rent or "royalty."

in period $t + 1$. Clearly observed rent on the marginal tons extracted in consecutive period rises more slowly than rate $r$. This is a consequence of quality decline as more ore is extracted and sold. We present additional details below but it is of interest that it is not inevitable that observed rent on the marginal ton rises at rate $r\%$. The $r\%$ rule is in fact rather special as opposed to general and should not be viewed as a most plausible result to corroborate or refute empirically. We have observed that the introduction of quality decline in the overall stock leads to rent on the marginal ton extracted across two consecurive periods rising more slowly than $r\%$ (though rent for two almost identical tons (one marginal and one intra marginal) will rise at rate $r\%$ but these two tons will not generally each be the marginal ton extracted in consecurive periods). This completes our introduction to the analysis of extraction programs under competitive conditions. The owners of the backstop have been taken to be passive.

The backstop is of interest because its presence presumes that actual exhaustion of an essential resource will not spell the end of economic activity and human existence. The backstop is the presumed "technical fix" which will obviate economic termination. The ultimate cost of backstop supply and its date of arrival are essential data to resource extractors. Changes in these conditions of future supply will affect current extraction activity. We reivew some cases including the effects of uncertainty in the date of arrival of the backstop.

Two central cases of non-competitive structure are monopoly and a dominant seller and a competitive fringe group. We analyze models in these contexts. We observe fairly complex departures from the competitive cases we reviewed above. An important difficulty is that of seepage from one underground stock to another as extraction proceeds. We examine how these imperfect property rights affect extraction paths.

Property rights are central to the analysis of exploration. A gold rush is a case of a discoverer having imperfect property rights on the object discovered. It is the "free" pickings surrounding the original find which induces the rush. The incentives to explore depend on the extent of property rights the discoverer acquires in the objects discovered. Part of property rights is the tax or royalty obligations associated with the find. We inquire into how these property rights issues affect the pace of exploration in some models. We also investigate the taxation of minerals and how extraction profiles are tilted by the presence or absence of certain types of taxes.

Finally we take up simple models of complete economies and inquire about the effects of resource depletion on the growth paths of the economy. We observe that population growth and finite essential stocks lead to a decline in per capita consumption. This can be viewed as T. R. Malthus with *shrinking* amounts of land. The special case of the current value of Hotelling rents being used to finance investment in new producible capital goods is investigated. This leads to paths displaying a plausible notion of intergenerational equity. Technical progress is shown above to obviate economic termination. We review procedures for measuring technical progress in growing economies and indicate that current practices in national accounting do not treat depletion or economic depreciation of exhaustible resource stock satisfactorily.

## 2. THE PRICE TAKING RESOURCE EXTRACTING FIRM

### Introduction

A resource extracting firm below is a price taker. The owner, decision-maker, or agent foresees an output price path into the finite future and plans how to deplete his or her stock of resources given the discount rate and his or her costs of extraction. For the firm extracted at any date rise with quantity currently extracted. An optimal extraction program is one for which the present value of profits (current revenue net of current extraction costs summed over all periods of extraction into the future) is a maximum. We investigate such paths and how they differ as conditions differ— conditions such as future interest rates, prices, and extraction costs. We consider both homogeneous initial stocks of known size and heterogeneous stocks and initial stocks of unknown size. We also inquire as to how uncertainty of future prices, interest rates, and costs affect the shape of extraction programs. In a subsequent section we consider how taxes and the possibility of exploration affect extraction paths.

### Details of the resource extracting firm

The firm is assumed to have a homogeneous stock $S$, of known size. The current and future price of output is known. We let it be constant at $p$ per unit output. Extraction costs $C(q)$ depend only on the amount mined or extracted. $dC/dq$ is denoted $C_q$ and $C_q(0) \geq 0$ and $C_{qq}(q) > 0$ or the marginal cost schedule is upward sloping. Profits at instant $t$ from mining and selling $q(t)$ tons from the stock $S(t)$ are $pq(t) - C(q(t))$ and the present value of profilts for extracting program $\{q(t)\}$ are

$$\pi = \int_0^T [pq(t) - C(q(t))]e^{-rt}\, dt$$

where

$$\int_0^T q(t)\, dt \leq S(O)$$

where $S(O)$ is the initial, known homogeneous stock and $r$ is the current interest rate used to discount current profits. The Euler equation defining an optimal extraction program $\{q^*(t)\}$ which maximizes $\pi$ subject to the stock constraint is

$$\frac{\overline{p - C_q(q(t))}}{p - C_q(q(t))} = r$$

which indicates that rent $p - C_q$ on the marginal ton extracted at date $t$ rises at a rate equal to the rate of interest. (The dot over a term indicates differentiation with respect to time.) In a discrete time formulation, this Euler equation is the first order condition

$$\frac{[p - C_q(q(t+1))] - [p - C_q(q(t))]}{p - C_q(q(t))} = r$$

We indicated in Figure 1 above how quantities $q(t)$ and $q(t + 1)$ in consecutive periods would be organized in light of this basic intertemporal efficiency condition (zero intertemporal profitable arbitrage condition).

The end-point condition defining an optimal extraction program is: $p - C_q(q(T)) = [pq(T) - C(q(T))]/q(T)$ or the marginal value of the last extraction $q(T)$ equals the average value of $q(T)$. For the above formulation, this occurs in the limit as $q(T) \to 0$. Hence $q(T) = 0$ and one can work back toward the initial time 0 using the Euler equation until $S$ is completely exhausted. We do this below.

The Euler equation expresses the basic zero arbitrage condition: the marginal ton extracted at $t$ is worth the same unextracted as it is if extracted. Intra marginal tons are worth more extracted in this view. The marginal ton in the ground rises in value by $\dfrac{\bullet}{p - C_q(q(t))}$ if unextracted. If extracted and the profits invested at rate $r$, it is worth $(1 + r)[p - C_q(t)]$ an instant later. The Euler equation indicates that there is zero profit from arbitraging the marginal ton "across time $t$".[2]

The above model was worked out in numerical examples by L. C. Gray [31] in 1914 (see Appendix I). It's logic is not changed if the constant price is permitted to move in a known trajectory into the indefinite future. Gray actually allowed marginal extraction costs decline for small initial quantities. This leads to a market failure at the level of the industry since it implies some initial returns to scale. We report on this below.

### Asset equilibrium along optimal programs

We can "break" an optimal extraction program at any point, formally, and expressed discounted profits as

$$\int_0^T [p\hat{q}(t) - C(\hat{q}(t))]e^{-rt}\, dt = V(T_1 - 0, S_1) + e^{-rT_1}V(T - T_1, S - S_1)$$

where $\hat{q}$ is an optimal extraction program and $V(\alpha, S_i)$ is the optimized present value of profit for extracting $S_i$ tons over interval $\alpha$. (We require appropriate initial quantities extracted over each interval to obtain the appropriate total optimized profit on the left hand side.) $T_1$ is arbitrary. If the right hand side is optimal, it

---

[2] With interest rates varying over time one still has an $r\%$ rule on rent for the marginal ton extracted but now simply across adjacent periods since the value of $r$ will vary over the life of the deposit. This can be seen readily in a discrete time framework in which there will be an $r_t$ rule as in

$$\frac{[p - C_q(t+1)] - [p - C_q(t)]}{[p - C_q(t)]} = r_t \qquad t = 1, \ldots, n.$$

satisfies

$$\frac{dV(T_1 - 0, S_1)}{dT_1} - re^{-rT_1} V(T - T_1, S - S_1) = 0$$

where

$$\frac{dV(T_1 - 0, S_1)}{dT_1} = [p\hat{q}(T_1) - C(\hat{q}(T_1))]e^{-rT_1}$$

$$+ \int_0^{T_1} [p - C'] \frac{dq(t)}{dT_1} e^{-rt} \, dt$$

$$+ \int_0^{T_1} [p - C'] \frac{dq(t)}{dq(T_1)} e^{-rt} \, dt \frac{dq(T_1)}{dT_1}$$

and $C' \equiv dC(q(t))/dq(t)$. Differentiation and substitution reveals that

$$e^{rT_1} \int_0^{T_1} [p - C'] \frac{dq(t)}{dT_1} e^{-rt} \, dt + e^{rT_1} \int_0^{T_1} [p - C'] \frac{dq(t)}{dq(T_1)} e^{-rt} \, dt \frac{dq(T_1)}{dT_1}$$

$$= [p - C'(q(T_1))]q(T_1).$$

This term is in fact *economic depreciation*, the decline in $V$ at $T_1$ arising from $q(T_1)$ being extracted. See Appendix II. At each date along an optimal program the quantity extracted $q(t)$ satisfies the *basic asset equilibrium condition*

$$pq(t) - C(q(t)) - [p - C']q(t) = rV(t).$$

Current income $pq(t) - C(q(t))$ net of economic depreciation equals the interest flow from the current capital value of the remaining stock. (This is an instance of the basic "dynamic efficiency condition" of Dorfman, Samuelson and Solow [20].)

Consider an example. $p = 10$, $C(q) = q + 0.5q^2$, $r = 0.1$ and total stock is 45 tons. We solved for $T = 11.98290437$ (see below "Solving the Model . . . " for details.) We now divide $S$ into $S_1$ and $S - S_1$ along an optimal extraction program and solve for $T_1 - 0$, $T - T_1$, $q(T_1)$. Then we calculate $pq(T_1) - C(q(T_1))$, $[p - C']q(T_1)$, and $rV(T - T_1, S - S_1)$. These are reported in the labelled columns in Table I.

We can make use of our construction on "breaking" an optimal path to *analyse set-up costs* associated with opening a new deposit.

TABLE I
Asset equilibrium and the extracting firm*

| $S_1$ | $T_1 - 0$ | $q(T_1)$ | $T - T_1$ | $pq(T_1) - C(q(T_1))$ | $[p - C']q(T_1)$ | $rV(T - T_1, S - S_1)$ |
|---|---|---|---|---|---|---|
| 40 | 8.45363195 | 2.67234518 | 3.529272427 | 20.50569486 | 16.9242831 | 3.581411772 |
| 35 | 6.867514764 | 3.60385065 | 5.115389606 | 25.9407861 | 19.44691634 | 6.493869737 |
| 30 | 5.596151894 | 4.248077232 | 6.386752481 | 29.209615 | 20.18653492 | 9.023080088 |
| 25 | 4.48564014 | 4.747537809 | 7.497264233 | 31.45828266 | 20.18872503 | 11.26955763 |
| 15 | 2.53856916 | 5.499901691 | 9.444335214 | 34.37465591 | 19.25019661 | 15.12445931 |

* Parameters: $p = 10$, $C(q) = q + 0.5q^2$, $r = 0.1$.

Consider two identical deposits with set-up costs $K_i$ associated with deposit $i$ and the same variable extraction costs $C(q)$. In maximizing the present value of profits, the first order condition defining the optimal moment $T_1$ for opening the second deposit is

$$pq(T_1^-) - C(q(T_1^-)) - [p - C']q(T_1^-) = -K_2 + rV(T - T_1, S_2).$$

The basic asset equilibrium condition indicates $rV(T - T_1, S_2) = pq^*(T_1^-) - C(q^*(T_1^-)) - [p - C']q^*(T_1^-)$. Hence $K_2 > 0$ implies $q^*(T_1^-) > q(T_1^-)$ or $p - C'$ jumps down across $T_1$. The set-up costs induce the firm to delay opening the second deposit and delay is achieved by raising the rent profile for deposit 1 or extracting stock size $S_1$ more slowly than would be the case in the absence of set-up costs. (There is no way to reallocate set-up costs associated with deposit 1 and thus $K_1$ has no effect on the extraction profile.)

### The output constrained firm and initial investments

Campbell [7] and Crabbé [8] have emphasized that resource extracting firms often have binding output capacity constraints. Ore must be extracted from a particular shaft of a specific size. The capacity is usually set before extraction commences by the firm incurring set-up costs. The capacity $\bar{q}$ becomes a function of the amount of set-up activity or $K(\bar{q})$ dollars of set-up activity yields capacity $\bar{q}$. There will be two phases of extraction for the simple case of a known stock of homogeneous quality. In the final phase marginal rent will rise at the rate of interest as the remainder of the stock is exhausted. The length of this phase is $\Delta_2$ in

$$p - MC(\bar{q}) = [p - A]e^{-r\Delta_2}$$

where $A$ is the intercept of the marginal extraction cost schedule and $MC(\bar{q})$ corresponds to the marginal extraction cost at quantity $\bar{q}$. Given $\Delta_2$ one can solve for $S^\Delta$ the stock depleted in the final phase. In the earlier phase stock will be extracted at rate $\bar{q}$ and the length of this phase will be $\Delta_1$ in

$$S - S^\Delta = \bar{q}\Delta_1$$

For any $\bar{q}$ we can define the discounted profits $V(\bar{q})$ with $dV/d\bar{q} > 0$. Then the optimal capacity $\bar{q}$ will satisfy

$$d[V(\bar{q}) - K(\bar{q})]/d\bar{q} = 0$$

With output price rising over time, one can save money by incurring set-up costs later and gain higher revenues for output at higher prices. In such cases, the date to incur the set-up costs or to open the deposit may be in the future. There is the similtaneous choice of an optimal starting date and an optimal capacity.

## Solving the model of the firm and comparative statics

The basic intertemporal efficiency condition for the model of the firm with a known homogeneous stock and extraction costs $C(q)$ with $M(q) = dC/dq > 0$ and $d^2C/dq^2 > 0$ is

$$p - M(q) = [p - A]e^{-r(T-t)}$$

where $A = M(0) \geq 0$. Thus $M(q) = p - [p - A]e^{-r(T-t)}$ and for $M(q)$ continuous and single valued, we have

$$q = g(p - [p - A]e^{-r(T-t)})$$

or the inverse of the marginal cost schedule $dg/d(\cdot) > 0$ for $(\cdot) > 0$. $d^2g(\ )/d(\cdot)^2$ has no obvious sign.

Equilibrium is defined by the efficiency condition being satisfied for all time values for which $q(t) > 0$ and the stock constraint

$$\int_0^T q(t)\, dt - S = 0$$

or

$$\int_0^T g(p - (p - A)e^{-r(T-t)})\, dt - S = 0.$$

(In addition the present value of profits will be a maximum when $q(t) = 0$.) Total differentiation of the stock constraint yields

$$\frac{dT}{dp} = \frac{-\int_0^T (1 - e^{-r(T-t)})g'\, dt}{\int_0^T (p - A)re^{-r(T-t)}g'\, dt} < 0$$

where $g' \equiv dg/d(\cdot)$, and

$$\frac{dT}{dr} = \frac{-\int_0^T (p - A)(T - t)e^{-r(T-t)}g' \, dt}{\int_0^T (p - A)re^{-r(T-t)}g' \, dt} < 0$$

and

$$\frac{dT}{dS} = \frac{1}{\int_0^T (p - A)re^{-r(T-t)}g' \, dt} > 0$$

(Note we made use of the fact that $g(T) = g(A) = 0$.)

In summary, an exogenous increase in the price of the mined mineral reduces the interval to stock exhaustion, an exogeneous increase in the interest rate reduces the interval to exhaustion and an exogenous increase in the size of the stock increases the interval to stock exhaustion.

Observe that $\frac{d^2T}{dp^2}$, $\frac{d^2T}{dr^2}$ and $\frac{d^2T}{dS^2}$ depend on $d^2g/d(\cdot)^2$ or on the shape of the marginal cost schedule, *not* just its slope. Since these second derivatives appear in the second derivatives of discounted profits

$$V = \int_0^T [pq(t) - C(q(t))]e^{-rt} \, dt$$

with $\int_0^T q(t) \, dt = S$, we observe that the convexity or concavity of $V$ turns on the shape or first derivative of the marginal extraction cost schedule. We have no prior knowledge of such "appropriate" marginal cost schedules. We turn to an example, first.

Example (Linear marginal extraction costs)

We specify the marginal cost as $A + Bq$ with $A > 0$ and $B > 0$. Then

$$q(t) = \left(\frac{p - A}{B}\right)[1 - e^{-r(T-t)}]$$

and

$$S = \int_0^T q(t)\,dt$$

$$= \left(\frac{p-A}{B}\right)\{T + (1/r)[e^{-rT} - 1]\}$$

and

$$V = \int_0^T \{pq - [Aq + 0.5Bq^2]\}e^{-rt}\,dt$$

$$= [BY^2/r](1 - e^{-rT})^2$$

where $Y \equiv (p - A)/B$.

We solve for $T$ for various parameter values in the stock constraint relationship and then for $V$ given $T$ and the corresponding parameter values. *We observe discounted profits convex in $r$, $p$ and marginal cost schedule intercept $A$ and concave in $S$.*

The parameters for our base case are $S = 10$, $A = 1$, $p = 10$ and $r = 0.1$. Below are four "runs".

– interest rate $r$ varying

| $r$ | $T$ | $V$ |
|------|------|------|
| 0.10 | 5.115389606 | 64.93869737 |
| 0.11 | 4.897619869 | 63.8742244(63.90451762) |
| 0.12 | 4.707815646 | 62.87033787 |

– output price $p$ varying

| $p$ | $T$ | $V$ |
|------|------|------|
| 10 | 5.115389606 | 64.93869737 |
| 11 | 4.831831682 | 73.4146702(73.45162799) |
| 12 | 4.589832808 | 81.96455861 |

– marginal cost intercept $A$ varying

| $A$ | $T$ | $V$ |
|------|------|------|
| 1.0 | 5.115389606 | 64.93869737 |
| 1.1 | 5.146494883 | 64.09562068(64.09605884) |
| 1.2 | 5.178159106 | 64.25342031 |

– stock size $S$ varying

| $S$ | $T$ | $V$ |
|---|---|---|
| 10 | 5.115389606 | 64.93869737 |
| 11 | 5.387381856 | 70.26164684(70.19155141) |
| 12 | 5.649378775 | 75.44440544 |

The value of $V$ in brackets is the equally weighted convex combination of the lowest and highest values of $V$ in each "run". For the value in brackets above (below) the observed value of $V$, we have $V$ convex (concave) in the parameter in question. We observe $V$ convex in $r$, $p$ and $A$ and concave in $S$.

The convexity of $V$ in $r$, $p$, and $A$ holds quite generally as Hartwick and Yeung [1985] demonstrated for the price variable. We set out the proof here for the interest rate $r$ variable and leave it to the interested reader to retrace the steps for the case of $p$ and $A$. We can exploit the fact, not used above, that $V(\bullet)$ is actually an optimized function. First preliminaries. We define three optimal programs for given stock $S$, $V(r_1, \{q^{r_1}\})$ given interest rate $r_1$, $V(r_2, \{q^{r_2}\})$ given interest rate $r_2$ and $V(\bar{r}, \{q^{\bar{r}}\})$ given interest rate $\bar{r} = \alpha r_1 + (1 + \alpha)r_2$, $0 < \alpha < 1$. We define two feasible values which are constructed as suboptimal: $V(r_1, \{q^{\bar{r}}\})$ and $V(r_2, \{q^{\bar{r}}\})$ are the *values with an extraction program optimal for $\bar{r}$ but evaluated with interest rates $r_1$ and $r_2$ respectively.*

Observe first,

$$V(r_1, \{q^{r_1}\}) \geq V(r_1, \{q^{\bar{r}}\})$$

and

$$V(r_2, \{q^{r_2}\}) \geq V(r_2, \{q^{\bar{r}}\})$$

since the values on the left hand side are for optimal extraction programs and those on the right for feasible (non-optimal) programs given $r_1$ and $r_2$ respectively. Thus

$$\alpha V(r_1, \{q^{r_1}\}) + (1 - \alpha)V(r_2, \{q^{r_2}\}) \geq \alpha V(r_1, \{q^{\bar{r}}\})$$
$$+ (1 - \alpha)V(r_2, \{q^{\bar{r}}\})$$

Now

$$\alpha V(r_1, \{q^{\bar{r}}\}) + (1 + \alpha)V(r_2, \{q^{\bar{r}}\}) = V(\bar{r}, \{q^{\bar{r}}\}) + \epsilon$$

where $\epsilon \geq 0$ because $e^{\alpha r_1 t} + e^{(1-\alpha)r_2 t} > e^{\bar{r}t}$ for $t > 0$. Hence the convexity of $V(r_i, \{q^{r_i}\})$ in $r_i$. (Note above that $V(r_1, \{q^{\bar{r}}\})$, $V(r_2, \{q^{\bar{r}}\})$ and $V(\bar{r}, \{q^{\bar{r}}\})$ each has the same time interval $(0, \bar{T})$ of integration and thus the magnitudes of the functions are readily compared as we proceeded above.)

## A production function for extraction for the resource extracting firm

We will introduce a production function for the activity "extraction" and work out a model of the present value profit maximizing extracting firm. This is a variant of the L. C. Gray model in which the extraction cost function $C(q)$ was taken as given. By working with a production function we can gain insights into the role that technical progress and scale economies might play. It is an exercise preliminary to doing econometric work on the production characteristics of resource extracting firms. We will set the model out and compute a version with neutral technical change and a Cobb–Douglas specification. Endogenous will be a stock of capital (buildings, elevators, and machines) as well as a variable input, "labor".

The firm faces a constant price of output $p$ dollars, a wage rate $w$ per unit of labor per unit of time and a rental rate $\eta$ per unit of capital per unit of time. Output $q(t)$ from stock $S(0)$ is produced with the production function $f(t, L, K) = q(t)$, where $K$ is the firm's capital stock and $L$ is the current labor being used. The firm maximizes the present value of profits by selecting $K$, $L(t)$ at each instant of time or implicitly an extraction program, $\{q(t)\}$. That is the firm's problem is to select $\{L(t)\}$ and $K$ to maximize

$$\int_0^T \{pf(t, L(t), K) - wL(t) - \eta K\}e^{-rt}\, dt$$

subject to

$$\int_0^T f(t, L(t), K)\, dt = S(0)$$

This problem can be solved in two stages. In stage $I$, $K$ is treated as a constant fixed at a positive value. The path $\{L^*(t)\}$ is solved for as a routine dynamic optimization problem. Then $K^*$ is solved for in stage II given the properties of $\{L^*(t)\}$ as established. The solution in stage I involves rent on the marginal ton rising at the rate of interest over time or $[p - MC(L(t))] = (p - MC(L(T)))]e^{-r(T-t)}$ where $MC(.)$ is marginal cost. $MC(.)$ is $(dwL/dL)/(df/dL)$ or $w/(\partial f/\partial L)$.

Consider the case of $q(t) = e^{\gamma t} K^\beta L(t)^{1/2}$. Here $\gamma$ is the rate of Hicks rental technical change and scale economies will exhibit increasing returns (decreasing returns) as $\beta > \frac{1}{2}(<\frac{1}{2})$. In this case

$$MC(L(t)) = 2wL^{1/2}/K^\beta e^{\gamma t}$$

and $MC(L(T)) = 0$ since $q(T) = 0$ and $L(T) = 0$. Then $p - MC(L(t)) = pe^{-r(T-t)}$ yielding $L(t)^{1/2} = \dfrac{e^{\gamma t} K^\beta p}{2w}(1 - e^{-r(T-t)})$ and given $K$ temporarily constant we can solve for $T$ in

$$\int_0^T e^{\gamma t} K^\beta L(t)^{1/2}\, dt = \int_0^T \frac{e^{2\gamma t} K^{2\beta} p}{2w}[1 - e^{-r(T-t)}]\, dt = S(0).$$

The solution $T^*(K)$ permits us to trace out $\{L^*(t); K\}$ and $\{q^*(t); K\}$. Given the stock constraint, we observe

$$\frac{dT}{dK} = \frac{-4\beta S(0)w(2\gamma + r)}{rpK^{2\beta+1}\{e^{2\gamma T} - e^{-rt}\}}$$

We can now solve for $K^*$ by solving the first order condition for $K$, $d\int_0^T [pK^\beta L(t)^{1/2} e^{\gamma t} - wL(t) - \eta K]e^{-rt}\, dt/dk = 0$.

Recalling $T$ is a function of $K$, this first order condition is:

$$-\frac{dT}{dK}\eta K e^{-rT} + \int_0^T \frac{rp^2 K^{2\beta}}{2w} e^{2\gamma t} e^{-2rT} e^{rt}\frac{dT}{dK}\, dt$$

$$+\frac{p^2 \beta K^{2\beta-1}}{2w}\int_0^T e^{(2\gamma-r)t}[1 - e^{-2r(T-t)}]\, dt - \eta\int_0^T e^{-rt}\, dt = 0$$

and on integration becomes

$$-\eta K^{-rT}\frac{dT}{dK} + \frac{dT}{dK}\frac{rp^2 K^{2\beta}}{2w(2\gamma+r)}[e^{(2\gamma-r)T} - e^{-2rT}] + \frac{p^2 \beta K^{2\beta-1}}{2w}$$

$$\times\left\{\frac{2re^{(2\gamma-r)T}}{(4\gamma^2 - r^2)} - \left(\frac{1}{2\gamma-r}\right) + \left(\frac{1}{2\gamma+r}\right)e^{-2rT}\right\} + \frac{\eta}{r}[e^{-rT} - 1] = 0$$

We solved for $T^*$ and $K^*$ using the above first order condition and the equation in $T$ and $K$ for the stock constraint. For $p = 10$, $w = 1$, $\eta = 1$, $r = 0.1$ we computed values for $T$, $K$, $L(0)$, $q(0)$ for various values of $\beta$ (the coefficient on $K$ in the production function), $S(0)$ and $\gamma$, the technical progress parameter. See Table II.

Note that for our specification (Cobb–Douglas) doubling $S(0)$ approximately doubles $L(0)$ but induces an increase in $K$ of only about 20%. Doubling aggregate output ($S(0)$) does not induce an approximate doubling in the level of $K$ selected. An increase in technical change ($\gamma$) lowers the level of $K$ chosen for small $S(0)$ and raises $K$ chosen for large $S(0)$. (This holds for values of the coefficient on $K$ greater and less than 0.5.) Otherwise, technical change tends to "shrink" the extraction program (i.e., $T$, $L(0)$, and $q(0)$ decline as $\gamma$ increases).

In contemplating estimating parameters in this model, one has to incorporate past history or initial conditions since both $K$ and $T$ depend on the initial stock size $S(0)$. If one observes a ten year old mine, the level of $K$ would reflect the past and future economic life of the mine. It would not be an efficient level selected for extracting the remaining stock, $S(t)$.

## TABLE II

| $\beta = 0.51$, $\gamma = 0.1$ | $K$ | $T$ | $L(0)$ | $q(0)$ |
|---|---|---|---|---|
| $S(0) = 20$ | 4.0660 | 4.6360 | 14.3879 | 7.75667 |
| $S(0) = 40$ | 4.8850 | 6.0704 | 26.1018 | 11.47239 |
| $\gamma = 0.02$ | | | | |
| $S(0) = 20$ | 4.0525 | 4.5657 | 13.9985 | 7.63799 |
| $S(0) = 40$ | 4.8941 | 5.9270 | 25.2554 | 11.29567 |
| $\beta = 0.47$, $\gamma = 0.01$ | | | | |
| $S(0) = 20$ | 4.2590 | 4.8074 | 14.2195 | 7.45107 |
| $S(0) = 40$ | 5.1132 | 6.3507 | 25.6149 | 10.89757 |
| $\gamma = 0.02$ | | | | |
| $S(0) = 20$ | 4.2421 | 4.7322 | 13.8219 | 7.33240 |
| $S(0) = 40$ | 5.1249 | 6.1927 | 24.7569 | 10.72510 |

The value of discounted profits is

$$V = \int_0^T [pK^\beta L^{1/2} e^{\gamma t} - wL(t) - \eta K]e^{-rt} dt$$

$$= \frac{p^2 K^{2\beta}}{4w} \left\{ \frac{2re^{(2\gamma - r)T}}{(4\gamma^2 - r^2)} + \frac{e^{-2rT}}{(2\gamma + 4)} - \frac{1}{(2\gamma - r)} \right\} + \frac{\eta K}{r} [e^{-rt} - 1]$$

along a "solution path".

We let $w$ and $\eta$ vary and observed $V$ to be *convex in w and concave in $\eta$*. The examples are reported in Table III below.

TABLE III

|            | $K$    | $T$    | $V$               | $L_0$   | $Q_0$    |
|------------|--------|--------|-------------------|---------|----------|
| $W = 1.5$  | 5.8257 | 7.1928 | 223.217           | 15.3197 | 8.96061  |
| $W = 1.0$  | 5.1249 | 6.1927 | 245.398(250.429)  | 24.7569 | 10.72510 |
| $W = 0.5$  | 4.1201 | 4.8002 | 277.641           | 55.0027 | 14.92775 |
| $\eta = 1.5$ | 5.2638 | 6.1117 | 234.299         | 24.9078 | 10.89381 |
| $\eta = 1.0$ | 5.1249 | 6.1927 | 245.398(245.242) | 24.7569 | 10.72510 |
| $\eta = 0.5$ | 5.0023 | 6.2671 | 256.185         | 24.6195 | 10.57420 |

* $s(0) = 40$, $p = 10$, $r = 0.1$, $\gamma = 0.02$, $\beta = 0.47$ and $\eta = 1.0$ for the first results and $w = 1.0$ for the second set. The number in brackets is the convex combination of high and low values for $V$ for each set of results.

### Uncertainty in the future value of a parameter

Suppose the mine owner is told that at date $T_a$ in the future, output price will be either $p^u$ with probability $\pi^u$ or $p^L$ with probability $\pi^L$; $\pi^u + \pi^L = 1$ and $\pi^u > 0$. The deposit owner must organize an extraction program between today and $T_a$. At $T_a$ the value of price will be revealed and the remaining stock can be extracted in a certainty environment. The decision problem is essentially how much stock should be extracted between today and $T_a$ and at what rate should this stock be extracted. The solution is to maximize discounted expected profit. Once solved this solution involves rent always rising at the rate of interest and at $T_a$, the rent on the ton extracted at $T_a^-$ just before the information is revealed, must equal the expected rent on the ton to be extracted just after the information is scheduled to arrive, or at $T_a^+$. Working backwards from complete exhaustion beyond $T_a$, we obtain the optimal

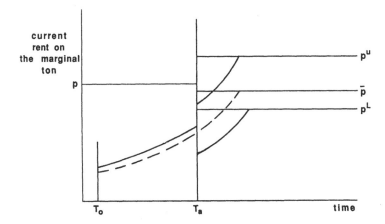

FIGURE 3 Beyond future date $T_a$, output price will be $p^u$ with probability $\pi^u$ or $p^L$ with probability $(1 - \pi^u)$. $\bar{p}$ is the mean price. A certainty extraction program is the dashed line and an uncertain program the solid line. At $T_a$ either of the two solid lines is followed as the "realized" extraction program.

contingent extraction program faced by the mine owner today, in the face of the uncertain price beyond $T_a$. We sketch with solid lines an optimal contingent rent profile in Figure 3 corresponding to an optimal contingent extraction program.

The convexity of $V$ in $p$ permits us to arrive at the following comparison of a situation with a certain future price $\bar{p} = \pi^u p^u + \pi^L p^L$ and an uncertain future price. For a specific stock left to be extracted after $T_a$, expected $V$ is larger with the uncertain price compared with the certain price. In equilibrium this leads to a larger stock being extracted beyond $T_a$ under uncertainty (smaller stock before $T_a$) and thus *a higher initial rent under uncertainty*. The broken line in Figure 3 corresponding to the certainty case has a lower initial rent than the corresponding program under uncertainty. Furthermore *expected profits at $T_0$* will be higher for the *firm under uncertainty than under certainty*, where certainty corresponds to the known price being the mean of the uncertain prices. This leads to the striking conclusion in Hartwick and Yeung [37], namely the risk neutral resource extracting firm prefers future price uncertainty to price certainty.

With complete futures markets and output price uncertainty

buyers will desire to enter into contracts before $T_a$ to receive stock at a "fair" price beyond $T_a$. Such a price corresponds to the expected rent on the marginal ton, the projection beyond $T_a$ of observed rent on the marginal ton before $T_a$. In other words with output price uncertainty, there will be a smoothly rising rent schedule across $T_a$, rising at rate $r$, with expected rent just beyond $T_a$ equal to observed rent just before $T_a$. Not only does this correspond to global expected present value of profit maximization for the extracting firm, but it corresponds to zero intertemporal arbitrage possibilities across $T_a$. Buyers will enter into such contracts to purchase a future expected prices to specific dates in order to avoid paying the high price *ex post* if the high price is realized. With an appropriate zero arbitrage profit contract, a consumer of output will be indifferent between buying a ton at $\hat{t}$ before $T_a$ and storing it for use (or sale) at $\hat{t} + \Delta$ beyond $T_a$ or writing a contract to buy a ton at $\hat{t} + \Delta$ at the expected price at $\hat{t} + \Delta$. (We assume no storage costs.) In the first case the price will be low but interest earnings will be foregone and in the second case the expected price will be high but payment will be made at $\hat{t} + \Delta$ and interest will have been earned on the outlay between $\hat{t}$ and $\hat{t} + \Delta$. The seller will be willing to enter into such zero profit arbitrage contracts because his or her expected profits will be unchanged from what they would be if he or she did not sell contracts before $T_a$ for delivery at dates beyond $T_a$. *Ex post* prices will have been observed to jump across $T_a$ but futures rents will have risen smoothly across $T_a$, moving up at a rate such that rent on the marginal ton extracted rises at $r\%$ per unit time.

Of importance in this analysis is the fact that beliefs about future prices, the "priors" about where prices will be after $T_a$ and the "degree" of belief about where they will be, directly affect the course of extraction, the time path of marginal rent, before $T_a$. Thus current extraction activity is a complex function of the known stocks, interest rate, and extraction costs as well as of current expectations about where future prices will be. Current rent per marginal ton reflects these beliefs, namely probabilities and possible future values of prices, as well as observable data. Understanding why current extraction levels are where they are requires an assessment of what current beliefs are about the future uncertain course of prices. Beliefs must be "netted out" or "factored in" in an empirical investigation of the course of extraction activity.

If some agent has special knowledge of where future prices will be, he or she can write contracts to have stock delivered at the prevailing expected price and realize excess profits when the price *ex post* is higher than most people expected. If this agent is greedy and enters into too many contracts, others will suspect he or she has inside knowledge of future prices and will stay out of the market for contracts for future delivery. This will result in a collapse of the market and the person with inside knowledge not being able to obtain contracts which guarantee excess profits. Inside knowledge will have thus revealed itself in the actions of the agent possessing the knowledge! It becomes common knowledge and new priors or beliefs are brought by futures buyers to the contract writing activity. The priors at which contracts are written tend to reflect a concensus of beliefs between buyers of stock at future dates and sellers of stock.

It should be clear that our argument does not turn on only two states being possible beyond $T_a$. There could be any number greater than two, each with its appropriate probability. In the limit there could be a continuum of uncertain states and the argument would remain unchanged through the techniques of analysis would need to be different in order to accommodate the continuum formulation. Our argument is also not dependent on the future being divided into a certain phase and a single uncertain phase. $T_a$ could be an hour away from $T_0$, a day, a week or whatever. The time phasing does not matter. Suppose beyond $T_a$ at $T_b$ there was another date at which subsequent uncertainty in price would be resolved. The optimal program in the face of uncertainty is solved backwards from the end. We illustrate in Figure 4. There are two uncertain prices beyond $T_b$ and two uncertain prices between $T_a$ and $T_b$. (Two states is a convenience, not a sacrifice of generality.)

There are two decision variables in maximizing expected present profits at $T_0$, namely, the stock to be extracted between $T_0$ and $T_a$ and between $T_a$ and $T_b$. The first order conditions indicate expected rent per ton is equal on each side of $T_a$ and on each side of $T_b$ for (i) the broken line schedules of rent in Figure 4 and (ii) the solid line schedules of rent. Just beyond $T_a$, corresponding to a high price is a contingent present value of profit depending on whether the high price is realized beyond $T_b$ or the low price. Similarly for the case of the low price just beyond $T_a$. Working back in time leaves the

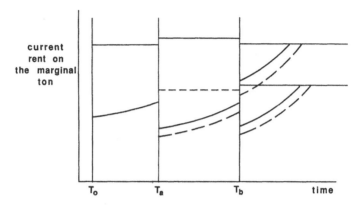

FIGURE 4   Uncertain prices in periods $(T_a, T_b)$ and $(T_b, \infty)$. If the lower price is realized in $(T_a, T_b)$, the broken rent schedule corresponds to the optimal extraction program. Expected rent per marginal ton is the same "across" $T_b$. The solid line corresponds to the case of the higher price being realized between $(T_a, T_b)$.

decision at $T_a$ essentially the same as if we were in a framework with no uncertainty beyond $T_b$. Thus our treatment above of just two phases, certainty before $T_a$ and uncertainty beyond $T_a$ captures all essentials of uncertainty in the future ranging over many future dates. Of course the analysis of mean preserving spreads in uncertain prices in a many phase problem would be complicated since the effects would work both forward in time and backward from the phase where the mean preserving spread (more uncertianty) was introduced.

The case of future interest rate uncertainty parallels that of price uncertainty precisely. Since $V$ is convex in $r$, given $S$, expected $V$ rises with variation in $r$, the mean of $r$ held constant. This implies a greater proportion of the initial stock will be extracted beyond $T_a$, the future date information on $r$ becomes available, under uncertainty in $r$, and uncertainty will thus drive up initial rent. At $T_0$, the firm will observe higher expected profits, the more uncertainty there is in $r$ beyond $T_a$ $(T_a > T_0)$ where more uncertainty leaves the mean of $r$ unchanged. We sketch the rent profiles for the certain case (broken line) and uncertain case in Figure 5.

For many competitive firms reacting to interest rate uncertainty, quantity supplied by each firm will respond *ex post* and *industry*

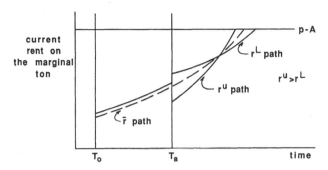

FIGURE 5 The certainty rent path corresponding to $\bar{r} = \pi^u r^u + \pi^L r^L$ is below the uncertainty rent path before the uncertainty in $r$ is realized. The broken line corresponds to the certainty path.

*price* in turn will respond. This has been investigated in Yeung and Hartwick [97]. The case of stock size uncertainty is quite different from the cases of price and interst rate uncertainty above. First, $V$ is concave in stock size, implying variability in $S$ lowers the expected value of $S$. In addition, *the date $T_1$* at which uncertainty is resolved is *usually endogenous* being dependent on how rapidly extraction proceeds. That is, to know whether there is more than contingent stock, say 1000 tons, one must extract 1000 tons and the observe whether there is more beyond that possible value. One learns the stock size by extracting. For the case of two stock sizes $S^L$ and $S^H$ with probabilities $\pi^L$ and $\pi^H$ respectively, the optimization problem is one of selecting date $T_a$ optimally or equivalently selecting the initial quantity to extract optimally. Between $T_0$ and $T_a$ (endogenous) an optimal program will correspond to one with rent rising at the rate of interest. At $T_a$, the remaining stock, either 0 tons or $S^H - S^L$ tons will be known and a standard optimal depletion program is appropriate if $S^H$ is observed. If zero additional tons are observed, the current value of the mine drops to zero. The essential first order condition defining $T_a$ in this problem is

$$pq(T_a) - C(q(T_a)) - [p - dC/dq]q(T_a)$$
$$= \pi^L \cdot 0 + \pi^H \cdot V(S^H - S^L, T - T_a) \cdot r$$

where $V(S^H - S^L, T - T_a)$ is the present value of profit for $S^H - S^L$

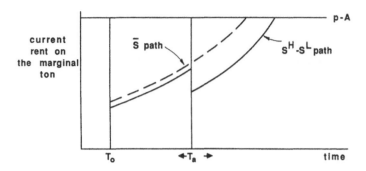

FIGURE 6   With certain stock $\bar{S}$, the broken line characterizes the rent profile for an optimal extraction program. The solid line corresponds to the contingent rent profile for the case of stock size uncertainty. $T_a$ is endogenous.

tons optimally depleted so that $q(T) = 0$. This is a variant of the *asset equilibrium condition* which we observed above. (Since $V$ is a capital value of $S^H - S^L$ tons and $pq - C(q)$ is current income, we have the basic condition that income net of depreciation divided by capital value (here expected capital value) equals the rate of interest.)

In Figure 6 we illustrate representative rent schedules for the case of certainty (the broken line) and uncertainty where $\bar{S} = \pi^u S^u + \pi^L S^L$.

For the case of stock size uncertainty and *information arriving exogeneously* at date $T_a$, the essential first order condition at $T_a$ is the same as that observed for interest rate and output price uncertainty, namely zero arbitrage across $T_a$ for the marginal ton extracted on either side of $T_a$. The mine-owner's decision is one of deciding how much of $S^L$ to extract before $T_a$, and the first order condition resolves this issue. In Figure 7 we indicate optimal rent profiles for the case of certainty, with $\bar{S} = \pi^u S^u + \pi^L S^L$ (the broken line) and uncertainty. We emphasize that with information on uncertain stock sizes obtained by mining, time $T_a$ is endogenous. When information on uncertain stock sizes arrives at known date $T_a$, the amount of stock to extract between $T_0$ and $T_a$ is endogenous. The certainty rent schedule in Figure 7 above lies above the uncertainty schedule between $T_0$ and $T_a$ because $V$ is concave in $S$ and an uncertain future $S$ induces more stock to be extracted

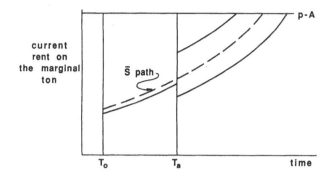

FIGURE 7 The broken line corresponds to the certainty schedule. Information on stock size arrives at known date $T_a$. Thesolid line is the rent schedule for the uncertain stock size.

between $T_0$ and $T_a$ that is the case under certainty (under certainty, $\bar{S} = \pi^u S^u + \pi^L S^L$.)

### Two deposits of uncertain size facing the firm

In what sequence should a firm exploit multiple deposits of uncertain size? Suppose extraction costs are the same for both of two deposits and the mineral is homogeneous in quality. Should the deposit with the largest mean size be tackled first? That with the highest variance of size? Lowest variance? The general problem with a continuum of states of arbitrary density function is too complicated to characterize in general largely because the solution involves switching from one deposit to the other. We shall see this below for an example with two deposits each with two possible sizes. However let us consider the case first of *one deposit of known size and one of uncertain size*. How should these deposits be exploited to maximize the expected present value of profits. Suppose the uncertain deposit has size 95 tons with probability $\pi_1$ and 150 tons with probability $\pi_2$. Let the certain deposit have 200 tons. We sketch the two possible optimal extraction programs in Figure 8a and 8b.

In Figure 8a the uncertain deposit is extracted first. At $T_a$ the extractor first discovers whether there is 55 additional tons in the uncertain deposit or not. There are two possible certainty rent

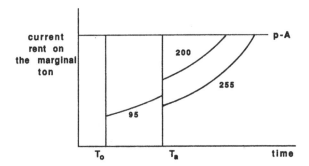

FIGURE 8a   Uncertain deposit first.

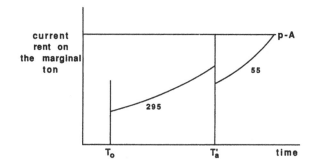

FIGURE 8b   Certain deposit first.

profiles beyond $T_a$, corresponding to 200 tons (a small stock size in the uncertain deposit realized) and to 255 tons (a large stock size in the uncertain deposit realized).

In Figure 8b, the certain deposit is depleted first and then extraction is switched to the uncertain deposit at time $T_a'$ (endogenous to the model). Which program is superior? Clearly not the case of the certain deposit first in Figure 8b. This follows because *formally* the program in Figure 8b could be traversed by exploiting the 95 tons from the uncertain deposit first and then the 200 tons from the certain deposit. But if this were actually done, information on future tons available would be made available when the 95 tons were extracted, well before $T_a'$, and this information is not acted upon in Figure 8b until much after it could be made available at zero cost. Thus the solution in Figure 8b squanders information of positive dollar value. Hence the solution with the uncertain deposit exploited first in Figure 8a is optimal. No information is wasted. The present value of expected profit will be higher for the solution with the uncertain deposit exploited first.

We can make use of the solution above for the case now of two uncertain deposits, each with two possible sizes. We will verify that it is optimal to plan to switch deposits *ex ante* before the first deposit is exhausted. Let there be two identical deposits, each with 95 tons with probability $\pi_1$ or 150 tons with probability $\pi_2 = 1 - \pi_1$, $0 < \pi_1 < 1$. Let deposit 1 be exploited first. After 95 tons are extracted, the firm knows whether there are 55 tons more or not. At this point the firm has either (i) a certain deposit wth 55 tons (those remaining in deposit 1) and an uncertain deposit or (ii) only an uncertain deposit with possibly 95 or 150 tons. We know how to construct optimal programs for each of these cases. In case (i) we know that the uncertain deposit should be extracted from first. But this implies switching deposits. Hence it is optimal for the firm to not plan to exhaust one deposit in an optimal extraction program. We illustrate the optimal program in Figure 9. Along each branch, rent on the marginal ton is rising at the rate of interest given output price constant and the extraction cost function stationary.

There will not be zero profit arbitrage across a node such as $T_1$ in Figure 9. Nevertheless the firm will be optimizing in the face of this apparent anomaly since it is controlling the information gathering

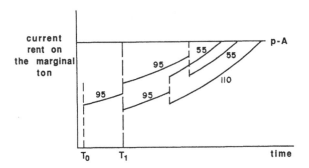

FIGURE 9   With two identical deposits of either 95 or 150 tons, it is optimal to arrange the extraction program to switch from one to the other after the first deposit has been revealed to be either 95 or 150 tons. Numbers on branches indicate tons extracted along the relevant branch.

about actual deposit sizes and it is this information "externality" which leads to the non-zero profit arbitage when stock size is uncertain and must be determined by extraction itself.

### Varying quality of ore in the model of the extracting firm

A more realistic model involves the stock declining in quality as the deposit is mined. A straightforward representation of this phenomenon is treating extraction costs as rising as the stock is depleted. One might think of a deposit as a series of layers and to extract the same quantity from a deeper layer is more costly. In place of extraction cost function $C(q(t))$ we have $C(q(t), S(t))$ where $\partial C/\partial S < 0$. Changing stock size might just affect the intercept in a rising marginal extraction cost schedule as in $C(q(t), S(t)) \equiv [A/S(t)]q(t) + \frac{1}{2}Bq(t)^2$. Two new properties of extraction programs emerge with declining quality of stock introduced. First rent on the marginal ton no longer rises at the rate of interest and secondly, there is no presumption that the known stock $S(0)$ will be exhausted.

The firm's optimization problem is to select an extraction program $\{q(t)\}$ such that

$$\int_0^T [pq(t) + C(q(t), S(t))]e^{-rt} dt$$

is a maximum subject to $\int_0^T q(t) dt \leqq S(0)$.

The Euler equation for this problem is

$$\frac{\dot{p - C_q}}{p - C_q} - \frac{C_s}{p - C_q} = r$$

which indicates that as $q(t)$ is extracted, rent on the marginal ton extracted at $t$ is rising at less than the rate of interest. The arbitrage relation here indicates that if the marginal ton at $t$ is left in the ground, it will yield capital gain $\dfrac{\dot{}}{p - C_q}$ along an optimal extraction program. If it is extracted and the proceeds invested for an instant, the marginal ton yields interest $(p - C_q)r$. However this extraction "degrades" subsequent tons by marginally increasing the extraction cost of the next $q(t)$ extracted. Hence $C_s$ must be netted out of $[p - C_q]r$ in order for the mine owner to be indifferent between extracting the marginal ton and investing the proceeds or leaving the marginal ton in the ground.

As quality declines, the marginal extraction cost schedule "shifts up". It is reasonable to expect that $p - C_q(q(T), S(T)) = 0$ with $S(T) > 0$. In this case the deposit becomes unprofitable at the margin before all the original stock $S(0)$ is exhausted. This alternate end-point condition usually implies $q(T) = 0$ and corresponds to *economic exhaustion* as distinct from physical exhaustion of the stock. In this latter case, the end point was

$$[p - C_q(q(T), S(T))]q(T) = pq(T) - C(q(T), S(T))$$

or marginal profit on $q(T)$ equals average profit on $q(T)$.

With *increasing* quality of stock, we can view the marginal extraction cost *schedule* as "shifting down" as $S(t)$ declines. As long as the marginal cost schedule is always upward sloping in $q(t)$ at each point in time (corresponding to the Hamiltonian being concave in $q(t)$ at each instant) we will have a well behaved optimization problem. It is possible then to have $q(t)$ increasing with time until near the end of the program, $q(t)$ declines to zero as physical exhaustion of $S(0)$ occurs.

Another realiatic element of heterogeneity in the quality of the stock involves multiple minerals in a ton of ore. The fixed proportion case is most straightforward formally. Let each ton of ore comprise $a_1, a_2, \ldots, a_n$ tons of mineral $1, 2, \ldots, n$ respectively. Let $c_1, c_2, \ldots, c_n$ be the cost of extracting a unit of mineral $1, 2, \ldots, n$ respectively from the ore. The firm's objective function is

$$\int_0^T [p_1 a_1 q + p_2 a_2 q + \cdots + p_n a_n q - c_1 a_1 q$$
$$- c_2 a_2 q - \cdots - c_n a_n q - C(q, S)]\, dt$$

and is to be maximized subject to $\int_0^T q(t)\, dt \leqq S(0)$. The new element in this formulation of variable quality is rent per marginal ton extracted is now $\sum_{i=0}^n a_i(p_i - c_i) - C_q(q, S)$. Rent is not associated with a particular mineral extracted and sold but with a quantity of ore distinctly different from a mineral on the market.

## 3. A RESOURCE EXTRACTION INDUSTRY

### Introduction

In the competitive industry there are many price taking firms, each with some small holding of resource of stock to extract, and each correctly projecting what industry prices must be into the future. The firms are price takers in the sense they were in the analysis of the firm above but output price emerges endogenously as each firm selects its quantity to extract period by period. With each firm optimizing intertemporally, it is *as if* a planner were maximizing the discounted social surplus in the market as a whole. Social surplus in a period is the sum of consumer surplus and producer surplus and dynamic rent. This permits us to analyze the competitive industry as if a benevolent planner were optimizing. This simplifies matters somewhat but we still keep in mind that the industry comprises many small resource extracting firms.

For the case of each firm having some stock of different quality, we shall be concerned with the emergence of differential or Ricardian rent as well as Hotelling or dynamic rent. We shall also be concerned about how uncertainty in different parameters affects extraction programs, including stock size uncertainty. We change assumptions at the conclusion and consider the industry operated by a single profit maximizing firm, the monopoly extraction case.

### The industry in detail

We shall set up a socially optimal extraction plan given a market demand schedule and consumers' benefit function and a known homogeneous stock $S$, and argue that an industry comprising many small competing extraction firms will replicate the extraction program under the socially optimal plan. Each firm will be assumed to regard the other firms in a particular manner currently and into the distant future since each firm is assumed to be maximizing the present value of his or her own profit within a large group of identical firms.

Given an inverted market demand schedule $p = g(Q)$. We define the instantaneous gross dollar benefit function

$$B(Q) = \int_0^{\bar{Q}} g(Q) \, dQ.$$

This then is the aggregate consumers' surplus for quantity $\bar{Q}$ being supplied to the market. Note $dB/d\bar{Q} = p(\bar{Q})$ or marginal benfits equal current price.[3] Assume that quantity demanded declines to zero beyond $\bar{p}$, the choke price.

Extraction involves cost $c$ dollars per ton mined and refined. The planning problem is to select extraction program $\{Q(t)\}$ such that

$$W = \int_0^T [B(Q(t)) - cQ(t)]e^{-rt}\, dt$$

is a maximum subject to

$$\int_0^T Q(t)\, dt \le S(0)$$

where $r$ is the discount rate, here assumed equal to the market rate of interest $r$ and $S(t)$ is the size of stock remaining below ground at time $t$. (Since $S(0)$ is known, it can be thought of as a large block of mineral sitting above ground, to be chipped at, at an optimal rate or a large tank of oil to be drained at an optimal rate, or a cake to be eaten at an optimal rate.) The Euler equation for the above dynamic optimization problem is

$$\frac{\overline{p(Q(t)) - c}}{p(Q(t)) - c} = r$$

where the dot over a term indicates differentiation with respect to time. Recall $p = dB/dQ$. This Euler equation is the Hotelling or $r\%$ rule indicating that rent per ton $p - c$ must rise at a rate equal to the rate of interest along an optimal extraction program. Such a condition implies zero profit to the owner of any ton arbitraging over time. If the ton were left in the ground at date $t$, its value would rise by $\dfrac{\bullet}{p(Q(t)) - c}$ over a subsequent short interval. If the

---

[3] It is well-known (e.g., Varian [95; pp. 207–213]) that changes in consumers' surplus is generally an approximation to change in utility in a static context. Blackorby, Donaldson and Maloney [4] have made precise the approximate nature of changes in the present value of consumers' surplus compared with the present value of utility. By working with consumers' surplus we can avoid dealing with changes in the *marginal utility of income* in addition to changes in prices and quantities—an approximation and simplification.

ton were extracted at date $t$ and the profit invested at rate $r$ for a short interval, it would earn $[p(Q(t)) - c]r$ a short interval later. The $r\%$ rule above indicates that these two sources of profit are the same at all times and for all tons. Thus any owner of a ton is indifferent between extracting and leaving his or her ton unextracted along a socially optimal extraction program. This is one argument for why a competitive group of firms comprising the industry replicates the socially optimal extraction program.

The end point condition characterizing an optimal program is

$$p(Q(T)) - c = \frac{B(Q(T)) - cQ(T)}{Q(T)}$$

or marginal net surplus from extracting $Q(T)$ equals average net surplus at terminal date $T$. This condition holds in the limit as $t \to T$ and $Q(T) \to 0$ is the above problem. Average return equals marginal return in the limit as the quantity extracted declines to zero. The last small unit extracted reaps the largest current rent available, namely $\bar{p} - c$ where $\bar{p}$ is the choke price or intercept of the demand schedule.

For individual resource owners to extract to satisfy this end point condition, they must have perfect foresight as to the evoluation of price $p(t)$. If the owners did not extract to satisfy this end point condition, current price would jump up from $p(T^-)$ to $\bar{p}$ at date $T$ or decline from $p(T^-)$ to $\bar{p}$. In the first case "excess" capital gains would be reaped by the last extractor or by waiting to extract one's ton until $T$. If all extractors waited to make this "killing" the initial price would rise rapidly and induce some to not wait until $T$. In equilibrium "excess" capital gains would be eliminated. An analogous argument establishes that price will not decline at $T$. Hence perfect foresight and profit maximization implies that the end point condition will be satisfied with many small resource owners.[4] Hence the market or perfect competition will replicate the socially optimal program.

---

[4] Kemp and Long [49] have emphasized that as the stock gets small near date $T$, the few owners remaining will be induced to band together and follow a monopoly extraction program. This seems logically irrefutable but does require a monopoly formation mechanism. Moreover if each owner wishes to be near the end to reap monopoly profits as with perfect foresight, then the competitive regime would breakdown. This same argument appears somewhat more clearly in Hartwick, Kemp, and Long [36]. We proceed above as if price taking behavior was followed by all resource owners without exception.

Implicit above was the demand curve stationary over time. In such a case with quantity demanded a continuous, negatively-valued function of price, quantity $Q(t)$ will decline over time toward zero at date $T$. The demand schedule might shift "out" over time. In this case the $r\%$ rule still governs the extraction program though $Q(t)$ could now rise over an interval. With interest rates varying over time, the $r\%$ rule "holds" across periods as in

$$\frac{[p(t+1)-c]-[p(t)-c]}{p(t)-c}=r(t)$$

in a discrete time formulation. $r(t)$ can change period by period. In a discrete time framework, the $r\%$ rule is illustrated in Figure 10. In continuous time with the interest rate varying the discount factor $e^{-rt}$ must be replaced by $\exp \int_{t_0}^{t} -r(y)\,dy$. Below we shall examine key properties of the model under the traditional assumptions of $r$ constant and demand stationary.

Another word on firms and the industry. For the case of $n \geq 2$ price taking firms with homogeneous and identically-sized stocks and extraction costs with upward sloping marginal costs as we considered earlier, we can view each firm as extracting at the same rate, "reading" current and future demands. Each firm's rent on the marginal ton extracted will be rising at the rate of interest as will "industry" rent. Suppose however that average extraction costs are U-shaped or there are some scale economies in extraction for small amounts mined. The optimal end-post condition for each firm continues to be where marginal benfits (profits) from $q(T)$ equal

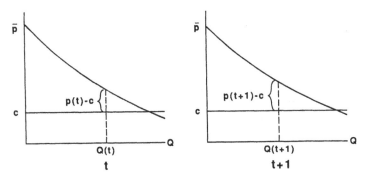

FIGURE 10   Quantity $Q(t)$ and $Q(t+1)$ across consequtive periods are related by the $r\%$ rule, i.e., $p(t+1)-c=(1+r)[p(t)-c]$.

average benefits. This will occur with each firm producing a *positive* quantity $q(T)$ at $T$ and the sum over all firms yields industry output $Q(T)$ positive at $T$. An instant later the quantity declines to zero at the industry choke price $\bar{p}$. Now $\bar{p} > p(Q(T))$. This necessary jump up in price could be foreseen by each firm and hence each producer would desire to reap the capital gain $\bar{p} - p(Q(T))$ by holding his or her ore off the market. *Hence the competitive path would not be followed,* given declining average extraction costs for each firm (Eswaran, Heaps and Lewis [23]). Scale economies in extraction lead to the non-existence of a competitive extraction program in the above sense. Another species of declining average extraction costs is pure set-up cost incurred before extraction takes place. This also leads to market failure as we observe below.

### Exhaustion of finite stocks and society's future

Economists resist the notion that exhaustion of essential stock $S$ implies termination of the life of an economy and its people. There are two ways economic death can be avoided. First exhaustion may never occur. There may instead be asymptotic depletion of a finite stock over infinite time. Lower quantities may induce conservation by users as higher prices are experienced. In place of an industry demand schedule with an intercept or choke price $\bar{p}$, we might postulate a demand schedule for which $p \to \infty$ as $Q \to 0$ and $\lim pQ \to 0$ as $Q \to 0$. The constant elasticity demand schedule $Q = kp^{\alpha}$ for $-\infty < \alpha < -1$ satisfies these conditions. A finite stock can be depleted over infinite time in such circumstances. (The physics of this phenomenon are unclear of course since teaspoons of say oil will be followed by eyedropperfulls and ultimately fractions of molecules followed by fractions of atoms.)

The other approach to exhaustion of a stock without the economic death of a society is to postulate that for every exhaustible resource, there is a substitute which can be brought into use if the price of the resource rises to the cost of producing the substitute. This is analogous to technological regress. For each commodity consumed there is an alternate process of production which can be appealed to if current price becomes sufficiently high. The alternate production mode has been labelled *the backstop*. In place of a choke price or intercept of the market demand schedule at $\bar{p}$ we introduce a backstop price or unit cost $E < \bar{p}$ with $Q(E) > 0$.

At any price above $E$, the backstop mode will be economically viable. The optimal strategy for competitive resource extracting firms is to arrange to exhaust the sum of their holdings of a homogeneous stock when price just rises to the backstop price and unit cost $E$. There is no unit revenue above $E$ and if a finite amount $S^E$ were left when the output price rose to $E$, these owners would observe a current price constant at $E$ and in present value terms, output price declining as the current price remained at $E$. Anyone holding a durable asset with a price constant into the indefinite future is incurring relative losses since the asset could be sold, the proceeds invested, and positive returns earned. Thus it does not pay to hold stock beyond the date price rises to $E$. More on this below.

## Solving the Hotelling model and comparative statics

The basic efficiency condition for the Hotelling model is the $r\%$ rule on rent which can be written

$$(E - c)e^{-r(T-t)} = p(t) - c \qquad 0 \le t \le T \tag{1}$$

where $E$ is the backstop price and $c$ is the constant extraction cost per ton. We know it is optimal to exhaust the stock when price just rises to $E$ or $q(T)$ satisfies $p(T) = E$. Given a demand function $q(t) = g(p(t); t)$ shifting over time, we can substitute for $p(t)$ and express $q(t)$ as a function of time $t$ and the parameters of the problem. Let us assume the demand schedule is stationary over time as is the interest rate and is $q(t) = f(p(t))$, then we have

$$q(t) = f[(E - c)e^{-r(T-t)} + c] \qquad 0 \le t \le T \tag{2}$$

along an efficient extraction path. Given the stock constraint $\int_0^T q(t)\,dt = S$, we obtain a non linear equation in $T$ defining a solved Hotelling model, namely:

$$\int_0^T f[(E - c)e^{-r(T-t)} + c]\,dt - S = 0. \tag{3}$$

Example: $q(t) = \alpha - \beta p(t)$ or a linear stationary demand schedule.

$$\int_0^T \alpha - \beta[(E - c)e^{-r(T-t)} + c]\,dt = wT - (\phi/r)[1 - e^{-rT}] = S$$

where $w = \alpha - \beta c > 0$ and $\phi = \beta(E - c) > 0$.

Consider comparative statics in the Hotelling model or how the extraction path responds to changes in the parameters of the problem. Here we solve for $dT/d\delta$ where $\delta$ is some parameter value (either $S$, $R$, $c$ or $E$) and one can infer the changes in the time path $\{q(t)\}$ given the changes in the one endogenous variable $T$. (Given changes in $T$ one can determine changes in $p(0)$ and $q(0)$ and thus the complete time path of $p(t)$ and $q(t)$). Consider the derivatives of the left hand side of (3).

i) with respect to $T$, we have

$$f[p(T)] + \int_0^T f'(\bullet)(-r)e^{-r(T-t)}(E-c)\,dt$$

which is positive since $f' \equiv df(\bullet)/d(\bullet) < 0$ because the demand curve slopes negatively in price.

ii) with respect to $E$, we have

$$\int_0^T f'(\bullet)e^{-r(T-t)}\,dt$$

which is negative since again $f'(\bullet) < 0$.

iii) with respect to $c$, we have

$$\int_0^T f'(\bullet)[1 - e^{-r(T-t)}]\,dt$$

which is negative.

iv) with respect to $r$, we have

$$\int_0^T -f'(\bullet)(T-t)e^{-r(T-t)}(E-c)\,dt$$

which is positive.

v) with respect to $S$, we have simply $-1$, obviously negative.

Thus we arrive at the basic results, holding $S$ constant

$$\frac{dT}{dE} > 0, \qquad \frac{dT}{dc} > 0, \quad \text{and} \quad \frac{dT}{dr} < 0$$

or the interval of extraction lengthens with exogenous increases in the price of the backstop and extraction cost per ton and declines with a rise in the interest rate. Also an exogenous increase in stock size $S$, lengthens the extraction period or $dT/dS > 0$.

Given $E$ constant, we can infer that $dp(0)/dc > 0$, $dp(0)/dr < 0$ and $dp(0)/dS < 0$. Since $dT/dE > 0$, the higher price of the backstop must result in the initial price $p(0)$ rising.

Remark: we can differentiate Eq. (2) with respect to time $t$ and after some rearrangement obtain

$$\frac{\dot{q}}{q} = \left\{ \left( \frac{p(t) - c}{p(t)} \right) \epsilon(t) \right\} \cdot r$$

where $\epsilon(t) \equiv \dfrac{df}{dp(t)} \cdot \dfrac{p(t)}{f} < 0$. We have then a relatively simple expression for the rate of extraction in a Hotelling model along an optimal path. For the case of zero extraction costs and $\epsilon$ constant (the constant elasticity of demand schedule) the rate of decline in quantity extracted is simply $\epsilon r$. The well-behaved case has $|\epsilon| > 1$ leaving the rate of extraction more rapid in absolute value than the rate of interest.

Observe that $d^2T/d\gamma^2$ for $\gamma = E$, $c$, $r$, and $S$ depends on $d^2f/dp(t)^2$ or on the *concavity or convexity of the demand schedule*. Since these second derivatives are required to evaluate $dW^2/d\gamma^2$ for $\gamma = E$, $c$, $r$, and $S$ where $W = \int_0^T [B(q(t)) - cq(t)]e^{-rt}\, dt$, we have the *a priori* result that the convexity of concavity of the present value benefit function depends on the shape (in addition to the slope) of the demand schedule. Since we do not have strong prior notions for the appropriate shape of the demand schedules, we turn to some examples in order to glean some not general results. The concavity or convexity of $W$ is required in order to analyze how uncertainty in the values of key parameters affects the pace of extraction.

**The constant elasticity of demand (zero extraction cost) example**

The demand schedule is

$$q = q^\epsilon - \infty < \epsilon < -1$$

where $q$ is quantity extracted and marketed and $p$ is the price per unit sold. Hotelling's Rule can be expressed as

$$p(t) = E^{-r(T-t)}$$

where $E$ is the cost equal to price of the backstop. We combine these equations to obtain

$$q = E^\epsilon e^{-r\epsilon T} e^{r\epsilon t}.$$

Since total quantity extracted must not exceed the given known stock $S$, we have

$$S = \int_0^T q(t)\, dt$$

$$= E^\epsilon e^{-r\epsilon T} \int_0^T e^{r\epsilon t}\, dt$$

$$= [1 - e^{-r\epsilon T}]\{E^\epsilon / r\epsilon\}$$

whence

$$Z \equiv e^{-rT} = \left[1 - \frac{Sr\epsilon}{E^\epsilon}\right]^{1/\epsilon}$$

$$\frac{dZ}{dE} = [\bullet]^{(1-\epsilon)/\epsilon} E^{-\epsilon-1} Sr\epsilon < 0$$

$$\frac{d^2 Z}{dE^2} = [\bullet]^{(1-\epsilon)/\epsilon} Sr\epsilon E^{-\epsilon-2}\left\{\left[\frac{Sr\epsilon}{E^\epsilon - Sr\epsilon}\right](1-\epsilon) - \epsilon - 1\right\}$$

We will use these derivatives below in our analysis of the convexity or concavity of the present value of welfare or surplus. Note however *a higher value of the backstop increases the interval for exhausting a given stock* (i.e., $dZ/dE < 0$). (This is an instance of our general result above.)

Instantaneous surplus is

$$\int_0^{\bar{q}} p(q)\, dq \equiv B(\bar{q}).$$

which for $q = p^\epsilon$ is $\int_0^{\bar{q}} q^{1/\epsilon}\, dq = kq^\alpha$ where $\alpha \equiv (\epsilon + 1)/\epsilon$ and $k \equiv 1/\alpha$. Substituting for $q$ from above yields

$$e^{-rt} B(q) = kE^{\epsilon\alpha} e^{-r\epsilon\alpha T} e^{r\epsilon t}$$

$$W = \int_0^T e^{-rt} B(q)\, dt = kE^{\epsilon\alpha} e^{-r\epsilon\alpha T} \int_0^T e^{r\epsilon t}\, dt$$

$$= k(E^\epsilon e^{-r\epsilon T})^\alpha \frac{S}{(E^\epsilon e^{-r\epsilon T})}$$

$$= \left(\frac{\epsilon}{\epsilon + 1}\right) SEe^{-rT}$$

$$= \delta EZ \quad \text{where} \quad \delta \equiv \epsilon S/(\epsilon + 1).$$

(Observe then that $W$ equals $\epsilon/(\epsilon + 1)$ of the present value of total rent on the $S$ tons, where $[\epsilon/\epsilon + 1] > 1$.) Recall that $Z \equiv e^{-rT}$ was defined above for an optimal extraction program. Routine differentiation yields

$$\frac{d^2W}{dE^2} = \delta \frac{dZ}{dE}(1 - \epsilon)\left\{\frac{E^\epsilon}{E^\epsilon - Sr\epsilon}\right\} < 0$$

Since $\epsilon < -1$ and $dZ/dE < 0$. Thus we arrive at the basic result: *the present value of welfare for an optimal extraction program given $S$ tons is concave in the price of the backstop.* (This has been established for the constant elasticity of demand case.) Randomness in the price of the backstop cannot increase the present value of welfare. Thus future backstop price uncertainty makes stock extracted in the future relatively less valuable in present value terms and induces more rapid extraction in the early certain period. See also Dasgupta and Heal [10] for an analysis of backstop price uncertainty leading to a "tilting" of extraction toward the present.

We illustrate the uncertain backstop result. Between time $t_0$ and $t_a$ the backstop price is known and beyond $t_a$ we consider two possibilities. First beyond $t_a$ the backstop is known at value $\bar{E} = \pi_1 E_1 + \pi_2 E_2$, $\pi_1 + \pi_2 = 1$ and $0 < \pi_1 < 1$. In the other case the backstop is uncertain beyond $t_a$, yet extraction must proceed optimally between $t_0$ and $t_a$ in the face of the future backstop price uncertainty. The uncertain extraction program is the solid line in Figure 11 and the certain program the broken line. Concavity in $W$ in the backstop value $E$ implies that the uncertain case has a lower initial price and more rapid extraction between $t_0$ and $t_a$ than the uncertain case with $E_1$ occurring with probability $\pi_1$ and $E_2$ with probability $\pi_2$. At $t_a$ the uncertain case has rent at time $t_a^-$ equal to expected rent at time $t_a^+$.

Note that since the constant elasticity of demand schedule is convex to the origin in price-quantity space, one assumes that it is a

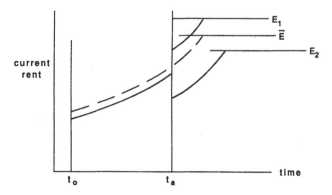

FIGURE 11 Uncertainty in the value of the backstop beyond $t_a$. The broken schedule is the certainty rent schedule. Uncertainty induces a lower initial price.

favorable candidate for observing a convex-in-the-backstop $W$ function. Such a result did not obtain and we conclude that the present value of welfare will generally be concave in the backstop price.

Consider now how $W$ varies with the interest rate $r$. From our derivation of $W$, we observe

$$\frac{d^2W}{dr^2} = \left(\frac{\epsilon}{\epsilon+1}\right) SE \frac{d^2(e^{-rT})}{dr^2}$$

We have an explicit expression for $e^{-rT}$ in the stock constraint relation above. Routine differentiation indicates

$$\frac{d^2(e^{-rT})}{dr^2} = \left(\frac{S}{E^\epsilon}\right)^2 (1-\epsilon)\left[1 - \frac{SR\epsilon}{E^\epsilon}\right]^{(1-2\epsilon)/\epsilon} > 0.$$

Hence $W$ *is convex in the interest rate* $r$. This result holds quite generally with any negatively sloped demand schedule since the method of proof of the convexity of the $V(\cdot)$ function for the firm can be applied to establish the convexity of the $W(\cdot)$ function in $r$. The convexity of $W$ in $r$ implies that discounted welfare with an uncertain interest rate beyond date $t_a > t_0$ will be higher than with a certain interest rate $\bar{r}$ beyond $t_a$ where $\bar{r}$ is the mean of the uncertain values. With many small deposit-owner, extractors, under rational expectations, the uncertain path will be traced out under a

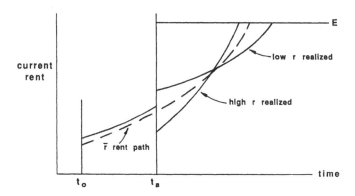

FIGURE 12 Interest rate uncertainty induces a high initial price in the constant elasticity of demand Hotelling model. The broken line is the certainty schedule.

decentralized market regime. The convexity of welfare or value makes the uncertain phase relatively more valuable than the certain phase and thus under uncertainty relatively more stock will be extracted beyond $t_a$. We illustrate in Figure 12. The solid lines correspond to the uncertain situation with two possible interest rate values beyond $t_a$. The broken line is the case of certainty. The certain rate $\bar{r}$ beyond $t_a$ is the mean of the two uncertain rates.

## The linear demand (constant extraction cost) example

We specify the inverse demand schedule

$$p = \alpha - \beta q$$

Aggregate surplus at a point in time is

$$B(q) = \int_0^q \alpha - \beta x \, dx = \alpha q - \frac{\beta}{2} q^2$$

and

$$W = \int_0^T [B(q(t)) - cq(t)]e^{-rt} \, dt$$

where

$$\int_0^T q(t) \, dt = S$$

The new result we observe is that $W$ *is convex is extraction cost* $c$ implying that discounted welfare and rent is higher with future extraction cost uncertainty than with extraction cost certainty (the certain value being set at the mean value of the uncertain possible values of $c$).

We will proceed to obtain an expression for $W$ which we can analyze in detail. Hotelling's Rule yields

$$p(t) - c = [E - c]e^{-r(T-t)}$$

or

$$\alpha - \beta q(t) - c = [E - c]e^{-r(T-t)}$$

yielding

$$q(t) = Y - Ue^{-r(T-t)}$$

where $Y = \dfrac{\alpha - c}{\beta} > 0$ and $U = \dfrac{E - c}{\beta} > 0$ with $Y > U$ since $E$ is the backstop cost or price and $\alpha$ is the choke price for the inverted demand schedule. Now

$$S = \int_0^T q(t)\, dt = YT + \frac{U}{r}[e^{-rT} - 1]$$

From this basic solution equation or equilibrium value of $T$ given parameters, we can obtain expressions for

$$\frac{dT}{dE}, \quad \frac{d^2T}{dE^2}, \quad \frac{dT}{dc}, \quad \frac{d^2T}{dc^2}, \quad \frac{dT}{dr}, \quad \frac{dT}{dr^2}, \quad \frac{dT}{dS}, \quad \text{and} \quad \frac{d^2T}{dS^2}.$$

To obtain an expression for $W$, we substitute $q(t)$ above in the expression for $W$, namely

$$W = \int_0^T \left[ (\alpha - c)q(t) - \frac{\beta}{2} q(t)^2 \right] e^{-rt}\, dt$$

and integrate to obtain

$$W = \frac{\beta Y^2}{2r}(1 - e^{-rT}) - \frac{\beta U^2}{2r} e^{-rT}[1 - e^{-rT}]$$

We proceeded to compute $W$ given the specification of $p = 10 - q$ with $C = 1$, $E = 9$, $r = 0.1$ and $S = 50$ as the base case. We systematically varied in respective inquiries $c$, $E$, $r$ and $S$ and examined the values of $T$ and $W$. In summary, *we observed $W$ convex in $c$, concave in $E$, convex in $r$, and concave in $S$*.

We report our examples below. In brackets is the value of $W$ for the case of $W$ hypothetically linear in the parameter in question. The observed value lying above (below) the "linear" value for $W$ implies concavity (convexity) of $W$ in terms of the parameter.

Extraction cost $c$ varying

| $c$ | $T$ | $W$ |
|---|---|---|
| 1.0 | 11.68014378 | 210.4842275 |
| 1.2 | 11.8300084 | 203.9348247(203.9534952) |
| 1.4 | 11.98561482 | 197.4227628 |

Backstop cost (price $E$) varying.

| $E$ | $T$ | $W$ |
|---|---|---|
| 9 | 11.68014378 | 210.4842275 |
| 9.2 | 11.89290589 | 210.510861(210.5055354) |
| 9.4 | 12.10791679 | 210.5268432 |

Interest rate $r$ varying

| $r$ | $T$ | $W$ |
|---|---|---|
| 0.1 | 11.68014378 | 210.4842275 |
| 0.12 | 10.97924954 | 194.8280518(195.9303337) |
| 0.14 | 10.43068137 | 181.3764398 |

Stock size $S$ varying

| $S$ | $T$ | $W$ |
|---|---|---|
| 50 | 11.68014378 | 210.4842275 |
| 52 | 11.98549987 | 215.4313877(215.3571537) |
| 54 | 12.28747691 | 220.2300798 |

In summary, *W is decreasing and convex in extraction cost c, is increasing and concave in backstop price E, is decreasing and convex in interest rate r and is increasing and concave in stock size S.* The convexity of $W$ in $c$ holds for any negatively sloped demand function and can be established by the reasoning used to establish $V$ convex in $r$ for the resource extracting firm, dealt with above.

Since we observed the same results for changes in $E$ and $r$ above for the case of the constant elasticity of demand and zero extraction costs, we need not comment again for this case of a linear demand schedule. Changes in stock size $S$ will have the same effect for both demand specifications; that is $W$ concave in $S$. There are two distinct specifications of the nature of stock size uncertainty. For the case of *exogenously supplied information,* the agent becomes informed at a specific date $t_a$ about actual stock remaining. In this case there will be zero profit arbitrage in rent across the date $t_a$. Because $W$ is concave, stock size uncertainty lowers expected welfare and rent at $t_0$ and leads to more stock being "used up" in the period before uncertainty is resolved. Thus uncertainty in the sense of a mean preserving spread results in a lower initial price and rent being observed at $t_0$ than would be the case with less uncertainty or no uncertainty.

The agent may however only learn about actual stock sizes by actually mining or extracting. This is the case of *information being obtained endogenously* or as a by-product of extracting mineral. In this case the pace of extraction affects the date which information on stock sizes becomes available. At these crucial dates, given discrete possible stock sizes, there is not zero profit arbitrage with information endogenous (Hartwick [34]) and the optimal planning solution will not be mimicked by the market solution. In each case, information exogenous or endogenous, the concavity of $W$ in stock size $S$ makes the future uncertain phases relatively unattractive from the viewpoint of the present program. We illustrate the case of information exogenously provided and stock size uncertain before date $t_a$. We treat the case of two possible stock sizes with mean size $\bar{S}$. At date $t_a$, the planner becomes informed whether the complete deposit, the amount extracted to $t_a$ plus the amount remaining, is large or small. The broken line is the certain case or that for $\bar{S}$ known at the outset. The solid line is for the case of uncertain stock

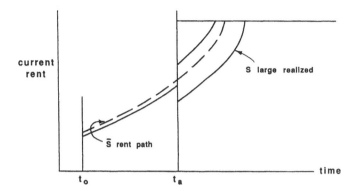

FIGURE 13   At date $t_a$ the planner or "market" becomes informed whether the deposit is large or small. The broken line is the corresponding rent path for extraction under certainty.

sizes in Figure 13. Observe that concavity of the objective function in the uncertain phase induces a "bird-in-the-hand" response or mineral is extracted more rapidly at the outset in response to the uncertain future. Epstein [22] explores the nature of risk aversion associated with this problem of stock size uncertain and information arriving endogenously.

For the case of future extraction cost uncertainty, the opposite result obtains because $W$ is convex in cost $c$. The uncertain future value of $c$ induces a lessening of extraction in the early phase. More of the known stock is shifted into the phase of uncertain costs. If for example extraction costs are directly related to wage rates and wage rates are uncertain, then this induces higher prices for the ore being extracted and less extraction in the initial period. We illustrate in Figure 14. We suppose two uncertain possibilities for costs $c$ and $\bar{c}$ or the mean as the corresponding certain value of $c$. The certain program which maximizes the present value of net surplus is the broken line in Figure 14. The solid lines trace out the corresponding uncertain program which maximizes the expected present value of net surplus. Across $t_a$, the date at which the uncertainty is resolved, rent on the last ton extracted before $t_a$ equals expected rent on the first ton extracted beyond $t_a$. Thus there is zero intertemporal arbitrage possible.

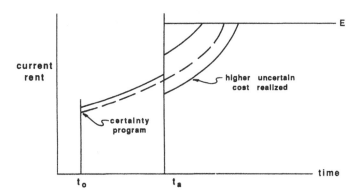

FIGURE 14   The uncertain future extraction costs induce higher initial prices and a reduction in the amount extracted relative to the case of certain future costs beyond $t_a$.

### Quality variation in the industry model

Declining quality of ore in the industry planning problem is often treated as a smoothly rising cost of extracting any positive quantity $Q(t)$. Formally this is done by introducing a shift in costs as the known stock is depleted. That is current extraction costs $C(Q(t), S(t))$ for extracting $Q(t)$ rise with $S(t)$ declining. The planner's problem is to select path $\{Q(t)\}$ subject to

$$\int_0^T Q(t)\, dt \le S(0)$$

to maximize

$$\int_0^T [B(Q(t)) - C(Q(t), S(t))]e^{-rt}\, dt$$

The Euler equation characterizing the optimal extraction path is

$$\frac{\overline{p(Q(t)) - C_Q(Q(t), S(t))}}{p(Q(t)) - C_Q(Q(t), S(t))} - \frac{C_s(Q(t), S(t))}{p(Q(t)) - C_Q(Q(t), S(t))} = r$$

Since $C_s < 0$, rent is rising at a rate less rapid than $r$. This is a revised Hotelling Rule. Note $-dC(q(t), S(t))/dS(t) \cong q(t)\Delta C_q(q(t), S(t))$. The term on the right is approximately a value of Ricardian or differential rent. We thus have a statement: "rental" income plus capital gains equal the interest rate multiplied by "price" of output, "price" being rent on the marginal ton. The end point condition is, for the case of $S(T) = 0$ or total exhaustion of the initial stock,

$$P(T) - C_Q(T) = \frac{B(Q(T)) - C(T)}{Q(T)}$$

which we have observed as marginal value of extracting $Q(T)$ equals average value at the terminal date. For the case of $S(T) > 0$ or economic exhaustion of the stock, one has the end point condition

$$p(Q(T)) - C_Q[Q(T), S(T)] = 0$$

or the marginal benefits of $Q(T)$ just equal marginal costs, and $Q(T) = 0$.

What about market equilibrium? Suppose many firms each hold a ton of ore, each of a slightly different quality. Will profit-maximizing, price-taking firms replicate the optimal planning extraction program? The answer is yes. Consider a discrete-time version of the problem.

We define $q(C)$ as the tons of ore of cost $C$ to extract and process. Then the size of the deposit is

$$S = \int_{\underline{C}}^{\bar{C}} q(Z) \, dZ$$

where $\underline{C}$ is the highest grade ore and $\bar{C}$ is the lowest grade. The total cost of extracting all of the ore at one point in time is

$$C(S) = \int_{\underline{C}}^{\bar{C}} Z q(Z) \, dZ$$

Consider a two period depletion strategy. The planner seeks to maximize

$$W = B(Q_1) - C(Q_1) + \left(\frac{1}{1+r}\right)\{B(Q_2) - C(Q_2)\}$$

by choice of $S$ where

$$Q_1 = \int_{\underline{C}}^{S} q(Z) \, dZ \quad \text{and} \quad Q_2 = \int_{S}^{\bar{C}} q(Z) \, d(Z),$$

and

$$C(Q_1) = \int_C^S Zq(Z)\,dZ \quad \text{and} \quad C(Q_2) = \int_S^{\bar{C}} Zq(Z)\,dZ$$

The first order condition is

$$(1+r)[p_1 - S] = [p_2 - S]$$

where $S$ is the cost of extracting and processing the marginal ton extracted in period 1 and the most intra-marginal ton in period 2. $p_i = dB/dQ_i$. With decentralized ownership to say each ton and price taking profit maximizing behaviour, this planning condition will clearly be minicked in the market. The owner of the marginal ton is indifferent between extracting in period 1 or in period 2. Intra marginal ton owners in period 1 are induced to extract their tons in period 1 and invest the proceeds of interest rate $r$. Those owners of tons with quality below or unit cost above $S$ will not be induced to extract in period 1. Intra marginal ton owners will receive a Ricardian or differential rent $S - Z$ for all $Z \le S$ on each ton with index or cost $Z$. Similarly in period 2, each ton owner will receive a Ricardian or differential rent equal to $P - Z$ for $Z \ge S$. There are then two sources of rent: rent arising from differences in quality (a static notion) and those arising from differences in the date which an identical ton is brought to market (an interest rate "wedge" or dynamic or Hotelling rent, often called a royalty.)

The stock size effect $C_s$ in the Euler equation above does not yield a market failure. Rather it represents a quality shift for an otherwise homogeneous unit of ore.

## Many certain deposits with distinct constant extraction costs

We consider the case of $n$ deposits each of known size $S_i$ and constant average extraction cost $c_i$. Herfindahl [39] first investigated this useful model and Nordhaus [69] applied it in a linear programming formulation to the long term analysis of world energy production and pricing.

An optimal planning solution which should be tracked by competitive markets involves

1. lower cost deposits developed before higher cost deposits, regardless of size

2. the pace of extraction being determined by resource rent rising at the rate of interest, and

3. no jumps in resource price along the path of prices for which rent per ton rises at a rate equal to the rate of interest

We sketch an optimal price profile given a demand schedule shifting, perhaps "in parallel," exogenously over time and a Backstop price B for the substitute competitively supplier. A demand curve shifting "in parallel" would be stationary over time.

The correct way to solve for the price profile in Figure 15 is to solve back from $T$ or to take the terminal rent a $T$ and let quantity rise from the high cost deposit as rent declines from $T$ as time moves toward the present. When $S_3$ is exhausted, there is a current price at $T_2$ to determine the terminal rent for deposit 2. Again rent declines as quantity supplied rises as time moves toward the present. When $S_2$ is exhausted, one proceeds to determine the optimal extraction program for deposit 1. The total interval $(0, T)$ is independent of calendar time. Thus the optimal profile can be slid back and forth until 0 is "the present".

We now consider a two deposit case in complete detail.

The two equilibrium conditions defining the optimal values of $T_1$

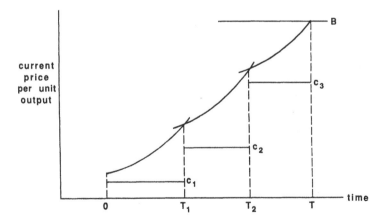

FIGURE 15 Profile of output price and rent for an output derived from three distinct progressively higher cost exhaustible sources (the Herfindahl model).

and $T$ are

$$\int_{T_1}^{T} f[(B - c_2)e^{-r(T-t)} + c_2]\, dt = S_2$$

$$\int_{0}^{T_1} f\big[((B - c_2)e^{-r(T-T_1)} + c_2 - c_1)e^{-r(T_1-t)} + c_1\big]\, dt = S_1$$

These yield differentials

$$\left[ f(B) + \int_{T_1}^{T} f'(\bullet)(-r)(B - c_2)e^{-r(T-t)}\, dt \right] dT$$

$$- f[(B - c_2)e^{-r(T-T_1)} + c_2]\, dT_1 = \left[ -\int_{T_1}^{T} f'(\bullet)[1 - e^{-r(T-t)}]\, dt \right] dc_2$$

$$\left[ \int_{0}^{T_1} f'(\bullet)(-r)(B - c_2)e^{-r(T-T_1)}e^{-r(T_1-t)}\, dt \right] dT$$

$$+ \left\{ f[(B - c_2)e^{-r(T-T_1)} + c_2] + \int_{0}^{T_1} f'(\bullet)(-r)(c_2 - c_1)e^{-r(T_1-t)}\, dt \right\} dT_1$$

$$= \left[ -\int_{0}^{T_1} f'(\bullet)e^{-r(T_1-t)}[1 - e^{-r(T-T_1)}]\, dt \right] dc_2$$

The determinant $D$ of the four terms on the left hand side above is positive since the sign pattern of the corresponding matrix is $\begin{bmatrix} + & - \\ + & + \end{bmatrix}$. In solving for $dT/dc_2$ by Cramer's Rule we have a system with sign pattern $\begin{vmatrix} + & - \\ + & + \end{vmatrix} \Big/ D$ which yields $dT/dc_2 > 0$. We solve for $dT_1/dc_2$ by Cramer's Rule and obtain after some manipulations

$$-(q(T)/D)[1 - e^{-r(T-T_1)}] \int_{0}^{T_1} f'(\bullet)e^{-r(T_1-t)}\, dt$$

$$+ (r/D)(B - c_2) \int_{0}^{T_1} f'(\bullet)e^{-r(T_1-t)}\, dt$$

$$\times \int_{T_1}^{T} f'(\bullet)[e^{-r(T-t)} - e^{-r(T-T_1)}]\, dt$$

which for $D$ and $-f'(\bullet)$ positive is positive or we obtain $dT/dc_2 > 0$.

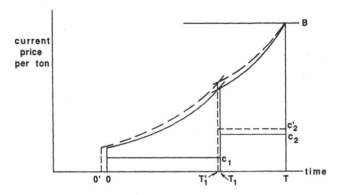

FIGURE 16 The broken line is the new price path after $c_2$ has risen slightly.

Running time in reverse, we illustrate these results in Figure 16. The broken line is the new price path after $c_2$ has risen slightly. One can obtain results in an analogous fashion for a rise in the interest rate $r$, an extraction cost $c_1$ and in the backstop price $B$. We sketch the new paths for each case in Figures 17, 18 and 19 respectively.

The recursive nature of the equilibrium system illustrated for two deposits with constant costs makes the $n > 2$ deposit case relatively easy to analyze. Comparative static results obtain with no ambiguity

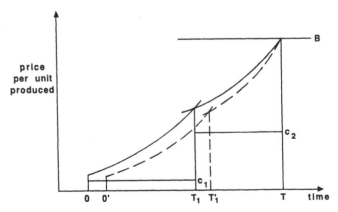

FIGURE 17 A rise in the interest rate $r$ results in the shorter extraction program indicated by the broken line.

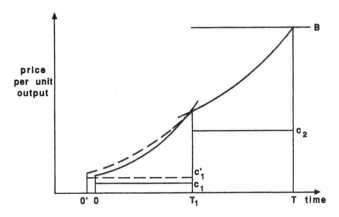

FIGURE 18  A rise in the extraction cost $c_1$ yields the new broken line path before $T_1$.

of sign for the general case. One only requires that the demand schedule $f(\cdot)$ be negatively sloped. See Hartwick [33] and Drury [21].

For deposits small in size and numerous, one can image a limiting case for the Herfindahl model in which a new higher cost deposit is brought into production at each instant of time. This model is in fact the Hotelling case for a stock steadily declining over time (see

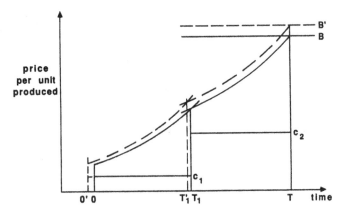

FIGURE 19  A rise in the backstop price $B$ lengthens the extraction profile to the broken line.

for example Levhari and Levitan [56]). Conversely, the Herfindahl model can approximate the more complicated case of continuously declining quality in industry or world supply. The Nordhaus [69] model can be interpreted as a Herfindahl model of world energy supply. We set out the basic Nordhaus linear programming model for the case of three future demand eras or periods and four sources of supply including a backstop technology in unlimited supply. Suppose each demand period is 50 years long. The quantity demanded in period $i$ is $\delta_i$ and the supply available from the source with extraction cost per ton $c_j$ is $S_j$. $c_4$ is the cost per unit with the backstop. The problem is to arrange sources or supplies from the different stocks to meet demands at minimum cost in present value terms. Let $x_{ji}$ be the amount of stock from $S_j$ used for demand $\delta_i$ in period $i$. We have then, select $x_{ji}$ ($i = 1, 2, 3, j = 1, 2, 3, 4$) non-negative subject to

$$\sum_j x_{ji} \geq \delta_i \qquad i = 1, 2, 3$$

$$\sum_i x_{ji} \leq S_j \qquad j = 1, 2, 3$$

$$\sum_i x_{4i} = \text{supply from the backstop}$$

to minimize

$$\sum_{j=1}^{4} x_{j1}c_j + \sum_{j=1}^{4} x_{j2}c_je^{-50r} + \sum_{j=1}^{4} x_{j3}c_je^{-100r}$$

For $\sum_{i=1}^{3} \delta_i > \sum_{j=1}^{3} S_j$, all sources including the backstop will be used. The dual variables or shadow prices on demands, $p_1$, $p_2$, $p_3$ and on supplies $\pi_1$, $\pi_2$, $\pi_3$ will vary systematically. For example, if $x_{11} > 0$, $p_1 - \pi_1 = c_1$ and if $x_{13} > 0$, $p_3 - \pi_1 = c_1e^{-100r}$. Since $p_3$ is a current price for a future period, it should be discounted to be made comparable with $p_1$. That is $p_1e^{100r} = p_3$ and we have rent per ton differing across demand periods by the rate of interst or discounted rate per ton, constant across demand periods. This is of course the Hotelling efficiency condition.

Diewert and Lewis [18] investigated the comparative dynamics of profit maximinzing programs in which terminal stock sizes were specified at the outset rather than a backstop price. They let the interest rate vary from period to period. Clear results were obtained only for the traditional case of a single stock being depleted, not for a multiple stock case in which extraction was pursed from many stocks simultaneously.

Does it ever make economic sense to exploit high cost deposits or low quality deposits before higher quality deposits? Certainly not in the Herfindahl model which is partial equilibrium. Lewis [58] addressed this question in a simple dynamic general equilibrium model after it was raised by Kemp and Long [50]. The question turns on whether once some part of a stock below ground is transformed into a stock or asset above ground, does it make sense to accumulate such stocks above ground? Lewis established that as long as such above-ground stocks are currently *useful* for production, it never pays to extract higher cost deposits before lower cost deposits. The usefulness criterion was implicit in the multiple deposit model of Solow and Wan [87].

Clearly if there are positive set-up costs for each deposit in the Herfindahl model as in Hartwick, Kemp, and Long [35] the variable costs indicating deposit quality do not necessarily signal which deposit is either lower cost of higher "quality". In such cases it may well be appropriate to extract a low quality (high variable cost) deposit with low set-up costs before a higher quality (low variable extraction cost) deposit with higher set-up costs.

In the classic Gray model of the resource extracting firm, though the stock is known and is homogeneous, extraction costs vary with quantity currently "mined". Thus if output price rose in response to an uncertain shock, quantity extracted would jump up and the average extraction cost per ton extracted would *decline* for the well-behaved case of ever-rising marginal extraction costs. In this sense lower "quality" quantitites can be observed extracted after higher "quality" (lower average extraction costs) in an optimal extraction program (see also Krautkraemer [52]).

### Asset equilibrium and two market failures

An optimal extraction program with stock $S$ has an optimal value

$$W = \int_0^T [B(Q^*(t)) - C(Q^*(t))]e^{-rt}\, dt$$

where $\{Q^*(t)\}$ is an optimized extraction program. (We will suppress the * from now on.) $W$ can be expressed as

$$W = W(T_1, S_1) + e^{-rT_1}W(T - T_1, S - S_1)$$

where $W(T_1, S_1)$ and $W(T - T_1, S - S_1)$ are themselves values corresponding to optimized extraction programs. Since $W$ is optimized, it satisfies $dW/dT_1 = 0$ or

$$\frac{dW(T_1, S)}{dT_1} - re^{-rT_1}W(T - T_1, S - S_1) = 0$$

where

$$\frac{dW(T_1, S)}{dT_1} = B(Q(T_1)) - C(Q(T_1)) - [p(Q(T_1)) - C_Q(Q(T_1))]Q(T_1).$$

(See Appendix II.) We have then the *basic asset equilibrium condition*:

$$B(Q(T_1)) - C(Q(T_1)) - [p(Q(T_1)) - C_Q(Q(T_1))]Q(T_1)$$
$$= W(T - T_1, S - S_1)r \qquad 0 \le T_1 \le T$$

This is a special case of the basic intertemporal efficiency condition discussed at length in Dorfman, Samuelson, and Solow [20; Chapter 12]; special because *economic depreciation or capital loss* takes the form $[p(Q(T)) - C_Q(Q(T))]Q(T)$. Extraction of $Q(T)$ induces a capital loss on $W(T)$ equal to the current dynamic rent or royalty associated with $Q(T)$. This holds for all $T$ along an optimal extraction program.

In deriving the basic asset equilibrium condition one also obtains an $r\%$ rule for quantities for models with homogeneous stocks, constant interst rates, and stationary demand and cost functions. This "rule" is

$$\frac{\dot{q}}{q} = \left\{ \frac{h'(q(t))}{qh''(q(t))} - \frac{1}{r\displaystyle\int_0^t \frac{h''(q(t))}{h(q(x))}e^{-r}(t - x)\,dx} \right\}r$$

where $h(q) = B(q(t)) - cq(t)$. For a linear, negatively sloped demand schedule and constant unit costs of extraction

$$\dot{q} = -q_0 r/(1 - e^{-rt})$$

where $q_0$ is the initial quantity extracted along a surplus maximizing program.

Our basic depletion or asset equilibrium condition $h(q(t)) - q(t)h'(q(t)) = rW(t)$ can be used to establish the market failure in Hotelling models associated with set-up costs (Hartwick, Kemp and Long [35]) and with stock size uncertainty (Hartwick [34]).

(i) *Set-up costs* Consider the case of two identical deposits in a Hotelling framework, each now with set-up costs $K_i(i = 1, 2)$. In the maximization of the present value of net surplus, the first order condition defining the optimal date $T_2$ for opening the second deposit is

$$B(q(T_2^-)) - cq(T_2^-) - \{p(q(T_2^-)) - c\}q(T_2^-) = rW(T - T_2, S_2) - K_2.$$

From our analysis above, we have

$$rW(T - T_2, S_2) = B(q(T_2^+)) - cq(T_2^+) - \{p(q(T_2^+)) - c\}q(T_2^+).$$

Thus for $K_2 > 0$ it follows that $q(T_2^-) > q(T_2^+)$ or price jumps down at the date the second deposit is opened. (Larger $K_2$ makes the second deposit less desirable and this is compensated for by prolonging the time over which the first deposit is depleted.) Since the deposits are physically identical, a jump down in price makes the rent per ton on the second deposit lower than on the first deposit. In a market situation, the owner of each deposit would demand to be first in the sequence of deposits, an impossibility. Hence the market failure associated with set-up costs in the Hotelling framework.

(ii) *Stock size uncertainty.* Suppose there is a deposit with either 100 tons or 150 tons in a Hotelling framework. Let $\pi_1$ be the probability that there is 100 tons and $\pi_2$ be the probability of 150 tons. $\pi_1 + \pi_2 = 1$ and $0 < \pi_1 < 1$. Extraction proceeds and after 100 tons are extracted it becomes apparent whether there are 50 more tons or not. Let $T_1$ be the date at which 100 tons are extracted. Beyond $T_1$, the problem is certain—one of two branches will be followed—one with 0 tons or 50 tons. Before $T_1$, extraction satisfies the $r\%$ rule but the initial quantity must be determined. $T_1$ satisfies the following analogies to the asset equilibrium condition:

$$h(q(T_1)) - q(T_1)h'(q(T_1)) = \pi_1 \cdot 0 + \pi_2 rW(T^{50} - T_1, 50)$$

where $W(T^{50} - T_1, 50)$ is the optimized surplus along the terminal branch with 50 tons. Our asset equilibrium condition indicates that

$$rW(T^{50} - T_1, 50) = h(q(T_1^+)) - q(T_1^+)h'(q(T_1^+)).$$

Thus the optimal $T_1$ (or initial quantity) satisfies the condition: net "income" $(h(q(T_1)) - q(T_1)h'(q(T_1))$ before $T_1$ is a convex combination of net "income" after $T_1$. It does *not* satisfy the condition $p(q(T_1)) - c = \pi_1 \cdot (p(0) - c) + \pi_2 \cdot (p(q(T^+)) - c)$ which is a market equilibrium condition (the zero intertemporal arbitrage condition). Hence the market failure associated with extraction involving endogenous revelation of stock size.

## Monopoly extraction

The monopoly problem has the single extractor seller taking the market demand schedule as his or her average revenue schedule. Marginal revenue plays the role which output price played in the social planning problem. With stock size effects or quality decline, the monopolist's problem is: select $\{Q(t)\}$ to maximize

$$\pi = \int_0^T [p(Q(t)) \cdot Q(t) - C(Q(t); S(t))]e^{-rt} \, dt$$

subject to

$$\int_0^T Q(t) \, dt \leq S(0).$$

Where $p(Q(t))$ is the inverse demand schedule and $S(t)$ is the stock remaining at date $t$. $C(.)$ is increasing and concave in $Q(t)$ and decreasing in $S(t)$. $p(.)$ is declining in $Q(t)$ for non-negative values.

The Euler equation for this problem is

$$\frac{\overline{MR(Q(t)) - C_Q(t)}}{MR(Q(t)) - C_Q(t)} - \frac{C_S(t)}{MR(Q(t)) - C_Q(t)} = r$$

where $MR(t) = d[p(Q(t)) \cdot Q(t)]/dQ(t)$ and $C_S$ and $C_Q$ are partial derivatives of $C(.)$ with respect to $S(t)$ and $Q(t)$ respectively.

For the case of a stock of homogeneous quality and constant

extraction costs $c$ per ton, the Euler equation is

$$\frac{\dot{\overline{MR(Q(t))-c}}}{MR(Q(t))-c}=r$$

or marginal revenue net of extraction cost per ton rises at the rate of interest. The end-point condition defining an optimal extraction program is

$$p(Q(T))-c=[MR(Q(T))-c]$$

or average equals marginal value of $Q(T)$ at $T$ which implies $Q(T)\to0$ as $t\to T$.

Clearly with quality declining as the stock is depleted, marginal revenue net of marginal cost rises at a rate less than $r$.

Hotelling [43] pointed out that for the case of the demand schedule linear in price, the monopolist would take longer to extract the same stock as would a planner or the competitive industry analogue. Examples worked out in Hartwick and Olewiler [36, Chapters 3 and 4] indicate that the extraction time of the competitors would be half that of the monopolist for a given deposit. Hotelling suggested that the monopolist was the "friend of the conservationist". However this result turns on the linearity of demand. For the case of demand with constant elasticity and zero costs of extraction

$$\frac{\dot{p}(t)}{p(t)}=\frac{\dot{MR}(t)}{MR(t)}$$

or the monopolist and the competitive industry would extract at the same rate (Sweeney [93] and Stiglitz [91]). See also Lewis, Matthews, Burness [60] for other cases.)

## 4. THE BACKSTOP AND OLIGOPOLY

### Introduction

We observed that exhaustible stock of type $i$ could be replaced by a substitute stock of type $j$, oil by coal for example. The ideal substitute can be produced at constant cost indefinitely, oil by say fusion power at some future date. Such a constant cost substitute has come to be known as the backstop supply source. Here we consider how different ownership arrangements for the backstop affect current extraction of the exhausting stock. Suppose oil producers developed fusion power and stood ready to implement the backstop. What is a welfare maximizing implementation scheme? We touch on these sorts of issues below. Games between current stock owners and backstop developers can arise.

We then consider non-price taking owners of portions of stock and how competition among them affects extraction paths. Scenarios with a dominant seller and fringe sellers are taken up. We also examine extraction paths among competitors when one extractor can draw down a competitor's stock as a result of underground seepage.

## The backstop supply and extraction programs

The modern view of potentially exhaustible stocks is that the resources from such stocks will ultimately be substituted for by a product producible into the indefinite future. Power derived from stocks of hydrocarbons will be produced from fusion power, for example. Such substitutes have been labelled backstop technologies. Attention is then directed to optimal programs of exhausting the stocks in the face of future substitutes or in the face of backstop technologies. In simple problems one might ask how the price of the backstop affects the depletion path of a stock. In more complicated cases one might ask how uncertainty about the date or cost of the backstop affects the depletion path of a stock. One might turn to strategic interactions between developers of the substitute and owners of the stock of resources. Complications can be multiplied. We turn to some representative cases.

i) Competitive resource extractors with a homogeneous stock of known size available at price $E$.

In this case the socially optimal program is to exhaust the stock as rent rises at the rate of interest at the rate such that as price rises to $E$, exhaustion is complete. The market will replicate such a program.

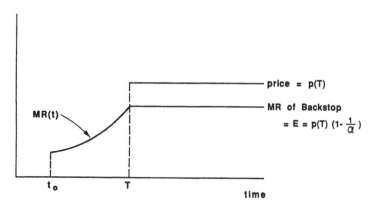

FIGURE 20 The monopoly resource stock owner owns the backstop. Stock is exhausted at date $T$.

ii) A monopolist resource extractor with a homogeneous stock of known size facing a known backstop with unit cost $E$ which the monopolist owns.

In this case $MR(t) - MC(t)$ should rise at the rate of interest, extraction proceeding as a consequence, so that exhaustion occurs at the instant the revenue from the sale of resources equals the marginal revenue from using the substitute. Monopoly profits are maximized. We illustrate in Figure 20. In Figure 20, exhaustion of the finite stock is planned to occur at $T$. For the demand schedule $q = p^{-\alpha}$ $\alpha > 1$, the marginal revenue of the backstop is $E = p(T)\left[1 - \dfrac{1}{\alpha}\right]$. Now

$$q(t) = \left(\frac{\alpha}{\alpha - 1}\right)^{-\alpha} E^{-\alpha} e^{(r/\alpha)(T-t)}$$

where $T$ satisfies

$$S = \int_0^T q(t)\, dt = -\frac{\alpha}{r}\left(\frac{\alpha}{\alpha - 1}\right)^{-\alpha} E^{-\alpha}[1 - e^{(r/\alpha)T}],$$

yielding

$$q(t) = \left[\frac{rS}{\alpha} + \left(\frac{\alpha}{\alpha - 1}\right)^{-\alpha} E^{-\alpha}\right] e^{-rt/\alpha} \qquad 0 \le t \le T$$

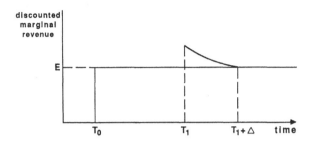

FIGURE 21 The monopoly resource stock owner faces a competitively supplied backstop. $MR(t)$ jumps up to the backstop price at $T_1$ and the remaining stock is exhausted between $T_1$ and $T_1 + \Delta$ with current $MR$ constant at the backstop price.

We sketch the schedule of marginal revenue rising at rate $r$ in Figure 20. Exhaustion of $S$ occurs at the moment the marginal revenue of the last ton equals the marginal revenue from using the backstop at marginal cost equals marginal revenue $E$.

iii) A monopolist resource extractor with a homogeneous stock of known size $S$ facing a known backstop controlled by a planner (or competitive group) who supplies the substitute at price $E$.

The case is novel because the monopolist maximizes profit by extracting over two phases—the first in which marginal revenue minus marginal cost rises at the rate of interest and the second in which current marginal revenue remains constant at level $E$, the price at which the backstop or substitute is available. We illustrate in Figure 21. Costs of extraction are zero. At $T_1$ in Figure 21, current marginal revenue to the resource supplier jumps from $(1 + (1/\epsilon))E$ where $\epsilon$ is the elasticity of demand to $E$. The length of the second interval is $\delta$ satisfying $Ee^{-r\delta} = (1 + (1/\epsilon))E$ or at $T_1$ the monopolist's discounted marginal revenue from his or her final quantity extracted equals the marginal revenue of the ton extracted just before $T_1$.

The Gilbert–Goldman [30] paradox has $q(T_0)$ in the model here below that in the model above when the backstop is controlled by the monopolist-extractor. The paradox is: potential entry by a competitor (the backstop supplier) induces a higher initial price from the monopolist currently supplying the commodity. We illustrate the paradox in Figure 22.

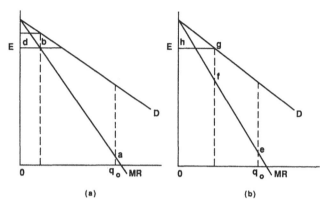

FIGURE 22 In (a) the backstop is owned by the monopoly resource producer and *abd* is the marginal revenue schedule. In (b) the backstop is competitively supplied at price *E* and *efgh* is the marginal revenue schedule.

In case (ii) the current time marginal revenue schedule followed is *abd* in Figure 22(a). For the case (iii), in which the planner provides the substitute at price *c*, the marginal revenue schedule followed is *efgh* with the jump occurring at *fg*, in Figure 22(b). The Gilbert–Goldman paradox is that in some cases the price at $q_0$ in Figure 22(b) is above that in Figure 22(a) or a competitively supplied potential substitute induces a higher price by the monopolist compared with the situation in which the monopolist resource owner also owns the substitute production process. The size of the stock controlled by the monopolist is of course the same in both situations.

Gallini, Lewis, and Ware [29] developed a simple game in which the planner with the substitute technology (the backstop) attempts to induce the monopolist resource supplier to deplete his earlier stock in a socially optimal, for consumers, fashion. The rules are that at $t_0$, the planner announces a specific future date at which the backstop will be implemented or "turned on" with the substitute being supplied at price *c*. This threat is credible and the monopolist arranges to deplete his stock $S_0$ in response to this announcement. There turn out to be three time periods within which the crucial date announced induces qualitatively similar behavior from the resource owning monopolist. Any date announced between $t_0$ and

$T_1$ induces the monopolist to follow the extraction plan as case (iii) above. For announcement dates between $T_1$ and $T_2$, the monopolist extracts some stock with price rising above $c$ and then some subsequently at $c$. Beyond $T_2$, the stock is exhausted precisely on the date of the substitute taking over.

What is the best announcement date, given these three types of response? It turns out that a date between $T_1$ and $T_2$ is optimal for consumers. This is true even if, at zero cost, the backstop implementation date could be moved forward in time. Implementation should be deferred well beyond $t_0$ even though it could be done at $t_0$. This is a binding contract game in which the owner of the backstop makes a credible first move (the announcement of the implementation date).

The game between substitute producers and a resource cartel above turned on a credible commitment to "turn on" the substitute (e.g., fusion power) on the date specified at the outset and at the cost or price specified. Suppose however resource producers interact with each other period by period. For example, the substitute producer can install productive capacity period by period to squeeze the market sought simultaneously by the resource producer. Lewis, Lindsay and Ware [59] investigate competitive interactions in such a setting. In their model, the resource cartel plans to exhaust its stock in three periods. A planner arranges a capacity expansion plan for the substitute. The cartel resource suppliers seek to maximize the present value of profit and the planner seeks to maximize net consumer surplus for the users of the commodity. Three scenarios are compared. In one scenario, the cartel commits itself to an extraction program at the outset, period by period and the planner–investor responds. In another scenario, the planner commits him or herself to a capacity expansion sequence and the cartel responds. In the third scenario, neither makes a multi-period commitment. The inquiry is made tractable by the use of quadratic benefit functions and linear decision rules. Lewis *et al.* discover that the cartel can be harmed by credibly precommitting to an extraction-sales path over the three periods examined. Also they indicate that private agents cannot be expected to arrange investment in capacity to take into account the benfits of strategy for consumers and thus see a role for government in the capacity expansion program. It is of course reassuring that these attractive prescriptions emerge from a carefully executed analysis of the cartel-substitute producer game.

## Uncertainty in the date of arrival of the backstop

The implementation of the backstop technology may turn on a technical discovery so that the date it "arrives" may be uncertain, though its cost may not be. Fusion power as a substitute source of energy has these characteristics, in part. Dasgupta and Stiglitz [13] examined a model in which a known stock is to be optimally depleted by a planner in the face of the competititve supply of a substitute, the backstop, arriving at an uncertain date but certain cost or price. The backstop can arrive at a date in the continuum of possible future dates. Demand is asymptotic to the price axis so the possible non-arrival of the backstop over the infinite future does not raise formal problems. Consumers can always make do with the finite stock. Of interest is the Hotelling Rule associated with this model, that is the time path of rent.

At each interval $(t, t + \theta)$ there are two possibilities. Either the backstop does not arrive and price (equal to rent in the absence of extraction costs) rises at the rate of interest, i.e.,

$$\frac{P_{t+\theta} - P_t}{P_t} = r_t\theta$$

which for $\theta \to 0$ becomes $\frac{\dot{p}_t}{p_t} = r$ or the backstop *does* arrive in $(t, t + \theta)$.

The probability of the backstop arriving in $(t, t + \theta)$ is $\lambda_t\theta$ where $\lambda_t$ is the instantaneous probability. Given its arrival, the planner sets a new price $\hat{p}_t(S_t)$ as a function of the remaining stock $S_t$ so as to just exhaust the $S_t$ as price rises to the price or cost of the backstop. This $\hat{p}_t(S_t)$ will generally be lower than the current price. Thus there will be a jump down in price on the date the backstop has been perfected. This capital loss on a ton will be $p_t - \hat{p}(S_t)$ occurring with probability $\lambda_t\theta$. Meanwhile without the backstop arriving in that interval, there will be the capital gain $dp_t$ with probability $(1 - \lambda_t\theta)$ for a ton left unextracted. Thus expected profit over the interval $(t, t + \theta)$ is $-\lambda_t\theta(p_t - \hat{p}(S_t)) + (1 - \lambda_t\theta) dp_t$ for an unextracted ton. For an extracted ton, the profit should be $r_t\theta p_t$. Given risk neutral extractors, these respective profits should be equal. Taking limits as $\theta \to 0$ yields

$$\frac{\dot{p}_t}{p_t} = r_t + (-\hat{p}(S_t)/p_t)\lambda_t$$

which is the basic arbitrage or Hotelling rule. Since $p_t - \hat{p}(S_t) > 0$, we have the result that uncertainty in the date of the backstop implies that uncertainty in the date of the backstop implies rent (price) rising faster than the rate of interest; extraction is sped up.

Note that to a first approximation for $\lambda_t = 0$ or there is no chance of the backstop arriving, $\frac{\dot{p}_t}{p_t} = r$. For the special case $\hat{p}(S_t) = 0$ or the remaining stock has no value, $\dot{p}_t/p_t = r + \lambda_t$ or uncertainty acts as a simple risk premium on $r$.

### Oligopoly and extraction programs

Non-competitive behavior of agents or non-price taking behavior results in extraction paths departing from those under competitive conditions. Monopoly ownership of a stock is a relatively straightforward "counter-case" to the competitive or Hotelling and related cases for the industry. (Hotelling in fact worked out the monopoly stock owner case in his original article.) We considered the monopolized industry in the section on the industry. Another straightforward variation on the competitive model is a symmetric oligopoly in which each of $n$ owners of stock take the extraction paths of the $n-1$ sellers as parametric and arrange their own extraction to maximize discounted profit in the "residual market". A variant of this model is one in which a feedback equilibrium is sought, a solution in which each firm's action is conditioned on the *current* market situation and future conditions. This differs from the closed loop solutions in which each firm's optimal plan is determined at time zero and is followed to the end of the program.

Another genre of oligopoly models have essentially two agents, a dominant supplier and a fringe group of suppliers acting competitively. These models have been developed to analyze OPEC (a cartel oil supplier) versus the West (a fringe group practicing price-taking behavior). These models have three modes of solution:

the fringe extracting alone before the cartel, the cartel extracting alone after the fringe has exhausted its holding of stock and an interval over which the fringe and cartel simultaneous extract, the cartel taking the fringe extraction program as given (a Cournot assumption). Of interest here is the possibility of dynamic inconsistency programs which become suboptimal to an agent after a passage of time. A feedback solution is required for this dynamic inconsistency to not arise.

Current extraction programs are conditioned on the nature of the backstop. If the owner of the backstop has market power, he or she can influence the actions of the resource extractors. This opens up another class of oligopoly models. Finally non-competitive considerations must be recognized in cases of oil seepage from one holding to another, a case of imperfect property rights. We will examine such "common property" models of resource extraction.

## Cournot oligopoly with $n$ extracting firms

If each of $n > 2$ sellers can compute the optimal quantity schedule of the remaining $n - 1$ extracting agents, then each agent can act as a monopoloist for the demand remaining. This would give us $n$ quasi-monopolistic extractors, each taking the $n - 1$ quantity programs of the other sellers as given and maximizing profits within this context. This is a dynamic Cournot oligopoly. With $n$ identical sellers the total output will be depleted more rapidly than for the pure monopoly and more slowly that for the pure competitive situation for the case of a linear industry demand schedule, constant extraction costs per ton and homogeneous stocks (Loury [62]). Each agent maximizes his or her present value of profits making use of the residual demand schedule defined at each point in time. The residual demand schedule is defined at date $t$ by taking the industry demand and netting out the quantities delivered or extracted by the $n - 1$ other extractors at that date. This is the open loop approach to oligopoly and a two firm three period example is set out two sections below.

## A dominant seller and a competitive fringe

A natural asymmetry in the Loury model of $n$ "quantity-taking" resource extracting firms is to assume that $n - 1$ firms constitute a

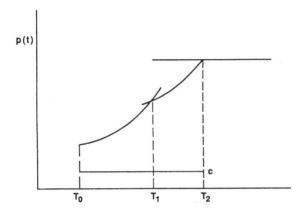

FIGURE 23   Between $T_0$ and $T_1$ the fringe supplies its stock and $p(t) - c$ rises at rate $r$. Between $T_1$ and $T_2$ the monopolist supplies its stock and $MR(t) - c$ rises at rate $r$.

price taking competitive fringe and the other firm acts as a quantity taking monopolist. This is a simple formulation of the idea of a resource extracting cartel and a competitive fringe group of extractors. We pursue this case introduced by Salant [75].

For the case of a fringe group and the monopolist with identical constant average extraction costs $c$, and given an industry demand schedule increasing in price, $p(t) - c$ rising at a rate of interest leaves the monopolist's $MR(t) - c$ rising faster than $r$. Hence when the fringe is motivated to supply stock as $p(t) - c$ rises at rate $r$, the monopolist is motivated to "horde" his or her stock in the ground since the capital gain per ton exceeds the alternate rate of return, $r\%$ per instant of time. We illustrate the industry equilibrium in Figure 23.

Consider the monopolist with a slightly higher extraction cost, $c + \epsilon$. In Figure 23, interval $(T_1, T_2)$ will be longer and the price at $T_1$ slightly higher. This will in turn lead to the interval $(T_0, T_1)$ being lengthened. The key point is that for the monopolist's cost higher, price over its interval of extraction will rise more slowly than before the price rise. The possibility emerges of the monopolist selling some stock jointly over an interval with the fringe in order to push down the fringe's initial price and speed the fringe's extraction to exhaustion. We are still in an environment of quantity-taking by the monopolist (a Cournot assumption). For the fringe, $p(t) - c$ will be rising at the rate $r$ and for the monopolist $\widehat{MR}(t) - c_M$ will over the same interval be rising at rate $r$. We use the notation $\widehat{MR}$ to denote the current marginal revenue to the monopolist defined for the industry demand net of the current quantity extracted and sold by the fringe. $c_M$ is now the monopolist's constant average extraction cost. Ulph [94] (see Newbery [68]) computed an instructive Cournot optimal program for the monopolist and fringe for certain respective initial stock holdings $S_F$ and $S_M$ and costs $c_F$ and $c_M$ ($c_M > c_F$), where subscript $F$ indicates fringe and $M$ indicates the monopolist. The monopolist's discounted profits were maximized by selling some stock over an inteval in which $p(t) - c_F$ was rising at rate $r$ but not $MR(t) - c_M$ or $\widehat{MR}(t) - c_M$. The monopolist was able to drive down the fringe's initial price and speed the fringe to exhaust its stock in so doing. We illustrate the Ulph [94] example in Figure 24.

The fringe acts as a price taking group in the solution in Figure 24, and the monopolist as a quantity taker. At $T_0$ each has maximum discounted profit given these competitive modes. However at $T_1$ it is in the monopolist's interest to renege on his announced optimal program. Since at $T_1$, the fringe has exhausted

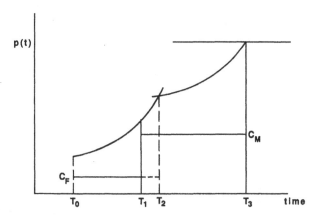

FIGURE 24   The fringe exhausts its stock between $T_0$ and $T_1$. The monopolist committed itself to the price path set out between $T_1$ and $T_3$ back at $T_0$ but given the exhaustion of the fringe at $T_1$ would wish to deviate beyond $T_1$ from its previous commitment.

its stock, the monopolist can act as a pure monopolist and let his or her price jump up so that between $T_1$ and termination of the program $MR(t) - c_M$ rises at rate $r$. This reneging action denotes *dynamic inconsistency*. The extraction program which is optimal at $T_0$ does not remain optimal as it is followed. A different solution concept is required in order to rule out this type of sub-optimizing or inconsistent behavior. In a *feedback solution*, each competitor reoptimizes period by period to the end of the program as in Levhari and Mirman [57] and Lewis, Lindsay and Ware [59].

## Oligopoly under alternative solution concepts

In the open loop (pre-commitment) solution, each extracting agent has his or her marginal revenue less marginal cost rising at the rate of interest. Each has the other extractors' quantity paths as given or parametric. Consider a 3 period, two firm case. (We assume that 3 periods are optimal for firm 1 to extract his or her stock and 2 periods are optimal for firm 2.) Firm 1's objective function is

$$Z_1 = \pi_1(Q_1(1), \bar{Q}_2(1)) + \beta\pi_1(Q_1(2), \bar{Q}_2(2)) + \beta^2\pi_1(S_1(1) - Q_1(2))$$

where $\pi_1 = p(Q_1 + \bar{Q}_2) \cdot Q_1 - C(Q_1)$ without time subscripts. $p(.)$ is the inverse industry demand curve and $C(Q_1)$ is firm 1's extraction cost function. $S_1$ is firm 1's initial stock. $\beta = 1/(1 + r)$. Terms for firm 2 are defined analogously.

Maximizing $Z$, by choice of $Q_1(1)$ and $Q_1(2)$ yields marginal revenue net of marginal cost rising at rate $r$. We have two equations in $Q_1(1)$ and $Q_1(2)$.

Firm 2's objective function is

$$Z_2 = \pi_2(Q_2(1), \bar{Q}_1(1)) + \beta\pi_2(S_2 - Q_2(1), \bar{Q}_1(2)).$$

Maximizing $Z_2$ by choice of $Q_2(1)$ yields marginal revenue net of marginal cost to firm 2 rising at rate $r$. If we combine the single first order condition for firm 2 maximizing profits with the two for firm 1, we have 3 simultaneous equations, $Q_1(1)$, $Q_1(2)$, and $Q_2(1)$. This is the solution to the oligopoly approach in considerable detail.

In the feedback solution to this oligopoly problem, firm 2 proceeds exactly as above but firm 1 condition's its choice of $Q_1(1)$ on the optimal value of $Q_1(2)$ selected to maximize

$$\pi_1(Q_1(2), \bar{Q}_2(2) + \beta\pi_1(S_1 - Q_1(1) - Q_1(2)).$$

Given $Q_1(2)$ optimally selected above, we can solve $Q_1(1)$ as a function of $Q_1(2)$. This yields a new problem. Maximize by choice of $Q_1(2)$,

$$Z_1 = \pi_1(Q_1((1), Q_1(2)), \bar{Q}_2(1)) + \beta\pi_1(Q_1(2), \bar{Q}_2(2))$$
$$+ \beta^2\pi_1(S_1 - Q_1((1), Q_1(2)) - Q_1(2))$$

The feedback solution is then two equations in $Q_1(2)$ and $Q_2(1)$. For firm 1, marginal revenue net of marginal cost no longer rises at the rate of interest in the first two periods.

Eswaran ad Lewis [25; Table 1] contains a numerical example like the one above but with six periods over which firm 1 is active and four over which firm 2 is active. In the open loop solution firm 1's initial output is lower than in the feedback solution. For firm 2, the opposite is true. Firm 1's profits are higher in the feedback or perfect equilibrium and firm 2's are lower. These results conform with our intuition. (Esweran and Lewis used a linear demand schedule, zero extraction costs and firm 1's initial stock twice that of firm 2's.)

With a constant elasticity of demand, demand schedule and each firm's extraction costs zero, the solutions are the same for the feedback or perfect equilibrium concept and the open loop or precommitment solution concept. Eswaran and Lewis derive an elegant rule for this specification, namely, each firm depletes its current stock by a time-invariant fraction period by period and the horizon is infinite. Furthermore this oligopoly solution is the same as the socially optimal solution since industry price rises at the rate of interest for the case of all firms identical. With stock sizes affecting extraction costs, the solutions are different under the alternative equilibrium concepts. Newbery [68] reports on a different feedback solution concept used to rule out dynamic inconsistency. Details have not been published.

### Oligopoly with imperfect property rights for stocks

Resources such as oil and gas occur in pools and are often exploited by distinct, competing extracting firms. There is a property rights imperfection. If firm $i$ extracts more slowly than all other firms it will in the end extract less than every other firm. Potential stock extracted by firm $i$ will be extracted and sold by other firms. To focus on the property rights-seepage problem alone, we can envisage the pool as a single tank of oil with $N$ taps distributed around the base of the tank. With each firm acting in a Cournot fashion, will in the symmetric case, the aggregate rate of depletion exceed the socially optimal rate? Intuitively one envisages a race in which each firm tries to prevent the $N-1$ other firms from pre-empting some of its potential stock. However Kemp and Long [51] discovered that for the open loop approach and symmetric firms, there was no departure from the socially optimal extraction rate when property rights imperfections (seepage) exist. Eswaran and Lewis [24] pointed out that under a feedback or perfect equilibrium concept, there would indeed by a speeding up of aggregate extraction caused by property right imperfections.

The case Eswaran and Lewis investigated involved each of $N$ identical firms with zero extraction costs and a constant elasticity industry demand schedule

$$p = Q^{-\alpha} \qquad 0 < \alpha < 1$$

where $Q$ is aggregate current output from the $N$ firms. Seepage is specified in the following equation of motion for firm $i$'s current stock:

$$S_t^i = (S_{t-1}^i - q_{t-1}^i) - \left(\frac{N-1}{N}\right)(S_{t-1}^i - q_{t-1}^i)k$$

$$+ \frac{k}{N} \sum_{j \neq i} S_{t-1}^j - q_{t-1}^j \qquad 0 \leq k \leq 1$$

where $S_t^i$ is firm $i$'s stock at period $t$

$q_t^i$ is firm $i$'s quantity extracted in period $t$

$k$ is a property rights parameter. $k = 0$ implies private property (no seepage) and $k = 1$ implies if ton $h$ is not extracted by firm $i$ this period, it will be added to the stocks of all other firms next period.

Backward induction established that at each date firm $i$ is maximizing

$$p_t q_t^i + \beta v_{t+1}^i$$

where

$$\beta \equiv 1/(1+r)$$

and

$$v^i_{t+1} = \frac{1 + Y/\psi}{1 + Y} p_{t+1} S^i_{t+1}$$

and

$$Y = \beta^{1/\alpha} \gamma^{1/\alpha} \psi^{1/\alpha}, \qquad \gamma = \frac{1 + \beta\gamma\delta^{1-\alpha}}{(1+\delta)^{1-\alpha}}, \qquad \delta = (\beta\gamma\psi)^{1/\alpha}$$

and

$$\psi = \frac{N(1-k) + k - \alpha}{N - \alpha}.$$

Of note is that $\psi = 1$ when $k = 0$ or perfect property rights are in effect. Thus for a private property regime, firm $i$'s future value of an extraction program is simple rent (price here) times future remaining stock.

Now $\frac{d\psi}{dk} = -N + 1 < 0$ which establishes that imperfect property rights imply $v^i_{t+1} > p_{t+1} S^i_{t+1}$. As $k$ increases (increased commonness of common property) aggregate extraction speeds up or price (rent) rises more rapidly in a further departure above the socially optimal rate $r$. Since price (rent) is rising faster than rate $r$, the firm is inclined to defer extraction according to the basic arbitrage principle but if it followed this rule the $N - 1$ other firms would appropriate firm $i$'s stock by seepage. Imperfect property rights ($k > 0$) does then induce a race to deplete the stock, an orderly race in the symmetric case however with the speed up of extraction varying directly with the value of $k$.

There is a paradox in these formal models. If extraction cost is zero, the complete pool could be extracted and divided equally among the $N$ symmetric competitors. Property rights imperfections would vanish at zero cost! Sinn [79] takes this paradox seriously and introduces storage costs in order to rule out the above elimination of property rights imperfections. Under two different types of competitive behavior (both open loop), Sinn establishes that commonness of property rights leads to aggregate extraction more rapid than is socially optimal.

## 5. EXPLORATION AND TAXATION

### Introduction

A rational agent explores at an intensity such that the marginal cost of a little more effort equals the expected marginal payoff from the extra effort. However when property rights on discoveries are imperfect or the organization of search is chaotic one expects much effort in exploration to be wasted or at least to exceed some sensible level. An extreme version of this argument is that the total costs of search may be very close to the average total payoff. In this case expected payoff is said to be dissipated by excessive search activity. We address some of these matters below. With decentralized exploration, agent $i$'s success can be agent $j$'s misfortune since additions to known stocks inevitably lower current prices. This spillover could be expected to affect the pace of exploration in total. Information spillovers lead to "gold rushes." If discoverer $i$ cannot realize or claim completely the value of his or her discovery, others rush in to free ride on $i$'s discovery by claiming part of the discovery for themselves.

Taxation affects the pace of exploration and the "tilt" of extraction programs. We report on these matters after we consider exploration in some detail. A tax which leaves an extraction program unchanged is said to be neutral and this neutrality concept serves as a benchmark for some of our analysis.

### The firm exploring under certainty

A straightforward extension of the basic model of the resource extracting firm is to add a second source of ore besides the known stock $S(0)$. Suppose there is a homogeneous long finite strip of land of area $R$ concealing minerals in the amount of "$a$" per unit land. Area $\Delta R$ can be explored at cost $X(\Delta R)$ revealing $a \Delta R$ of ore. This ore can be extracted at cost $C(a \Delta R)$ and sold at exogenously given price $p$.

Clearly the present value of profit will be maximized by a path $\{q(t)\}$ which has two distinct phases. Since discovery is certain but costly, the optimal strategy is to deplete the initial stock $S(0)$ with rent $r$ on the marginal ton rising at the rate of interest. That is, in phase I,

$$\frac{\overset{\bullet}{\overline{p - C_q}}}{p - C_q} = r \qquad S(t) > 0.$$

In the second phase $S(0)$ is exhausted and the ore beneath the land is then hunted down period by period so that the amount currently discovered matches the amount extracted and sold at price $p$. Thus, in phase II,

$$\frac{\overset{\bullet}{\overline{p - C_q - aX_{\Delta R}}}}{p - C_q - aX_{\Delta R}} = r \qquad S(t) = 0, \qquad R(t) > 0$$

where $C_q$ and $aX_{\Delta R}$ are derivatives with respect to quantity and $R(t)$ is the amount of land remaining at date $t$. *Exploration and extraction are simultaneous in this second phase.* (The problem is most straightforward formally for the case of $C_{qq}$ and $X_{qq} > 0$.) Exhaustion of the land will occur as $q(T) \to 0$ at date $T$ as marginal and average profit approach the same value for an optimal program.

Clearly exploration operates simply as an additional cost of "producing" ore. The stock beneath the land is simply an alternate higher cost deposit. A minor extension would have extraction costs lower with $S(t)$ positive. This would provide an incentive to explore and extract before exhausting the initial known quantity $S(0)$. There would then be a stock size effect term in our Euler equations above. However in the second phase the amount explored for and extracted would still be approximately the same at all dates— approximately because $S(t)$ will change over time, supplementing the amount discovered on the land. Without stock size effects on extraction costs, the rule for exploring is: explore until the marginal ton discovered yields a current quantity that when this quantity is extracted, rent per marginal ton discovered and extracted is rising at the rate of interest. If one multiplies rent per ton by '$a$,' tons per unit land, one has in the second phase, land rent rising at the rate of interest.

A natural way to break the simultaneity of search and discovery of $q(t)$ tons and extraction of that $q(t)$ quantity is to assume that at the outset of each period search and discovery of a stock $\Delta S(t)$ takes place at cost $X(a \Delta S(t))$ and this stock is exhausted over the period in question. This would correspond to our phase II above. In phase I, the initial stock would be exhausted. (We assume no stock size effects on extraction costs, now.) We still assume that search turns up a *known* amount given the appropriate expenditure on search. Let us take up a formulation in which there is no exogenously given initial stock. The firm starts by exploring for stock. With certainty, the amount explored for will match the amount extracted over the current interval. In a discrete time framework the firm's objective function is

$$Z = \sum_{i=0}^{n} \beta^{i+1}[-X(a(S(i) - S(1 + i))) + V(S(i) - S(1 + i))]$$

where $\beta = 1/(1 + r)$ and $S(i)$ is the stock remaining at the beginning of period $i + 1$. That is amount $S(i) - S(i + 1)$ is explored for in period $i + 1$ at the outset of the period.

The solution involves, search done instantaneously at the beginning of each period and rent on the marginal ton extracted rising at the rate of interest over the interval. The amount discovered and extracted in each interval, namely $\{S(i) - S(i + 1)\}$, satisfies

$$\frac{[\{p - C_1(t + 1)\}e^{-\Delta tr} - aX_{a\Delta S(t+1)}] - [\{p - C_q(t)\}e^{-\Delta tr} - aX_{a\Delta S(t)}]}{\{p - C_q(t)\}e^{-\Delta tr} - X_{\alpha\Delta S(t)}} = r$$

where $\Delta t$ is the length of an interval and $X_{a\Delta S(t)}$ is the derivative of $X(\,)$ with respect to its argument. $p - C_q(t)$ is defined at the end of the interval $t$ and $X_{a\Delta S(t)}$ at the beginning of the interval. The rule governing the exploitation over time is an amended $r\%$ rule. It is of interest largely as an introduction to the realistic case of uncertainty in the payoff to search.

## Uncertainty in exploration by the firm

It is realistic to assume that the payoff from exploring $Y$ square miles (we shall use hectare units here after) is uncertain. A straightforward formalization of this idea is exploration of area $Y$ yields $\lambda_j Y$ tons of ore with probability $\pi_j$ with $\pi_j > 0$ and $\sum_{j=1}^{m} \pi_j = 1$. Arrow and Chang [3] investigated a variant of this model. They let each unit of land yield either 1 ton of ore or 0 tons with a

constant probability. They then set the model in continuous time
and the essential questions at each instant were (i) whether to
search the next unit of land or wait until later and (ii) how much of
the current discovered stock should be sold off in the market. The
Arrow–Chang formulation is technically complicated because of the
0–1 choice, not explore—explore, at each instant of time. No
special economic insights are provided by this tricky formulation of
the problem. The essential economic issue with uncertainty is
whether to carry some discovered stock in period $t$ over into period
$t + 1$ in order to (a) keep prices or rents higher in period $t$ and (b)
reduce the amount of exploration that might have been pursued in
period $t + 1$. (These are basically "continuous" analogues to the
Arrow–Chang question: should the potential 1 ton be explored for
now or later at each instant $t$.) Note that even with a positive
amount of discovered stock available at the outset of any period, it
will often pay to explore for more stock in that period. There
remains the possibility of a high stock being discovered in one
period and no exploration being undertaken in a number of
subsequent periods, periods, however. Note also that we can rule
out the curious case of no ore being offered for sale in a period
intermediate in the life of the area to be explored by (i) arranging
for exploration to always yield some positive amount of ore and (ii)
arranging for demanders to make do with infinitesimal amounts of
ore over periods of time and at very high prices. Consider a two
period example with two possible states for each period. The
problem involves (1) the optimal choice of exploration at the outset
of period 1 and then (2) the allocation of discovered stock between
periods 1 and 2 and its depletion at an optimal rate. Solving
recursively backwards in time, the problem reduces to selecting the
initial level of exploration optimally, given the subsequent divisions
of stocks optimally arranged as a function of a given level of
exploration in period 1. Three types of solutions can obtain:

a) an interior solution in which for both states in period 1, some
stock is held over to period 2 and exploration is completed in
period 2.

b) a corner solution in which for the small stock state being
realized in period 1, no stock is carried over into period 2.

c) a corner solution in which all land is explored in period 1 and there is no exploration in period 2. Stock discovered in period 1 is exhausted in period 2.

Most plausibly some scale economies in exploration are required in order to have stock carried over from the first period to the second. Otherwise costs can be minimized by deferring exploration of stock used in the second period to the second period because of the bite of discounting. We turn to a detailed statement with a specific model inspired by Arrow and Chang.

Our firm has $L$ units of land to explore. The firm selects $\lambda L$ units to explore today at cost $C = (\lambda L)^\epsilon\ 0 < \epsilon \leq 1$, Once exploration is complete either $\alpha_1 \lambda L$ tons of ore are discovered with probability $\pi_1$ or $\alpha_2 \lambda L$ tons are discovered with probability $\pi_2 (\pi_1 + \pi_2 = 1$ and $0 < \pi_2 < 1)$.[5] The firm mines and sells either $\alpha_1 \lambda L - S_{R1}$ over period $(t_0, t_1)$ of given fixed length or $\alpha_2 \lambda L - S_{R2}$ over this period. $S_{R1}(\geq 0)$ and $S_{R2}(\geq 0)$ are "excess" discoveries carried over to period 2 for mining and selling. Rent on the marginal ton mined and sold rises at the rate of interest over $(t_0, t_1)$ as either $\alpha_1 \lambda L - S_{R1}$ is mined and sold or $\alpha_2 \lambda L - S_{R2}$ is mined and sold. So far, endogenous variables are $\lambda$, the fraction of land selected for exploration at $t_0$ (exploration takes no time), $S_{R1}$ and $S_{R2}$, stocks discovered at $t_0$ but not mined in the interval $(t_0, t_1)$ and $q_{01}$ and $q_{02}$, initial quantities extracted at $t_0$ as the $r\%$ rent path over $(t_0, t_1)$ is first established.

At $t_1$, the remaining land is explored at cost $C = ((1 - \lambda)L)^\epsilon$ and either $\alpha_1 (1 - \lambda)L$ tons are discovered with probability $\pi_1$ or $\alpha_2 (1 - \lambda)L$ tons are discovered with probability $\pi_2$. The firm now has either of four stock sizes to exhaust:

$$S_{R1} + \alpha_1 (1 - \lambda)L \text{ over interval } (t_1, T_{11})$$

$$S_{R1} + \alpha_2 (1 - \lambda)L \text{ over interval } (t_1, T_{12})$$

$$S_{R2} + \alpha_1 (1 - \lambda)L \text{ over interval } (t_1, T_{21})$$

$$S_{R2} + \alpha_2 (1 - \lambda)L \text{ over interval } (t_1, T_{22})$$

---

[5] It is unaesthetic to have say $k$ square land units explored and find only either all $k$ units yield much ore, unit by unit, or little ore. A more attractive formulation would have say a probability density function of a binomial form relating the probability of $x$ successes (high quantity discovered on a unit) in $k$ trials (or $k$ units of land). But this richer model would be much more complicated to examine and not yield economic insights that we do not see in our less aesthetic formulation.

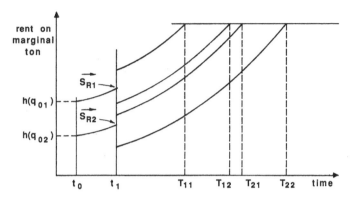

FIGURE 25   At $t_0$ either much or little ore is discovered under land $\lambda L$ yielding two possible branches over $(t_0, t_1)$. At $t_1$ again either much or little ore is discovered under land $(1 - \lambda)L$ yielding two possible rent branches for each branch over the $(t_0, t_1)$ interval. In general more ore is discovered at $t_0$ than is used over the interval $(t_0, t_1)$. This "over-exploration" reduces future stock size uncertainty.

where the intervals are determined by rent on the marginal to rising at $r\%$ to the terminal exogenous rent value, given by the demand and extraction cost schedules. We have then four more endogenous variables, namely $T_{11}$, $T_{12}$, $T_{21}$, $T_{22}$ making nine in total. The nine equations characterizing the firm's present value profit maximizing exploration-extraction program comprise six "materials balance" equations on stocks used up over the six $r\%$ rent branches of the program and three first order conditions in $\lambda$, $S_{R1}$ and $S_{R2}$ (See Appendix III). We sketch the rental branches of a possible solution[6] in Figure 25.

In Figure 25 $h(q_{01})$ and $h(q_{02})$ are each rent per marginal ton extracted when $q_{01}$ and $q_{02}$ are the quantities extracted respectively. The notation $\vec{S}_{R1}$ indicates that an amount $S_{R1}$ of stock is discovered at $t_0$ are carried over to the second period for exploitation by the firm. That $S_{R1}$ and $S_{R2}$ are in general positive indicates that "over exploration" at $t_0$ is optimal for the firm even though exploration is

---

[6] Pindyck [71] explored the resource extracting firm facing demand uncertainty, stock uncertainty, and exploration pay-off uncertainty using Ito's Lemma for underlying Weiner processes for modelling uncertainty. No end-point issues were explored or reported on, just generalized Euler equations, essentially. Arrow and Chang [3] paid attention to how exhaustibility feeds back on the trajectory of extraction and exploration as we have done above in our model.

costly. This holds true whether there are returns to scale ($\epsilon = 1$). "Over exploration" is a response to future stock size uncertainty. "Over exploration" reduces future uncertainty and this reduction is a positive pay-off to the firm. The payoff is represented by the firm being able to set out an extraction program which more closely approximates an extraction program under perfect certainty. The closer an extraction with uncertainty resembles the corresponding extraction program with certainty, the higher the firm's present value of profit will be.

We report examples solved on a computer (our nine nonlinear equations in $\lambda$, $q_{01}$, $q_{02}$, $S_{R1}$, $S_{R2}$, $T_{11}$, $T_{12}$, $T_{21}$, $T_{22}$ in Appendix III). The runs have (i) exploration costs scale economies varying and (ii) the degree of uncertainty (values of probabilities in our two states) varying. The planner's[7] instantaneous benefits are

$$Aq - 0.5Bq^2 - cq$$

and we set $A = 10$, $B = 1$ and $c = 1$ yielding a linear demand schedule $A - Bq$. Terminal rent per ton is $A - c = 9$. Exploration costs are $C = (\lambda L)^\epsilon$ with the single parameter $\epsilon$ between 0 and 1. The interest rate $r = 0.1$ and land $L$ is 60 units. Each unit of land yields $\alpha_1 = 1$ ton with probability $\pi_1$ or $\alpha_2 = 3$ with probability $\pi_2$. $t_0 = 0$ and $t_1 = 2.0$.

(i) With uncertainty set so that $\pi_1 + \pi_2 = 0.5$, we investigated the response to changes in the exploration cost scale parameter $\epsilon$. We observe that as $\epsilon$ declines from 1.0 (constant returns in exploration) to a small positive number (increasing returns in exploration) the fraction of land initially explored rises to $\lambda = 0.61721$ ($\epsilon = 0.35$) and then declines slightly.

| $C$ | 1.0 | 0.75 | 0.55 | 0.35 | 0.15 | 0.01 |
|---|---|---|---|---|---|---|
| $q_{01}$ | 5.38252 | 5.38252 | 5.26010 | 5.25837 | 5.26001 | 5.26107 |
| $q_{02}$ | 7.39662 | 7.39662 | 7.48226 | 7.48335 | 7.48231 | 7.48166 |
| $T_{11}$ | 4.76700 | 4.76700 | 4.80877 | 4.80935 | 4.80879 | 4.80844 |
| $T_{12}$ | 12.18788 | 12.18788 | 11.24184 | 11.22913 | 11.24124 | 11.24895 |
| $T_{21}$ | 13.23939 | 13.23936 | 14.16877 | 14.18113 | 14.16936 | 14.16186 |
| $T_{22}$ | 19.77731 | 19.77231 | 19.74989 | 19.74960 | 19.74986 | 19.75005 |
| $\lambda$ | 0.55304 | 0.55304 | 0.61637 | 0.61721 | 0.61641 | 0.61589 |
| $S_{R1}$ | 23.19156 | 23.19156 | 27.26231 | 27.31688 | 27.26491 | 27.23175 |
| $S_{R2}$ | 85.09702 | 85.09702 | 96.30646 | 96.45631 | 96.31358 | 96.22258 |

---

[7] For the case of a firm facing a constant price for mined output and a linear rising marginal extraction cost schedule, A would be the firm's price per ton, $c + Bq$ would be the linear marginal extraction cost schedule.

In each case a substantial amount of ore discovered at $t_0$ is not mined in the interval $(t_0, t_1)$. $S_{R1}$ and $S_{R2}$ are these amounts discovered but not mined in the first period. We see the same now with the degree of uncertainty varying.

(ii) (a) Under constant returns to scale ($\epsilon = 1.0$) in exploration we let uncertainty vary ($\pi_1$ varying between 0.15 and 0.95 with $\pi_1 + \pi_2 = 1.0$). The lowest value of $\lambda$ occurred at $\pi_1 = 0.95$

| $\pi_1$ | 0.15 | 0.35 | 0.50 | 0.65 | 0.85 | 0.95 |
|---|---|---|---|---|---|---|
| $q_{01}$ | 5.19334 | 5.53488 | 5.38252 | 5.16724 | 4.84731 | 4.67546 |
| $q_{02}$ | 7.71424 | 7.54109 | 7.39662 | 7.23360 | 6.88195 | 6.01228 |
| $T_{11}$ | 4.83148 | 4.71498 | 4.76700 | 4.84037 | 4.94897 | 5.00715 |
| $T_{12}$ | 8.95311 | 11.48204 | 12.18788 | 12.74110 | 13.95620 | 17.05238 |
| $T_{21}$ | 16.24571 | 13.84534 | 13.23936 | 12.79656 | 11.75298 | 8.71735 |
| $T_{22}$ | 19.68898 | 19.73441 | 19.77231 | 19.81508 | 19.90729 | 20.13504 |
| $\lambda$ | 0.76109 | 0.59588 | 0.55304 | 0.52088 | 0.44644 | 0.23962 |
| $S_{R1}$ | 36.09364 | 25.42476 | 23.19156 | 21.73871 | 17.98026 | 5.95172 |
| $S_{R2}$ | 121.84351 | 92.48871 | 85.09702 | 79.66946 | 67.04768 | 31.74606 |

(b) Under increasing returns to scale ($\epsilon = 0.5$) in exploration, we let uncertainty vary. The lowest value of $\lambda$ now occurred at $\pi_1 = 0.98$.

| $p_1$ | 0.20 | 0.35 | 0.50 | 0.70 | 0.90 | 0.98 |
|---|---|---|---|---|---|---|
| $q_{01}$ | 4.94036 | 5.33197 | 5.25887 | 5.01073 | 4.71130 | 4.59098 |
| $q_{02}$ | 7.72378 | 7.65061 | 7.48304 | 7.31846 | 7.14575 | 6.77690 |
| $T_{11}$ | 4.91744 | 4.78425 | 4.80919 | 4.89356 | 4.99502 | 5.03569 |
| $T_{12}$ | 8.24024 | 10.39053 | 11.23273 | 11.82837 | 12.25080 | 13.92126 |
| $T_{21}$ | 16.94243 | 14.92131 | 14.17763 | 13.71667 | 13.43474 | 11.89210 |
| $T_{22}$ | 19.68648 | 19.71748 | 19.74968 | 19.79285 | 19.83812 | 19.93480 |
| $\lambda$ | 0.80906 | 0.66916 | 0.61697 | 0.58322 | 0.56133 | 0.45349 |
| $S_{R1}$ | 39.53146 | 30.27069 | 27.30139 | 25.82532 | 25.17508 | 18.97130 |
| $S_{R2}$ | 130.45549 | 105.53593 | 96.41382 | 90.70187 | 87.14467 | 68.55080 |

The "force" of increasing returns to scale in exploration is to induce relatively more exploration at $t_0$, that is $\lambda$ larger for $\epsilon = 0.5$ compared with $\epsilon = 1.0$.

The Arrow–Chang model resembles the above model in the following senses: (i) there is a finite amount of land and under each unit is 1 ton of ore with probability $\delta$ or 0 tons with probability $1 - \delta$ (ii) there is a concave instantaneous benefit function defined on ore mined (iii) there are costs associated with discovering whether ore exists or not beneath each unit of land. The salient difference is that Arrow and Chang formulate the planner's explore-extract problem in continuous time rather than in our discrete time fashion. Their problem abounds in technical detail. One can in both problems view the $L$ units of land as set as linearly as a string. The planner works his or her way along the string at a certain rate in Arrow and Chang's model depending on whether many units are discovered initially or not. Their only qualitative conclusion is that rent will rise as the end of the string is approached. The complexity of the analysis precludes them observing the phenomenon of exploration leading current "usage"—the "over exploration" which we focussed on above. Part of the technical difficulty in the continuous time formulation stems from the fact that at each instant the planner must decide whether to explore the next unit or wait and run down current stocks only. There is a band-bang control at each instant—proceed one square or wait and proceed at a later instant.

A distinctive feature of exploring for deposits of an exhaustible resource is the closing off of the search as exploration proceeds. Since the resource is finite in amount what is discovered today implies roughly speaking less to search for tomorrow. Moreover what is discovered today represents a durable stock which will be there tomorrow to be mined and so the penalty from "over exploring" today is simply the interest costs of not deferring the marginal discovery. The pay-off from "over-exploring" today is finding out sooner how much future stock will be available and we know that the pay-off from running down a known stock $\bar{S}$ is greater than running down an unknown stock of possible sizes $S_1$ and $S_2$ where $\pi_1 S_1 + \pi_2 S_2 = \bar{S}$ and $0 < \pi_1 < 1$ and $\pi_1 + \pi_2 = 1$. In each period with *uncertain* discovery, there is in general the incentive to "over explore" in order to reduce future stock size uncertainty. If exploration were costless, it would be completed "today" and a certainty extraction program followed. This is the logical extreme of "over exploring" today relative to current demands or needs. This "over exploration" is distinct from inventory holding or "precautionary" stock accumulation which is motivated by future demand uncertainty. In our case "over exploration" is simply buying information today about stock size tomorrow and using this information in arranging the current extraction program contingent on future discoveries.

Devarajan and Fisher [16] and Lasserre [53] have exploration take place over an undiscovered stock with search costs varying with cumulative search effort. Exhaustibility can be viewed as search costs rising over time as cumulative effort increases. The special case of unlimited stock results in expected rent equalling zero over time as in Deshmukh and Pliska [15].

### Search and rent dissipation

Exploration above is necessary to obtain stocks. Suppose there is an uncertain distribution of stock underground and exploration can reveal which state or size is correct. In this case exploration provides only information, not both stock and information about the state of stocks. In this case the issue is: at what date is it optimal to commit resources to exploration activity. Dasgupta and Heal [11; Chapter 14] investigated this matter. Consider a two state example. Suppose there are 90 tons with probability $\pi_1$ and 140 tons with probability $\pi_2$. Let $K$ be the dollar cost of exploring. Given any date $T$ of exploration fixed, there is an optimal amount of the known 90 tons to exploit beyond $T$ in an interior solution. Let this amount be $S(T)$ and it is selected according to the optimality condition: expected rent per ton just beyond $T$ equals rent per ton just before $T$. The problem of selecting the optimal date is then maximize by choice of $T$

$$R(T) = V(90 - S(T))$$
$$+ e^{-r(T-T_0)}\{\pi_1 V(S(T)) + \pi_2 V(50 + S(T)) - K\}$$

Using the Envelope Theorem ($S(T)$ has been optimized given $T$) we obtain the basic condition for selecting $T$

$$K = \pi_1 V(S(T)) + \pi_2 V(50 + S(T))$$

or exploration costs equal expected future rent at the optimal date. This is a striking rent dissipation result: at the optimal date to explore, exploration costs equal the total of expected future rents (profits for the firm). This of course removes the incentive for the agent to explore.[8] Whatever future rents there may be are exactly

---

[8] This result is presented as equation 14.18, p. 431 in Dasgupta and Heal [11] and receives no comment in the text. The other first order condition (equation 4.17) concerning expected rent at $T$ equal to rent just before $T$ receives two pages of comment.

dissipated by the cost of ascertaining their precise magnitude. The above may be a local maximum only and the global maximum involves no search at all. Deposit size is revealed simply by mining.

The above treatment of information is of course special. One is either fully informed by expending $K$ dollars or fully uninformed. Being partially better informed can involve a revision is one's prior notion of the mean size of the deposit or of the higher moments such as the variance. Being fully informed reveals the mean precisely and reduces the higher moments to zero. In the above model there is no margin for becoming slightly better informed at an additional cost, except moving the date of information revelation forward.

Resources expended in search for deposits turn crucially on the property rights arrangements over (a) the area over which an agent may search or prospect and (b) the deposit or deposits discovered. The classic free-for-all gives the ownership of what is discovered to the discoverer. In such a situation, we expect (a) each agent to dissipate expected returns completely in search costs (as in the free access fishery) and (b) there to be duplication of effort as more than one agent searches over territory already searched by one or other agents. A way to avoid excessive entry and the dissipation of rent in (a) is to tax entry or restrict the number of searchers by requiring licences to be held. To avoid resources wasted in (b), a public agency can subdivide a large area into subareas and lease rights to one or a specific number of agents to conduct a search in the subarea. This latter procedure goes under the name, letting "claims" to prospectors. The claim holder usually has exclusive rights to search an area. The exclusivity is enforced by granting exclusive rights to the claim holder to deposits uncovered in his or her claim. These rights represent leases with a horizon. They are often renewable. If the lease price is very low and renewable, overall search intensity can be made small because the cost of holding an unsearched claim is small. Leasing subareas avoids duplication of search effort but can retard the speed of search overall.

A formalization of a search free-for-all is the Lee and Wilde [54] model of a patent *race*. In place of winning a patent we consider an exploration firm winning a new deposit. In the Lee and Wilde [54] race, each of $n$ firms spends $x$ dollars per unit time searching and wins the single prize of capitalized value $V/r$ by being first to discover a single deposit. There is a constant probability per unit time of a firm discovering the deposit. The probability of discovery on or before date $\tau$ for $\tau \leq t$ is $1 - e^{-th(x)}$, where $h(x)$ increases in dollars expended in search per unit time. Up to $\bar{x}$, $h(x)$ is convex in $x$ and beyond $\bar{x}$, $h(x)$ is concave and $h(0) = 0$.

For firm $i$ to be the first to discover the deposit at date $\bar{\tau}_i$ on or before $t$, the probability is $1 - e^{at}$ where $a \equiv \sum_{j \neq i} h(x_j)$. We assume all firms are identical. Then the expected gross payoff from firm $i$ being in the race is

$$EB = \int_0^\infty ae^{-at} \left\{ \int_0^t he^{-hs} e^{-sr} \, ds \right\} dt = \frac{Vh}{a+h+r}$$

where $r$ is the constant discount rate.

There is a set up cost of $F$ dollars for a firm to enter the race plus the $x$ dollars expended per unit time. Total expected costs are then

$$EC = \int_0^\infty \left\{ \int_0^t xe^{-rs} \, ds \right\} (a+h)e^{-(a+h)t} \, dt + F = \frac{x}{a+h+r} + F.$$

Maximization of $E\pi = EB - EC$ yields $\hat{x}$ satisfying

$$\frac{h - xh'}{(a+r)h} = F$$

and with free entry, $E\pi = 0$ at $\hat{x}$. Rent net of search costs is ex ante, zero. There is complete dissipation of rent by the search costs to find the deposit. There is a classic externality here. Entry by firm $i$ changes the probability of every other firm winning the prize and this spill-over is unpriced.

Expected social payoff can be thought of as the expectation of $V$ being discovered by one of $n$ firms searching on or before $t$. This is

$$V \sum [1 - e^{at}] = nV \cdot [1 - e^{at}]$$

Expected social costs are then $nEC$ where $a = (n-1)h(x)$. Maximization of net expected social payoff yields a pair $(n, x)$ to compare with the untaxed entry equilibrium above.

The above model is an illustration of a race with complete rent dissipation *ex ante* and no property rights over the terrain being searched. Optimal search involves (a) an optimal division of the total terrain into subareas each sub area being leased to an optimal number of searchers (possibly one) and (b) a lease which encourages search to be conducted methodically and quickly. Different distributions of ore underground require different subdivisions and leases. Some deposits are widely dispersed over an area and others are highly concentrated. Small area subdivisions for dispersed ore are associated with search externalities. One searcher finds evidence of valuable ore and others rush in staking claims in the surrounding area. Followers often free ride on the work done by the first discoverer. The followers incur almost no search costs but reap substantial benefits. If claim areas were large in such cases, the first discoverer could assume property rights for the complete dispersed deposit and the free riders would be left out of the benefits.

Unexpected discoveries of new stock drive down the current price of resource output and lower the value of known remaining stock. Thus current stock owners have an aversion to new unexpected discoveries. A sure method of avoiding price-lowering unexpected discoveries is to defer any exploration until current stocks are exhausted. Aside from the out of pocket costs of exploration, this is an additional incentive to current owners to defer exploration until current stocks are exhausted. Unexpected non-discoveries cut in the opposite direction. The value of current known stocks will rise if expected discoveries are not realized. A monopolist who also owns the areas of unexplored minerals could arrange the timing and intensity of exploration to take account of future surprises in discovery of new stocks. A game emerges however when exploration is pursued by agents who do not own current stocks. These latter are interested in the value of discoveries *per se* and not in the capital losses or gains on current stocks directly. Clearly there are significant parallels in such a game and the one discussed between developers of a backstop supply and current owners of mineral stocks.

## Auctions and resource tract sales

Auctions play a significant role in organizing use of deposits of exhaustible resources. Governments auction uncertain stocks in an effort to distribute fairly an asset in the public domain to persons in the private property sector. In this transfer some fraction of the value of the deposit or asset is transferred to the public treasury and represents government revenue. In these auctions one is interested in how each bidder arrives at his or her bid submitted and given the auction with many participants, how much of the value of the asset gets transferred to the public treasury. A first glance would suggest that all rents would be transferred to the public treasury because on average the winning bidder could expect no surplus or excess profit. The process of bidding would drive the marginal bidder, the owner, to end up with no excess profit. However given inherent uncertainty about the value of the asset, since it is below ground when bidding takes place, each bidder must enter without certain knowledge of the value of the deposit. This introduces the issue of each bidder trying to decide how reasonable his or her subjective evaluation of the value of the asset is relative to say what values he or she thinks others are assignming to the asset. There is always the hazard of bidding more than the value of the marketable ore is worth. This is referred to as "winner's curse" in the literature on auctions. But great caution in bidding usually leads to small chance of winning the auction, that is submitting the highest bid.

We will sketch some results in optimal auctions for the case in which the winner has a valuation $v_i$, a bid $b(v_i)$, a distribution function $F(v_i)$ from which $v_i$ and other bidders' valuations are drawn, and a number $n - 1$ of competing bidders excluding the owner, who him or herself has a reserve bid. We ignore here the problem that *ex post* the winner discovers that his or her $v_i$ exceeds the market value of the deposit or asset he or she won in the earlier auction. In these simpler auctions which we consider first, it never pays the bidder to set his or her bid $b(v_i)$ in excess of his or her valuation $v_i$ and $v_i$ in this model is not "contradicted" by a subsequent market realized value.

There are a variety of institutional arrangements for organizing an auction. The English auction is oral and the highest bidder wins and pays his final bid while other bidders pay and receive nothing. A second price auction involves the highest bidder winning and paying a price set equal to the bid of the second highest bidder. A Dutch auction involves a "price" being lowered by the auctioneer until one bidder enters. At that price which a bidder first entered, the item is sold to this first bidder.

The principal results which hold in these simpler auctions with risk neutral bidders are (Riley and Samuelson [74]):

a) with open English auctions and second price sealed bid auctions, each bidder's best strategy is to bid his or her valuation $v_i$ and in his sense these auctions are then equivalent.

b) with a high bid win and pay the high bid auction, each bidder optimally shades his or her bid $b(v_i)$ below his or her valuation $v_i$ as in

$$[v_i - b(v_i)]\left\{\frac{F(v_i)^{n-1}}{\int_{b_0}^{v_i} F(x)^{n-1}\,dx}\right\} = 1 \qquad \text{for all } i$$

where $F(v_i)^{n-1}$ is the probability that the $n-1$ competing bids are below $v_i$ and $\int_{b_0}^{v_i} F(x)^{n-1}\,dx$ is the range over which winning bids are feasible. That is bids below $b_0$ may "win" but not be accepted as sufficiently high (above $b_0$) by the seller.

c) Given bidders bidding optimally in the face of the institutional rules of the auction, expected revenue to the seller is

$$n\int_{v_*}^{\tilde{v}} (vF'(v) + F(v) - 1)F(v)^{n-1}\,dv$$

where $v_*$ is the reservation value for which a bidder is indifferent between bidding and not bidding.

d) $v_*$ satisfies

$$v_* = v_0 + 1 - \left\{\frac{F(v_*)}{F'(v_*)}\right\}$$

where $v_0$ is the seller's reserve value. For high bid and second price auctions, the seller will set $b_0 = v_*$ where $b_0$ is the reserve price or bid of the seller

Let us consider the derivation of these results.

(a) In an ascending bid oral English auction the winner bids marginally above the second highest bidder. In other words the winner bids the second person's bid to win. To establish that each should bid his or her reservation value $v_i$, one asks given person $i$ winning with bid $b = v_i$ could he or she have gained either surplus $(v_i - b_i)$ or a higher probability of winning by altering his or her bid slightly above $v_i$ or below $v_i$. Inquiry on this point reveals the answer to be negative. Hence each bidder should bid his or her value if he or she bids in his or her best interest.

The next two results follow from two considerations. First all $n$ bidders are identical as they enter the auction in the sense that each bidder draws his or her $v_i$ from the same density function (generalized urn) and each seeks to maximize his or her net gain or surplus. Thus *ex ante*, each bidder should at the margin expect to gain the same amount from entering the auction ("playing the game"), if the $v_i$ selected yields a rational bid above the seller's reservation price. Result (b) above captures this outcome of an optimal bidding function "selected" by each bidder.

If the seller knows the density function $f(v)$ and the number of players, he or she can calculate expected revenue for each reservation price he or she sets. An optimal reservation price will maximize the seller's net surplus and result (d) follows. Let us then derive the seller's revenue for a general $n$ person auction. Results (b) and (d) are corollaries to this result. In obtaining expected revenue, we consider a representative bidder's optimal bid. Each bidder seeks to maximize expected net surplus

$$\pi(x, v) = [F(x)]^{n-1}v - P(x)$$

for any $v$ drawn from the density function $f(v)$, where $[F(x)]^{n-1}$ is the probability that $v$ is at least as high as the $v$'s of the $n-1$ competing bidders and $P(x)$ is expected payment for the article being auctioned.

$$P(x) \underset{v_2, \ldots, v_n}{E} p(b(x), b(v_2), \ldots, b(v_n))$$

where we, for specificity, consider the representative bidder to be person 1 or the person who draws $v$ labelled $v_1$. $E$ is the expectation or expected value operator. $P(x)$ is then bidder 1's average or expected payment and it is this function which we derive properties for in the optimal bidding "game".

We suppose bidder 1 maximizes his or het net surplus by choice of $x$ which in equilibrium must be equal to $v_1$. Thus $\partial \pi / \partial x = 0$ yields

$$P'(v_1 = x) = v_1 \frac{d[F(v_1)]^{n-1}}{dv_1} \qquad v_1 \geq v_*$$

where $v_*$ is the value of $v$ at which a bidder is indifferent between entering the auction and staying out.

$$[F(v_*)]^{n-1}v_* - P(v_*) = 0$$

Using this boundary condition on $v$ and integrating $p'$ yields

$$P(v_1) = [F(v_*)]^{n-1}v_* + \int_{v_*}^{v_1} x d[F(x)]^{n-1} \qquad v_1 \geq v_*$$

$$= [F(v_1)]^{n-1}v_1 - \int_{v_*}^{v_1} [F(x)]^{n-1} dx \qquad v_1 \geq v_*$$

The seller's expected revenue is in turn

$$R^1 = \int_{v_*}^{v_1} P(v_1)F'(v_1) \, dv_1$$

which upon substituting for $P(v_1)$ from above yields

$$R^1 = \int_{v_*}^{\bar{v}} [F'(v)v + F(v) - ][F(v)]^{n-1} \, dv.$$

where $\bar{v}$ is the upper bound of the density function.

Since person 1 was an arbitrary selection, total expected revenue for the seller is $n$ times expected revenue from one person or the result in (c).

If the high bid wins and is paid, it must satisfy

$$P(v) = b(v)F^{n-1}(v).$$

Substituting this value of $P(v)$ in the individual's optimal $P(v)$ above yields the high-bid bidding rule in (b) above.

If the seller maximizes the net expected surplus, net of his reserve value $v_0$, with respect to $v_*$, we obtain the result in (d) above which indicates that $v_* > v_0$ and when $v_*$ is the reserve price or bid as in high and second price auctions.

In the above simple auction scheme $v_i$ was considered a true estimate of value. In many cases it is more reasonable to view $v_i$ as a signal upon which the bidder makes his estimate of value of the item being auctioned. The signal then is "translated" into an estimate and on the basis of that estimate, a bid is made. For example we might imagine the case of $k$ contiguous resource tracts to be auctioned. A macro survey of the area suggests an average value for each tract with a density function associated with this average, the same over all tracts, *a priori*. Bidder $i$ then surveys tract $j$ and receives a signal $v_i^j$ and on the basis of this signal constructs an estimate $\hat{v}_i^j$. This could be a Bayesian estimate as in Hoel [41; p. 374–77]. A bid is developed on the basis of this estimate, say $b(\hat{v}_i^j)$. It remains then for the bidder to arrive at a probability of winning each tract. There are a variety of approaches of assigning a probability of $b(\hat{v}_i^j) > b(\hat{v}_h^j)_{h=1,\ldots,n}^{h \neq i}$ depending on how the bidding function is constructed. However a basic equilibrium condition is that for bidders with identical characteristics, expected profit should equal zero when evaluated over all $k$ tracts. (Free entry of bidders implies this zero expected profit condition.) This is the analogue to the equilibrium condition in (b) above. Since it is implausible to bid more than one's assessed value of tracts, one concludes that the bid should equal the Bayesian-determined value for each bidder on each tract. This leaves open the possibility that *ex post* the bid exceeded the true market value on one or more deposits. Winner's curse can be hedged against but not eliminated. Reece [72] developed a quite different model of $n$ agents bidding for a resource tract and concluded that *ex post* the winning bid would fall well short of the market value of the tract.

### Taxation of exhaustible resources

Taxation can affect the rate of extraction of known deposits, the timing of development of known deposits and the intensity of exploration for new deposits. We shall take up these matters separately although from a practical stand point, they are related. The decision-maker who faces the tax, the taxee if you will, is the extracting firm in the first instance. Thus attention is focussed on how the firm adjusts its extraction plan is to the presence of a tax. We consider the firm's action before and after the tax is imposed.

A tax is said to be *neutral* if it leaves the firm's profit maximizing extraction plan unchanged from the no-tax situation. Neutrality originates in the classical literature of economics and is associated with taxes on land. Under seemingly reasonable assumptions, a landowner will work a fixed amount of land with the same variable input before and after the tax on land is imposed and output from the land is thus unchanged after the tax is imposed. A land tax is thus said to be neutral in its impact on resource allocation and output levels. (A counter argument is that land is a capital good and a land tax alters the *rate of return* of this asset (land) relative to other assets such as factories and/or mineral deposits. Wealth will be allocated out of assets whose rate of return is driven down. In this context, a land tax is not neutral.) A basic result is a tax on the extracting firm's cash flow is neutral in the sense that a land tax is neutral. Thus after the imposition of a tax $\tau$ on cash flow, the firm's problem is

$$\max_{\{q(t)\}} \int_0^T [p(t)q(t) - C(q(t))]e^{-rt}(1 - \tau)\, dt$$

$$\text{subject to} \int_0^T q(t)\, dt = S.$$

Now $(1 - \tau)$ factors out of the firm's objective function leaving it selecting the same $\{q(t)\}$ before and after the tax. Hence a cash-flow tax is neutral.

A *royalty* is a tax on current output such as a tax of 50¢ per barrel of oil extracted currently. A royalty is not neutral since it represents an extra cost of production which can be reduced by deferring extraction. The Euler equation for the profit maximizing firm becomes

$$\frac{\overline{p(t) - C_q(t)}}{p(t) - C_q(t) - \$0.5} = r$$

which differs from the pre-tax Euler equation by the presence of $0.5 in the denominator. The firm's extraction program will differ in the pre and post tax situation.

A typical cost of the firm is interest payments on its debt. If lenders pay personal income tax on interest payment receipts, this will generally raise the cost of borrowing to firms. To achieve neutrality for the resource extracting firm in these circumstances, Samuelson [76] and others established that deduction of "true economic depreciation" from current income before taxes were paid was the desired instrument. "True economic depreciation" in the absence of taxes is

$$\lambda(t)q(t) = rV(t) - \{p(t)q(t) - C(q(t))\}$$

where $q(t)$ is the quantity along the optimal extraction program at $t$ and $V(t)$ is the value of the deposit remaining at $t$ along an optimal extraction program. For a perpetually-lived asset, current income is $r\%$ of the capital value of the asset. For a "wasting" asset, current income exceeds $rV$ by "true economic depreciation" to be deducted from income before taxes. This "balances" the distorting wedge caused by interest payments being taxed as income to lenders. Neutrality can be preserved with depreciation allowances in these circumstances. Long and Sinn [61] take issue with this view when they examine the argument in an intertemporal general equilibrium setting. In general equilibrium, there is the issue of how taxes in one sector affect the relative attractiveness of assets in other sectors. *Intersectoral neutrality* involves maintaining the rate of return on assets in distinct sectors $i$ and $j$ the same after the imposition of taxes as before. In the absence of intersectoral neutrality the size of the sector whose return declines most after tax will shrink relative to the sizes of other sectors. Asset holders shift out of assets whose net rates of return decline.

In general equilibrium intersectoral neutrality involves capital being invested in each sector at each date so that $MP_{K,i} = MP_{K,j} = r$ where $MP_{K,i}$ is the marginal product of capital in sector $i$. Across periods, intertemporal efficiency requires satisfaction of the Dorfman, Samuelson, Solow [20] conditions (see Appendix II) of which the Solow–Stiglitz (Hotelling) efficiency condition $\dot{MP}_{R,i}/MP_{R,i} = MP_{K,i}$ for exhaustible resources is a special case. Finally individuals save along optimal paths to equate the $MP_{K,i}$ to the rate of time preference of households (a social rate of time preference). Clearly what the government spends its tax receipts on affects the nature of the past tax equilibrium. A neutrality assumption here is that the revenues are returned to citizens as lump sum (not conditioned on any characteristics of the recipient) payments.

Long and Sinn [6] argue verbally (and mathematically) as follows. The allowance of true economic depreciation in the face of taxation of interest payments may achieve intersectoral neutrality in general equilibrium, but the saving-consumption margin is distorted in this regime. Hence achieving intersectoral neutrality by these means may not be desirable in this second best world. In fact, in a fully specified model, they argue that allowance for deductability from taxes of true economic depreciation of exhaustible resources is not desirable to balance the taxation of interest payments. "All of this shows how little is known about the structure of dynamically efficient tax systems". (Long and Sinn [61; p. 245]).

With a spectrum of deposits of varying quality and thus aggregate profitability, taxation can affect the timing at which "fallow" deposits are brought into production. The rate of taxation affects the rate of return each deposit yields. Lower yielding assets will be brought into active life later than higher yielding assets.

The issue of taxing the output of exhaustible resource deposits can be viewed quite broadly. One might consider the extracting firm as leasing the deposit from the public and resource taxation is payment for the lease. Since this form of lease payment has strong negative incentive effects on exploration by firms compared to a world of no taxation of output (royalties), one might look for an optimal lease or schedule which involves the firm paying for its lease which still exploring relatively vigorously. This approach, the construction of an optimal contract or lease between the public (government) and the extracting firm or lessor, has been examined by Leland [55] and Hyde and Markusen [45].

Suppose beneath a claim is an amount of mineral, possibly zero comprising $n + 1$ possible sizes. The firm pays a bonus bid $\delta_i$ in state $i$ (possibly a negative sum) and incurs exploration costs. If state $i$ is realized then the firm incurs extraction costs $K_p$ as a function of the amount discovered and receives gross revenues $q_i F(K_p)$ in state $i$. Thus production costs are determined *ex post* whereas exploration costs are selected *ex ante*. An optimal lease is a risk sharing contract in which rents (revenues less production costs) are shared between the government and the firm, exploration costs are shared between the two parties and a "bonus bid" or fixed fee is levied for the right to mine.

In the plausible case of no risk aversion on the part of the government, the contract merely specifies a fixed charge to the firm independent of the state, or amount discovered and mined. An interesting risk sharing contract then requires risk aversion on the part of both parties to the contract and in fact a richly detailed contract requires that the government and firm have different priors over the states that can be realized and thus different degrees of risk aversion. Hyde and Markusen discover that the details of the optimal lease are state dependent and thus remark that the royalty rate for a deposit and the bonus bid should be deposit specific or "governments should negotiate these two instruments as a package" (p. 233). For government less risk averse, a negative bonus bid may be warranted, and as in Leland [55] the optimal payments schedule should be increasing and convex in total resource rents. The more risk averse agent should other things being equal bear a relatively large share of the exploration costs. ("This may not be obvious." (Hyde and Markusen)).

## 6. ECONOMIC GROWTH AND EXHAUSTIBLE RESOURCES

### Introduction

Sustaining a prosperous economy in the face of an essential input which is both finite and being depleted is the issue in an economy wide consideration of exhaustible resource use. If population is growing, economic growth *per capita* in the long run seems impossible without much technical improvement. Thus one tends to look first at the case of a constant population and reproducible capital (buildings, machines, infrastructure) being accumulated to offset reductions in the use of exhaustible resources in the long run. We can suppress the introduction of population or labor in production in these latter problems and focus attention on ac- cumulation of reproducible capital, resource use, consumption, investment, and output. One might view a fixed population as standing on the sidelines, consuming but not laboring. Needless to say, consumption cannot be increased indefinitely with an unchang- ing techology. Generally, per capita consumption must decline in the face of a finite stock of resources and output positive over infinite time. However in one special case, accumulation of re- producible capital can offset a steady decline in resource use (oil consumption by firms?) and allow per capita consumption to be maintained at a constant positive level indefinitely. This case involves society investing all rents from exhaustible resources reproducible capital instant by instant. We will then set out an analysis of aggregate growth with population constant first and later consider the extension to situations of population growth. We then turn to accounting procedures for measuring economic growth and its sources when exhaustible resources are essential.

## Accumulation of reproducible capital (population and technology unchanging)

The planning problem is to (1) run down the nonrenewable resource stock $S(t)$, and (2) add to the reproducible capital stock from output each period in order to maximize the discounted utility from consuming $C$ of output $Q$ period by period into the future. $Q(t) = f[K(t), R(t)]$ and $C(t) + \dot{K}(t) = Q(t)$ at each date $t$. We have formally

$$\text{maximize } W = \int_0^\infty e^{-rt} U(C(t))\, dt$$

$$\text{subject to } \dot{K} = f[K(t), R(t)] - C(t)$$

$$\text{and } R(t) = -\dot{S}(t)$$

where

$$\int_0^\infty R(t)\, dt \le S(0)$$

$U[C(t)]$ is the utility of consumption at time $t$

$r$ is the discount rate

The Hamiltonian function defined at each instant of time $t$ for this dynamic optimization problem is

$$H(t) = e^{-rt} U[C(t)] + \Psi[f(K, R) - C] - \lambda R$$

At each date $H(t)$ is maximized by choice of $C$ and $R$, yielding

$$e^{-rt} U_c - \Psi = 0 \tag{4}$$

$$\Psi f_R - \lambda = 0 \tag{5}$$

and the differential equations, $\dfrac{\partial H}{\partial \Psi} = \dot{K}$ and $-\dfrac{\partial H}{\partial K} = \dot{\Psi}$ must be satisfied as well as transversality and boundary conditions [transversality conditions on $K(t)$ and $S(t)$ at $t \to \infty$ and boundary conditions on initial stocks of $K(t)$ and $S(t)$]. Thus we have

$$\dot{K} = f(K, R) - C \tag{6}$$

$$\dot{\Psi} = -\Psi f_K \tag{7}$$

Equations (4) to (7) characterize the family of optimal paths for our dynamic system. The optimal path is the member of the family that satisfies initial conditions and traversality conditions. From (4) and (5), we get, respectively:

$$\dot{\Psi} = -re^{-rt}U_C + e^{-rt}U_{CC}\dot{C}$$

$$\dot{\lambda} = \dot{\Psi}f_R + \dot{f}_E\Psi = 0$$

Substituting in (7) yields

$$\frac{U_{CC}\dot{C}}{U_C} - r = -f_K \tag{8}$$

which is called the Ramsey optimal savings relation, and substituting in (7) using the second expression above yields

$$\frac{\dot{f}_R}{f_R} = f_K \tag{9}$$

which is the efficiency condition for using up the nonrenewable resource (a variant of the Hotelling rule). Since $\dot{f}_R = f_{RR}\dot{R}$, Eq. (9) is a dynamic equation in $R$. The revised equations for the family of optimal paths are (6), (8), and (9), three dynamic equations in $C(t)$, $R(t)$, and $K(t)$. These could be analyzed using standard methods. (When a dynamic system involves only two variables, time paths can be plotted in two dimensions as the phase plane and a full analysis performed. With three equations, such methods can be applied only if the system can somehow be reduced to two equations in a precise fashion.)

For the case of the particular utility function

$$U(C) = \frac{1}{v^2}C^v \qquad -1 < v < 0$$

and Cobb–Douglas production function, $Q = K^\alpha R^{1-\alpha}$, our three dynamic equations in (6), (8) and (9) can be written, respectively, as

$$g_K = \frac{Q}{K} - \frac{C}{K} \tag{10}$$

$$(v - 1)g_C = r - \alpha\left(\frac{Q}{K}\right) \tag{11}$$

$$g_R = -\frac{Q}{K} \tag{12}$$

where $g_x \equiv \frac{\dot{x}}{x}$ is a growth rate for variable $x$. Since $g_C$ and $g_R$ are linked by a simple equation, we can analyze $g_C$ separately and $g_R$ will follow.

It is convenient to put things in ratios of $C/K = y$ and $Q/K = \eta$. Now

$$g_Q = \alpha g_K + (1 - \alpha)g_R \tag{13}$$

Substitute (12) in (13), and we have $g_Q = \alpha g_K - (1 - \alpha)\frac{Q}{K}$, giving us $g_K$, $g_C$, and $g_Q$ in terms of $C/K = y$ and $Q/K = \eta$. Since $g_y = g_C - g_K$ and $g_\eta = g_Q - g_K$, we can obtain

$$g_y = \left(\frac{r}{v - 1}\right) - \left(\frac{\alpha + v - 1}{v - 1}\right) \tag{14}$$

$$g_\eta = (\alpha - 1)(2\eta - y) \tag{15}$$

For $g_y = g_\eta = 0$, Eqs (14) and (15) become, respectively:

$$y = \left(\frac{r}{1 - v}\right) + \left(\frac{\alpha + v - 1}{v - 1}\right)\eta \tag{16}$$

$$y = 2\eta \tag{17}$$

We plot these schedules in the $y - \eta$ plane in Figure 26. $g_K = 0$ divides the space in half. Points above $g_K = 0$ have $\dot{K} < 0$, which we rule out. Paths originating in region A rise and hit the $g_K = 0$ boundary with $C/K$ rising and $Q/K$ falling. This would presumably never be optimal, since collapse seems inevitable unless the path moved down along the $g_K = 0$ boundary with no accumulation taking place. In region B, paths move toward the origin, with $C/K$ and $Q/K$ declining continually. Such behavior seems potentially optimal, since $C$ and $Q$ would presumably decline but not necessarily go to zero in infinite time. This might be called asymptotic decline in the economy. (Recall $g_R = -\eta$, so the growth rate in $R$ declines as $\eta \to 0$ in the figure.)

From region G, a path could rise to the northwest and then bend down to decline toward the origin. An initial rise in $C(t)$ is possible,

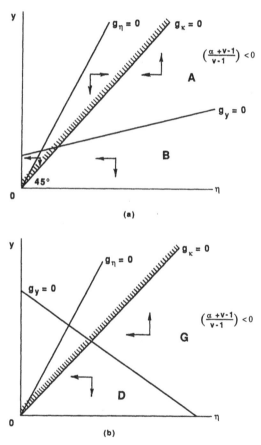

FIGURE 26  Phase planes for the model of growth with an exhaustible resource. Both $y = C/K$ and $n = Q/K$ collapse as $K$ grows and resource stocks are depleted.

as Dasgupta and Heal [10] point out for large initial endowments of resource stock $S(0)$ and capital stock $K(0)$. Paths originating in region D behave the same as those originating in region B. Optimal paths must end in regions B and D with asymptotic decline as $C(t)$ approaches zero, since $\eta \to y$ as time passes.

### Investing resource rents

Solow [86] established that if the social discount rate $r$ above were zero and that preferences over time were Rawlsian (each generation received the same per capita consumption) aggregate consumption could be maintained at a positive level indefinitely for the case of a Cobb–Douglas production with $\alpha > 1 - \alpha = \beta$. The interpretation of this striking result is that if each unit of reproducible capital is sufficiently productive relative to the exhausible resource input, new reproducible capital goods can compensate for the steady decline in resource use and sustain output and consumption above an infinitesimal level indefinitely. Cairns [6] established this result for the case of exhaustible resources which decline in quality as the stock is depleted. In such trajectories, resource use declines asymptotically so that in the limit infinitesimal amounts of resources are sustaining the economy. Casual observers have objected to the reasonableness of such results from the standpoint of physics, an economy functioning on an eyedropper of oil, then a fraction of an eye-dropper etc.

An interesting property of this basic Solow model is that the implicit savings-investment rule which maintains aggregate consumption (and also per capita consumption) constant is: resource rents, instant by instant, are invested in reproducible capital goods. In other words, if the current net value of resources used up at time $t$ is used to purchase new reproducible capital goods at current prices of date $t$, consumption can be maintained constant. What the generation at date $t$ uses up in terms of resources is passed on dollar for dollar as additional buildings and machines. To see this, we observe from the basic national accounting identity holding at each instant $C + \dot{K} = f(K, R)$

$$\dot{C} + \ddot{K} = f_K \dot{K} + f_R \dot{R}$$

Our savings-investment relation is $\dot{K} = f_R R$ yielding

$$\ddot{K} = \dot{f}_R R + \dot{R} f_R.$$

The basic efficiency condition for using the exhaustible resource is $\dot{f}_R = f_R f_K$. Now substitute the $\dot{f}_R$ relation in $\ddot{K}$ and the $\ddot{K}$ relation in the $\dot{C} + \ddot{K}$ relation and we observe $\dot{C} = 0$ or given resource rents invested in reproducible capital and efficient depletion of the exhaustible stock, per capita consumption remains constant over time.

In a multiple capital goods setting there is a net national product function

$$Y^*(t) = Y(K^*(t), p(t)) = C^*(t) + p(t)\dot{K}^*(t)$$

where $p(t)$ is a vector of shadow prices of capital goods with the consumption good as numeraire. Intertemporal efficiency conditions are satisfied as $Y^*(t)$ evolves over time. Investing rents from natural resource flows in reproducible capital now takes the form

$$p(t)\dot{K}^*(t) = 0$$

$\dot{K}_i < 0$ would be an exhaustible resource flow. Using a result in Weitzman [96], Solow [86] shows that $\dot{C}^*(t) = 0$ under this savings-investment rule in this multiple capital goods model.

One observes in turn

$$\dot{Y}^*(t) = r(Y^*(t) - C^*(t)) = rp(t)\dot{K}^*(t)$$

which upon integrating yields

$$Y^*(t) = Y^*(0) + r \int_0^t p(s)\dot{K}^*(s)\, ds$$

or the increment in net national product since $t = 0$ is representable as interest on the accumulation of capital value since $t = 0$. For the case of $p(t)\dot{K}(t) = 0$ (accumulation of new reproducible capital equals resource rents) the stock of value that is being maintained intact can be thought of as

$$V(t) = \int_{-\infty}^t p(s)K^*(s)\, ds$$

which is to be interpreted to include the initial endowment of resources and if there is any, reproducible capital. These "as if" exercises have made use of the interest rate $r$ constant and would have to be amended for the case of $r$ variable over time.

## Population growth and technical progress

Consider now population growing at a constant rate $n$ and working in the economy. Per capita consumption must collapse given a finite stock of resources. Let us then introduce exogenous technical change to offset the population growth. Aggregate output $Q$ is now a function of technical progress, reproducible capital $K$, resource flow $R$ and labor services $L$. Production takes place under constant returns to scale with Hicks neutral technical change at rate $\lambda$. For simplicity, the production function is still taken to the Cobb–Doublas. In this case, each input is *essential*. We have then

$$Q = F(\lambda, K, L, R) = e^{\lambda t} K^{\alpha_1} L^{\alpha_2} R^{\alpha_3}; \qquad \alpha_1 + \alpha_2 + \alpha_3 = 1$$

where $\alpha_i$ is the share of input $i$ in output $Q$, $K$ is the current stock of reproducible capital yielding a constant flow of services proportional to $K$ (the factor of proportion being unity), $L$ is the flow of labor services taken to be proportional to the current population (the factor of proportion being unity) and $R$ is the flow of natural resource services (e.g., oil consumed per unit time) and is drawn from a current stock $S(t)$ of known homogeneous quality and size.

Output $Q$ at each instant is divided into amount $C$ currently consumed by population $L$, net investment in new reproducible capital $\dot{K}$, replacement of depreciated capital $\delta K$, and resource discovery, extraction and processing costs $xR$. That is

$$Q = C + \dot{K} + \delta K + xR.$$

The basic intertemporal efficiency condition (generalized Hotelling Rule or zero profit intertemporal arbitrage condition) is

$$\frac{\overset{\bullet}{\overline{F_R - x}}}{F_R - x} = F_K - \delta$$

$$\alpha_1 \beta - \delta = \frac{\alpha_3[g_Q - g_R] - uZ}{\alpha_3 - Z}$$

where

$$\beta = \frac{Q}{K}, \qquad Z = \frac{xR}{Q}, \qquad u = \dot{x}/x \quad \text{and} \quad g_Q = \frac{\dot{Q}}{Q} \left( g_R = \frac{\dot{R}}{R}, \text{etc.} \right)$$

Since $\dot{K} = sQ - xR - \delta K$ we have

$$g_K = s\beta - \beta Z - \delta$$

where $s$ is the savings rate, and from the production function,

$$g_Q = \lambda + \alpha_1 g_K + \alpha_2 n + \alpha_3 g_R$$

where $n = \dot{L}/L$ and is the exogenously given rate of population (and labor force) growth. Note also that $\dot{\gamma}/\gamma = g_R + \gamma$ where $\gamma = R/S$.

For the *rate* of extraction costs $Z$ to be constant given $\dot{x}/x = u$ constant, we require

$$g_Q - g_R = u.$$

This balancedness requirement implies, from the efficiency condition on resource depletion,

$$\beta = \frac{u - \delta}{\alpha_1}$$

and $g_Q$ can be written

$$g_Q = \frac{\lambda + \alpha_2 n + \alpha_1 \beta(s - Z) - \alpha_1 \delta - \alpha_3 u}{\alpha_1 + \alpha_2}.$$

Balancedness in $K/Q$ or $g_K = g_Q$ implies

$$s - Z = \frac{g_Q + \delta}{\beta}$$

Hence an efficient, balanced $K/Q$ path grows at rate

$$g_Q = \frac{\lambda + \alpha_2 n - \alpha_3 u}{\alpha_2}$$

We have the important result that *more rapid technical change increases the growth in output* and *increased scarcity of the stock of exhaustible resources* (higher $u$) *decreases the growth in output.*

$s - Z$ is the *net rate* of saving, the rate of saving from current output net of the rate at which current output must be set aside for resource extraction costs. Given $s$ exogenously set, then aggregate consumption grows at the same rate as aggregate output, i.e., $g_Q = g_C$. Then

$$Z = s - \left[\frac{\lambda + \alpha_2(n + \delta) - \alpha_3 u}{\beta \alpha_2}\right].$$

where $\beta = (u - \delta)/\alpha_1$.

Thus the growth rate is independent of the net and gross savings rate (as in the standard model without exhaustible resources). The savings rate influences the *level* of consumption in output given $C$ and $Q$ growing at the same rate. Also the savings rate affects the level of extraction costs in output, $Z$, a higher savings rate being associated with a higher $Z$. That is, given $Q$ growing at its technically determined rate, a higher savings rate permits a higher rate of extraction costs to be sustained.

Given $s$, *per capita consumption grows at rate* $\dfrac{\lambda - \alpha_3 u}{\alpha_2}$ and we obtain the stark result that $\lambda/\alpha_3$ must exceed $u$ for per capita consumption to *grow*. Since $Q = K^{\alpha_1} L^{\alpha_2} R^{\alpha_3} e^{\lambda t} = K^{\alpha_1} L^{\alpha_2} (Re^{(\lambda/\alpha_3)t})^{\alpha_3}$, $\lambda/\alpha_3$ is effectively the rate of resource augmenting technical change. Hence resource augmenting technical change must exceed the rate of degradation $u$ of the resource stock. Observe that neither the rate of population growth nor the rate of depreciation of reproducible capital affect the rate of growth of per capita consumption.

Since $g_Q - g_R = u$ and $g_Q$ has been solved for, we can solve for $-\gamma = g_R$ in a steady state. Thus the ratio of resources used in current stock available, i.e., $R/S$ remains constant.

The rationale for the constancy of the capital-output ratio has been defended in the first instance by Solow [83]. We have in addition *imposed* a steady state condition on extraction costs. We postulated a cost degradation coefficient which increased at a constant rate. This is an approximation to some form of steadily rising extraction costs. Each ton extracted or utilized in production required more output for extraction and processing as *time* passed. To preserve a steady state quality to our problem we imposed the condition that each increase in degradation charges was balanced by a decrease in the resource output ratio so that the rate of extraction costs remained constant. This is an approximation to a realistic situation since we expect the ratio of resources extracted to aggregate output to decline over time. We took the real world trends and imposed balancedness for the purposes of model building. We have not derived an economic mechanism which might cause a constancy in the rate of extraction costs to obtain. Our imposition of this constancy does not appear to be at odds with general empirical regularities. To summarize: we imposed an exponentially rising degradation or resource extraction cost and a constancy in the extraction rate. These requirements plus a constant saving rate and constant capital-output ratio and a constant labor force growth rate yielded a constant growth rate in output. The growth in output was independent of the rate of savings. This was a case of rising extraction costs, an ultimately plausible scenario. Many observers have noted that technical progress has resulted in a secular trend toward declining extraction costs over much of the twentieth century. This may well be an important source of increased aggregate output but we have not modelled this phenomenon. It does not fit in our steady-state framework. We now consider a case of no extraction costs, a case of a known homogeneous stock being depleted. This model was set out and investigated by Stiglitz [90].

### Growth without extraction costs (positive population growth and neutral technical change)

We have the same Cobb–Douglas production function.
   Now

$$Q = C + \dot{K} + \delta K$$

Intertemporal efficiency is now

$$\alpha_1 \beta - \delta = g_Q - g_R,$$

and $\dot{K}/K$ or

$$g_K = s\beta - \delta$$

Now

$$g_Q = \frac{\lambda + \alpha_2 n + \alpha_1 \beta(s - \alpha_3) - \delta(\alpha_1 - \alpha_3)}{\alpha_1 + \alpha_3}$$

and

$$g_\beta = g_Q - g_K = \frac{\lambda + \alpha_2 n - \beta(\alpha_2 s + \alpha_1 \alpha_3)}{\alpha_1 + \alpha_2},$$

and

$$\dot{\gamma}/\gamma = g_R - \gamma.$$

Following Stiglitz [90] a steady state is characterized by an exponential growth in aggregate consumption and output and a constant output-capital ratio. Thus the savings rate and $\beta$ are constant. We solve the two equations $g_Q = \bar{g}_c$ and $g_\beta = 0$ and obtain

$$\beta = \frac{(\alpha_1 + \alpha_2)[\lambda - \alpha_2(g_C - n)] - \delta\alpha_2(\alpha_1 - \alpha_3)}{\alpha_1 \alpha_3 (\alpha_1 + \alpha_2)}$$

and

$$s = \frac{(\lambda + \alpha_2 n)\alpha_1 \alpha_3 (\alpha_1 + \alpha_2)}{\alpha_2(\alpha_1 + \alpha_2)[\lambda + \alpha_2 n - \alpha_2 g_C] - \delta\alpha_2(\alpha_1 - \alpha_3)\alpha_2} - \frac{\alpha_1 \alpha_3}{\alpha_2}.$$

Alternatively, given $s$ exogenous, we can define $g_C = g_Q$ and solve for the rate of growth of per capita consumption, namely

$$g_C - n = \frac{(\lambda s - \alpha_1 \alpha_3 n)(\alpha_1 + \alpha_2) - \delta(\alpha_1 - \alpha_3)[s\alpha_2 + \alpha_1 \alpha_3]}{(\alpha_1 + \alpha_2)(\alpha_1 \alpha_3 + s\alpha_2)}$$

which represents an awkward expression indicating when $g_C - n > 0$. An alternative form of $g_C - n$ is of course

$$\frac{\lambda s - \alpha_1 \alpha_3 n}{\alpha_1 \alpha_3 + s\alpha_2} - \frac{\delta(\alpha_1 - \alpha_3)}{\alpha_1 + \alpha_2}$$

and when $\delta = 0$, we obtain the condition set out below. A condition for $g_C - n > 0$ is

$$\lambda s > \alpha_1 \alpha_3 n + \frac{\delta(\alpha_1 - \alpha_3)(s\alpha_2 + \alpha_1 \alpha_3)}{(\alpha_1 + \alpha_2)}$$

We presume $(\alpha_1 - \alpha_3) > 0$ and we observe $s$ has to be higher when $\delta > 0$ in order to yield the same $g_C - n > 0$.

For the special case of zero depreciation of reproducible capital,

$(\delta = 0)$,

$$\beta = \frac{g_C}{s} = \frac{\lambda + \alpha_2 n}{\alpha_1 \alpha_3 + \alpha_2 s}$$

$$s = \frac{\alpha_1 \alpha_3 g_C}{\lambda - \alpha_2 (g_C - n)}$$

$$\gamma = \frac{(\alpha_2 n + \lambda)(\alpha_1 - s)}{\alpha_1 \alpha_3 + \alpha_2 s}.$$

Given $g_C$ exogenous then *for per capita consumption to grow, we must have*

$$\frac{\lambda}{\alpha_3} > \frac{n\alpha_1}{s}.$$

Recall that $\lambda/\alpha_3$ can be interpreted as resource augmenting technical progress. In efficient balanced growth, $s > 0$ and $g_R < 0$ implies $s < \alpha_1$. Thus $\lambda/\alpha_3 > n$ is necessary for growth in per capita consumption. (Stiglitz [90; p. 128] proves that if $g_C - n = 0$, then $\lambda > \alpha_3 n$ ("necessity" in Stiglitz's words); and if $s = \alpha_1 \alpha_3 n / \lambda < \alpha$ then $g_C - n = 0$ ("sufficiency"). Clearly the interesting result: if $\lambda > \alpha_3 n$ then $g_C - n > 0$ is not true in general.)

Solow [86] refers to $\dfrac{\lambda - n\alpha_1}{1 - \alpha_3}$ as the "natural rate of growth" in this model ($\delta = 0$ and extraction costs zero) and observes that if $s = \alpha_3$ or resource rents are invested in new reproducible capital, then $g_C - n = \dfrac{\lambda - n\alpha_1}{1 - \alpha_3}$. That is the investment rule, invest resource rents in new reproducible capital goods, yields the "natural" rate of growth of per capita consumption. *For growth in per capita consumption to indeed be positive, capital goods augmenting technical change, $\lambda/\alpha_1$, must exceed the rate of growth of population.*

There is an interesting inverse optimum problem associated with the investing resource rents rule with population growth and technical change. Stiglitz solves the optimal growth problem with the above Cobb–Douglas technology and objective function

$$\int_0^\infty [C^v/v] e^{-(\delta - n)t} dt \qquad 0 < v < 1$$

where $C$ is per capita consumption and $\delta$ is the rate of time preference. The solution with $\dot{C}/C$ constant is

$$Q/K = \frac{\delta\alpha_2 + \lambda(1-v)}{\alpha_1(1-\alpha_1-\alpha_3 v)}$$

and

$$\dot{K}/Q = \frac{\alpha_1[(1-\alpha_1-\alpha_3 v) + \lambda - \alpha_3\delta]}{\lambda(1-v) + \alpha_2\delta}$$

For the case of $\dot{K}/Q = \alpha_3$ (investing resource rents)

$$Q/K = \frac{\lambda + n\alpha_2}{\alpha_3(1-\alpha_3)}$$

(which equals incidentally $[\dot{C}/C\alpha_3]\alpha_3^{-1}$). Thus one can solve for the $v$ and $\delta$ which generate a savings rate $\alpha_3$.

## Growth accounting with exhaustible resources

It might be useful to attempt to estimate the "drag" on economic growth which resource stock depletion of an exhaustible stock represents. Many estimates of the contribution of various factors to economic *growth* have been developed but in these pieces, specific attention to the "drag" on growth arising from stock depletion, has not been paid. Presumably this is because the magnitudes are assumed to be small and can be averaged into magnitudes such as reproducible capital augmentation. However for say oil producing countries, stock depletion could be a large item in the national accounts. Hulten [44] presents an accounting framework which can be used to work up estimates of multi-factor productivity growth over many periods. It is an extension of the single period Hicksian index developed by Solow. Hulten's framework is in fact a system of accounts for presenting a one commodity growth model in a way in which annual data can be inserted and estimates of observed productivity growth derived. Given the accounts, "the dynamic residual" or measure of productivity growth over many periods can be arrived at and estimated if data are available. We incorporate exhaustible resources in Hulten's schema. We work with a special case of exhaustible resources for simplicity. We will have no extraction costs or stock heterogeneity, no exploration activity or discoveries, and no uncertainty. This special case can be reworked to incorporate the elements abstracted from in actual empirical work. We will also assume our exhaustible resource is nondurable (i.e., oil, coal, etc., but not copper, bauxite, etc.). This permits us to abstract from the cascading "productivity" of the amount extracted currently. Durable machines are directly productive for many periods with the future. Our nondurable resource flow is not. It simply contributes to production in the current period.

Hulten simplifies matters by assuming "radioactive decay" depreciation of produced capital goods and a single commodity which can be consumed or invested in new machines. An illustrative four period case is presented in Table IV.

We define terms in the Table. The prices are all in present values discounted at period rate $r_t$

$\delta$ is the constant rate of depreciation

$R_t$ is the present value of rental per unit of capital used in period $t$ defined with respect to period 1.

$I_t$ is the investment set aside in period $t$ for use in period $t + 1$.

$p_t$ is the present value price of a unit of output consumed or used in period $t$.

Note price $p_t$ is equal to discounted net rentals plus end-period value. For example

$$p_0 = R_1 + (1 - \delta)R_2 + (1 - \delta)^2 R_3 + (1 - \delta)^3 R_4 + (1 - \delta)^4 p_4$$

and

$$p_2 = R_3 + (1 - \delta)R_4 + (1 - \delta)^2 p_4$$

Since the numeraire in period 1 is unity,

$$p_t = \frac{1}{\pi_{s=1}^t (1 + r_s)} \qquad t = 1, \ldots, 4.$$

where $r_s$ is the rate of discount on consumption goods implied by preferences of consumers and equals the marginal product of capital.

$K_t$ is amount of capital used in production in period $t + 1$. $K_t$ equals depreciated $K_0$ plus depreciated investments in previous periods. For example

$$K_3 = I_3 + (1 - \delta)I_2 + (1 - \delta)^2 I_1 + (1 - \delta)^3 K_0.$$

$C_t$ is aggregate consumption in period $t$.

## TABLE IV
### Intertemporal accounting system

| | (1) | (2) | (3) | (4) | (5) | (6) | (7) |
|---|---|---|---|---|---|---|---|
| | Delivery of investment to year $t$ (intermediate demand) | | | | Final demand export of capital | Consumption | Value of product sum of (1) through (6) |
| Year | 1 | 2 | 3 | 4 | | | |
| 1 Delivery of Investment — 1 | | $R_2 I_1$ | $R_3(1-\delta)I_1$ | $R_4(1-\delta)^2 I_1$ | $p_4(1-\delta)^3 I_1$ | $p_1 C_1$ | $p_1 Q_1$ |
| 2 From Year $t$ — 2 | | | $R_3 I_2$ | $R_4(1-\delta)I_2$ | $p_4(1-\delta)^2 I_2$ | $p_2 C_2$ | $p_2 Q_2$ |
| 3 | | | | $R_4 I_3$ | $p_4(1-\delta)I_3$ | $p_3 C_3$ | $p_3 Q_3$ |
| 4 | | | | | $p_4 I_4$ | $p_4 C_4$ | $p_4 Q_4$ |
| 5 Import of Capital | $R_1 K_0$ | $R_2(1-\delta)K_0$ | $R_3(1-\delta)^2 K_0$ | $R_4(1-\delta)^3 K_0$ | | | |
| 6 Total Capital Outlay (Rows 1–5) | $R_1 K_0$ | $R_2 K_1$ | $R_3 K_2$ | $R_4 K_3$ | | | |
| 7 Total Labour Outlay | $w_1 L_1$ | $w_2 L_2$ | $w_3 L_3$ | $w_4 L_4$ | | | |
| 8 Ex. Res. Use | $v_1(S_0 - S_1)$ | $v_1(S_1 - S_2)$ | $v_1(S_2 - S_3)$ | $v_1(S_3 - S_4)$ | | | |
| 9 Total Outlay (Rows 6–8) | $p_1 Q_1$ | $p_2 Q_2$ | $p_3 Q_3$ | $p_4 Q_4$ | | | |

$Q_t$ is aggregate output produced in period $t$.

$L_t$ is the labor used in production in period $t$.

$w_t$ is the wage rate in period $t$ discounted to period 1.

$S_t$ is the stock of exhaustible resources available at the end of period $t$. $S_t - S_{t-1}$ is resource use in period $t-1$. It might be oil used up in the period. $v_1$ is the rent per unit of exhaustible resources in period $t$ discounted to period 1. By "Hotelling's Rule" this price is constant across periods.

Now the present value of gross product over the four periods is

$$\sum_t p_t Q_t = \sum_t p_t I_t + \sum_t p_t C_t$$

and the present value of factor payments "originating" is

$$\sum_t p_t Q_t = \sum_t w_t L_t + v_1 \sum_t (S_t - S_{t-1}) + \sum_t R_t K_{t-1}$$

Substitution reveals

$$\sum_t p_t C_t + p_4 K_4 - p_0 K_0 = \sum_t w_t L_t + v_1 (S_0 - S_4) = W_4 \qquad (18)$$

$W_4$ is total value added over the four periods and has its counterpart in a value of factors used, namely $\sum_t w_t L_t$ and $v_1 (S_0 - S_4)$.

Hulten defines the percentage increase in $W_4$ (or $W_N = \sum p_t C_t + p_N K_N - p_0 K_0$) net of the weighted sum of percentage changes in factor inputs (here labor and exhaustible resources) as "the dynamic residual" which is viewed as a measure of productivity growth over the four (or $N$) periods. We proceed to this expression. Total differentiation of (18) yields

$$\sum_{t=1}^{N} \frac{p_t C_t}{W_N} \left[ \frac{Dp_t}{p_t} + \frac{DC_t}{C_t} \right] + \frac{p_N K_N}{W_N} \left[ \frac{Dp_N}{p_N} + \frac{DK_N}{K_N} \right] - \frac{p_0 K_0}{W_N} \left[ \frac{Dp_0}{p_0} + \frac{DK_0}{K_0} \right]$$

$$= \sum_{t=1}^{N} \frac{w_t L_t}{W_N} \left[ \frac{Dw_t}{w_t} + \frac{DL_t}{L_t} \right] - \frac{v_1 S_N}{W_N} \left[ \frac{Dv_1}{v_1} + \frac{DS_N}{S_N} + \frac{v_1 S_0}{W_N} \right] \left[ \frac{Dv_1}{v_1} + \frac{DS_0}{S_0} \right]$$

Note $Dv_1/v_1 = r_1$ and $DS_N = Z_N$ and $DS_0 = Z_1$. The former is the Hotelling Rule—dynamic efficiency condition and the latter indicates that an increment of stock at period $t$ equals the amount that the change in the stock at period $t$ equals the flow $Z_t$ drawn from the stock. Clearly then $S_0 - S_4 = Z_1 + Z_2 + Z_3 + Z_4$. The dynamic residual is

$$T(0, N) = \sum_t \frac{p_t C_t}{W_N} \frac{DC_t}{C_t} + \frac{p_N K_N}{W_N} \cdot \frac{DK_N}{K_N} - \frac{p_0 K_0}{W_N} \frac{DK_0}{K_0} - \sum_t \frac{w_t L_t}{W_N} \frac{DL_t}{L_t}$$

$$- \frac{v_1}{W_N} [Z_1 - Z_N]$$

or the percentage increment in value-added between period 0 and period $N$, net of the weighted percentage increases in primary factors used (or used up) in production over the time span. Note that in balanced growth with exhaustible resources (as in Stiglitz [90]) $Z_t > Z_{t+i}$ and thus other things being the same exhaustible resource conservation is roughly a substitute for technical progress (as measured by the dynamic residual). We say roughly because one cannot impose alternative exhaustion strategies on an economy and still satisfy the intertemporal efficiency conditions although one can impose alternative rates of say Hicks-neutral technical progress and observe different exhaustion trajectories.

Hulten makes two important observations following his derivation of $T(0, N)$ (without of course exhaustible resources). First $T(0, N)$ can be derived in a continuous time framework using Malinvaud's intertemporal possibility frontier and assuming linear homogeneity of the underlying aggregate production function net of technical progress. In this case prices equal value of marginal products and are proportional to marginal utilities in a static context and zero intertemporal arbitrage (the Dorfman, Samuelson, Solow conditions) holds across periods. Secondly, the dynamic residual $T(0, N)$ can be shown to be a weighted sum of period by period Solow residuals. That is

$$T(0, N) = \sum_t \frac{p_t Q_t}{W_N} T_t^*$$

where $T_t^*$ is a single period residual first analyzed by Solow [84] and expressible as the rate of Hicks-neutral technical progress in period $t$. The weights sum to a number greater than or equal to one and were introduced by Domar in a related aggregation problem. Thus in balanced growth in a model with a production function exhibiting constant Hicks-neutral technical progress $\lambda$ (e.g., Stiglitz [90]) the dynamic residual for $N$ period growth will be $\eta\lambda$ with $\eta \geq 1$ and

$\eta\lambda \geq \lambda$ reflects the induced investment (and capital accumulation) occasioned by technical progress occurring at rate $\lambda$ per "period". In any case we have a precise relationship between period by period measures of productivity change (the period by period Solow residual) and the measure $T(0, N)$ relevant to the complete multi-period context. We noted that the reason that the multi-period measure is a complicated magnification of the single period measures is that once over technical progress in a period not only "releases" extra output, it also induces more investment because there is more product to divide between current consumption and current investment.

In (18), we observe that $S_0 - S_4 = Z_1 + Z_2 + Z_3 + Z_4$ and $v_1 \sum Z_t$ is the value of rentals over the four periods expressed in period 1 resource rental rates. We discounted values to period 1. Also $v_1(S_0 - S_4)$ is the diminution in future stock value expressed in period 1 for resource use over the four periods. Thus $v_1(S_0 - S_4)$ is economic depreciation of the exhaustible resource stock arising because of resource use over the four periods. Rentals on resources equals the negative of stock depreciation, $\delta V(S)/\delta t$, where $V(S(t))$ is the value of the remaining stock $S(t)$ at date $t$. Ambiguity arises in the measurement of an economy's output in the sense that it is not obvious on which side of the first equality $v_1 \sum Z_t (= v_1(S_0 - S_4))$ should be placed in defining the multiperiod product-income accounts. If $v_1 \sum Z_t$ is put on the income side with a positive sign we have gross multiperiod "product" measured on the income side as $\sum_t w_t L_t + v_1 \sum_t Z_t$. However if depreciation of resource stock is placed on the output side we have multiperiod "product" measured as $\sum_t p_t C_5 + [p_4 K_4 - p_0 K_0] - v_1[S_0 - S_4]$. In this latter case a resource producing nation's product would be viewed as much smaller than if the former accounting convention were followed.[9] People have commented that Kuwait would be viewed as very rich or very poor, depending on how stock depletion is factored into the accounts. This "paradox" is clear in our four period framework but occurs as well in the one period accounts. Should annual depletion be viewed as negative investment (placed on the product side) or as

---

[9] If investment gross of depreciation of reproducible capital (equal to savings) equals resource rents, then over the four periods $\sum_t p_t C_t = \sum w_t L_t$ and for $L_t$ constant, $C_t$ will be constant. This procedure, invest resource rents in reproducible capital was discussed by me and has been recently reanalyzed in Solow [86].

positive income (rents placed on the income side). Clearly the calculation of $T(0, N)$ is not affected. However the definition of annual and multiperiod "product" is affected. For countries with a relatively small mineral extraction sector, the magnitudes involved will be small on an annual basis since it is dynamic or Hotelling rents that are involved as income and these Hotelling unit rents are used to compute economic depreciation of the stock. Much of value added in the mineral extraction sectors is labor and capital used in mining and refining and is not Hotelling rent. However in countries specialized in say oil production, much of the price of oil is Hotelling rent and the magnitudes are large relative to say a nation's annual wage bill It seems clear to this contributor that a nation's "product" should be defined net of economic depreciation of the resource stocks or resource stock disinvestment should be combined with positive investment in new buildings and machines (reproducible capital). That is, Hotelling rents should not be treated as income symmetric with wage payments, but as expressed in their "dual" guise as economic depreciation and netted out of the product side of the accounts. A group of people living off declining oil stocks be very well off as consumers but are in an obvious sense impoverishing themselves over time and this will show up if economic depreciation is placed on the product side of the accounts and not as resource rents on the income side.

In 1981, Kuwait's GNP was 9041 and GDP was 6904 (IMF *International Financial Statistics Yearbook* 1987). Petroleum exports were 4778.3 money units. Petroleum production was 56 931 thousand metric tons and domestic consumption 15 822 metric tons (*U. N.* 1984 *Energy Statistics Yearbook,* pp. 159–160, Table 14). This yields exports of 41109 metric tons fetching $4778.3/41109 = 0.116$ money units per ton. Hence the value of oil production is $0.116 \times 56931 = 6604.0$ money units. Suppose extraction costs are 0.1 of this value of output and extraction costs are constant. Then $0.9 \times 6604 = 5943.6$ money units is resource rent and is 66% of GNP and 86% of GDP. Most of this rent is Ricardian or differential rent representing the relative cost advantage of Kuwait oil over the marginal oil extracted in 1981 in the world. The marginal ton extracted in the world would command a Hotelling rent of its selling price minus its cost of extraction. This number multiplied by Kuwait's production is Kuwait's Hotelling rent in a textbook world of no capacity constraints, uncertainty or discoveries. It is this Hotelling rent which should be netted out of reported GNP and GDP to allow for economic depreciation of the stock. In the United States, Hotelling rents are treated as income in the national accounts. (See Soladay [82].) As is appropriate, there is no entry for stock depreciation given the entry for rent. However, the correct method would place stock depreciation as disinvestment in the product side of the accounts and omit Hotelling rents from the income side.[10]

What about residual income ascribable to land? (Differential land rent or Ricardian land rent?) This return is of course income and should be added to labor income $\sum_t w_t L_t$. These natural resource rents arise from differences in quality of land and are not related time as are Hotelling Rents and their variants. If exhaustible resources are heterogeneous in quality, part of the rent is a dynamic or Hotelling rent and part is a differential rent. In this case the part ascribable to qualify differences should be treated as income symmetric with land rent and the part ascribable to exhaustibility should be treated as economic depreciation and placed in the output side of the accounts (i.e., netted out of the value of consumption and net accumulation of reproducible capital). The conceptual problem of separating dynamic or Hotelling rent from differential or Ricardian rent with heterogeneous exhaustible resources is discussed in the Introduction above and in Chapter 3 of Hartwick and Olewiler [36].

## 7. THEORY AND FACTS (STYLIZED AND OTHERWISE)

Theory is supposed to provide a convincing explanation of observed phenomena and to provide predictions which can be verified. The phenomena to explain in the study of exhaustible resources are historically given paths of extraction and of output prices. Slade [80]

---

[10] Depletion allowances for tax purposes are not entered as stock depreciation in the national accounts. Soladay [82] advocates entering stock depreciation as negative investment and stock discoveries as positive investment but he is imprecise in his criticism of the treatment of exhaustible resources in the U.S. national accounts overall. Note that part of exploration expenditures are treated as investment in the U.S. accounts and are depreciated in a manner similar to that for other durable investments.

has reported on long time trends in quantities and prices. An explanation of quantity trends would seem most straightforward—quantities consumed increase with industrial output, population growth, and technical changes which make certain resources such as oil essential in the production of say transportation services. There remains the question of whether low priced oil made internal combustion engines ideal in some sense or whether the development of the engines made the development of oil sources economically attractive. Quantities produced are of course presumed to reflect stock-flow adjustment assuring the owner of the stock a maximum of the present value of profits.

The stock-flow adjustment reflects the basic zero profit arbitrage condition

$$y(t) + \dot{p}(t) = p(t) \cdot r$$

where $y(t)$ is income from capital good, $p(t)$ is the price of the capital good and $r$ is the interest rate. This equation appears so simple that a statistical test of its validity appears easy to pursue. This seems particularly so for the Hotelling Rule specialization

$\dfrac{\dot{}}{p(t) - c(t)} = (p(t) - c(t)) \cdot r$ where $c(t)$ is the cost of extracting the

marginal ton of $q(t)$ extracted at date $t$.

Nordhous [69] suggested the Hotelling rule could be invalid over the long run for two reasons. He first suggested that oligopolization of supply would result in some departure of marginal revenue from $p(t)$ in the Hotelling formula. Hence the time path of quantities extracted would be somewhat flatter than the Hotelling Rule would imply. This we have seen, in theory. A monopolist in many cases extracts a given stock over a longer period than would a group of competitive extractors. In such a case if $\dfrac{\dot{}}{p(t) - c(t)} / [p(t) - c(t)]$

where regressed on $r$, the left hand side would be larger than $r$. The intercept might pick this *a priori* discrepancy up. Nordhous solved for a long term price trajectory under competitive assumptions and observed a discrepancy between the observed price path and the path predicted under competitive conditions.

The second reason Nordhous suggested for the Hotelling arbitrage rule to not be valid was that speculative activity could be destabilizing. He suggested that futures markets are incomplete and as a consequence the putative stabilizing effect of speculative activity may not be observed. We will return to this point below when we take up the question of how expectations of future values and trends are formed. We introduced this topic in our analysis of output price uncertainty and the firm.

Clearly a third reason is simply that with declining quality of stock $\dfrac{\dot{}}{p(t)-c(t)} < (p(t)-c(t)) \cdot r$ since $-C_S(q(t), S(t)) > 0$ in the more general intertemporal arbitrage condition. Nordhaus incorporated this discrepancy by considering a series of distinct exhaustible sources each with a constant $c(t)$ but with $c(t)$ different for each distinct source (the Herfindahl model). But it remains an open question as to how to incorporate these cost shifts in a complete statistical test since data are few on the exent and timing of the shifts. Since $+\partial C(q(t), S(t))/\partial S(t) \cong -q(t)\Delta C_q(q(t), S(t))$ one observes that the cost shift term is a function of current Ricardian or differential rent and could easily exceed $\dfrac{\dot{}}{[p(t)-c(t)]}$. This raises the question of the relevance of the simple Hotelling rule in markets with declining quality of stock. In these latter cases, differential rent terms may swamp the capital gain terms or the capital gains on rent may be a "second order order smalls".

Speculation involves owners of stock holding their stock off the market under the belief that capital gains will exceed normal interest income obtainable by selling the stock today and investing the proceeds. Cornering the market involves a single speculator buying up *all* available stock and supplying demanders at relatively high prices. This makes sense in exhaustible resource markets in principle. If all stock could be bought up at the current market price for output the purchaser could supply the market as a monopolist and in the change of regimes reap a large once over capital gain. But the buying up of all stocks is generally very difficult and successful monopolization in resource markets is not a widespread phenomenon though cartelization of diamond supply, nickel supply, uranium supply, and oil supply has been successful over certain limited periods.

The central quality of speculation as a bubble is that of a lottery.

It takes many entrants to make prices move up and only a few reap the substantial capital gains before the speculative bubble bursts. Just as many people willingly play lotteries, speculations attract the needed critical mass of players regularly. This is basically destabilizing speculation. It is only an irrational activity to the extent one thinks of lotteries as games played by fools. The difference between a speculative bubble and a pure lottery is that in the latter people enter, generally aware of the risks, whereas in a speculative bubble, an entrant is never sure whether price reflects some basic underlying value or opportunity cost or the value plus speculative froth resulting from the rapid entry of bidders. Stabilizing speculation is essentially arbitrage activity which averages out different beliefs of different people about values of future prices. Thus if half of potential buyers believe the price will be $p + \alpha$ next period and half believe it will be $p - \alpha$, arbitrageurs can sign contracts to supply both sides in the future, implicitly buying stock today at known prices, and make some profit *ex post* or some loss. These arbitrageurs are speculators who live by implicitly aggregating distinct beliefs into a group or average belief. It is this type of speculation which is endorsed by economists as price stabilizing and socially desirable. This is essentially what stock markets and commodity brokerages accomplish. They transform different beliefs of agents into a single market clearing price, instant by instant. Needless to say in markets with no transactions costs or "drift", speculative profits will equal speculative losses over the long run.

We noted in our analysis of the firm and future output price uncertainty how beliefs about levels of future uncertain prices (essentially probabilities linked to various possible future prices) actually fed back and in part determined the level of current prices in the period before uncertainty was resolved. There is a simple illustration of the aggregation of diverse beliefs. Given a person's subjective probabilities on where prices will be at any date in the future and discount rates, we can translate these beliefs into a bid at the current date. For example if person A believes that the price of a share in a company paying a dividend will be $20 five years from now with probability 0.5 or $15 with probability 0.5 then $\left(\dfrac{1}{1.1}\right)^4 (10 + 7.5)$ is the current discounted expected price. Allowing for a premium for risk, person A will enter a bid today somewhat below $\left(\dfrac{1}{1.1}\right)^4$ $17.50 for a share. This is the registration today of one person's beliefs about the future course of prices. All owners of stock will also have beliefs about the future and thus current bids, and all potential purchases of stock will have beliefs about the value of future prices and thus current bids. The intersection of these schedules of "bids" and "asks" will provide a price at which sellers will willingly surrender their ownership claims and purchaser take on the claims. Distinct beliefs become aggregated into a single price, arrived at a central clearing house or brokerage agency. In Figure 27, we illustrate.

In Figure 27, the flats are *quantities* bid for or asked on and the levels indicate prices at which bids and asks are registered. Any belief about future prices can be "translated" into a current bid or ask and quantities can be thought of a part of the strength of the belief about the location of futures prices. A broker who receives the bids and asks can reap the "producer surplus" and "consumer surplus" as personal profit since he or she can perfectly price discriminate given knowledge of the precise bids. This is a digres-

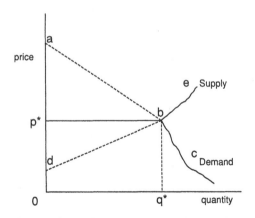

FIGURE 27 At the end of a trading period, bidders (purchasers) along *ab* expect the future price to rise above $p^*$ and asker (sellers) along *db* expect the future price to be below $p^*$. Along *be*, current askers expect the future price to lie above $p^*$ and along *bc*, current bidders expect the future price to lie below $p^*$. ("Above" and "below" must be adjusted for interest rates i.e. future expected prices are discounted.)

sion however. Our point is that different beliefs about the future get aggregated into a current observed market price. Note that two relatively steep schedules would reflect much uncertainty about future prices and small shifts in such schedules would result in relatively wide price movements. Relatively flat schedules reflect a relative concensus among participants as the future course of prices. Small shifts in schedules would have little effect on price per share but could have relatively large effects on the volume of shares traded. These observations about the degree of concensus about the future levels of price could be refined if we considered one schedule relatively flat and one relatively steep and *vice versa*. The point is that there are institutions for "aggregating" diverse views among participants as to the future course of events in markets into a single "composite" view. Current prices reflect a diversity of beliefs about future prices.

How are expectations of future prices formed? It is only information available from the past and current periods which can be "processed" to provide expectations. A basic rationality postulate is that those who form "good" expectations survive and those who are poor at forming expectations lose money. Those whose expectations are fulfilled do not lose money and those who expectations are not fulfilled make losses and withdraw from the market. One would like to infer from these considerations that the current equilibrium price is an accurate predictor of the price next period, subject to interest rate adjustments. Such arguments have been made for *individuals*. Roughly speaking, rationality implies that the current price is the best estimate of the average price next period. This is the *efficient markets* hypothesis. However one would require additional assumptions on how individuals react to bidding by other members of a group of investors before one could argue that the current price was the "most rational" price for a security. Of course how "rational" the current price is, is at the heart of price volatility. The observed "excess volatility" of stock market prices suggests that the formation of expectations by individuals in groups may have substantial "group effects" built in. For example, estimating the price of gold tomorrow by extrapolating its value from the past three prices builds into the estimate any rule of thumb other agents are using to predict. The estimators are correlated.

In exhaustible resource markets there is a necessary degree of stock size uncertainty at a point in time because the future stocks are generally hidden below the surface. Uncertainty is not resolved each year as it is in say cocoa markets in which supplies are ultimately harvests. There is never a complete harvest for an exhaustible resource except when a deposit is completely depleted and that is usually only known a short time before it occurs. It is generally learning about stock size by extracting. Thus endemic stock size uncertainty presumably makes for more uncertainty reflected in current market prices than in other types of commodities. Moreover uncertainty about the pace of development of backstops also plagues exhaustible resource markets. We argued that socially optimal extraction programs would differ from competitive paths for stock size uncertainty. There seems to be no reason why this should lead to increased market price volatility although we did not pursue this topic in detail. Stiglitz [89] made formal investigations of output price instabilities but not in terms of endemic market failure. Solow [85] speculated about whether durability *per se* of exhaustible resources would lead to excess volatility in output prices but did not reach a definite conclusion. Above we noted that future output price and interest rate uncertainty resulted in higher average profits for firms. On the face of it, one might surmise that this would induce "excess" volatility of prices in exhaustible resource markets. There may be arbitrage possibilities which "neturalize" these possible "excess" volatilities and we have not explored this line of argument. Though such preference by firms for output price uncertainty has been observed for non-resource industries, such industries did not have outputs emerging. from durable stocks. They involved industries such as bread and shoes in which the output price did not involve dynamic rent and interest rate effects. Thus our results on a resource extracting firm's preference for interest rate and output price uncertainty await integration into models which include shareholders and a financial side of the firm. Shiller [78] has argued that there is "excess" volatility in prices in markets for shares in companies such as the New York Stock Exchange. Such "excesses" may be compouned in markets involving exhaustible resource stocks. We note also that the basic zero profit intertemporal arbitrage equation does not fit well for stock market data (see for example Marsh and Merton [63] who work with aggregate data).

There remains the questions of whether "noise" in such series swamps "trend" and that we will only observe the basic arbitrage relationship on series that have been smoothed or averaged over long periods. Ultimately we expect prices for exhaustible resources to rise as stocks run down and the precise form of the price rise may be difficult to discover though some zero profit intertemporal arbitrage relationship must hold. With free entry people do not consistently make "excess" profits!

We turn now to the phenomenon of declining price for exhaustible resources. Such trends were observed in the first half of the twentieth century for prices for many exhaustible resources. Technical progress in the extraction process can yield this result. Though rent on the marginal ton extracted must rise in Hotelling's model, this can occur with *declining* extraction costs and declining prices. In our analysis of the extracting firm, we provided a formulation with an explicit extraction production function with a technical progress parameter. Ingenious econometric sleuthing might provide estimates of technical progress in extraction, an apparently important source of productivity growth in general in industrialized economies. Men and mules were replaced in mines by machines.

There are two other plausible explanations for declines in resource prices. A shrinkage in demand such as that associated with the Depression of the 1930's will do it. Though we generally take the demand schedule for a resource as unchanging over time, this is only a convenience and does not reflect known facts. In addition, unanticipated discoveries of new sources of stock will drive down current prices. We noted above how current prices reflect beliefs about future stocks and discoveries. If these expectations are contradicted by subsequent events, current prices will adjust to the new information. A few large unanticipated discoveries of stock will show up as declines in current price in a Hotelling framework with stock size uncertainty.

Finally we turn to an issue raised by Adelman [1]. Does not theory predict that low cost sources of supply of an exhaustible resource should be exhausted before higher cost sources are tapped? With no set up costs and no uncertainty the answer is yes. With uncertainty a new low cost source of supply may emerge. But let us remain with no set up costs and certainty. With a variety of small deposits with different extraction costs, we expect there to be simultaneously extraction within a period for the period defined for more than an instant. The good quality deposits will earn a differential or Ricardian rent compared with the marginal deposit. All will earn a dynamic or Hotelling rent. This we have observed and discussed. However in a subsequent period there should be a new array of higher cost deposits being worked. No intramarginal deposit from the previous period should still be worked. This is Adelman's point. Low cost deposits should be exhausted within the period before higher cost deposits are worked in a subsequent period. Resource markets are non-competitive in Adelman's view if a low cost deposit, an intramarginal deposit is operated while higher cost deposits are opened in a subsequent period. It is hard to disagree with this view. A possible way to explain the departure from competititve behavior is that national security and national development exigencies intrude and over-ride the purely economic issues. A country with high cost deposits should buy the resource from abroad until the low cost deposits are exhausted. However a high cost country may wish to develop its sources to protect itself from a politically inspired breach in supply. Alternatively a poor country may develop its relatively high cost supply in order to sell and gain revenues to be used in a national development. It may not be able to borrow for development using its stocks in-ground as collateral. Thus Adelman's argument makes good sense. Much observed extractive activity contradicts predictions from competitive economic models of extraction and should be attributed to a non-competitive mode of resource development. But political exigencies have often over-ridden plain economic consideration.

## References

[1] Adelman, M. A. [1986] "Scarcity and World Oil Prices," *Review of Economics and Statistics*, 68, pp. 387–397.
[2] Anderson, James [1777] "An inquiry into the Nature of the Corn Laws, with a View to the Corn Bill proposed for Scotland."
[3] Arrow, K. J. and S. Chang [1982] "Optimal Pricing Use and Exploration of Uncertain Natural Resource Stocks," *Journal of Environmental Economics and Management*, 9, pp. 1–10.
[4] Blackorby, Chas., D. Donaldson and D. Malony [1984] "Consumer's Surplus and Welfare Change in a Simple Dynamic Economy," *Review of Economic Studies*, 51, January, pp. 171–176.
[5] Blaug, M. [1968] *Economic Theory in Retrospect*, Revised Edition, Homeword Illinois: Irwin.

[6] Cairns, Robert [1986] "Intergenerational Equity and Heterogeneous Resources," *Scandinavian Journal of Economics*, **88**(2), pp. 401–416.

[7] Campbell, H. F. [1980] "The Effect of Capital Intensity on the Optimal Rate of Extraction of a Mineral," *Canadian Journal of Economics*, **13**, pp. 349–356.

[8] Crabbé, P. J. [1982] "The Effect of Capital Intensity on the Optimal Rate of Extraction of a Mineral Deposit," *Canadian Journal of Economics*, **15**, No. 3, August, pp. 534–540.

[9] Crabbé, P. J. [1983] "The Contribution of L. C. Gray to the Economic Theory of Exhaustible Natural Resources and Its Roots in the History of Economic Thought," *Journal of Environmental Economics and Management* **10**, pp. 195–220.

[10] Dasgupta, P. and G. Heal [1974] "The Optimal Depletion of Exhaustible Resources," *Review of Economic Studies*, Symposium, pp. 3–28.

[11] Dasgupta, P. and G. M. Heal [1979] *Economic Theory and Exhaustible Resources*, Cambridge: Cambridge University Press.

[12] Dasgupta, P., G. Heal and J. Stiglitz [1980] "The Taxation of Exhaustible Resources," in G. A. Hughes and G. M. Heal, eds., *Public Policy and the Tax System*, London: Allen and Unwin.

[13] Dasgupta, P. and J. E. Stiglitz [1981] "Resource Depletion Under Technological Uncertainty," *Econometrica*, **49**, 1, January, pp. 85–104.

[14] Dasgupta, S. and T. Mitra [1983] "Intergenerational Equity and Efficient Allocation of Exhaustible Resources," *International Economic Review*, **24**, pp. 13–54.

[15] Deshmukh, S. D. and S. Pliska [1980] "Optimal Consumption and Exploration of Nonrenewable Resources Under Uncertainty," *Econometrica*, **48**, pp. 177–200.

[16] Devarajan, S. and A. C. Fisher [1982] "Exploration and Scarcity," *Journal of Political Economic*, **90**, pp. 1279–90.

[17] Devarajan, S. and A. C. Fisher [1982] "Measures of Natural Resource Scarcity under Uncertainty," in V. K. Smith and J. V. Krutilla, eds., *Explorations in Natural Resource Economics*, Baltimore: John Hopkins University Press.

[18] Diewert, E. and T. Lewis [1982] "The Comparative Dynamics of Efficient Programs of Capital Accumulation and Resource Depletion," in W. Eichhorn, R. Henn, K. Neumann and R. W. Shephard, eds., *Economic Theory of Exhaustible Resources*, Wien: Physica-Verlag, pp. 301–326.

[19] Dixit, A., P. Hammond and M. Hoel [1980] "On Hartwick's Rule for Regular Maximum Paths of Capital Accumulation and Resource Depletion," *Review of Economic Studies*, **47**, 3, April, 347–54.

[20] Dorfman, R., P. A. Samuelson and R. M. Solow [1958] *Linear Programming and Economic Analysis*, New york: McGraw-Hill.

[21] Drury, R. C. [1982] "Exploitation of Many Deposits of an Exhaustible Resource: Comment," *Econometrica*, **50**, 3, May, pp. 769–774.

[22] Epstein, L. G. [1983] "Decreasing Absolute Risk Aversion and Utility Indices Derived from Cake-Eating Problems," *Journal of Economic Theory*, **29**, 2, April, pp. 245–264.

[23] Esweran, M., T. Heaps and T. Lewis [1983] "On the Non Existence of Market Equilibria in Exhaustible Resource Markets with Decreasing Costs," *Journal of Political Economy*, **91**, pp. 145–167.

[24] Eswaran, Mukesh and Tracy lewis [1984] "Appropriability and the Extraction of a Common Property Resource," *Economica*, **51**, pp. 393–400.

[25] Eswaran, Mukesh and Tracy Lewis [1985] "Exhaustible Resources and Alterna-

tive Equilibrium Concepts," *Canadian Journal of Economics*, **XVIII**, No. 3, August, pp. 459–473.

[26] Farrow, S. [1985] "Testing the Efficiency of Extraction of Stock Resource," *Journal of Political Economy*, **93**, pp. 452–87.

[27] Fetter, Frank A. [1934] "Rent" in E. R. A. Seligman, editor, *Encyclopedia of Social Sciences*, **XIII**, New York: Macmillan, pp. 289–292.

[28] Flux, A. W. [1913] "Rent, Basis of," in Sir. R. H. I. Palgrave, editor, *Dictionary of Political Economy*, Vol. **III**, London: Macmillan, pp. 282–284.

[29] Gallini, N., T. Lewis and R. Ware [1983] "Strategic Timing and Pricing of a Substitute in a Cartelized Resource Market," *Canadian Journal of Economics*, **16**, 3, August, pp. 429–446.

[30] Gilbert, R. J. and S. Goldman [1978] "Potential Competition and the Monopoly Price of an Exhaustible Resource," *Journal of Economic Theory*, **17**, pp. 319–331.

[31] Gray, L. C. [1914] "Rent under the Assumption of Exhaustibility," *Quarterly Journal of Economics*, **28**, May, pp. 466–489.

[32] Halvorsen, R. and T. R. Smith [1984] "On Measuring Natural Resource Scarcity," *Journal of Political Economy*, **92**, pp. 954–64.

[33] Hartwick, J. M. [1978] "Exploitation of Many Deposits of an Exhaustible Resource," *Econometrica*, **46**, No. 1, January, pp. 201–218.

[34] Hartwick, J. M. [1983] "Learning About and Exploiting Exhaustible Resource Deposits of Uncertain Size," *Canadian Journal of Economics*, **16**, 3, August, pp. 391–410.

[35] Hartwick, J. M., M. C. Kemp and N. V. Long [1986] "Set-Up Costs and the Theory of Exhaustible Resources," *Journal of Environmental Economics and Management*, **13**, 3, September, pp. 212–224.

[36] Hartwick, J. M. and N. D. Olewiler [1986] *The Economics of Natural Resource Use*, New York: Harper and Row.

[37] Hartwick, J. M. and David Yeung [1985] "Preference for Output Price Uncertainty by the Nonrenewable Resource Extracting Firm," *Economics Letters*, **19**, pp. 85–89.

[38] Heal, G. and M. Barrow [1980] "The Relationship Between Interest Rates and Metal Price Movements," *Review of Economic Studies*, **47**, pp. 161–81.

[39] Herfindahl, O. C. [1967] "Depletion and Economic Theory," in M. Gaffney, ed., *Extractive Resources and Taxation*, Wisconsin, University of Wisconsin Press.

[40] Hoel, M. [1983] "Future Conditions and Present Extraction," *Resources and Energy*, **5**, pp. 303–311.

[41] Hoel, P. G. [1984] *Introduction to Mathematical Statistics*, 5th Edition, New York: Wiley.

[42] Hotelling, H. [1925] "A General Mathematical Theory of Depreciation," *Journal of the American Statistical Association*, **XX**, pp. 340–353.

[43] Hotelling, H. [1931] "The Economics of Exhaustible Resources," *Journal of Political Economic*, **XXXIX**, April, pp. 137–175.

[44] Hulten, Chas. R. [1979] "On the "Importance" of Productivity Change," *American Economic Review*, **69**, No. 1, March, pp. 126–136.

[45] Hyde, R. and J. Markusen [1982] "Exploration versus Extraction Costs or Determinants of Optimal Mineral Rights Lenses," *Economic Record*, September, pp. 224–234.

[46] Jevons, W. S. [1871] *The Theory of Political Economy*, London: Macmillan.

[47] Jorgenson, D. [1974] "The Economic Theory of Replacement and Depreciation," in W. Sellekaerts, *Econometrics and Economic Theory*: *Essays in Honor*

*of Jan Tinbergen,* White Plains, N.Y.: International Arts and Sciences Press, pp. 189–222.

[48] Kames, Lord (Henry Home) [1788] *The Gentleman Farmer,* 3rd Edition, Edinburgh: printed for John Bell and G. G. J. and J. Robinson.

[49] Kemp, M. C. and N. V. Long [1978] "The Optimal Consumption of Depletable Natural Resources," *Quarterly Journal of Economics,* **92,** No. 2, May, pp. 345–353.

[50] Kemp, M. C. and N. V. Long [1980] "On Two Folk Theorems Concerning the Extraction of Exhaustible Resources," *Econometrica,* **48,** pp. 663–674.

[51] Kemp, M. C. and N. V. Long [1980] "Resource Extraction Under Conditions of Common Access," in M. C. Kemp and N. V. long, eds., *Exhaustible Resources, Optimality and Trade,* Amsterdam: North Holland.

[52] Krautkraemer, J. A. [1985] "The Cut-Off Grade and the Theory of Extraction," Working Paper # 1284-1, Economics, Washington State University (revised).

[53] Lasserre, P. [1985] "Discovery Costs as a Measure of Rent," *Canadian Journal of Economics,* **XVIII,** August, pp. 474–483.

[54] Lee, T. and L. L. Wilde [1980] "Market Structure and Innovation: A Reformulation," *Quarterly Journal of Economics,* March pp. 429–436.

[55] Leland, H. [1978] "Optimal Risk Sharing and the Leasing of Natural Resources with Application to Oil and Gas on the OCS," *Q.J.E.,* **XCII,** September, pp. 413–38.

[56] Levhari, D. and D. Leviatan [1977] "Notes on Hotelling's Economics of Exhaustible Resources," *Canadian Journal of Economics,* **X,** May, pp. 177–192.

[57] Levhari, D. and L. Mirman [1980] "The Great Fish War: An Example Using a Dynamic Cournot–Nash Solution," *Bell Journal of Economics,* **11,** pp. 322–334.

[58] Lewis, T. [1982] "Sufficient Conditions for Extracting Least Cost Resource First," *Econometrica,* Vol. **50,** No. 4, July, pp. 1081–1083.

[59] Lewis, T., R. Lindsay and R. Ware [1986] "Long Term Bilateral Monopoly: The Case of an Exhaustible Resource," *The Rand Journal of Economics,* **17,** Vol. 1, Spring, pp. 89–104.

[60] Lewis, T., S. A. Matthews and H. S. Burness [1979] "Monopoly and the Rate of Extraction of Exhaustible Resources: Comment," *American Economic Review,* **69,** March, pp. 227–230.

[61] Long, N. V. and H. W. Sinn [1984] "Optimal Taxation and Economic Depreciation: A General Equilibrium Model with Capital and an Exhaustible Resource," Essay 13 in M. C. Kemp and N. V. Long, eds., *Essays in the Economics of Exhaustible Resources,* Amsterdam: Elsevier, pp. 227–246.

[62] Loury, G. [1986] "A Theory of 'Oiligopoly': Cournot–Nash Equilibrium in Exhaustible Resource Markets with Fixed Supplies," *International Economic Review,* **27,** 2, June, pp. 285–301.

[63] Marsh, T. A. and R. C. Merton [1985] "Dividend Behavior for the Aggregate Stock Market," Sloan School Working Paper # 1670, MIT.

[64] Marshall, A. [1916] *Principles of Economics,* Seventh Edition, London: Macmillan.

[65] Mill, J. S. [1878] *Principles of Political Economy,* Vol. I, New York: Appleton and Company.

[66] Miller, M. H. and C. W. Upton [1985] "A Test of the Hotelling Valuation Principle," *Journal of Political Economy,* **93,** pp. 1–25.

[67] Muth, Richard F. [1968] "Rent" in D. L. Sills, editor, *International Encylopedia of the Social Sciences,* Vol. **13,** New York: Macmillan, pp. 454–461.

[68] Newbery, D. [1981] "Oil Prices, Cartels and the Problem of Dynamic Inconsistency," *Economic Journal,* **91,** September, pp. 617–646.

[69] Nordhous, W. D. [1973] "The Allocation of Energy Resources," *Brookings Paper on Economic Activity,* **3,** pp. 529–570.

[70] Orchard, J. E. [1922] "The Rent on Mineral Lands," *Quarterly Journal of Economics,* Vol. **XXXVI,** pp. 290–318.

[71] Pindyck, R. S. [1980] "Uncertainty and Exhaustible Resource Markets," *Journal of Political Economy,* Vol. **88,** No. 61, pp. 1203–1225.

[72] Reece, D. K. [1978] "Competitive Bidding for Offshore Petroleum Leases," *Bell Journal of Economics,* **9,** Autumn, pp. 369–384.

[73] Ricardo, D. [1951] *On the Principles of Political Economy and Taxation,* edited by P. Sraffa, Volume I of *The Works and Correspondence of David Ricardo,* Cambridge: Cambridge University Press.

[74] Riley, John G. and William Samuelson [1981] "Optimal Auctions," *American Economic Review,* No. 3, June, pp. 381–392.

[75] Salant, S. [1976] "Exhaustible Resources and Industrial Structure: A Nash–Cournot Approach to the World Oil Market," *Journal of Political Economy,* **84,** 5, pp. 1079–1093.

[76] Samuelson, P. A. [1964] "Tax Deductability of Economic Depreciation to Insure Invariant Valuations," *Journal of Political Economy,* **72,** pp. 604–606.

[77] Scott, A. [1973] *Natural Resources: the Economics of Conservation,* Toronto: McCelland and Stewart.

[78] Shiller, R. J. [1981] "Do Stock Prices Move Too Much to be Justified by Subsequent Changes in Dividends?," *American Economic Review,* **71,** 3, June, pp. 421–436.

[79] Sinn, H. W. [1984] "Common Property Resources, Storage Facilities and Ownership Structures: A Cournot model of the Oil Market," *Economica,* **51,** pp. 235–252.

[80] Slade, M. [1982] "Trends in Natural-Resource Commodity Prices: An Analysis of the Time Domain," *Journal of Environmental Economics and Management,* **9,** pp. 122–37.

[81] Smith, V. K. [1981] "The Empirical Relevance of Hotelling's Model for Natural Resources," *Resources and Energy,* **3,** pp. 105–117.

[82] Soladay, John J. [1980] "Measurement of Income and Product in the Oil and Gas Mining Industries," in Dan Usher, editor, *The Measurement of Capital,* National Bureau of Income and Wealth, Chicago: University of Chicago Press, pp. 347–376.

[83] Solow, R. M. [1956] "A Contribution to the Theory of Economic Growth," *Quarterly Journal of Economics,* **70,** pp. 65–94.

[84] Solow, R. M. [1957] "Technical Change and the Aggregate Production Function," *Review of Economics and Statistics,* **39,** August.

[85] Solow, R. M. [1974] "The Economics of Resources and the Resources of Economics," *American Economic Review,* May.

[86] Solow, R. M. [1986] "On the Integenerational Allocation of Natural Resources," *Scandinavian Journal of Economics,* **88,** 1, pp. 141–149.

[87] Solow, R. M. and F. Ware [1977] "Extraction Costs in the Theory of Exhaustible Resources," *Bell Journal of Economics,* Autumn, Vol. **7,** No. 2, pp. 359–370.

[88] Sorley, W. R. [1889] "Mining Royalties and their Effects on the Iron and Coal Trades," *Journal of the Royal Statistical Society,* March, pp. 60–98.

[89] Stiglitz, J. E. [1974] "Growth with Exhaustible Natural Resources: The Competitive Economy," *Review of Economic Studies*, Symposium, pp. 123–138.

[90] Stiglitz, J. E. [1974] "Growth with Exhaustible Natural Resources: Efficient and Optimal Growth Paths," *Review of Economic Studies*, Symposium, pp. 123–137.

[91] Stiglitz, J. E. [1976] "Monopoly and the Rate of Extraction of Exhaustible Resources," *American Economic Review*, Vol. **66**, No. 4, pp. 655–661.

[92] Stollery, K. R. [1983] "Mineral Depletion with Cost as the Extraction Limit: A Model Applied to the Behavior of Prices in the Nickel Industry," *Journal of Environmental Economics and Management*, **10**, pp. 151–65.

[93] Sweeney, J. L. [1977] "Economics of Depletable Resources: Market Forces and Intertemporal Bias," *Review of Economic Studies*, **44**, pp. 125–142.

[94] Ulph, A. M. [1980] "Modelling Partially Cartelised Markets for Exhaustible Resources," mimeo, Southampton University, Economics.

[95] Varian, H. [1978] *Microeconomic Analysis*, New York: Norton.

[96] Weitzman, M. [1976] "On the Welfare Significance of National Product in a Dynamic Economy," *Quarterly Journal of Economics*, **90**, pp. 156–62.

[97] Yeung, D. and J. M. Hartwick [1988] "Interest Rate and Output Price Uncertainty and Industry Equilibrium for Nonrenewable Resource Extracting Firms," *Energy and Resources*, (forthcoming).

## Appendix I: Notes on the historical background to rent on exhaustible resources

The notion of rent or income from a piece of land as a return in excess of paying for capital and labor on the poorest land emerged clearly in Anderson [2] and Kames [48]. Good quality land could yield "two or three bushels per acre more than ordinary product (on marginal land); the value of which goes entirely to the landlord as rent" (Kames [48; p. 312]). The terms are here and the understanding is clear. In Anderson's words "as the expense of cultivating the least fertile soil is as great, or greater than that of the most fertile field, it necessarily follows, that if an equal quantity of corn, the produce of each field, can be sold at the same price, the profit on cultivating the most fertile soil must be much greater than that of cultivating the others . . . the expense of cultivating some of the inferior soils will equal the value of the whole produce" (p. 45). Moreover the ethical correctness of who should reap the return due to good quality is emphasized. "Fertility is a quantity of land; and a subject belongs to the proprietor with all its qualities. As fertility depends not on the tenant's skill nor industry, he is entitled to no benefit from it" (p. 307). The notion of a range of pieces of land of declining fertility leads to a notion of diminishing returns to labor. Given Malthus' emphasis on labour force growth and a natural wage at subsistence, observers realized the logical connectedness of rent, declining fertility and labor force size. Blaug [5; p. 80] summarizes the contemporary textbook interpretation. "These two ideas (ground rent and diminishing returns) are so intimately connected that they emerged simultaneously as part of the reaction to the publication of Malthus' *Principles*. The year 1815 saw the appearance of four publications by West, Torrens, Malthus, and Ricardo, each of which independently formulated the theory of differential rent. Each tract was in its own way a reaction to committees appointed by both Lords and Commons to report on the recent fall in grain prices." Since the notion of differential rent was explict in Kames and Anderson, the 1815 contributors merely had to redevelop ideas which were much in the air. Instead of "independently formulated" Blaug might more accurately say "each of which independentlý integrated the theory of labor force size and payment into the theory of land rent." Actually Ricardo [73; pp. 70–72] clarified the nature of diminishing returns. In chapter II he makes clear that land rent can arise on a piece of land of fixed size as the intensity of the variable factor ("capital" in his case) is varied. He distinguishes between working three distinct parcels of land of equal size with "an equal employment of capital and labour" and the case of "doubling the original capital employed on No. 1" and observing declining marginal product. In this second case the residual revenue arising after paying for the extra variable input is also land rent. In any case 1815 is considered the year that differential land rent became widely understood in the theory of factor payments and income distribution. Jevons [46; p. 209] produced the diagram with labor on the horizontal axis and the marginal product of labor on the vertical axis, for the first time.

How did the theory of land rent get extended to cover exhaustible resources such as mineral deposits? It was ninety-nine years later that L. C. Gray [31] was able to combine the notion of diminishing returns with exhaustibility of a mineral stock, and his analysis was not easy to follow and went unrecognized for many years. There is no doubt that Adam Smith confused matters by asserting more than once that "the price both of the precious metals and of the precious stones is regulated all over the world by their price at the most fertile mine in it." Chapter IV, part II. His analysis otherwise seemed sound. "Fertile" deposits yielded more rent than less "fertile" deposits. But at no time did Smith try to extract a notion of rent related to the notion of exhaustibility. Even the word "royalty" which by 1890 was identified with the loss in value of a deposit due to current mineral extracted does not appear in Smith's discussion of mines and rents on those entities. Above extraction costs, Smith considered the "highest price" of a metal "seems not to be necessarily determined by anything but the actual scarcity or plenty of those metals themselves." That exhaustibility will make a metal more scarce in the future did not occur to Smith as a matter to analyze. Part of the problem was rooted in Ricardo's equivocation on the matter of rent and mineral resources. In Chapter ii of his *Principles* Ricardo avers that rent from mines are distinct from rent on land and in Chapter iii, he indicates that both land and mineral deposits yield the same stream of income, namely rent. Adam Smith was criticized in Chapter ii for including rent in the same class of income as wages and profits. Ricardo neglected to observe elsewhere in *The Wealth of Nations* (Book I, Chapter XI) that Smith remarks that "it is because its price is high or low "relative to" what is sufficient to pay those wages and profits, that it affords a high rent, or a low rent, or no rent at all." Ricardo attacks Smith's view that "the most fertile mine regulates the price of coals at all other mines in the neighbourhood." It is clear that Ricardo in Chapter iii "On the Rent of Mines" entertained no notion of a rent on minerals being related to its abundance today relative to its abundance at a future date. At the end of his fourth paragaph he moves from a discussion of mineral rent being a return for relatively more accessible deposits (differential rent) to a new topic. But the new topic is not rent arising from intertemporal considerations *sui generis* but a discussion of other miscellaneous issues involving technical improvements in mining, the price of products using metals as inputs, the abundance of precious metals in different parts of the world and gold as a standard of value. These miscellaneous topics are taken up in a little more than a page. The word "royalty" does not appear in the analysis. The problem as Marshall later made clear was that mineral deposits involved quality differences as with plots of land but had the additional element of exhaustibility. The former quality should be associated with differential rent as in the analysis of land whereas the second was novel and perplexing. Ricardo emphasized the first quality of mineral deposits and thus in

Chapter iii associated mineral deposits with differential rent. By 1889 the term royalty was associated with exhaustibility *per se*. "The last ton of coal or ironstone raised pays the same royalty as the first. The royalty system thus prevents the theory of rent from holding true of mines as it does of agricultural land; and the royalty system itself is rendered necessary by the fundamental difference between a farm and a mine, that the latter is, while the former is not, deteriorated by working" (Sorley [88; p. 77]). This is very explicit. Not only is royalty associated with exhaustibility *per se* but every ton of mineral extracted yields the same royalty! J. S. Mill [65; III, V, 3] contributed virtually nothing to the development of this doctrine. He was concerned with the different quality of mines and raised the tricky question as to why mines of quite different quality would be worked simultaneously rather than in sequence.

The concept of royalty emerged as a payment to the crown by a person working a mineral deposit as a use or rental payment for that working of the deposit. Originally it was one tenth of the value of output. Later when mineral deposits were made alienable from the crown, the royalty became a rental or use payment made by the individual working the deposit or mine to the owner of the mine. Sorley [88; p. 66] summarizes the contemporary view at the time of Marshall's first edition of his *Principles*.

In a system which admits of the possession of minerals by others than those who work them, the royalty rent finds its obvious justification in the deterioration of the mine by each quantity of mineral removed. The royalty protects the landlord against the rapid exhaustion of the mine, as the certain rent protects him against its lying idle. The royalty is nearly always estimated at so much per ton or other quantity of mineral extracted.

The royalties in different parts of the country vary largely with the quantity of the mineral, the thickness of strata, freedom from "troubles" or faults in the strata, accessibility of markets, etc.

Marshall [64; p. 439] explains that "the royalty itself [as distinct from rent] on a ton of coal, when accurately adjusted, represents that diminution in the value of the mine, regarded as a source of wealth in the future, which is caused by taking the ton out of nature's storehouse." He is uncertain how to measure this quantity as a practical matter and suggests it be "calculated in regard to those seams in the mine which are neither exceptionally rich and easy of working, nor exceptionally poor and difficult." Orchard [70;

p. 294] restates Marshall's view and in addition makes the claim with no evidence that "Ricardo undoubtedly believed that mine royalties had a dual character—that they were partly payment for minerals removed and partly a differential return due to the superior location or the greater fertility of particular mines" (p. 291). This was eight years after Gray [31] made explicit the relationship between the income flow from extracting $q(t)$ tons from stock $S(t)$ and a present value surplus maximizing extraction program.

Gray [31] identifies his "two antagonistic forces" for theoretically "determining the rate of utilization" of a homogeneous known stock: "diminishing productivity and the discount on the returns from future removal (assumed to be ten per cent)" (p. 475). By diminishing productivity he means marginal cost per ton extracted rising with quantity currently extracted. He is careful to make clear that "the basis of comparison" of different quantities potentially extracted at a point in time "must be the net return from the removal of an additional quantity of coal (marginal net dollar pay off), not the average net return" (p. 475).

Gray explains the determination of "the rate of utilization" with three examples (three different initial stocks) and two sets of parameters (two different prices for output and one set of cost data).[11] Gray has a U-shaped average cost curve for extraction and a constant price of output. He has then "maximum average net returns" at the minimum point of his average cost curve. Gray argues that the last quantity extracted given the initial stock will always be at this "maximum average net return." Given a constant discount factor this "maximum average net return" can be identified at any earlier period and serves as a benchmark to compare marginal net returns, interest rate adjusted, for any other quantity extracted. The principle Gray implicitly invokes is given the horizon of extraction and the "maximum average net return" for the last quantity extracted, the current time marginal net return for any

[11] The Hotelling [42] problem on optimal depreciation is formally the same as Gray's problem on depletion except (a) Hotelling's problem ends with a known scrap value function for the machine being depreciated and (b) the intertemporal time paths of all key variables are given in Hotelling's problem and he only solves for an intertemporally constant output price and date for scrapping the machine. Hotelling's is *not* the question of how intensively a machine should be operated to maximize the present value of its profit.

earlier quantity extracted must not exceed this interest rate adjusted "maximum average net return." In fact Gray has the rate of utilization satisfy the current time marginal net return for any earlier quantity extracted *equal*, approximately, the interest rate adjusted "maximum average net return." Gray only allows integer quantities rounded to the nearest 100 tons to be extracted in his examples and thus his numbers do not yield strict equality of the marginal values. Furthermore Gray only discounts his first column precisely and his examples are approximate because of the approximations in the other columns.

The first two examples are only illustrative because the quantities or initial stocks considered were relatively small compared with the key quantity to be extracted in the final period (first a stock of 1200 compared with a final quantity of 400 and then a stock of 3700). Moreover given a stock of 3700 tons, the complete extraction program is not worked out—Gray asserts that 600 tons is the correct initial quantity because "the sixth hundred tons could not be removed at any time in the future so as to yield a greater net return than thirty dollars" (p. 476). Gray thus illustrates one principle of constructing an optimal extraction program: current time rent on the marginal 100 tons extracted should never exceed the interest rate adjusted "maximum average net return" for that current period. Gray's first two illustrations are of this principle and are not fully specified optimal extraction programs.

Gray's third example has a higher output price and an optimal extraction program. There is an initial stock of 3700 tons. The example is given in Table IV and one sentence directs the reader to it. There is no mention that there is a central principle involved: namely the constancy of the marginal net returns, interest rate adjusted.[12] In fact this principle is difficult to discern in the example because there is considerable truncation to fit the extraction program to the nearest hundred tons, period by period. Gray never states the second key principle in words (the equality of discounted rent on the marginal amount extracted period by period), though it

---

[12] Crabbé [9] contains an excellent survey of the history of the economic theory of exhaustible resource use and discusses Gray's key paper in detail. I believe Crabbé attributes more to Gray than is in Gray's paper when he asserts "Gray evolved the first order conditions for an optimum in the discounted case, i.e., the equality of marginal discounted profits" (p. 205).

is related to the first principle (rent on the marginal amount extracted in any period, interest rate adjusted, must never exceed the "maximum average net return" in the final period).

Gray's example has a complicating feature. The two "natural examples" with Gray's data involve either 3900 tons of stock or 3000 tons. These examples are "natural" because the present value of rent on the marginal one hundred tons are approximately constant. Since Gray's 3700 tons falls between these two values, he is required to arrange an optimal extraction program for which the present value of rent on the marginal hundred tons deviates "unnaturally" from the relatively constant values. The "natural" program involving 3900 tons is circled in Table 1, constructed from Gray's data (a corrected version of Gray's very similar Table IV) Gray's extraction program lies just above the broken line.

Present value by period of net profit on marginal 100 tons*

| Tons | Period 1 | 2 | 3 | 4 | 5 | 6 |
|------|------|--------|--------|--------|--------|--------|
| 400  | 150 | 136.36 | 123.97 | 112.70 | 102.45 | 93.14 |
| 500  | 140 | 127.27 | 115.70 | 105.18 | 95.62 | |
| 600  | 130 | 118.18 | 107.43 | 97.67 | 88.79 | |
| 700  | 117 | 106.36 | 96.69 | 87.90 | | |
| 800  | 101 | 91.82 | 83.47 | 75.88 | | |
| 900  | 100 | 90.91 | 82.64 | 75.13 | | |
| 1000 | 82 | | | | | |

* based on Gray's parameters and a corrected version (slightly amended) of Gray's Table IV.

Note that if we amend Gray's hypothetical solution by reducing period 1 production by 100 tons and increasing period 3 production by 100 tons, the present value of profit declines by 3.306 dollars. In other words Gray's hypothetical solution appears correct. The interested reader would have to be perceptive to discern the principle of equality of the present value of rent on the marginal 100 tons, period by period. Moreover at no time does Gray interpret his principles as conditions for maximizing the present value of profits subject to a given stock. Gray arrived at the correct solution but failed to communicate his method and rationale clearly. He was in fact solving a simple constrained dynamic optimization problem correctly, a remarkable accomplishment. Moreover by re-solving his problem with different parameters, he was correctly undertaking comparative dynamics. Gray obscured his contribution by touching on real world complications such as variation in the quality of the ore being extracted. Hotelling [43] makes no reference to Gray or hints that a problem in determining the optimal extraction program for an exhaustible resource had been correctly solved. Gray attempts to put his results on the nature of optimal extraction program in historical context. Early on he identifies the rising marginal extraction cost schedule as embodying Ricardian diminishing returns. After presenting his examples, he asks the long-standing question of whether a marginal mine would in fact yield a positive rent or a "royalty." Here Gray seems confused by the claims of others. He argues that his examples are independent of calendar date. He then asks whether there is an obvious depreciation charge in his model, a depreciation charge being identified as a positive royalty. He concludes: "the coal in the mine on the margin which yields no rent, except in the cases above-noted, has no value which could be made the basis of a charge for depreciation" (p. 481). Hence Gray concludes, marginal mines yield no positive rent or a positive "royalty" (depreciation charge) in spite of claims that such mines yield a positive royalty in Sorley [88], Marshall and Flux.

He examines Ricardo's position on the nature of income from mines and notes a contradition between adjacent chapters. Ultimately Gray adheres to Ricardo's second view "that the entire net return from a mine is rent" (Gray, p. 483). In spite of those who inject a separate income labelled royalty, Gray asserts: "The true rent, indeed, in the present . . . is the whole surplus as determined by the difference between the gross product in the present and the expenses of production." Gray understood the essence of depreciation. ("The business man . . . desirous of keeping intact his fund of capital, charges to depreciation the amount by which the total value of the mine or farm has been reduced by utilization" (p. 484)). But he was unable to link his maximization of the present value of "surplus" to "royalty" or "depreciation."

Flux [28] did not address the issue of rent on mineral deposits in his brief survey. Fetter [27] mentions neither mineral rent or rent from exhaustible resources nor L. C. Gray. Muth [67] also fails to mention exhaustible resources or L. C. Gray. Blaug [5] mentions neither Gray or Hotelling on the subject of rent and exhaustible resources. Hotelling [43] avoided using the term rent or royalty.

### Appendix II: Economic depreciation and asset equilibrium

The basic efficiency condition for accumulating (or decumulating with exhaustible resources) discussed at length in Dorfman, Samuelson and Solow [1958; Chapter 12] is

$$r_i(t) + \dot{p}_i(t) = rp_i(t) \qquad (i = 1, \ldots, n) \qquad (19)$$

where $r_i(t)$ is current income derived from capital good $i$
$p_i(t)$ is the current selling price of capital good $i$
$r$ is the numeraire interest rate
$\dot{p}_i(t) \equiv dp_i(t)/dt$ and is a capital gain or loss.
Observe that in a static world $\dot{p}_i(t) = 0$ and we have the very basic relation: current income is simply $r$ times the current price of capital good $i$. The essential message in Dorfman, Samuelson and Solow was that investment or capital goods accumulation in general should be arranged so that (19), a price relationship, was always satisfied. Thus (19) was shown to be an efficiency condition, not merely an accounting identity.

We show (i) exhaustible resource models of the Gray and Hotelling type (homogeneous known stocks, stationary demand, cost and interest rates) satisfy (19) at each instant of time where $r(t) = B(q^*(t)) - cq^*(t)$ and $p(t) = \int_t^T [B(q^*(t)) - cq^*(t)]e^{-rt} dt$ for the Hotelling model (stars indicate optimal extraction programs) and (ii) $-\dot{p}(t) = \left[ \dfrac{dB(q^*(t))}{dq^*(t)} - c \right] q^*(t)$ along such optimal paths. Thus $\dot{p}(t)$ is the loss in future capital value, equal to dynamic rent, from extracting $q^*(t)$ from the remaining stock. $\dot{p}(t)$ is *economic depreciation* and we derive a precise expression for it. Current dynamic rent represents the diminution in capital value from extracting $q^*(t)$ along an optimal extraction program.

We will now establish that an optimal (surplus maximizing) extraction program satisfies (19) for a continuous time formulation.

Given $S(0)$, demand and cost conditions into the indefinite future, we define an optimal extraction program (one which maximizes the present value of surplus) $\{q(t)\}_{t=0}^{t=T}$ which satisfies

$\int_0^T q(t)\,dt = S(0)$. Associated with this program is a present value of surplus $V(S(0); t)$ at time zero or a present value of surplus $V(S(t); T - t)$ where $S(t)$ is the stock remaining at date $t$. That is, $V(S(t); T - t)$ is the maximized $\int_t^T r(q(t))e^{-rt}\,dt$ subject to $S(t) = \int_t^T q(t)\,dt$. Given an arbitrary $t_1$ satisfying $0 < t_1 < T$, we have

$$V(S(0), T) = V(S(0) - S(t_1), t_1) + e^{-rt_1}V(S(t_1), T - t_1) \quad (20)$$

where $V(S(0) - S(t_1), t_1)$ is the present value of surplus accruing in the optimal program between time $0$ and $t_1$ and over which $S(0) - S(t_1)$ is used up. Since the above extraction program is optimal, it satisfies the following first order condition

$$\frac{V(S(0), T)}{dq_1} = \frac{dV(S(0) - S(t_1), t_1)}{dt_1} \cdot \frac{dt_1}{dq_1} + \frac{\partial V(S(0) - S(t_1), t_1)}{\partial q_1}$$

$$- re^{-rt_1}V(S(t_1), T - t_1)\frac{dt_1}{dq_1} = 0$$

where $q_1$ is the quantity extracted at $t_1$ in $V(S(t_1), T - t_1)$, and

$$\frac{dV(S(0) - S(t_1), t_1)}{dt_1} = r(q_1)e^{-rt_1} + \int_0^{t_1} \frac{\partial r(q(t))}{\partial t_1} e^{-rt}\,dt$$

and

$$\frac{\partial V(S(0) - S(t_1), t_1)}{\partial q_1} \cdot \frac{dq_1}{dt_1} e^{rt_1} + e^{rt_1}\int_0^{t_1} \frac{\partial r(q(t))}{\partial t_1} e^{-rt}\,dt$$

will be written as $\dot{V}(t_1)$. This first order condition can be expressed then as

$$r(q_1) + \dot{V}(t_1) = rV(S(0) - S(t_1), t_1) \quad (0 \le t_1 \le T) \quad (21)$$

which is the continuous time statement of the efficiency condition in (19) above.

With appropriate regularity conditions and end point conditions, the converse theorem is false. If (21) is satisfied, the corresponding $\{q(t)\}$ defines an extraction program, not necessarily optimal.

$\dot{V}(t)$ is the capital value "wasted" at date $t_1$ from extracting $q(t_1)$ from the finite stock. As such it is depreciation in the capital value $V$ and has been labelled by early observers of the economics of mineral use, as a "royalty" (e.g., Marshall [1916; p. 439]). $r(q_1) + \dot{V}(t)$ was identified by these same observers as "rent," rent analogous to that associated with "diminishing returns" by Ricardo.

Modern parlance identifies $r(q_1)$ as surplus or profit at date $t_1$ comprising static "surplus" (static net consumer surplus in a Hotelling model or static net producer surplus in a Gray model) and a dynamic "surplus" associated with the finiteness of the aggregate stock. The sum of both surpluses is aggregate rent $r(q_1)$ associated with $q_1$. Of considerable interest is that along an optimal path $-\dot{V}(t)$ is exactly the dynamic rent $q(t)r'(q(t))$, where $r'(q(t)) = dr(q(t))/dq(t)$, or in Marshall's words "that diminution in the value of the mine, regarded as a source of wealth in the future, which is caused by taking [q] (JMH insert) out of nature's storehouse" (p. 439). We now establish this formally in

PROPOSITION I $\quad V(t) = -q(t)r'(q(t))$ in regular resource models with homogeneous stocks.

By regular, we mean models in which the instantaneous payoff $r(q(t))$ is increasing and strictly concave in $q(t)$. This rules out models with marginal extraction costs declining over some range of $q(t)$. The proof simply involves obtaining the correct expressions for $dq(t)/dt_1$, $dq(t)/dq_1$ and $dq_1/dt_1$, and substituting them in the expression above for $\dot{V}(t_1)$. We will proceed first to obtain the correct expressions.

(1) Since we are dealing with extraction paths which satisfy the appropriate Euler equations ($r\%$ rule), we have

$$r'(q(t)) = r'(q_1)e^{-r(t_1-t)} \qquad 0 \le t \le t_1$$

Thus

$$r''(q)dq = -rr'(q_1)e^{-r(t_1-t)}\,dt_1$$

and

$$r''(q)dq = e^{-r(t_1-t)}r''(q_1)dq_1$$

whence

$$\frac{dq}{dt_1} = -\frac{e^{rt}}{r''(q(t))}r'(q_1)re^{-rt_1} \tag{22}$$

and

$$\frac{dq}{dq_1} = \frac{e^{rt}}{r''(q(t))}r''(q_1)e^{-rt_1} \tag{23}$$

Since $\int_0^{t_1} q(t)\,dt = S_1$, we obtain

$$q(t_1)\,dt_1 + \int_0^{t_1}\frac{dq}{dt_1}\,dt\,dt_1 + \int_0^{t_1}\frac{dq}{dq_1}\,dt\,dq_1 = 0$$

or

$$\frac{dq_1}{dt_1} = \frac{-q(t_1) - \int_0^{t_1} \frac{dq}{dt_1} dt}{\int_0^{t_1} \frac{dq}{dq_1} dt}$$

which upon substituting from (22) and (23) becomes

$$\frac{dq_1}{dt_1} = \frac{-q(t_1) + H(t_1)r'(q_1)e^{-rt_1}r}{H(t_1)r''(q_1)e^{-rt_1}} \tag{24}$$

where

$$H(t_1) = \int_0^{t_1} \frac{e^{rt}}{r''(q(t))} dt$$

(2) We now substitute (22), (23) and (24) in $\dot{V}$.
Recall that by definition

$$\dot{V}(t_1) = \left[ \int_0^{t_1} r'(q(t)) \frac{dq(t)}{dt_1} e^{-rt} dt + \int_0^{t_1} r'(q(t)) \frac{dq(t)}{dq_1} e^{-rt} dt \frac{dq_1}{dt_1} \right] e^{rt_1}$$

and upon substituting from (22), (23) and (24)

$$= -rH(t_1)[r'(q_1)e^{-rt_1}]^2 e^{-rt_1} + H(t_1)r'(q_1)e^{-rt_1}r''(q_1)e^{-rt_1}e^{rt_1} \frac{dq_1}{dt_1}$$

$$= -q(t_1)r'(q(t_1)) \quad \square.$$

The proof of our main proposition is thus established. Recall that in either the Gray model or Hotelling model $r'(q(t)) = p(t) - mc(q(t))$ where $p(t)$ is the current price per unit extracted from the stock and $mc(q(t))$ is the marginal cost of extracting $q(t)$ at time $t$.

Example: An extracting firm faces a constant price for each ton of output $p$ and extraction costs $C(q) = Aq + (B/2)q^2$ yielding marginal extraction cost schedule $A + Bq$ with $A$ and $B$ positive. Thus $r(q) = pq - [Aq + (B/2)q^2]$.

(i) given $S(0)$, we solve the complete optimal extraction program. We then divide $S(0) = S_1 + S_2$ to solve the two sections of the overall optimal extraction program. This gives us for a specific $S_1$ and $S_2$, $t_1$, $T_1$ and $q_1$ and we can solve for $\dot{V}(t_1)$, $pq_1 - C(q_1)$, and $[p - mc(q_1)]q_1$. We repeat these calculations for various alternative divisions of $S(0)$ into two components.

Using the fact that $p - mc(q(t)) = [p - A]e^{-r(T-t)}$, we solve for

$T - t$, in

$$\left(\frac{p-A}{B}\right)\left\{(T - t_1) - \frac{1}{r}[1 - e^{-r(T-t_1)}]\right\} - S_2 = 0$$

and

$$q_1 = \left(\frac{p-A}{B}\right)[1 - e^{-r(T-t_1)}]$$

Given $q_1$, we solve for $(t_1 - 0)$ or $t_1$ in

$$\left[\frac{p-A}{B}\right]t_1 - \left[\frac{p-A-Bq_1}{Br}\right][1 - e^{-rt_1}] - S_1 = 0$$

For $p = 10$, $A = 1$, $B = 1$, $r = 0.1$ and $S(0) = 45$, we have $T - t_1 = T = 11.98290437$. We proceed to break $S(0)$ into two components $S_1$ and $45 - S_1$. The corresponding values for $T - t_1$, $q_1$ and $t_1$ are reported in the appropriately labelled columns in Table I in the text above.

(ii) We proceed to calculate $\dot{V}$ for our example of output price constant and marginal extraction costs linear. From the definition of $\dot{V}$ we have for our example

$$\dot{V} = \int_0^{t_1} \left[[p - A]\frac{dq(t)}{dq_1}e^{-rt} - Bq(t)\frac{dq(t)}{dq_1}e^{-rt}\right]dt\frac{dq_1}{dt_1}e^{rt_1}$$

$$+ \int_0^{t_1} \left[[p - A]\frac{dq(t)}{dt_1}e^{-rt} - Bq(t)\frac{dq(t)}{dt_1}e^{-rt}\right]dte^{rt_1}$$

Since

$$q(t) = \left[\frac{p-A}{B}\right] - \left[\frac{p-A-Bq_1}{B}\right]e^{-r(t_1-t)}$$

we observe

$$\frac{dq(t)}{dq_1} = e^{-r(t_1-t)}$$

and

$$\frac{dq(t)}{dt_1} = \left[\frac{p-A-Bq_1}{B}\right]re^{-r(t_1-t)}$$

Also one observes from the equation defining $t_1$ above that

$$\frac{dq_1}{dt_1} = \frac{-r\left\{\left(\frac{p-A}{B}\right)(1 - e^{-rt_1})q_1e^{-rt_1}\right\}}{(1 - e^{-rt_1})}.$$

The term in braces is incidentally $q(t = 0)$ which we shall indicate as $q_0$. Thus $dq_1/dt_1 = -rq_0/(1 - e^{-rt_1})$. $\dot{V}$ can now be written as

$$-\{[p - A]t_1 - BS_1\}rq_1/(1 - e^{-rt_1}) = -[p - A - Bq_1]q_1$$

and numerical values are reported in the column labelled $\dot{V}$ in Table I in the text.

(iii) We now obtain values for $V(S_2, T - t_1)$ in order to obtain $rV$.

$$V = \int_{t_1}^{T} \{pq(t) - [Aq(t) + (B/2)q(t)^2]\}e^{-rt} \, dt$$

where

$$q(t) = \left(\frac{p - A}{B}\right)[1 - e^{-r(T-t)}]$$

Substituting in $V$ and integrating yields

$$V = \frac{(p - A)^2}{2rB}[1 - e^{-r(T-t_1)}]$$

and values for $rV$ are listed in Table I in the text. This ends our example.

We have in passing derived a rule characterizing the percentage decline in $q(t)$ for regular exhaustible resource models with homogeneous stocks. This was the statement in (24) which can be written as

PROPOSITION II    *Present value surplus maximizing solutions satisfy*

$$\frac{\dot{q}(t)}{q(t)} = \left\{ \frac{r'(q(t))}{q(t)r''(q(t))} - \frac{1}{r\int_0^t \frac{r''(q(t))}{r''(q(x))} e^{-r(t-x)} \, dx} \right\} r.$$

Clearly such a rule lacks the elegance of the $r\%$ or Hotelling Rule for the motion of rent per ton. However for linear $r'(q)$ (with negative slope for strict concavity of $r(q)$) we obtain

$$\frac{\dot{q}(t)}{q(t)} = -rq_0/[q(t)(1 - e^{-rt})] \tag{25}$$

where $q_0$ was defined as the initial quantity extracted in a maximizing program. Thus the model of the firm with constant output price and linear marginal extraction costs (as worked out above) and the Hotelling model with a constant extraction cost per ton and linear demand schedule both have extraction programs characterized by (25).

For the case of the Hotelling industry model, $r(q(t))$ equals $B(q(t)) - cq(t)$ where $B(q(t))$ is gross surplus or the area under the demand schedule between 0 and $q(t)$ and $c$ is the constant cost of extracting a unit of $q$. $r'(q) = p(q) - c$ which for a linear inverse demand schedule $\alpha - \beta q$ yields $r''(q) = -\beta$. In this case $\dot{V} = -[p(q) - c]q$ and again $\dot{q} = -rq_0/(1 - e^{-rt})$.

Without exhaustibility, $\dot{V} = 0$ and we are in a "land framework" in which current net income from the land (rent) equals $rV$ where $V$ is the *price* for land, price being a capitalization of net income. Thus $r(q) + \dot{V}(q)$ is analogous to a perpetual net income stream from a capital good. Current gross dollar benefit from using $q(t)$, namely $r(q(t))$ induces a future diminution of earning capacity in the stock and net benefits, inclusive of future "wastage," are $r(q(t)) + \dot{V}(q(t))$. $\dot{V}$ has been labelled *true economic depreciation* which is the loss in future income generating capacity of a capital good.

### Appendix III: Costly exploration and extraction

At $t_1$ all information on stock size becomes known and one of four Hotelling paths are followed. Thus we have four certainty paths with rent on the marginal ton rising at the rate of interest $r$. Given terminal time $T$ (to be determined for each of the four branches), the rent rule yields

$$[A - c]e^{-r(T-t)} = p(t) - c$$
$$= A - Bq(t) - c$$

yielding

$$q(t) = \frac{A - c}{B} - \left[\frac{A - c}{B}\right]e^{-r(T-t)}$$

The industry demand schedule is $A - Bq(t)$ and unit extraction costs are $c$. Corresponding to terminal time

$T_{11}$ stock size along the branch is $\alpha_1(1 - \lambda)L + S_{R1}$
$T_{21}$ stock size along the branch is $\alpha_1(1 - \lambda)L + S_{R2}$
$T_{12}$ stock size along the branch is $\alpha_2(1 - \lambda)L + S_{R1}$
$T_{22}$ stock size along the branch is $\alpha_2(1 - \lambda)L + S_{R2}$

Thus

$$\int_{t_1}^{T_{11}} q(t)\, dt = \alpha_1(1 - \lambda)L + S_{R1}$$

or

$$\left[\frac{A-c}{B}\right](T_{11} - t_1) + \left[\frac{A-c}{Br}\right][e^{-r(T_{11}-t_1)} - 1] = \alpha_1(1 - \lambda)L + S_{R1}$$

There are three more analogous equations corresponding to $T_{21}$, $T_{12}$, $T_{22}$ and the related stock sizes. These comprise *four materials balance equations* of the nine equation system.

Since $\lambda$ and $S_{R1}$ and $S_{R2}$ can be considered parametric above we obtain "comparative static" expressions

$$\frac{dT_{11}}{d\lambda} = \frac{-\alpha_1 LB}{[A-c]\{1 - e^{-r(T_{11}-t_1)}\}} = -\alpha_1 L \frac{dT_{11}}{dS_{R1}}$$

$$\frac{dT_{12}}{d\lambda} = \frac{-\alpha_2 LB}{[A-c]\{1 - e^{-r(T_{12}-t_1)}\}} = -\alpha_2 L \frac{dT_{12}}{dS_{R1}}$$

$$\frac{dT_{22}}{d\lambda} = \frac{-\alpha_2 LB}{[A-c]\{1 - e^{-r(T_{22}-t_1)}\}} = -\alpha_2 L \frac{dT_{22}}{dS_{R2}}$$

$$\frac{dT_{21}}{d\lambda} = \frac{-\alpha_1 LB}{[A-c]\{1 - e^{-r(T_{21}-t_1)}\}} = -\alpha_1 L \frac{dT_{21}}{dS_{R2}}$$

We require these derivatives below in our definitions of the first order conditions.

Between $t_0$ and $t_1$ there are two branches with rent on the marginal ton rising at rate $r$. We have

$$q(t) = \left[\frac{A-c}{B}\right] - \left[\frac{A - Bq_0 - c}{B}\right]e^{r(t-t_0)}$$

and $q_0 = q_{01}$ if $\alpha_1$ is tons per acre revealed and $q_0 = q_{02}$ if $\alpha_2$ is tons per acre revealed. The two materials balance equations, when integrated are

$$\left[\frac{A-c}{B}\right](t_1 - t_0) - \left[\frac{A - Bq_{01} - c}{rB}\right][e^{r(t_1-t_0)} - 1] = \alpha_1 \lambda L - S_{R1}$$

$$\left[\frac{A-c}{B}\right](t_1 - t_0) - \left[\frac{A - Bq_{02} - c}{rB}\right][e^{r(t_1-t_0)} - 1] = \alpha_2 \lambda L - S_{R2}$$

These comprise two additional equations in the nine equation system. For the moment, $\lambda$, $S_{R1}$ and $S_{R2}$ can be treated as parameters and we obtain "comparative static" results

$$\frac{dq_{01}}{d\lambda} = \frac{\alpha_1 Lr}{[e^{r(t_1-t_0)} - 1]} = -\alpha_1 L \frac{dq_{01}}{dS_{R1}}$$

$$\frac{dq_{02}}{d\lambda} = \frac{\alpha_2 Lr}{[e^{r(t_1-t_0)} - 1]} = -\alpha_2 L \frac{dq_{02}}{dS_{R2}}$$

There are six branches over which to calculate the present value of net surplus: $\omega = \int [B(q(t)) - cq(t)]e^{-rt} dt$ where

$$B(q(t)) = Aq(t) - 0.5Bq(t)^2$$

Recall from above

$$q(t) = R - We^{rt}$$

where $R = \dfrac{[A-c]}{B}$

$$W = \begin{cases} W_{01} = [R - q_{01}]e^{-rt_0} & t_0 \leq t \leq t_1 \\ W_{02} = [R - q_{02}]e^{-rt_0} & t_0 \leq t \leq t_{11} \\ W_{11} = Re^{-rT_{11}} & t_1 \leq t \leq T_{11} \\ W_{12} = Re^{-rT_{12}} & t_1 \leq t \leq T_{12} \\ W_{21} = Re^{-rT_{21}} & t_1 \leq t \leq T_{21} \\ W_{22} = Re^{-rT_{22}} & t_1 \leq t \leq T_{22} \end{cases}$$

Integrating yields six values of discounted surplus corresponding to six branches of the extraction program. Thus

$$\omega_{01} = -\frac{B}{2r}(R^2[e^{-rt_1} - e^{-rt_0}] + W_{01}^2[e^{rt_1} - e^{rt_0}])$$

and $\omega_{02}$ is analogously defined.

$$\omega_{11} = -\frac{B}{2r}(R^2[e^{-rT_{11}} - e^{-rt_1}] + W_{11}^2[e^{rT_{11}} - e^{rt_1}])$$

and $\omega_{12}$, $\omega_{21}$, $\omega_{22}$ are analogously defined.

Expected total discounted surplus is

$$\phi = \pi_1\omega_{01} + \pi_2\omega_{02} + e^{-r(t_1-t_0)}\pi_1\{\pi_1\omega_{11} + \pi_2\omega_{12}\}$$
$$+ e^{-r(t_1-t_0)}\pi_2\{\pi_1\omega_{21} + \pi_2\omega_{22}\}$$

and is to be maximized by choice of $\lambda$, $S_{R1}$ and $S_{R2}$. Recall that $q_{01}$ is a function of $\lambda$ and $S_{R1}$, $T_{11}$ is a function of $\lambda$ and $S_{R1}$, $T_{21}$ a function of $\lambda$ and $S_{R2}$, etc. We have the derivatives defined above, namely $dq_{01}/d\lambda$ etc. We require the following derivatives in the maximization of expected discounted surplus.

$$\frac{d\omega_{01}}{dq_{01}} = \frac{B}{r} W_{01}e^{-rt_0}[e^{rt_1} - e^{rt_0}]$$

$$\frac{d\omega_{02}}{dq_{02}} = \frac{B}{r} W_{02}e^{-rt_0}[e^{rt_1} - e^{rt_0}]$$

$$\frac{d\omega_{11}}{dT_{11}} = -\frac{B}{2}\{W_{11}^2e^{rT_{11}} - R^2e^{-rT_{11}}\} + BW_{11}^2\{e^{rT_{11}} - e^{rt_1}\}$$

$$\frac{d\omega_{12}}{dT_{11}} = -\frac{B}{2}\{W_{12}^2e^{rT_{12}} - R^2e^{-rT_{12}}\} + BW_{12}^2\{e^{rT_{12}} - e^{rt_1}\}$$

$$\frac{d\omega_{21}}{dT_{21}} = -\frac{B}{2}\{W_{21}^2e^{rT_{21}} - R^2e^{-rT_{21}}\} + BW_{21}^2\{e^{rT_{21}} - e^{rt_1}\}$$

$$\frac{d\omega_{22}}{dT_{22}} = -\frac{B}{2}\{W_{22}^2e^{rT_{22}} - R^2e^{-rT_{22}}\} + BW_{22}^2\{e^{rT_{22}} - e^{rt_1}\}$$

The final three equations in our nine equation system are $\frac{d\phi}{d\lambda} = 0$, $\frac{d\phi}{dS_{R1}} = 0$, and $\frac{d\phi}{dS_{R2}} = 0$. These are, then

$$\pi_1\frac{d\omega_{01}}{dq_{01}} \cdot \frac{dq_{01}}{d\lambda} + e^{-r(t_1-t_0)}\pi_1\left\{\pi_1\frac{d\omega_{11}}{dT_{11}} \cdot \frac{dT_{11}}{d\lambda} + \pi_2\frac{d\omega_{12}}{dT_{12}} \cdot \frac{dT_{12}}{d\lambda}\right\}$$

$$+ \pi_2\frac{d\omega_{02}}{dq_{02}} \cdot \frac{dq_{02}}{d\lambda} + e^{-r(t_1-t_0)}\pi_2\left\{\pi_1\frac{d\omega_{21}}{dT_{21}} \cdot \frac{dT_{21}}{d\lambda} + \pi_2\frac{d\omega_{22}}{dT_{22}} \cdot \frac{dT_{22}}{d\lambda}\right\}$$

$$- \frac{dC^1}{d\lambda} - e^{-r(t_1-t_0)}\frac{dC^2}{d\lambda} = 0$$

$$\frac{d\omega_{01}}{dq_{01}} \cdot \frac{dq_{01}}{dS_{R1}} + e^{-r(t_1-t_0)}\left\{\pi_1 \frac{d\omega_{11}}{dT_{11}} \cdot \frac{dT_{11}}{dS_{R1}} + \pi_2 \frac{d\omega_{12}}{dT_{12}} \cdot \frac{dT_{12}}{dS_{R1}}\right\} = 0$$

$$\frac{d\omega_{02}}{dq_{02}} \cdot \frac{dq_{02}}{dS_{R2}} + e^{-r(t_1-t_0)}\left\{\pi_1 \frac{d\omega_{21}}{dT_{21}} \cdot \frac{dT_{21}}{dS_{R2}} + \pi_2 \frac{d\omega_{22}}{dT_{22}} \cdot \frac{dT_{22}}{dS_{R2}}\right\} = 0$$

where $C^1 = (\lambda L)^\epsilon$ and $C^2 = ((1-\lambda)L)^\epsilon$, $0 < \epsilon < 1$.

The last two equations are first order conditions indicating that rent on the marginal ton extracted immediately before $t_1$ equals expected rent on the marginal tons extracted immediately after $t_1$. These are zero profit intertemporal arbitrage conditions. They can be used to simplify the other first order condition. It becomes

$$\pi_1\pi_2 e^{-r(t_1-t_0)}(\alpha_1 - \alpha_2)L\left\{\frac{d\omega_{12}}{dT_{12}} \cdot \frac{dT_{12}}{dS_{R1}} - \frac{d\omega_{21}}{dT_{21}}\frac{dT_{21}}{dS_{R2}}\right\}$$
$$= \frac{dC^1}{d\lambda} + e^{-r(t_1-t_0)}\frac{dC^2}{d\lambda}.$$

With exploration cost minimization alone, we would have $\frac{dC^1}{d\lambda} + e^{-r(t_1-t_0)}\frac{dC^2}{d\lambda} = 0$. The "extra" term above reflects the information value of marginally more exploration. By exploring somewhat more than merely cost minimization requires, information is acquired which reduces the level of remaining stock size uncertainty beyond $t_1$. The "extra" term is a formal statement of the motive for the planner or firm to "over explore" in order to reduce future stock size uncertainty.

The last three equations above complete the nine equation system defining an equilibrium for the model in the text.

# INDEX

# MODELS OF THE OIL MARKET

JACQUES CRÉMER AND
DJAVAD SALEHI-ISFAHANI

# Models of the Oil Market

Jacques Crémer

and

Djavad Salehi-Isfahani
*Virginia Polytechnic Institute and State University,
Blacksburg, Virginia, USA*

A volume in the Natural Resources and Environmental Economics
section
edited by
C. HENRY
*Ecole Polytechnique,
Paris, France*

 **Harwood Academic Publishers**
Australia • Canada • China • France • Germany • India •
Japan • Luxembourg • Malaysia • The Netherlands •
Russia • Singapore • Switzerland • Thailand •
United Kingdom

First published 1991
Second printing 1996

Emmaplein 5
1075 AW Amsterdam
The Netherlands

---

**Library of Congress Cataloging-in-Publication Data**
Crémer, Jacques, 1949–
    Models of the oil market / Jacques Crémer and Djavad
Salehi-Isfahani.
        p.   cm. — (Fundamentals of pure and applied economics,
    ISSN 0191–1708;
    v. 44. Natural resources and environmental economics section)
    Includes bibliographical and references (p.    ) and index.
    ISBN 3-7186-5072-X
    1. Petroleum industry and trade—Mathematical models.   I. Salehi-Isfahani, Djavad.
    II. Title.   III. Series: Fundamentals of pure and applied economics; v. 44.   IV. Series:
Fundamentals of pure and applied economics. Natural resources and environmental economics
section.
HD9560.5.C74   1991                                                                           90-5132
382′.42282′0724—dc20                                                                          CIP

# Contents

# Introduction to the Series

Drawing on a personal network, an economist can still relatively easily stay well informed in the narrow field in which he works, but to keep up with the development of economics as a whole is a much more formidable challenge. Economists are confronted with difficulties associated with the rapid development of their discipline. There is a risk of "balkanization" in economics, which may not be favorable to its development.

*Fundamentals of Pure and Applied Economics* has been created to meet this problem. The discipline of economics has been subdivided into sections (listed at the back of this volume). These sections comprise short books, each surveying the state of the art in a given area.

Each book starts with the basic elements and goes as far as the most advanced results. Each should be useful to professors needing material for lectures, to graduate students looking for a global view of a particular subject, to professional economists wishing to keep up with the development of their science, and to researchers seeking convenient information on questions that incidentally appear in their work.

Each book is thus a presentation of the state of the art in a particular field rather than a step-by-step analysis of the development of the literature. Each is a high-level presentation but accessible to anyone with a solid background in economics, whether engaged in business, government, international organizations, teaching, or research in related fields.

Three aspects of *Fundamentals of Pure and Applied Economics* should be emphasized:

—First, the project covers the whole field of economics, not only theo-retical or mathematical economics.
—Second, the project is open-ended and the number of books is not predetermined. If new and interesting areas appear, they will gener-ate additional books.

—Last, all the books making up each section will later be grouped to constitute one or several volumes of an Encyclopedia of Economics.

The editors of the sections are outstanding economists who have selected as authors for the series some of the finest specialists in the world.

*J. Lesourne*                                        *H. Sonnenschein*

# Acknowledgements

Over the years, we have discussed and debated the economics of the oil markets with too many colleagues and friends to name all of them. Their ideas and encouragement made this book possible and we are very grateful. Our first joint work had an eventful career. We are especially thankful to our colleagues who supported us through unpleasant times.

Claude Henry asked us if we would write a volume for this series and encouraged us to pursue our ideas. Raj Sah convinced us to go ahead with the project when we were weighing the pros and cons. A conversation with Alan Manne provided useful information about the large models that he so ably surveys in the International Energy Project. Graduate students at VPI suffered through a course on the economics of the oil market where we developed some of the ideas discussed here. Cathy Johnson and Kyusig Han provided able research assistance.

The monograph was completed before the Iraqi invasion of Kuwait in August 1990. We have included some comments on this 'third oil crisis' in the Epilogue.

# Models of the Oil Market

JACQUES CRÉMER and DJAVAD SALEHI-ISFAHANI

*Department of Economics*

*Virginia Polytechnic Institute and State University*

*Blacksburg, Virginia, USA*

## 1. INTRODUCTION

Any poll of academics, business executives, politicians or journalists would identify the 'oil crisis' as the economic event of the 1970s. Section 2 will detail the story, but it may be worthwhile reminding the reader of the main facts. Figure 2.1 shows the path of oil prices between 1973 and 1987; not shown is the long preceding period of stability before 1970, and a progressive increase between 1970 and 1973. We observe a large jump around December 1973 and January 1974. A long period of stability is interrupted by a spectacular increase at the change of decade and an even more spectacular decrease from 1982 onwards. The changes in market shares illustrated by Figure 2.2 are nearly as spectacular.

Even before the crisis broke out, in 1973, following the Club of Rome report on the long-run growth of the economy, Professor Solow saw economists descending as lemmings in huge crowds on the field of natural resource economics. In 1974, attracted by the smell of the largest cartel in history, the lemmings had multiplied manyfold. Fifteen years later, most have swam away and the beach has recovered its customary calm. Indeed, the quantitative changes in the economic literature are very impressive. Figure 1.1 traces the number of articles on natural resources referenced in the *Journal of Economic Literature*. We see two sharp increases, induced both by curiosity and availability of research funds, which follow with a one-year lag the shocks in the market. In this volume of the *Encyclopedia*, we would like to take stock of this work. What have we learned? Did economists build a coherent framework for analyzing this market? What are the reflexes of our profession when faced by a sudden and important puzzle?

1

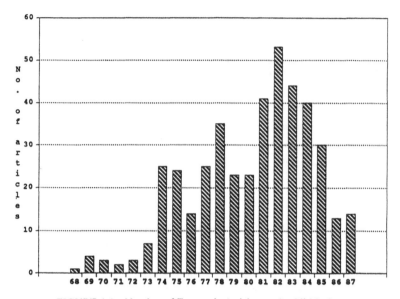

FIGURE 1.1    Number of Economic Articles on the Oil Market.

The first objective of this review is to serve as a reference to the efforts of economists to make sense of the events of the last 15 years, to find the framework that accounts for as many facts as possible, and in some cases to influence policies. There is no agreement on the proper model or mode of analysis. The importance and influence of collusion among producers is still subject to debate. The econometric evidence is very weak. The value of simulation models is open to doubt. Our grid of analysis will proceed by submitting the different theories to a rather stringent test: do they provide an economically coherent explanation for *all* the events of the last 15 years? Let us elaborate. First, the theory, whether formal or informal, must be based on sound economics. Second, it should provide an integrated view of the different events of the last 15 years. One can sometimes find in the literature a disconcerting tendency to build a new theory to fit every movement in prices, and we want to know whether it is possible to build a theory that is stable when confronted with new developments. Of course, no mode of analysis passes perfectly our test, but its systematic application will provide a good measure of the road still ahead.

The first reflex of economists in 1974 was to grab and use two sets of existing tools. The first contained a sophisticated analysis of markets for natural resources, first developed systematically by Hotelling in his admirable and classic 1931 paper. The second contained the tools developed over the years by industrial organization specialists, and the insights they had developed about the internal structure of cartels. These fertilized each other, and it is the result of this union that we study. Both parent literatures are extremely vast and interesting, and we can only hope to survey the parts that apply directly to the oil market. In particular, we will not explore the interesting and important literature on the optimal use of natural resources, except for the small part that we will directly need. We will also focus our attention on studies of the structure of the market, that is the main forces that affect the price charged and outputs chosen by the main actors. We will ignore the extensive discussions of the macroeconomic effects of the oil shocks, of stockpiling strategies, of exploration, except as they directly inform our study of the structure of the market. We also for the most part bypass the non-economic literature. We do not feel competent to survey the abundant work of the other social scientists.

The literature is challenging and especially interesting because it mixes all modes of economic discourse from informal discussions to high theory through simulation models and some econometrics. We have tried to give the proper weight to each of these and to show their benefits and shortcomings. We have also tried to explain how the different strands have influenced each other.

Section 2 briefly surveys the history of the last 15 years, with enough background on previous periods when warranted. It serves as reference for the rest of the book. Section 3 surveys what, for lack of a better word, we call 'informal models' of the oil market, defined as those models that are presented without the use of mathematics or computer simulation. Most of what is written on the oil market fits into this category. While this style allows for careful attention to institutional details, it does not provide the automatic checks on the rigor of the arguments that more formal approaches provide.

In Section 4 we turn to simulation models, an approach imported from development economics and very popular during the 1970s. Simulation models are composed of a number of equations which represent the behavior of the agents, and they are solved numerically, in general with representative data. They allow formalizing of some arguments while obtaining more specific answers than would be possible through more general theoretical models. In the oil literature, simulation models have proved extremely useful, and their recent decline in popularity is difficult to understand.

Section 5 discusses 'theoretical models' of the market, that is economic theory directly built to throw light on some of its aspects. Whereas there has been much literature on natural resources in general (see the survey by Hartwick (1989) in volume 33 of this *Encyclopedia*), very little theoretical work has actually been devoted to issues relating specifically to the oil market. The conceptual issues involved in the modeling of oligopolies in natural resource markets are fascinating, and extremely challenging.

Section 6 studies the econometric evidence that has been presented by different authors. The literature is very small, composed of two published papers and a few working papers, and we give it more space than its quantitative importance warrants in order to showcase the difficulties of empirical testing and to call attention to the need for more work.

Section 7 stresses the open questions and the challenges that we face in developing a better understanding of this market, and we conclude in Section 8 by taking stock of our profession's approach to the analysis of the oil market.

The classification by style of analysis would not be successful in many fields of economics, as we would want to stress the main message of the different papers involved. In the present case the questions that have been tackled with these different methods have been separate enough that this simple-minded criterion works well.

We also caress the ambition that this book will serve as a case study of the functioning of our profession. In 1973, economists found themselves facing a gigantic puzzle: a would-be cartel that had been rather unsuccessful in the past suddenly increased the price four-fold, with seemingly little difficulty. On the basis of past experience, a number of prominent economists promised a quick collapse of the cartel, and although prices did eventually decrease the scenario was far from what was predicted. At the same time, a flurry of papers appeared which tried to describe the decision-making process in this market, and to predict the long-run future of oil prices. Now that the dust has settled, we can appraise our first reflexes, and see whether and how we could have done better. We can also reflect on the way in which the inner dynamics of our profession help or hinder our approach to a fashionable topic.

Finally, we should mention that we are not disinterested bystanders in the debates we survey. In previous work, we have expressed rather strong views on the functioning of this market. We have tried hard not to use this occasion to show that our thesis is correct. We do want to look at the internal logic of each of the main currents in the literature, and understand their weaknesses and strengths.

## 2. HISTORICAL OVERVIEW OF THE MARKET

### 2.1. Introduction

This section summarizes the history of the oil market in the last 40 years in order to provide a factual basis for the evaluation of the models in the next sections. Our account is limited to the salient events, and the reader familiar with this history may wish to skip this section and return to it for reference as need arises without missing the essential points of our survey. For more detailed accounts, the less expert reader is referred to any of the several good books on the oil market (Stocking, 1970, Rouhani, 1971, Adelman, 1972a, Schneider, 1983, Skeet, 1988).

We will examine with special care the events surrounding the sharp changes in the price of oil, in 1973, 1979–1980, and 1986. Indeed, most models are motivated by the desire to explain them and in particular to determine if they were the consequence of structural changes in the market.

Economists have been especially interested in two historical developments. First, in 1973, after thirteen years of unsuccessful attempts the oil producing countries, grouped in OPEC, succeeded in raising prices. Second, the contractual arrangements between the international oil companies and the producing governments have been overhauled over the years. Many analysts of the oil market contrast the incentives of companies and governments, and stress the importance of the transfer of the control of supply from one group to the other. For example, governments and companies may have different costs and benefits of cooperation through cartel agreements. Also, governments who view oil as belonging to several generations of their citizens, and companies who fear nationalization of oil may have different discount rates (Johany, 1980). Furthermore, in many countries, foreign companies, although they have lost most of their control on output, still conduct the actual extraction under contract from the governments, and the terms of these contracts influence heavily the supply side of the market.

To focus attention on specific events, we divide our survey into six different periods: 1945–1970, 1970–1973, 1973–74, 1974–1978, 1979–1980, and 1981 to the present.

## 2.2. 1945 to 1970

The period between the end of World War II and 1970 is marked by two major developments. First, a drastic expansion of demand, caused by substitution of oil for coal, most of which was satisfied by production in the Middle East. Second, the formation of OPEC in 1960, which at that time, more than anything else, was a signal of the changing relationship between the international oil companies and the producing governments.

At the beginning of the period, extraction and marketing were conducted by a few international oil companies, the majors. The governments of the producing countries did not participate in production or pricing, but merely acted as competing sellers of 'licenses to produce' (Adelman, 1972b), known as 'concessions'. The majors operated a highly profitable oligopoly, using informal agreements to control prices for final products as well as rents going to the governments.

The high profits enjoyed by the majors caused entry into the international crude market. Smaller companies, known as independents, were offering better terms in order to break into the protected market for concessions. The number of companies with international concessions increased from 33 in 1953 to 337 in 1969 (Jacoby, 1974). As the oligopsonistic power of the majors in the market for concessions declined, government revenues from concessions increased. Increased competition caused oil prices to fall both in real and nominal terms throughout the 1960s.

Before 1950, the revenues of the countries were computed as royalties based on the volume of production. As a result, they were more interested in output than price. In the 1950s the concessions were changed to 50/50 profit-sharing agreements, but the computations of profits were difficult. Because the spot market was very small at the time, the market price could not be determined unambiguously. The transfer prices which the companies used to value the purchase of crude from the countries were not an acceptable basis for calculation of the payments to the countries. The operating companies were all part of vertically integrated multinational firms, and could minimize their tax obligations by manipulating internal transfer prices. The calculations were therefore simplified by using a 'posted price,' which was computed from the value of oil sold in different markets around the world. Because market prices did not affect their profits directly, the countries still showed little interest in the price at which their oil was sold.

Under the new scheme each government benefited from increases in its own production, but a new collective interest was created around the posted price, over which the companies had considerable discretion. In 1959 and 1960, prompted by a declining market price for oil, itself brought about by increased competition in the crude market, the companies announced two consecutive cuts in the posted price. The oil exporting governments formed OPEC in 1960 in order to pressure the companies to restore posted prices as well as to stabilize market prices (in the words of the first OPEC communiqué) 'by, among other means, regulation of production.'

OPEC did not succeed in increasing market prices: the price of crude oil declined throughout the ensuing decade to its lowest point of $1.29 per barrel[1] in 1969. But it did accomplish its other objective. Acting as a collective bargaining agency on behalf of the governments, the posted price, on which their revenues depended, remained unchanged at $1.80. For all practical purposes, the situation had reverted to a fixed per-barrel fee.

At different times, some members tried to convince the organization to seize control of the volume of production from the companies. These efforts were totally unsuccessful, because individual countries were bound by the terms of their contracts with the companies, and lacked the necessary technical know-how. It is also possible that each country thought that it could do better on its own, pressuring companies to increase the output from its fields, rather than cutting it to bring up the world price. Indeed, companies perceived that they had to resist the demands for output increases by individual countries, and frequently voiced fears that prices would decline if countries gained control of production (Penrose, 1968).

---

[1] The barrel is the standard unit of measurement of volume of oil. It is equal to 42 US gallons.

Although these unsuccessful attempts were not important factors in the history of the market during the 60s, they have important implications for the interpretation of the events of the 70s. They suggest that in the 1960s the governments were acting in a competitive manner. Therefore, the formation of a successful cartel in 1973 must have been preceded by some important change in the relation of the countries to each other and in the role of OPEC.

## 2.3. 1970 to 1973

Between 1970 and 1973, the world demand for OPEC oil increased at a fast rate, as European and Japanese demand surged and US production peaked. Most of this increase was met from Middle Eastern sources, whose production rose by 11% in 1972 and 17.5% in 1973. This led to two major changes. First, the decline in market prices was reversed, with market prices doubling between 1970 and 1973. This pushed up the posted price of the marker crude, which had stayed constant at $1.80 during the 1960s and rose sharply to $3 in the summer of 1973. Second, the countries stopped pressuring the companies to increase the rate of extraction, as their revenues soared due to increases in posted prices and production. The countries also found their bargaining position *vis-à-vis* the companies strengthened and increased their control over production.

Several countries used various opportunities to assert their control over output through abrogation of old concession agreements and/or through increased 'participation' in production. (Through participation, governments became part-owners of the operating companies previously wholly owned by the foreign multinationals.) For instance, in 1970 Libya cut the exports of Continental, a small independent company, by 50% to pressure it to pay more for Libyan oil. Continental eventually conceded to Libya's demand. In 1971 Algeria nationalized the interests of the French oil company, Companie Française de Pétrole, and acquired complete control over all its oil supply. With the exception of Iraq, the Arab oil producers, comprising half of OPEC's membership, used this control for political purposes two years later, when they asked the operating companies to cut production in order to force the Western supporters of Israel to modify their policies in the Arab–Israeli conflict.

In 1971, OPEC approved a resolution urging its members 'to take immediate steps toward the effective implementation of the principle of Participation in the existing oil concessions' (OPEC, 1984, p. 89). While forming a united front in their effort to control production, the members agreed to split in two separate groups to negotiate posted prices and tax rates, because their interests were not homogeneous. Since the closing of the Suez canal in 1967, transportation costs to the Western consumers were much lower for the North African members than the Persian Gulf countries. In 1971, the first group negotiated a separate agreement in Tripoli, while the other met with the companies in Tehran.

The resulting Tehran–Tripoli agreements were hailed as a success by companies and countries alike. Designed to last for five years, they offered stability for the companies, and raised revenue per barrel for the governments. The tax rates were raised from 50% to 55% and the posted price for the Gulf countries from $1.80 to $2.18, with an even greater increase in price for the North African countries.

But the agreements lasted less than two years. Based on tradition and the experience of a stable international economic environment in the 1960s, the Tehran–Tripoli agreements had fixed the posted price in dollars, allowing only a 2.5% annual increase for inflation. Following the effective devaluation of the dollar as a result of the Smithsonian Agreement of December 1971 and inflation rates in the industrialized countries far higher than the 2.5% envisaged, the system of profit sharing on the basis of a fixed posted price denominated in dollars came under increasing distress. The companies and governments reopened negotiations. Between 1971 and 1973 a series of meetings were held at heavy cost to both sides until the last round of talks was interrupted by the break-out of the October 1973 war in the Middle East.

## 2.4. The 1973 price increase

In the aftermath of the October war, in December 1973, the countries raised the price of oil four-fold. The events surrounding this price increase are important because it is this phenomenon that most models of the oil market have tried to explain.

Soon after the start of the hostilities, the Arab oil-exporting countries, with the exception of Iraq, imposed production cutbacks and an embargo on shipments to the United States and the Netherlands. The cumulative effect of these cuts was a 5% drop in total world supply (Stobaugh, 1975). Coupled with nervousness in the market and a very low short-run elasticity of demand, this modest decrease induced a sharp rise in the spot market price: Whereas in October the countries were trying to negotiate a posted price of $5 per barrel, by December some oil was traded at $17 per barrel! On December 22, the governments unilaterally announced a new posted price of $11.69 per barrel for the Saudi marker crude.[2] The cutbacks ended in March 1974, and subsequently the world supply increased to its previous level without reversing the price increase.

However dramatic its consequences, the December 22 meeting was even more remarkable for what it did not discuss. There was no mention of any coordination of output to support the new price, nor of price differentials for other types of oil. Countries were left free to set prices in relation to the marker crude as they wished.

## 2.5. 1974 to 1978

For several years after the price increase the market was relatively calm with the price increasing in nominal terms but falling slightly in real terms (see Figure 2.1). Demand was generally slack following the deep recession of 1975 in the industrialized countries, which many attributed to the oil price increase itself. The substitution of other fuels for oil and conservation measures had slow effects which were felt later. OPEC continued to meet periodically during this period to set the price of the marker crude. Despite two minor price increases, the real price of oil fell by 29% between 1974 and 1978.

The reduction in demand required some countries to cut production. Kuwait and Libya announced production ceilings. Saudi Arabia, who before the 1973 price increase had unveiled plans to increase capacity to 20 mbd (millions barrels per day), announced that it would keep production under 8.5 mbd. The record seems to indicate that the countries that cut production did so voluntarily and unilaterally, without expecting in return similar measures by other OPEC members: Despite the market slackness between 1975 and 1978, no formal agreement bound

---

[2] The marker crude refers to a specific type of oil (34° Arab Light), produced in Saudi Arabia, which served as a standard until 1985. Other types of oil were priced above or below its price according to quality differentials and location.

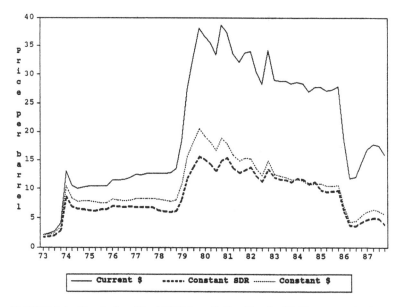

FIGURE 2.1 Nominal and Real Oil Prices. Deflated by the OECD export price index.

individual countries (except Saudi Arabia), and they were free to set output and prices for their own oil as they wished (Mabro, 1975a; Jaidah, 1982, p. 110). For instance, in 1975, when demand for oil was at its lowest, OPEC countries reduced their production by 11%, without explicit rationing or even, as far as we know, discussion of output shares in OPEC meetings. While most members reduced production, the shares did not remain constant. Of the eight OPEC members depicted in Figures 2.2a and 2.2b, all except one (Iraq) lost output share. More than half of the 2.5 mbd decline in OPEC output came from reduced output by Saudi Arabia.

OPEC meetings were the scene of substantial disagreements. With its huge reserves and the price of its oil fixed by OPEC, Saudi Arabia, who lost output share with every price increase, opposed large adjustments in the marker price. Others, notably Iran and Algeria, with smaller reserves and the flexibility to set their own prices, asked for large increases without fear of losing output. The most vehement

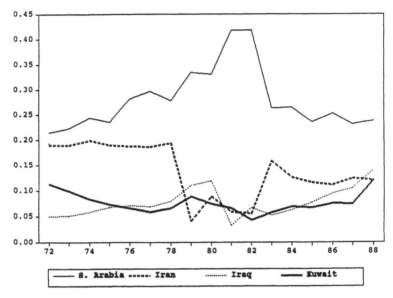

FIGURE 2.2(a)   Production shares in OPEC 1973–88.

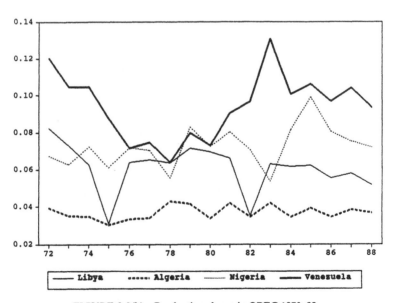

FIGURE 2.2(b)   Production shares in OPEC 1973–88.

disagreement occurred in Doha, Qatar, in 1976. Eleven countries raised their prices by about 15%, while Saudi Arabia and United Arab Emirates raised theirs by only 5%. There would not be another price increase until December 1978, when the Iranian revolution reduced the supply of oil.

In the meantime, producing countries gradually solidified their control of production, and by the end of 1975 all decisions concerning price, output, and capacity had come under the exclusive control of the governments.

### 2.6. The 1979–1980 price increases

The years 1979 and 1980 saw two consecutive rounds of price increases which pushed the price from $12.00 to $36.00 per barrel. First, a strike by oil workers beginning in the fall of 1978 reduced Iranian supply. By December exports had completely stopped as production fell below domestic needs. Iran's output increased slightly in the first quarter of 1979, but still averaged only 1.2 mbd compared to 6.1 mbd six month earlier. As percentage of world output, this reduction in production was nearly twice as large as the worldwide shortfall due to the embargo and cutbacks of 1973 at their worst point. However, spot prices rose only moderately because other producers made up all but 1.5 mbd of the loss (Schneider 1983, p. 436).

By spring 1979, Iranian production had resumed, albeit at half its pre-revolutionary rate, but prices continued to increase, reaching a high of $38 later that year. Although the new leaders announced plans to stabilize output at 3 mbd, there was still uncertainty regarding their ability to maintain output even at this level.

As in 1973, during this crisis OPEC's actions lagged behind the market. At the December 1978 meeting, after the oil workers' strike had already cut by half the Iranian production for the quarter. OPEC decided to increase the marker price by only 10%. By June, while spot prices had risen to $38, OPEC announced a ceiling of $23.50 for the official price. Saudi Arabia kept its price even lower at $18. However, as the crisis worsened, several countries increased their prices without regard to this agreement, charging up to $38. Successive OPEC meetings aiming at unification of the price structure would fail until October 1981.

These conservative increases in the official price relative to the spot price reflected the belief of most OPEC members that the market would soon stabilize and spot prices would decline. Most countries sold about half of their exports at official prices through long-term contracts, the rest closer to the spot price.

The first supply disruption was quickly followed by another. In September 1980, Iraq attacked Iran, and occupied much of its oil producing region, starting a war that would last until 1988. Iranian exports fell immediately to less than 1 mbd and then ceased completely in the last quarter of 1980. Iraqi output soon followed suit and fell from 3.5 mbd to 0.5 mbd by end 1980. The aggregate cuts in Iran and Iraq accounted for a loss of output close to 9 mbd in 1980 compared to 1978. Prices that had declined during the early part of 1980 to about $33 jumped back up to $38. OPEC set its official price at $36, while Saudi Arabia sold its oil for $32 per barrel.

Whereas OPEC output remained constant for two years after the 1973 price increase, after 1979 it declined continuously, and never regained its all-time high of 32 mbd in mid-1979. In this period also, production shares changed drastically (see Figures 2.2a and 2.2b). Virtually all the decrease in the shares of Iran and Iraq was picked up by Saudi Arabia, who produced less than 30% of OPEC output in 1978 and more than 47% in mid-1981, its output reaching a record 10.6 mbd in the last quarter of 1980 after both Iran and Iraq had ceased to export. The proximate cause for the explosion in Saudi Arabian output was a price several dollars per barrel lower than its competitors'. Of course, price and output are determined simultaneously, and the decision to charge less may have been taken in order to sell more oil in a short period. It is remarkable that, except for Iraq, all other major OPEC suppliers reduced production, choosing a strategy opposite to that of Saudi Arabia.

## 2.7. 1981 to the present

The 1980s have been marked by a continuous decline in demand for OPEC oil, by a decline in Saudi production both in volume and as share of OPEC, by the introduction of output rationing by OPEC, and by a drastic fall in the real price of oil.

In the beginning of 1981 OPEC tried to unify prices, and Saudi Arabia agreed to raise the price of its marker crude by $2 to $34. Realizing that with declining demand other countries would lower their prices so as to increase sales, OPEC for the first time set specific differentials for various crudes and explicitly required its members to observe them. However, later in the year the British National Oil Company (BNOC) lowered the price of its North Sea oil, and Nigeria responded by cutting its own price by $5.50 without consulting OPEC. First Iran and later other countries followed suit.

With the breakdown of the price agreement OPEC tried to control output, behaving for the first time like a textbook cartel. In March 1982 OPEC set output quotas for its members with an aggregate ceiling of 17.5 mbd. Although a monopolist needs only set price or output, OPEC was now trying to set both—with little success.

The agreement was loosely applied at first. Iraq was explicitly allowed to produce more than its quota when its capacity permitted. Iran, limited to 1.2 mbd, responded by aggressive marketing and increased its output from 1.1 mbd to 2.8 mbd by December 1982. Libya and Venezuela also denounced their quotas, and by the end of 1982 aggregate OPEC production exceeded the ceiling by nearly 2 mbd. In February 1983 the glut in the oil market induced BNOC to cut its price again, to $30.50, and once more Nigeria responded immediately, cutting its price by $5.50 to $30.

During all this period, Saudi Arabia was not explicitly assigned a quota; it was understood that it would produce 7 mbd, the difference between the aggregate OPEC ceiling and the sum of the quotas of the other members. However, its actual production was always below this level. Still continuing to defend the marker price, Saudi Arabia was put in the position of the swing producer, accommodating the resumption of exports from Iran and Iraq, increases in non-OPEC sales, as well as decline in worldwide demand. As a result, its output dropped from over 10 mbd in 1981 to 2.7 mbd in the third quarter of 1985, its share of OPEC output falling from 47% to 18%.

In March 1983 OPEC reduced the marker price to $29, and announced a second agreement with the same aggregate ceiling of 17.5 mbd but higher quotas for Iran, Libya, Kuwait and Venezuela at the expense of Saudi Arabia, whose implied quota was brought down to 5 mbd. Iraq was limited to its maximum production capability of 1.1 mbd, with the stipulation that its quota would increase as its capacity increased.

In October 1984 the ceiling was lowered to 16 mbd, and Saudi Arabia, whose output was rapidly dwindling, was for the first time given an explicit quota, 4.35 mbd. Up to 1985, OPEC had set the price of the Saudi Light crude, known as the marker crude. In 1985, at the request of Saudi Arabia, this practice was abandoned and in its place a somewhat vague average target price was announced. This placed Saudi Arabia on the same footing as the other members. The responsibility for defending the 'OPEC price' was off Saudi shoulders; it could stop acting as the swing producer.

Lower ceilings and Saudi production below quota were not sufficient to prevent a decline in spot prices. In February 1985 the British government announced that BNOC, which had been acting as the *de facto* price leader in the contract market, would be disbanded effective July 1, 1985, implying that in the future British oil would be sold at spot prices. OPEC's hopes for cooperation with Britain as 'the fourteenth OPEC member' (as *The Financial Times* had once referred to Britain) were dashed, and shortly thereafter prices collapsed.

While OPEC publicly blamed the United Kingdom and the other non-OPEC suppliers for the falling oil price, it was well aware of lack of discipline within its own ranks. Cheating was widespread. A 1985 OPEC report described 23 ways in which members cheated on price (*Petroleum Intelligence Weekly Special Supplement*, October 21, 1985, p. 1). The Ministerial Executive Council of OPEC was given the task of improving adherence to agreements (with the help of an international auditing firm). But members did not cooperate and refused to provide access to the information that was necessary to measure their price and output, and the council proved ineffective. The market, which for a few months in 1985 was relatively stable, soon began to discount the new monitoring system. Furthermore, even if it had been able to identify cheaters, the Council would have been unable to punish them, except by exposing them to quick reaction from other countries.

By summer of 1985 overproduction by several OPEC members had forced Saudi output down to 2 mbd, prompting King Fahd to give an ultimatum: his country would claim its full quota and prices would fall unless others reduced production. In September Saudi Arabia made good on its threat and increased production to 4.7 mbd causing prices to collapse from $28 to $11 in a matter of weeks. To win back customers lost during the years when it was the highest priced seller, it adopted the so-called netback pricing rule in which all sales were priced on the basis of the prices at which refiners sold the final products.

Oil prices hit a floor in August 1986 when they fell below $10. At this price some high-cost output, mainly from the stripper wells in the US, was shut off. In time demand picked up, keeping prices fluctuating between $15 and $18. OPEC seems to have given up hope of recovering the loss suffered in 1985–86 and to have chosen $18 as a best attainable target price. The group has met several times since 1986, revising at intervals the quota allocations, but there is little evidence that it has influenced the market significantly.

## 3. INFORMAL MODELS

### 3.1. Introduction

In this section, we survey the 'informal' models of the oil market. They are exposed with little or no mathematical symbolism, and with careful attention to institutional detail, at the cost of assumptions which are not always explicitly stated, and some blurring of the distinction between assumptions and results. The majority of economists who write on the oil market employ informal modeling. Because they are not constrained by the necessity to find a mathematical formulation, they can address directly, if sometimes with limited rigor, the puzzles of the oil market. As a result, the informal literature has been able to define a different set of questions than the theoretical literature. It has been much less concerned with the implications of exhaustibility, and instead has concentrated on institutional issues, such as the organization of OPEC, closer to the subject matter of industrial organization. This literature is also important because of its impact on policy, due to its easier accessibility for a lay audience. Most policy issues have been debated in terms of informal models and it is mainly through this literature that our profession has influenced policy and the perceptions of the public on oil and energy questions.

Comparison of the writings surveyed here and the theoretical models of Section 5 reveals what may be relatively commonplace in economics: The dialogue between the theorists and the applied practitioners is weaker than one would expect. The influx of theoretical papers in response to the issues raised by the oil price revolution failed to influence the direction or the level of the discourse of the applied economists. As a result, there is substantial dissimilarity between the topics treated by theorists and the applied energy economists. Whereas theorists dealt mainly with the oil market from the viewpoint of the exhaustible resource literature, energy economists concentrated on questions of market structure and organization. Except for a limited effect on the stimulation models, all of which incorporate exhaustibility in one way or another, the non-theoretical literature has benefited little from the findings of theorists. Nor is there much of a detectable influence in the reverse direction.

The informal literature on the oil market is very extensive, and almost no two accounts describe the oil market in exactly the same way. However, most models fall into two basic types: those that emphasize monopolistic behavior and those that emphasize competitive behavior. The former category, much larger in volume, includes models that describe OPEC as a textbook cartel—a group of producers acting in a unified manner—as well as those that stress the influence of a 'dominant firm', Saudi Arabia (acting alone or in unison with its close Persian Gulf allies). The models in the competitive category are of three types: backward-bending supply curve (multiple equilibria), property rights, and supply shock models.

Before discussing these models, we must address two basic analytical issues which are used as building blocks for many of the theories that we will discuss. First, we study the importance of exhaustibility for the oil market. There is a finite amount of oil available on earth; how important is this scarcity in explaining the recent history of the market? Second, we study the shape of the supply curve as it would exist if the market were competitive. This preliminary work will greatly simplify our comparison of the industrial organization implications of the models.

## 3.2. The relevance of exhaustibility

A good is exhaustible if greater consumption today implies less consumption tomorrow. The consequences of this intertemporal link were first studied formally by Hotelling (1931). Considering a competitive economy with perfect foresight and perfect capital markets, he showed that, in equilibrium, the difference between the price of an exhaustible good and its marginal cost of extraction is strictly positive and rises at the rate of interest. Therefore, contrary to what happens for standard goods, even under perfect competition the price of an exhaustible resource would be different from its marginal cost of production.[3] Thus, even an exhaustible good that is costless to extract would command a positive price, which is the reward to the resource owners for having held to their stocks up to the present date. In the literature this difference between price and marginal cost is known as the 'scarcity rent'. The sum of the marginal cost of production and the scarcity rent is known as the 'user cost', which is the proper definition of the opportunity cost of selling oil in any given period.

Of course, in a world with uncertainty the actual price path will also reflect the influence of demand-and supply-side shocks. Furthermore, when capital markets are imperfect and reserves cannot be traded, the consumption and production decisions of the resource owners are interdependent, and individual discount rates rather than the market rate of interest influence production. Reserve owners will extract to satisfy their revenue needs because they cannot borrow or sell their stocks. As we shall see in Section 5, the theory is much less well developed when these complications are introduced. But nevertheless an important implication of Hotelling's finding remains: the marginal cost and the price will differ.

All this implies that attempts to prove monopoly pricing in exhaustible resource markets on the sole basis of comparisons between production costs and price are theoretically unsound, as long as some estimate of the scarcity rent is not included. To understand price behavior in such markets we must isolate the effects of exhaustibility and market structure, both of which result in a premium of price over marginal cost.

Indeed, oil price increases have been attributed both to scarcity and to monopoly depending on the analyst's point of view. OPEC used exhaustibility as justification for the first price increase in 1973, in order to mollify the outcries against the resulting huge shift in the worldwide distribution of income. The Shah of Iran proclaimed oil too precious a resource to burn, and other OPEC spokesmen wished the world would thank them for reminding it of the rapid rate of depletion in petroleum reserves (see, for example, Ortiz, 1982, p. 1).

---

[3] It should be pointed out that other reasons besides exhaustibility may account for a difference between marginal cost and price. Constraints on production capacity arising from dynamic adjustments of exploration and investments in capacity, as well as technical limits on the rate of extraction from a given reservoir, would still be important even if oil were not exhaustible.

Everyone agrees that the stock of oil is finite. But in practical terms, we need to determine whether this significantly influences present market behavior. A natural first step in answering this question is to examine the data on oil reserves. This turns out to be a murky area, and the literature contains much confusion on the topic.

At the end of 1988, worldwide proved reserves were 907 billion barrels (*Oil and Gas Journal*, December, 1988). Compared to a consumption of approximately 20 billion barrels per year, this is not a large amount, but such comparisons are misleading. Estimates of oil reserves are highly uncertain and must be used with caution. As Adelman (1972b, pp. 74–75) observed, while in 1950 the Persian Gulf reserves were estimated at 42 billion barrels, in 1971, after 47 billions had been extracted, 367 billion barrels remained! By the end of 1988, after an additional 98 billion barrels had been extracted, 552 billion still remained!

The paradox of the previous paragraph was built by using proved reserves, defined as the portion of known reserves that can be profitably extracted at current prices and technology. This implies that proved reserves are not a measure of the physical scarcity of oil, as they are influenced by economic decisions. Companies and governments who desire better predictions of future revenues may carry exploration farther in advance from extraction, and proved reserves will be increased. Furthermore, for given fields, and at given technology, reserves change not only with discovery and improved technology, but also with price. Price increases extend the amount that can be profitably extracted.

Not only is the definition of proved reserves subject to criticism, often the quality of the data is poor. Because of its legal implications for the value of company assets, the amount of proved reserves in private hands is carefully estimated. However, this legal requirement does not exist for OPEC reserves since they are owned by governments. And, because proved reserves are an important factor in the determination of the production quotas that have been imposed since the early 1980s, its members have an incentive to overestimate them. For example, most observers believe that the 1988 increases in estimated proved reserves by Saudi Arabia (50%), the United Arab Emirates (100%), and Iraq are motivated in part by this bargaining problem (*Wall Street Journal*, January 10, 1989, p. A2).

Because of its dependence on price, even a reliable measure of proved reserves would be of limited value. Other more comprehensive measures—such as probable reserves, ultimately recoverable reserves, and oil in place (Danielsen, 1982)—show that there is much more oil than indicated by proved reserves. For example, oil in place for the Persian Gulf has been estimated at four-times the proved reserves (Fesharaki and Isaak, 1983). But these estimates do not provide much more economic information since they do not relate availability to cost. Ideally, we would like to know a function that would inform us of the amount of oil available at different costs.

Optimists believe that, for all practical purposes, there exists an endless supply of oil reserves. Pessimists calculate the life of the reserves by dividing current reserves by consumption, and, depending on the estimate of reserves that they choose, predict depletion within 50 to 100 years. Even if we discount the enormous uncertainty associated with such long-run predictions, these figures are very poor estimates of the actual longevity of reserves because as the stock nears exhaustion the price will increase, consumption will decline, and the life of the reserve will be prolonged.

In any case, an accurate estimate of the life of known reserves is not very crucial for our purposes, because the economic significance of exhaustibility does not really stem from eventual exhaustion, but rather from the fact that prospects of future scarcity and increasing costs influence current prices. Expectations of higher future prices encourage resource owners to hold on to their reserves, thereby driving up the current price and the scarcity rent. If this effect is significant, oil is exhaustible, if it is not significant, oil is not exhaustible.

On the whole, energy economists have treated oil as exhaustible, but this is much more evident in their forecasts of future supplies and prices than in their descriptions of the functioning of the market. Almost all price forecasts, whether they are made with simulation models or intuition, predict price increases over the medium and long run. In the mid-1980s, when prices were falling, analysts lowered the projection path but continued to predict increasing prices in the future (see the survey by Manne et al, 1986).

Influential writings by Professors Adelman (1972b, 1979, and 1986) and Houthakker (1983) have provided a notable exception to this general acceptance of exhaustibility. Even before the oil price revolution of 1973, treating oil like a standard, renewable commodity, Adelman argued that the marginal cost of production in the Middle

East, properly defined to take into account all stages from exploration, development, to extraction, was somewhere between 10 to 20 cents per barrel, less than one-tenth of the price in 1972 (see Adelman 1972a, p. 6). For Adelman oil is 'produced' when it is discovered, hence the use of the term inventory to refer to oil reserves: 'Depletion of reserves at the Persian Gulf is only about 1.5% a year. It is uneconomic to turn over an inventory so slowly.' (1972b, p. 76). This view is also shared by McKie (1978, p. 39) who believes that oil 'reserves are only working inventory.'

Adelman rejects exhaustibility in part because he does not believe that oil prices are determined according to Hotelling's model. Most economists, even some proponents of competitive behavior, actually agree with him and use the Hotelling model as a benchmark of analysis rather than a description of the world we live in. Prices in their models are influenced by exhaustibility of oil, but they are not the same prices that would prevail in a Hotelling-type competitive equilibrium. For instance, no one has argued that the 1973 price increase was caused by a sudden realization that oil is exhaustible. All the informal models, whether of the monopoly or competitive variety, that explicitly take into account exhaustibility provide a separate explanation for the 1973 price increase.

Exhaustibility is often confused with shortages that have appeared from time to time in the oil market. Adelman (1972b), Danielsen and Selby (1980), and others have quite reasonably objected to the identification of 'shortages', which may arise from price controls or accidental factors, with the long-term scarcity that arises because oil is exhaustible. Such identification may lead to counterproductive policies. For instance, governments in consuming nations have often responded to market crises, such as the 1973 price increase, with long-term policies of conservation which may be besides the point.

Exhaustibility only influences the supply side of the market. Economic models study the interaction of the supply and demand sides, and it is only in such models that we can understand how exhaustibility influences present prices. As it turns out, we understand demand for oil much better than its supply. We know quite a bit about the long-term price elasticity of demand, in part thanks to academic research (Pindyck, 1979b, Hogan, 1989a) and in part because the experience of two price increases has taught us much about substitution possibilities.

### 3.3. The competitive supply of oil

In any market, before answering questions about market structure, economists try to identify the competitive supply curve. In the case of the market for oil, the analysis of supply depends crucially on whether or not we decide that oil is exhaustible. If oil is treated as a renewable resource, its supply price would simply be its marginal production cost and the supply curve the marginal cost curve. This implies, among other things, that there is a well-defined, unique competitive equilibrium, and that a price above marginal cost signals imperfect competition.

But if oil is treated as a non-renewable resource, as we think it should be, the problem is substantially more complex as individual supply curves are determined by complex intertemporal optimization problems, and the supply price (opportunity cost) in any period will differ from the marginal cost of production. The amount supplied will depend not only on the current price but also on future prices and on the investment opportunities available to producers. As noted in the previous section, to capture the opportunity cost (user cost) of selling a barrel today, a scarcity rent must be added to the cost of extraction. Unfortunately, this does not say much as the scarcity rent must be determined endogeneously.

We will find it convenient to use the term 'supply curve' to describe producer behavior, and so have many writers on the oil market. This should be only understood as an expository device as the supply in any period depends not only on the current price but also on expected future prices.

If we define the equivalent of the static supply curve as the function relating current supply to current price, we should take into account two complications due to exhaustibility. First, current supply depends on future prices. This implies that a change in the current price has two effects on current supply: a standard price effect due to the change in the price of the product relative to its cost, and an intertemporal effect due to the resulting changes in future expected prices, and therefore the opportunity cost of oil. If, for example, a price increase is expected to last for a long time, the opportunity cost of extracting a barrel today increases, because the value of oil in the ground has risen. If the discounted increase in future prices is larger than the increase in the current price, producers may even decide to conserve and sell later, thus creating a negatively sloped 'supply curve.' On the other hand, if a price increase is expected to last for only a short time, the opportunity cost of selling in this period is not increased, and the supply curve will have the normal upward sloping shape.

The second complication concerns the role of capital markets. In an exhaustible resource market, the producers' reaction to price changes depends on their investment opportunities. Consider the following example. A price increase is followed by expectations of equivalent increases in the future, i.e. a proportional shift in the expected price path. With perfect capital markets, there is no intertemporal effect and there would be no change in extraction. With imperfect capital markets producers may not be able to invest present revenues profitably, and may decide to cut back on current supply. Similarly, if prices drop temporarily, supply may not fall if producers are unable to borrow to finance expenditures they consider necessary.

The recent experience of the oil market has underlined the importance of taking into account both expectations and imperfect capital markets. Because of the special circumstances that surrounded it, the price increase of 1973 induced a parallel increase in the expected price of oil. Energy crisis, the OPEC revolution, the end of cheap oil, were all phrases that made the price hike appear as the harbinger of a new era rather than a temporary aberration. Whatever one's favorite description of the market, it is impossible to understand supply behavior after 1973 without reference to these expectations. Had the price increase been regarded as temporary, countries would have faced strong incentives to sell as much as possible in a short period of time. This would have put considerable pressure on any cartel agreement and hence on prices. On the other hand, if the price increase had signaled even larger future increases, some resource owners would have been tempted to postpone production.

Having said this, it should be recognized that the theoretical literature provides little guidance on the best way to think about expectations. Theorists agree that the best modeling strategy is generally to use rational expectations, but they are very difficult to handle. Rational expectations models have been successful in applications, for instance in monetary economics, where the information set of the agents is easy to define and where similar decisions are repeatedly taken by the agents. This was clearly not the case in the oil market in 1973 or 1980!

Before discussing in detail the shape of the supply curve, we need to understand better the relevant imperfections in the capital markets. Oil producers can invest domestically or abroad. We begin by the limitations of foreign investments. They are a very useful tool for the purpose of intertemporal smoothing of expenditures, but in several respects domestic capital and oil in the ground are superior for storing the country's wealth. Because foreign investments are under the control of host governments, both their value and the rate of return are subject to manipulation. The freezing of Iranian assets in 1979 by the United States government provides a somewhat extreme example. Indeed, after the price increases of 1973 and 1979–80 the richer OPEC members invested abroad large proportions of their suddenly expanded revenues. Very quickly, they realized the limits of foreign investment as a substitute to domestic investment or to oil in the ground (see Crémer and Salehi-Isfahani, 1980 and 1989, Teece, 1982, and Noreng, 1982). This led Hogan (1982) to suggest that better returns on the oil-exporters' investments in the West would encourage them to increase production.

The countries that did take substantial advantage of the international capital markets, such as Saudi Arabia and Kuwait, also realized that their holdings of wealth in foreign assets was costly in terms of political pressure from both foreign and domestic sources. On the foreign front, OPEC was perceived as having disrupted the international system and of having caused severe balance of payments difficulties for the poorer Third World nations. To improve their image, OPEC countries embarked on a hasty aid program, spending as proportion of their GNP more than any other group of countries. On the domestic front, large holdings of foreign assets were unpopular and seemed inconsistent with gradual and prudent expenditure of oil revenues.

Therefore, foreign investment is a limited outlet for oil revenues. So is domestic investment (Crémer and Salehi-Isfahani, 1980, Ezzati. 1976, Moran, 1978, and Scott, 1981). The fact that in any given year there are only a limited number of productive investment opportunities is a familiar theme in development economics, where the phenomenon is described as limited absorptive capacity (see Eckaus, 1973). The time needed to learn to operate new equipment and to train personnel with specific skills limits the speed with which investment expenditures can be turned into productive capital. Some oil exporting countries tried to beat this bottleneck by importing labor, or by buying turn-key factories, but tales of corruption and inefficiencies later prompted them to reduce investment. In addition, there are limits on the proportion of this investment that the government could or would like to undertake itself, and there are few efficient or politically feasible ways of channeling large parts of the oil revenues to the private sector for investment (Salehi-Isfahani, 1989).

Governments also face a choice between expenditure on investment and consumption. Like investment, consumption is subject to declining marginal benefits. At the margin, the benefits of extra consumption are weighed against more investment expenditures, both of which are subject to diminishing returns, and must in turn be compared with benefits of keeping oil in the ground.

The implication of these constraints on the useful expenditure of revenues for supply behavior is now straightforward. At low prices, and therefore low revenues, the marginal benefits of current consumption and investment are high and price increases may encourage more extraction. At high prices these benefits are lower and it is likely that an increase in price will trigger a perverse supply response. This results in a backward bending supply curve for the individual country (Crémer and Salehi-Isfahani, 1980 and 1989).

To give a simple illustration of this hypothesis, assume that capital markets do not exist, that marginal utility of consumption drops to zero beyond some level $\bar{C}_t$, and that annual investment above $\bar{I}_t$ is unproductive. Then, the country will always choose a rate of extraction such that in period $t$

$$p_t R_t + Y_t \leq \bar{C}_t + \bar{I}_t$$

where $Y_t$ is non oil GNP, $p_t$ is price and $R_t$ the rate of extraction of oil. The left hand side of this inequality represents total income available and the right hand side the total potential productive use of this revenue. The inequality states that the country will never choose to extract so much oil that its revenue cannot be fruitfully used. This results in a downward sloping supply curve because when the price becomes large enough, $R_t$ has to decrease. Of course, the supply behavior implied by this extreme version[4] is not realistic because the supply curve is negatively sloped for all prices. The more elaborate

---

[4] It is the basis of the 'target revenue' model of the oil market (Teece, 1982) to be discussed later.

model by Crémer and Salehi-Isfahani allows for smooth utility and absorptive capacity functions, takes into account future price expectations, and still produces a backward bending supply curve.

The idea of a negatively sloped supply curve has found increasing support in the literature and has been widely used in analyzing the oil market (Adelman, 1980 and 1982, Bénard, 1980, Reza, 1981, Scott, 1981, Bohi and Montgomery, 1982, Noreng, 1982). Adelman believes it explains the behavior of some countries some of the time, particularly the low absorbers, such as Saudi Arabia and Kuwait. Noreng (1982, p. 199) believes this is a reasonable approximation even for Norway and Mexico. Numerical simulations have also confirmed these intuitions. Incorporating absorptive capacity constraints and imperfect capital markets in a dynamic programming model, Salehi-Isfahani (1986) has shown that, even for a country with high absorptive capacity (Algeria), the supply curve should be backward bending at the range of prices observed after 1973. It should be stressed that this hypothesis is logically and practically separate from the diagnosis of the market structure.

However, the assumption of an upward sloping supply curve remains in wide use (see, for instance, Erickson, 1980, and Singer, 1985, who assume rising supply curves for the competitive fringe, although this is not necessary for their models to make sense). Some simulation models (MacAvoy, 1982 and 1983, Pindyck, 1978, and Verleger, 1982a) also assume positively sloped supply functions. However, MacAvoy, who estimates his supply responses econometrically, finds that the estimated coefficient is negative for some countries. Although he dismisses these estimates because they have 'the opposite sign from what can be expected' (p. 26), he provides implicit support for the hypothesis of a backward-bending supply curve.

### 3.4. Demand

Two characteristics of the demand curve for oil have played an important role in the informal literature on the oil market. First, the short-run elasticity is very low. A limited supply shock, such as the 1973 cutbacks by Arab producers, can lead to a sharp increase in the spot market price. The long-run elasticity is considerably larger due to substitution of other energy sources and conservation.

Second, the demand for oil has a high income elasticity, generally believed to be around unity; everything else equal, the rate of growth of demand for oil is equal to the rate of growth of world GNP. Rapid expansion in the world economy increased consumption in the industrialized countries by 5.2% per year between 1965 and 1973. As a consequence, many believed that the price was too low before the oil crisis, and Penrose (1975) argues that rising demand was an important contributor to the price increase.

Demand plays an important role in simulation models used to forecast the price of oil. For example, Hogan (1989b) forecasts an interesting cyclical pattern for the price of oil which is almost entirely caused by demand behavior. Demand adjusts to price with a lag; as a result high prices shift future demand curves to the left. This causes prices to fall some years later. The resulting low prices encourage consumption (shift future demand curves to the right) causing prices to rise, thus creating a cyclical pattern which fits the recent experience of the market rather well.

Although we understand demand for oil much better than its supply, our poor understanding of the latter has serious implications for the accuracy of our estimates of the demand function. Attempts to measure the elasticity of demand without reference to supply presents familiar econometric problems. Existing estimates are based on the assumption that OPEC sets the price, and this price is used as an exogeneous variable in the estimation. If price is determined simultaneously with quantity, this methodology is not legitimate, as the demand function is not identified. Furthermore, it is generally difficult to disentangle price and income effects, in part because the two periods of sharp decline in demand for oil, 1975 and 1981–1986, were preceded by a sharp price increase in price and coincided with a recession.

### 3.5. Models emphasizing monopoly behavior

Most authors explain the recent history of the oil market through the use of market power by OPEC or some subset of its members. It is convenient to distinguish two basic variants of this approach, cartel and dominant firm theories. The cartel version is by far the most widely used but, as it became increasingly clear that interactions within OPEC did not correspond to the classic cartel theory, the dominant firm version recently gained in acceptance.

Before reviewing the literature dealing with the application of these models to the oil market, let us briefly describe the basic theory behind each. In keeping with the spirit of the informal literature we focus on their static versions.

### 3.5.1. *The cartel model: theory*

Cartels are groups of producers who cooperate to reduce the quantity supplied of a commodity and thereby raise the price. As a consequence, price exceeds marginal cost, cartel members are kept to the left of their competitive supply curves and have incentives to increase sales through price discounts. The cartel's task is to 'absorb' the excess supply at the high price (*AB* in Figure 3.1).

As Pindyck (1979a) has put it, the success of a cartel depends on whether it 'can agree on an optimal aggregate production level ... agree on a division of output and profits and find a means to detect and deter cheating.' More precisely, it must:

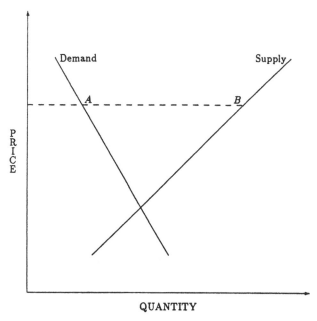

FIGURE 3.1   Cartel model.

1. Determine a price and a production level for the group as a whole. If the cartel does not include all the suppliers, this determination requires some calculation of the 'residual demand' left after subtracting from the market demand the supply of the producers that are not part of the cartel, the so-called 'competitive fringe'. Because the incentives of the members of the cartel depend on future as well as present prices, OPEC must devise an agreement over a sequence of future prices, and differences in discount rates can make this problem very complicated. Countries with larger reserves tend to be more farsighted and have a lower discount rate. Thus Saudi Arabia wants lower current prices than Algeria or Iran.
2. Allocate output between members. If OPEC were run as a unified profit maximizing entity, it would produce mainly from the lower cost reserves in Saudi Arabia and Kuwait and some form of redistribution of the profits to the other members would be necessary. In turn, those who would produce later would promise to pay part of their future profits to the early producers. Because such intertemporal transfers are difficult to enforce, in any period all countries must generate their share of profits from the sales of their own products.
3. Detect and punish cheaters. This is the most vexing issue faced by the cartel. Whatever agreement is reached, some members can improve their welfare by cheating, and a comparison is often drawn with the prisoners' dilemma where the 'all cheat' solution is an equilibrium. Members are not necessarily deterred from cheating by the fact that if they all did so everyone would be worse off. A system of enforcement in which they all have confidence is needed.

### 3.5.2. *Dominant firm: theory*

In this family of models, all firms except one, the dominant firm, behave competitively. This firm computes its own demand curve, $D_{DF}$, by subtracting the supply of the competitive fringe, $S_{CF}$, from the market demand, $D_F$, and then finds the maximum profit point, $P_1$, on this derived demand curve (see Figure 3.2).

This is the well-known Stackelberg equilibrium.[5] In contrast to the

---

[5] In contrast to the simulation and theoretical literatures, the informal literature has not found much explicit use for the concepts of Cournot and Bertrand equilibria.

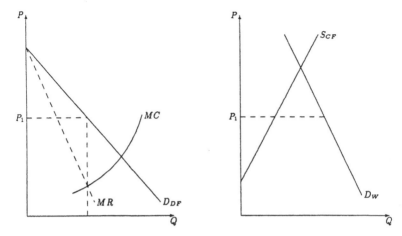

FIGURE 3.2 Dominant firm model.

cartel theory, in this version of monopolistic behavior all complications related to cooperative behavior are bypassed. The dominant firm faces a more elastic demand curve than a cartel that would include it, and would therefore choose a lower price. If its market share is very small, we revert to the competitive solution.

### 3.5.3. *The cartel model: application to the oil market*

Cartel is by far the most widely used term to describe OPEC. This description came naturally to mind in 1973, 13 years after OPEC's formation, when it decided to set the price of oil unilaterally, at four-times its previous level, without negotiation with the international oil companies. The price increase came with all the indications of a cartel in control: at the time of the announcement in December 1973, the cutbacks by OAPEC, the Organization of Arab Petroleum Exporting Countries, were at their height, and the 13 OPEC nations only made official the resulting increase in the spot price.

However, there is general agreement that the textbook definition of a cartel does not apply to pre-1982 OPEC, and specialists have spent much time identifying the internal features that make OPEC successful despite this fact, although the subtlety of the issue is not apparent in many textbooks or policy discussions (for an example of textbook treatment, see Hirshleifer 1988, pp. 254–256, and for an example of a policy discussion, see Darmstadter *et al*. 1983, pp. 129–133). We will examine in detail the treatment in the literature of two important questions: the determination of the cartel price and output, and the nature of the output-sharing agreement that supports the cartel price.

## (a) Price and output determination

A cartel chooses a price and aggregate output along its demand curve, and allocates this output among its members. However, until 1982, OPEC set the price of oil, and let its output be determined by the market. There was no allocation of the output among member countries. In 1982, OPEC adopted output rationing, but did not abandon the habit of announcing the price it wanted to defend. In 1989, proposals were made (especially by Saudi Arabia) that OPEC only determine output without specifying a target price.

While OPEC only set the price, disputes over this price were common, and informal models have paid much attention to these disputes. The main disagreement was between the so-called price moderates, led by Saudi Arabia, and the price hawks (Libya, Iran, and Algeria). Price disputes are generally believed to result from differences in discount rates. Discount rates diverge for a number of reasons, development strategy (investment policy and need for foreign exchange), size of reserves (the longer the time until exhaustion, the less myopic the country) and political system (the horizon of the decision makers). Some countries (Saudi Arabia, Kuwait) do not seem to discount the future heavily because they have large stocks of oil relative to their current revenue needs, and therefore expect their oil to last for many decades. For them a high current price may be undesirable because it causes substitution of other forms of energy for oil. Others (Algeria, Venezuela, Iran) are less affected by future substitutions because they have relatively less oil and/or a development strategy that requires a heavy expenditure of foreign exchange in the present (Algeria). A number of studies incorporate these differences in discount rates, see Hnyilicza and Pindyck (1976) and Daly *et al*. (1982). If unlimited intertemporal side payments were possible, for all practical purposes all reserves would be pooled, countries would not sell oil individually, and each would receive a share of the total revenues according to an agreed upon formula. Conflicts over the price path, which are linked to differences in discount rates, would be reduced. Of course, such side payments are extremely difficult if not impossible for OPEC.

Saudi Arabia's position as the leading price moderate, of which Chapter 2 gives many examples, has also been studied by non-economists. Many studies by political scientists and oil historians have dwelled on the motives for this price policy (see Choucri, 1976, Moran, 1982, Schneider, 1983, Skeet, 1988). They do not necessarily refute the more fundamental low discount rate explanation of Saudi price policies offered by economists, but they add event specific explanations of Saudi Arabian motives in which arms purchases and the politics of the Arab-Israeli conflict figure prominently.

A number of other authors have provided descriptions of OPEC's pricing policy, less well grounded in economic theory or political science. For instance, Danielsen and Selby (1980) believe that OPEC sets the price simply by following the spot market. Calling OPEC a 'viable price-setting and output restricting organization', they nevertheless argue that 'there has been no master plan . . . and no predetermined prive level toward which [OPEC] aims.' OPEC does not determine prices but views whatever level the spot market has reached as the 'minimum acceptable' and uses its production restricting abilities to maintain that price level. The timing of OPEC price increases, especially the 1979–80 rounds, coming shortly after supply disruptions, lends some support to this view. In these instances, OPEC decisions were focused on the short run and were not the result of some long run plan similar to those computed by the simulation literature surveyed in Chapter 4. This relationship between spot and official prices has also found econometric support in Lowinger and Ram (1984) and Verleger (1982b). Danielsen and Selby derive some policy implications from this theory. Governments of consuming countries could reduce increases in contract prices by reducing the impact of oil supply shocks on the spot market. Because supply shocks, such as the Iranian crisis of 1979, are exacerbated by inventory behavior, a federal agency could use stockpiles to stabilize the price, much like the Federal Reserve System stabilizes exchange rates. It should be stressed that this theory falls well short of a general theory of oil price determination, as it does not explain the spot prices themselves.

The cartel models have found it difficult to explain the 1979–1980 price increases. The earlier simulation models argued that the 1973 price increase was in line with a cartel maximizing the present value of its wealth. Once the optimal price path is chosen, the adjustments should only come as a result of changes in the variables in the optimization problem. What caused OPEC to make the drastic adjustments in 1979–80? The disruptions of Iranian and Iraqi supply cannot explain the price increase in the cartel framework. If the pre-1980 price were the profit maximizing price, reduction in the supply of any cartel member should have been made up by increase in output of other members, as long as production capacity was available. Informal models have not given a satisfactory answer to this question.

### (b)  Output sharing

Because the cartel theory of OPEC asserts that the high price is above the competitive price, the joint output of the cartel must be below its competitive level. Cartel theories must explain the allocation of output among OPEC members.

We distinguish two periods. The decade between 1973 and 1982 include OPEC's most successful years. Although there was no prorationing of output, the price increase of 1973 was never seriously threatened by cheating, nor was there even the usual type of tension between cartel members that became commonplace later in the 1980s. As a result, OPEC earned the image of a happy-go-lucky cartel. Explaining the 'missing excess supply' is the main puzzle faced by the cartel theory with respect to this period.

After 1982 several output quota systems were adopted, but none really functioned well and the price continued to decline, until it collapsed in 1986. Why did OPEC fail to achieve with explicit output rationing what it had succeeded to do without in the previous period?

*The pre-1982 period*    The literature offers several explanations for OPEC's success in the absence of explicit output rationing during this period. Well before the price revolution of 1973, Adelman (1972a and 1972b) argued that international oil companies performed output restriction for OPEC. He claimed that 'the producing nations have become a cartel that sells a license to produce', but, because they lack the ability to proration or police cartel agreements, the licensees conduct these tasks for them. The price floor was determined by the tax OPEC imposed on the companies, hence his description of the role of the oil companies as 'OPEC tax collectors'. Thus the companies maintained the price far above its cost of production and, unwittingly, helped police the cartel: OPEC members could not cheat because their agreements with the companies that determined the price they received and the amount they produced were public information (Adelman, 1972b; see also Schneider, 1983, p. 9 and p. 318).

While there is some truth to the argument that before 1973 the major oil companies did restrict production in certain countries, for several reasons it is difficult to think of the governments as the master-minds behind the cartel. First, as Adelman himself has noted elsewhere (1982, p. 39), the company-imposed rationing was done in opposition to the wishes of the host governments. Second, the idea of OPEC tax as floor to price is contradicted by the evidence that, 'Between the spring of 1970 and the summer of 1973, market prices for crude oil more than doubled measured in dollars, and nearly doubled in terms of other currencies, but the fiscal income of the host governments accounted for less than half of the increase.' (Penrose, 1975, p. 47). Also, Adelman's prediction based on the above argument that direct sales by national oil companies would increase cheating and drive the price of oil down to its competitive level was not confirmed in the mid-1970s. Third, because by the mid-1960s many countries had entered into complex profit-sharing agreements with a number of smaller independent companies, it was very difficult to determine their total output from company data. Finally, easy detection of cheating is not by itself sufficient to guarantee cartel stability; punishment of cheaters is necessary. This is the most difficult problem for a cartel made up of independent governments because submission to punishment undermines sovereignty (Eckbo, 1976, p. 49, Hartshorn, 1985, p. 67).

After 1973, when OPEC began setting the price unilaterally and without consulting the companies, many more explanations were provided. Most economists described OPEC as a classic cartel, with the usual internal coordination problems endemic to all cartels, and as a result the cheating problem received a lot of attention. This basic dilemma of cartels is nicely described by Adelman:

'Each member is always tempted to chisel and sell at a somewhat lower price to increase volume and profits ... hence the cartel must have a machinery to detect cheating or register non-cheating, and to assure each member that all others are observing the price.' (Adelman, 1972a, p. 210)

To stimulate cheating he later proposed that consuming countries require oil exporting countries to purchase import tickets (Adelman, 1976). This would allow members of OPEC to give secret discounts and thereby undermine its stability. This argument—and many other proposals to break up OPEC—assumed that there existed an implicit quota system maintained by implicit threats of punishment and made possible by the transparency of the market.

However, by the mid-1970s OPEC's staying power gradually raised doubts about its vulnerability to cheating, and by the same token about the appropriateness of its description as a classic cartel. Many authors with intimate knowledge of its organizational structure noted that OPEC's lack of attention to quantity supplied did not conform to cartel theory (Mabro, 1975b, Mikdashi, 1975, Penrose, 1975, and Moran, 1978). Whereas in the beginning cartel references were typically to the textbook case, later OPEC was presented as a unique and unusual cartel. Adelman's views appear to have undergone a similar change as he de-emphasized cheating and began referring to OPEC as a 'clumsy cartel' and a 'loosely cooperating oligopoly' (Adelman, 1980, 1982).

Similarly, Robert Mabro, who has written extensively on the oil market, does not want to remain within the confines of strict definitions. He rejects the interpretation of OPEC as a classic cartel and offers his own interpretation:

> 'The term cartel may suggest to the uninformed that controls in the form of pro-rationing or an agreed cut-back by a significant producer are the instruments applied by OPEC. OPEC . . . has never implemented such measures. Its preferred instruments are taxes and prices.' (1975a, p. 14).

Thus, in his mind, there is a simple interpretation for OPEC's behavior:

> 'OPEC tries to do what a primary producer faced with a less than perfectly elastic demand curve for its product would always be recommended to do: impose an export tax.' (1975a, p. 14).

The idea of a 'tax floor' set by OPEC for the price is also part of Adelman's argument noted above (1972b). The emphasis on manipulations of prices and taxes is quite common in the literature (see also Mikdashi, 1975, p. 209, Moran 1982), and is consistent with the fact, already mentioned above, that before 1982 output was not discussed in OPEC meetings.

The need for coordination between OPEC members is not lessened by the interpretation in terms of export tax. Since the demand curve faced by an individual country is elastic, any increase in one country's export tax not matched by others would increase its price over the market price and cut its sales substantially. Raising tax rates requires coordinated restriction of the supply of crude to the extracting companies in the same way that raising the price requires coordinated action in the supply of crude to the refiners. Without coordination, any single members's attempt to raise its tax rate above others will only result in reduced output and revenues. Furthermore, higher tax rates achieved by common action are unstable because of cheating in the form of lowering the tax rate. Therefore, the export taxation paradigm, although very suggestive, does not by itself provide a description of OPEC's solution to the cartel coordination problem. Griffin and Steele (1980) seem to disagree with us on this issue. Although they are aware of the power of the companies before 1970 to switch countries as source of crude (p. 106), they discuss OPEC's successful attempts at raising tax revenues during this same period without any reference to the coordination problem (pp. 102–103).

Another solution to the problem of excess supply is to argue that it is too small to create any coordination problem. Arguing that the short-run elasticities of both supply and demand are very low, many authors maintained that immediately following the price increase of 1973 there would be no excess supply, as this statement by Houthakker (1974) demonstrates:

> 'There are markets in which price can be doubled or tripled without changing the balance of supply and demand, but the petroleum market is certainly not one of them. In the very short run not much can be done, but at prevailing OPEC prices we are likely to see a surplus of oil within the next year or two.'

Clearly, Houthakker's predictions about the medium-run evolution of the market were not realized, and other authors argued that the excess supply stayed low because the elasticity of supply is small, possibly negative, even in the long run as OPEC members have limited revenue needs (see our discussion of supply behavior in Section 3.3). An early statement of this argument, without explicit mention of the size of the excess supply, is in Mabro (1975a, p. 19):

'The natural strength of OPEC arises from the distribution of oil production capacity among members. Countries with large populations and considerable development needs tend to have either small oil reserves . . . or large reserves but small installed capacity. Countries with large reserves . . . are cushioned . . . by financial reserves.'

The statement of the same argument by Moran (1978, p. 1) comes very close to saying there is no excess supply:

'OPEC has had a special advantage in dealing with the question of market shares and with the problem of cheating: the member states with the greatest ability to expand output have not 'needed' the revenues that additional production could have generated; the member governments that have 'needed' the revenues the most have been able to produce at near capacity.'

This account is similar to the competitive equilibrium described by Crémer and Salehi-Isfahani (1980 and 1989).

In his more recent writings, Professor Adelman (1980 and 1982) has also stressed the small size of the excess supply in his explanation of OPEC stability:

'Worldwide, supply elasticity does not greatly differ from zero. In some countries, higher prices do elicit greater supply: an orthodox forward-sloping supply curve. In other countries, the richer they get the easier it becomes for them to be good cartelists and restrain output. The more they change, the less they produce: a backward bending curve. In still other countries, both forward and backward bending curves are at work.' (Adelman 1980, p. 46)

The size of the excess supply is just one of the multitude of factors that affect cartel stability. It is implicit in the work of many others that it is also influenced by the size of the gains from cartelization (Pindyck, 1978, and Mackie-Mason and Pindyck, 1987). But there is no direct connection between the size of the excess supply or of the gains from cartelization and the strength of the incentives to cheat, which is really the important factor. A more systematic approach would be to compare the benefits of cooperative play with those for non-cooperative play, but the literature does not contain much by way of analysis of these incentives.

Some authors explain the price stability by resorting to loosely defined concepts such as OPEC unity, Arab solidarity, or implicit threats (e.g., Griffin and Steele, 1980, and Adelman, 1982). The term OPEC unity has been used in a somewhat tautological manner. Unity prevails when OPEC is successful, and disunity prevailed after the price collapse of 1986. Clearly, unity—in culture, political goals, etc. —has a lot to do with.cartel strength, and may well be a good explanation of how OPEC might have functioned well as a cartel in one period and not in another. But in its present form the argument is not persuasive.

Finally, on this point we should also note the contributions of political scientists. Moran (1982) argues that the political interactions within the cartel are a very important determinant of its stability. In periods of falling prices, pressure from the hawks forced Saudi Arabia to reduce its output (pp. 122–23). This may explain the pre-1985 decline in Saudi output but not the subsequent increase in production that caused the price collapse. More generally, we should point out that if Moran is correct and strategic considerations affect Saudi oil policies significantly, our modeling effort becomes very difficult, as it must also include the behavior of the US and perhaps other Western powers.

*The post-1982 period*    Soon after the 1980 price increase, demand for OPEC oil began to decline as world demand fell and supply from Mexico and the North Sea increased. Although OPEC production declined from 32 mbd in mid-1979 to 21 mbd in late 1981, mostly because of reduction in Iranian and Iraqi output, there was excess supply at the high price of $34 per barrel. Beginning in 1982, in a clear break with tradition, OPEC started to assign output quotas to its members. Ten years after the price increase, OPEC had finally begun to behave like the cartels described in the economic literature. However, no enforcement mechanism was implemented at first, and the allocation system failed to restrict the collective output of OPEC. There was little change in the output shares of members, or in total production, but for the fact that Saudi Arabia absorbed the slack created by overproduction and saw its own share decrease.

Although the agreements signed by OPEC since 1982 are more typical of cartel agreements, they still raise important and difficult questions:

1. Does the adoption of explicit prorationing throw light on the cartel mechanism that operated before this date?

2. Most members decreased production, well below the average for the 1970s, albeit not as much as the quotas required, and not enough to prevent the price collapse of 1986. What accounts for the lower level of output despite obvious coordination failure?

3. Until 1988, Iraq was excused from adherence to its quota, as it insisted on maximizing its sales in order to finance its war with Iran. This is tantamount to temporary suspension of Iraq's membership in OPEC. In 1988, after the war ended, Iraq decided to respect its quota. What persuaded Iraq to participate in the production restricting program after several years of absence? More broadly, what are the incentives for countries to join OPEC? Why have Mexico or Oman not shown interest in OPEC membership?

4. Agreements on quotas have been reached easily, and have fallen apart rapidly. Are there incentives to sign agreements and not obey them? While Iran may have had serious reservations about accepting its quota, when Iraq did not have to, for two reasons it may have found it worthwhile to sign agreements that at least committed others to production cuts. First, a few countries did respect their quotas. Second, consumers and speculators react to the signing in such a way that prices increase, at least for a few months. There may of course be costs in signing but not respecting agreements; if these costs are low enough, agreements will be reached but not respected.

Predictably, with the introduction of specific quotas, cheating became a major problem for OPEC, which it has tried hard to solve, but without much success. Two classic problems of cartels have been responsible, inability to detect cheaters and inability to punish them. While there have been attempts to solve the detection problem, no discussion of a punishment mechanism has been reported. The first quota agreements were not supported by explicit mechanisms to detect cheating. Price cutting and overproduction became so widespread as to threaten the entire market share of Saudi Arabia whose output dropped from 10 mbd in 1981 to 2.7 mbd in the third quarter of 1985. In response, it adopted the netback pricing formula, and soon after followed the price collapse of 1986.

As noted in Section 2, sometime before the price collapse, in December 1984, OPEC made a serious attempt to prevent cheating by setting up the Ministerial Executive Council, and hired an international auditing firm to assist the monitoring of compliance with price and output agreements. The Council did not have actual disciplinary powers, and, because of lack of cooperation from member countries, it even failed in its limited role of identifying cheaters. One OPEC report seemed very pessimistic about accurate monitoring and enumerated 23 ways in which countries could hide their price cutting and overproduction, including the widespread use of countertrade, i.e., direct exchange of oil for products. The last few years have taught OPEC that detection of cheating is very difficult, if not impossible.

An even more difficult obstacle for OPEC is effective punishment of cheaters. The difficulties of setting up explicit punitive systems of sanctions in a cartel composed of governments are fairly obvious. Sovereign nations do not easily submit to sanctions for fear of appearing submissive to external pressure.[6] OPEC is therefore forced to depend only on indirect measures such as threats of overproduction by others if any member cheats.

Osborne (1976) has considered in detail a 'tit-for-tat' strategy which might enable a cartel to survive without an explicit enforcement mechanism. He proposes a rule in which each member produces max $(q_i^*, q_i^* + (s_i/s_j)\Delta q_j)$, where $q_i^*$ is the output quota of the $i$th country, $s_i$ is the production share of country $i$, equal to $q_i^*/\Sigma q_j^*$, and $\Delta q_j$ is production over quota of country $j$. According to Osborne such a rule provides a sufficient threat of retaliation to deter cheating and to stabilize the cartel. But, as Mackie-Mason and Pindyck (1987) have pointed out, Osborne's solution is not consistent because once one party has deviated from the agreement, it may no longer be in the interest of the others to actually carry out the threat of increasing their production.

On the other hand, it is conceivable that in a dynamic game threats similar to those considered by Osborne would provide the right incentives for compliance, and further research is needed on this topic. It could throw light, for instance, on the price war of 1986 initiated by Saudi Arabia, who ended up with less revenue while doubling its output. Price wars are not uncommon in cartels and they are often seen in relation to enforcement of cartel agreements (see Porter's 1983 study

---

[6] Although the 1985 output expansion by Saudi Arabia has been generally seen as a punishment for overproduction by other producers, it has never been described as such by OPEC. Instead, it was officially defended as a policy to win back market share for Saudi Arabia and for OPEC (Skeet, 1988, p. 215).

of the Joint Executive Committee that operated a freight cartel in the US in the late 19th century, before cartels became illegal).

### 3.5.4. *The dominant firm model: application to the oil market*

Because of the lack of concordance between the textbook version of a cartel and the organization of OPEC, some authors have argued that Saudi Arabia (with or without the assistance of a few neighboring countries) is best understood as a Stackelberg price leader (Mabro, 1975a, Erickson, 1980, Plaut, 1981, Singer, 1983 and 1985).[7]

There are two important questions to consider in applying this model to the oil market.

1. Is the elasticity of the residual demand curve faced by Saudi Arabia small enough that it has significant market power? The answer depends on the elasticity of world demand for oil, Saudi Arabia's share in the world market, and the elasticity of supply of the competitive fringe (Plaut 1981). In the short run, even with less than 15% of the supply of the non-communist world, Saudi Arabia has considerable market power because demand and the supply of the competitive fringe are both inelastic. In the long run, the influence of Saudi production is smaller because world demand and the supply of the competitive fringe are more elastic.

2. Does the behavior of producers other than Saudi Arabia approximate that of a competitive fringe? It may be argued that this question does not really arise for certain countries, such as Kuwait and the United Arab Emirates, who for political reasons may be acting in unison with Saudi Arabia. But it is more difficult to argue that larger producers such as Iran, whose output during the 1970s was only 20% below that of Saudi Arabia, behaved substantially differently. One should also explain how the behavior of these larger, politically more independent countries differs from the non-OPEC competitive fringe, such as Mexico, Great Britain, and Norway (Noreng, 1982). These two groups certainly behaved differently with respect to capacity: while the latter expanded its capacity in response to the 1973 price increase, the former did not.

---

[7] In most simulation models based on the cartel theory OPEC is also modeled as a dominant firm. But this dominant firm is a composite unit with the same internal organization problems raised in the previous section.

Mabro (1975a) was the first to advance a dominant firm view of the oil market. He noted that, although OPEC seemed to fix the price of oil, in fact it only fixed the price of the so-called marker crude, the Saudi light, and that other OPEC members were free to set their own prices and force Saudi Arabia to reduce its output of light crude.[8] Why, then, was Saudi Arabia not priced out of the market altogether? Mabro answered this question implicitly by arguing that most OPEC members were in 1974 producing at full capacity. This answer does not apply to later years since capacity can change, and should be considered endogenous in the long run.

Erickson (1980) gives a more straightforward interpretation of the dominant firm view. He leaves price determination to Saudi Arabia and, like Mabro, he seems to think that other countries set their own production. Stating that 'OPEC is cartel in name only,' he argues that the wide swings in market shares of its members show that there is no internal coordination. For Erickson, the small Saudi market share of 15% is not an impediment to its role as a price leader because 'swings in Saudi rate of output meet about 50% of the swings in world demand' (p. 13). Accordingly, other large producers, such as Iran with a market share close to that of Saudi Arabia, act as competitive suppliers because their output does not fluctuate as widely as that of Saudi Arabia. The fluctuations in production of other countries are adjustments to changing world prices and shifts in the type of oil demanded.

As Saudi output declined in response to decline in demand in the mid-1980s, the dominant firm model gained in popularity. An early influential supporter of cartel theory, Professor Adelman, in his later writings accepted a larger role for Saudi Arabia. Still labeling OPEC as a 'loosely cooperating oligopoly', he proposed the interesting hypothesis that the oil market changes its behavior between two extremes of cartel and dominant firm in which Saudi Arabia acts as the 'swing producer' (Adelman, 1982). This implies that when the cooperative agreement fails to prevent members from cheating and thereby expanding output, Saudi Arabia acts as the residual supplier.

There is some difficulty in combining the two models in this way. When OPEC is acting as a cartel, the other members have a greater

---

[8] Acting in a similar fashion, in 1978 Saudi Arabia reduced the share of the light crude whose price was fixed and increased its production of other crudes whose price it was free to set (Mabro, 1978, p. 41).

incentive to cheat if they know that Saudi Arabia will reduce its output in response. There would be a strong tendency to return to the dominant firm mode of behavior. This theoretical difficulty does not arise in the models presented by other writers who interpret the change from one regime to the other as a structural change in the oil market and therefore view only one of the two models as being true at any one moment of time. By 1985, Adelman too seemed to have picked the dominant firm model as the only true one: 'The Saudis are the chief of the price makers, the cartel of OPEC nations—not OPEC itself, which is of no importance.' (Adelman, 1985, p. 17).

The models described above pay scant attention to the supply behavior of the competitive fringe, which includes every country except Saudi Arabia. The difficulty of modeling competitive supply, noted earlier in this section, has led some authors of simulation models to make *ad hoc* assumptions. For example, Daly, Griffin, and Steele (1982) have Saudi Arabia and several low-absorbers such as Kuwait and Libya—'the Cartel Core'—act as the residual supplier. The non-OPEC competitive fringe as well as a subset of OPEC producers are given a standard supply curve with a positive price elasticity. The rest of OPEC countries follow a supply rule according to which their production varies inversely to price when the ratio of reserves to production falls below a certain level.

Another weak point in the treatment of the supply of the competitive fringe is the lack of attention paid to capacity. It is often treated as an exogeneous variable which affects supply (e.g., Mabro, 1975a), but it is actually a decision variable under the control of suppliers. To be credible the dominant firm theory must explain why countries such as Kuwait, Libya, Iraq and Iran did not imitate Mexico and the North Sea producers, and increase capacity as well as production. Had they done so, the Saudi share would have fallen even below 15%.

As its proponents argue, the dominant firm theory explains well the role of Saudi Arabia as a 'price moderate' within OPEC. Plaut (1981, p. 22) has pointed out that, because it is its own output that must be restricted in order to support the price, the dominant firm prefers smaller price increases. However, the dominant firm theories have difficulty explaining Saudi Arabia's role in the 1986 price collapse (see Section 2). Saudis certainly could predict the effect of the doubling of their production on prices. How could their action be made consistent with the dominant firm model? Green (1988) answers that the price collapse can be explained by a change in the elasticity of demand facing Saudi Arabia. Because of the increase in non-OPEC production and the overall decline in world demand during 1980s, the dominant firm's demand became more elastic, causing its profit maximizing output to increase. The difficulty with this explanation is that from 1980 onward, long before Saudi Arabia decided to increase production, its demand was becoming more elastic but its production was declining rather than increasing. In addition, the suddenness of the 1986 production increase gives more support to a strategic interpretation for this move as a punishment for other producers. In all fairness, it should be stressed that all economic models of the oil market have great difficulty explaining this Saudi decision.

### 3.6. Models emphasizing competitive behavior

We present in this subsection a family of 'competitive' models that do not resort to restrictions on the behavior of individual countries imposed either by explicit agreements, implicit agreements, or implied threats of retaliation. In one form or the other they ague that there is no excess supply at the high price. Most of these competitive descriptions of the oil market appeared in response to apparent lack of output restrictions by OPEC before 1982.

### 3.6.1. *Backward bending supply curve*
In the early 1980s several papers appeared arguing that OPEC was not a cartel because its members had no incentive to increase production at the high price. Bénard (1980), Crémer and Salehi-Isfahani (1980), Scott (1981), and Teece (1982) all used the idea of absorptive capacity and imperfect capital markets to note that oil exporting countries had more revenues than they could spend. Crémer and Salehi-Isfahani (1980) presented a more formal argument, identifying the several competitive equilibria resulting from the backward bending supply curve discussed above.

With a backward bending supply curve the possibility of multiple equilibria emerges. Figure 3.3 depicts the simplest case with two stable equilibria, one at the low price and the other at the high price. The only equilibrium prices of interest are $P_1$ and $P_3$, since $P_2$ is unstable.

If this basic picture is accepted, it makes sense to identify $P_1$ with the price at the beginning of 1973, and $P_3$ with the price that OPEC picked

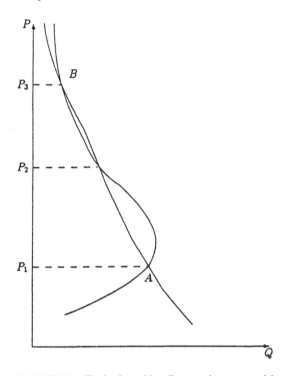

FIGURE 3.3    The backward bending supply curve model.

in December of that year. According to this model, since there is no excess supply at this high price, OPEC does not have any role in output coordination, but it has another critical role. After the price increase in 1973, producers would only limit production if they expected prices to remain at their high level for some time. OPEC was instrumental in the formation of such expectations by providing a forum where the producers could discuss their plans.

Although the competitive models do not explain how they are formed, expectations are crucially important for them. If producers believe that the price will fall in the short to medium run, they will try to take advantage of current conditions by increasing output immediately, thus pulling the price down. The way expectations enter in the analysis may distinguish the oil market from other commodity markets, where prices exhibit well established cyclical patterns. In

1973-74 the price of several commodities increased by factors ranging from two to four, and two of them (zinc and rice) experienced even larger price increases than oil. However, it is only in the oil market, in part thanks to the control exercised by the international oil companies, that the price had not fluctuated prior to 1973. Coupled with the widespread talk of an 'energy crisis', this fact made it easy for the members of OPEC to convince themselves that the change in price was permanent. Paradoxically, the post-1973 belief that OPEC was a powerful cartel and would be able to maintain the high price can be integrated into a competitive model: it eliminates incentives for producers to increase production. The popularity of the cartel model may be in part responsible for the existence of a competitive price!

The competitive theory has some difficulty dealing with the responses of individual countries to the 1979-80 price hike, when Saudi Arabia increased output while Kuwait and several others cut back. Crémer and Salehi-Isfahani (1989) argue that Saudi Arabia may have perceived (correctly, as it turned out) that the price increase was temporary, while others saw it as another permanent gain. Of course, it is a major weakness of the theory that the anticipations are not determined endogenously when it relies so heavily on them. On the other hand, the competitive theory presents a rather natural interpretation of the huge size of the 1979-80 price increases which would be due to the near parallelism of the supply and demand curves at the high price. In turn, the price decline of 1985-86 can be interpreted as a consequence of the emergence of excess supply at the high price. The demand and supply curves shifted away from each other as oil producers expanded their absorptive capacity and demand for OPEC oil declined.

Another obvious criticism that can be levelled against the competitive model is that it ignores the market power of some large producers, notably Saudi Arabia. In the absence of output coordination, as was the prevailing situation before 1982, the competitive outcome could be defended as a better approximation to the market outcome than an implicit agreement. But, the fact that Saudi Arabia faces a downward sloping demand curve needs to be taken into account.

According to the competitive story, oil extraction capacity is explained by output rather than the other way around. Those OPEC countries, Kuwait and Saudi Arabia, that stopped capacity expansion plans after 1973, are precisely those with the lowest absorptive capacity.

### 3.6.2. *Property rights model*

The property rights model was developed in direct response to the 1973 price increase. Let us sketch the argument. The countries have lower discount rates than the oil companies. Indeed, their rights to the oil are more secure (companies fear nationalization), and, because their access to capital markets is limited, they have less use for oil revenues. As a consequence, for a given price, the countries wish to produce less than the companies, and the transfer of control over production during the 1960s shifted the supply curve to the left. Thus the equilibrium price increased.

Mabro (1975b) was the first to note the importance of property rights in oil supply, and Johany (1980) and Mead (1979) developed the full model. Mabro pointed out that producers may want to increase the price if 'present prices diverge from expected future prices properly discounted. The oil price increase of 1973 may have been partly motivated by such considerations and thus may be construed as an attempt by oil producing countries to react to long-term interests endangered by non-economic rates of production.' (p. 14). For Mabro the 'proper' rate of discount is the rate reflecting the governments' preferences, and 'non-economic' refers to rates of extraction that are too high.

Johany emphasized the companies' fear of expropriation as the source of divergence between the rates of extraction of the companies and the governments. Implicitly, he argued that governments, living in an infinite horizon world, would want to produce at the rate implied by the market rate of interest which exceeded the rate at which the companies, fearing nationalization, discounted future profits from their oil concessions. Mead noted that the change in control of oil resources also placed the production decision in the hand of the parties with fewer opportunities for profitable investment.

Johany and Mead have identified an important determinant of supply: property rights. However, these property rights are only one of the determinants of the incentives of the suppliers, and the existing expositions have not dealt with the following problems:

1. Before 1970, the governments did have some influence over production at the time of renegotiation of the contracts.
2. In the same period, the actual terms of the contracts and competition with other governments actually gave the countries incentives to pressure companies to *increase* production, contrary to the predictions of the model. Thus, in 1966, to gain a 20% increase in pro-

duction, the Iranian Prime Minister threatened the companies that, 'We cannot stand by idly while our own oil resources are kept unexploited underground and not utilized for the country's development.' (Stocking, 1970, p. 140, see also Adelman, 1982, p. 39).

3. Although the property rights of the countries are permanent, some governments have shorter horizons, as their tenure may be limited and uncertain.

4. More careful attention should be paid to the timing of the first price increase. As noted in section 2, change in control over supply was gradual between 1970 and 1975, whereas the price increase in December 1973 was very sudden.

In conclusion, the property rights hypothesis falls short of providing a complete model of the oil market, while proposing a very interesting interpretation of the 1973 oil price revolution. Other equally important events, such as the price changes in 1979–80 and 1986, cannot be explained by changes in control of supply, and require more detailed modeling of the supply behavior of the governments.

### 3.6.3. *Supply shock models*

Our last category includes models that explain all oil price increases since 1973 by supply disruptions (MacAvoy, 1982, Verleger, 1982a), and we label them supply shock models. These disruptions (the embargo and cutbacks of 1973, the Iranian oil strike of 1979 and the Iran–Iraq war of 1980) are considered exogenous, consequences of essentially political events. These models assume upward sloping supply curves, and therefore, in contrast with the backward bending supply curve model, have only one equilibrium price for each set of supply and demand curves. They explain price changes through shifts in these curves, focusing principally on the supply side.

MacAvoy argues that OPEC did not control production in the 1970s, and therefore is not responsible for the price increases of 1973 and 1979–80. He simulates a model in which OPEC countries behave according to his supply specification and finds that the actual price path can be approximated without assuming cartel action. He generates lasting effects from temporary supply shocks, such as the embargo and cutbacks of 1973, by introducing lagged output and reserves, themselves dependent on past output, in the supply function. Thus, the embargo of 1973 reduces supply for several years, and explains the stability at the high price during the 1970s. This effect is reinforced by stockpiling behavior on the part of consumers. In response to an (unforeseen) cut in supply consumers increase their demand for inventory, causing a shift in demand and a larger price increase than is otherwise justified by the original shift in supply.

Verleger argues that OPEC followed price increases rather than lead them. Supply shocks first affect the spot market and, with some delay, OPEC adjusts its official price to reflect the changed market circumstances. He argues, rather unconvincingly, that OPEC prices which were too low compared to spot prices delayed consumer adjustment and encouraged speculative behavior which contributed, in 1973 and 1979, to larger price increases than were necessary.

### 3.7. Conclusion

Despite their shortcomings, informal models have been the main vehicle for discussing the important institutional and policy issues related to the oil market. Concentrating on issues of market structure, they have offered three different explanations of the 1973 price increase. First, the cartel models emphasize joint OPEC action, but do not spell out the way in which coordination problems within the cartel are solved. This is particularly surprising for the period when explicit output quotas were not in effect. Second, dominant firm models limit monopolistic action to Saudi Arabia, in conjunction with one or two other countries closely tied to it. The entire weight of the price revolution is shouldered by producer(s) with less than 20% of the market. Third, competitive models deny collusion altogether and describe the high price equilibrium by price-taking behavior. These models ignore the market power of individual producers and the way in which they can influence the market price.

If one may fault the literature with one shortcoming, it is its lack of integration. While trying hard to present the writings of diverse authors in relation to each other, we were struck by the degree to which the authors themselves failed to build on each other's work. Very few authors have attempted to compare and contrast their own work with those of others, maybe because the informal nature of the methodology makes this difficult.

## 4. SIMULATION MODELS

### 4.1. Introduction

Simulation models are quantitative models, composed of a system of equations representing the behavior of the agents, and whose solution describes the equilibrium of the market. The system of equations is usually solved by using a computer, although one could imagine useful models that would be simple enough to be solved by hand or with the use of a calculator.

Simulation models differ from theoretical models because they use functional forms especially adapted to the analysis of a particular market. This modeling strategy stems from an interest in the specific situation at hand, as opposed to the derivation of general results. In practice the difference between the two types of models is rather sharp, although one could imagine a continuum of models between the two extremes.

Contrary to econometric models, simulation models do not allow for easy testing of their validity by comparison with data. This removes a useful discipline on the modeler, but the use of the models to predict a long-run future which might be very different from the past justifies this relaxation of the standard test. Furthermore, even when the interest lies in the re-examination of history, the use of simulation models allows a closer description of the actual objectives of decision makers, and of the constraints under which they operate, even when the data is poor.

In the literature on the oil market, simulation models were used extensively just after the 1973–74 crisis to get a handle on the long-run price. As some analysts were predicting a rapidly increasing price over the long run, they were used principally to test whether this was indeed the optimal strategy for OPEC. Prediction continues to be a prime motivation for model builders, though they show less optimism in the possibility of obtaining good long-run forecasts. A more modest aim, which will be the focus of this survey, is to develop a better intuition for the market under study and to compute the sensitivity of the equilibrium to some exogenous variables. For instance, a model may teach us how the present price varies with changes in proved reserves. It may also teach us what is the subset of the embodied relationships that are critical to the evolution of the system as a whole. Finally, the models can be used to provide better informed policy advice. For instance, support for R&D in alternative energy sources will affect the elasticity of demand, and a well constructed model can offer some insights on the consequences for oil prices.

Models can be more or less comprehensive. One extreme is summarized by Ezzati (1978): 'This book presents an analytical framework for evaluating energy policy issues concerning world energy markets. The framework is designed to closely approximate the behavior of all important aspects of those markets.' Others build specialized models that focus on one or two relationships that they find essential. In any case, for the reader to be able to understand the economic intuition behind the main conclusions, the critical assumptions that drive the principal results must be clearly identified.

To explain the precise coverage of this section, it is convenient to use a classification developed by Gately (1979)—we change his terminology to fit our needs. Models in his first category use reduced form representations of the behavior of the agents; they are 'formal models with explicitly stated functional relationships among the variables, which are used to evaluate the implications over time of various price-paths for world markets for energy and oil.' The second category includes optimization models, 'similar in structure', but which 'employ some optimizing procedure to select an "optimal" price-path for OPEC', that is, models that explicitly study the decision making processes. Finally, 'energy balance models' have 'no explicit functional relationships among the variables, nor any equilibrating mechanism to ensure consistency among supply and demand in the various markets'. The largest models are of this last type; they basically take the decisions of OPEC countries as given, and check for consistency.

Although there exists a very large variety of energy balance models, we will for the most part ignore them. The International Energy Workshop, organized by Professor Allan Manne of Standford, regularly polls the authors of many of them and summarizes their predictions. In January 1988, 69 predictions were polled, most supported in part by a formal simulation model. To the best of our understanding their builders concentrate most of their effort in giving a precise description of the demand side. Like the rest of this book, this section only considers models designed to study explicitly the structure in the market, and this includes a good proportion of the reduced form models, nearly all the optimizing models, but almost no energy balance models.

Our survey is also constrained by the need to have access to a rather complete set of the equations so that we can describe the mechanics of the models. As a consequence, we will mention at one point or the other the following models: Ben-Shahar (1976), Blitzer, Meeraus, and Stoutjesdijk (1975), Crémer and Weitzman (1976), Daly, Griffin and Steele (1982), Ezzati (1978) for which a preliminary version is available in Ezzati (1976), Gately, Kyle and Fisher (1977), for which a revised version is used in Gately (1983), Hnyilicza and Pindyck (1976), Houthakker and Kennedy (1978), Kalymon (1975), Kennedy (1973), MacAvoy (1982), Pindyck (1978), and Salant (1982).

Before proceeding we should point out that Salant (1982) presents a technology for solving a family of models sharing a common structure rather than a specific model, as the author does not commit himself to specific values of the coefficients. This creates some difficulty in integrating the discussion of this work with that of the other models. On the other hand, the work is very important as it is very clean methodologically, and we will discuss it.

As the reader will shortly see, the models that we discuss are very different in methodology and in sophistication, but they do share certain conclusions. First, the lags of adjustment in consumption and in non-OPEC production are crucial for determining the amount of monopoly power and for predicting the price path. This is of great importance, as the informal and theoretical literatures have not paid much attention to this phenomenon. Second, there will be no rapid and persistent price increase. While they do not rule out violent temporary aberrations in the price path such as that due to the loss of production capacity in 1979–80, they predict a relatively slow average increase in price up through the first decade of the 21st century.

The rest of this section will be divided in two main subsections. We will first review the techniques of model building, before turning our attention to the main results of the different models. A number of good surveys of the literature have been published, among them Fisher, Gately and Kyle (1975), Gately (1984) and Moran (1982). We try to focus on areas less stressed by these authors.

## 4.2. Model building for the oil market

A model does not represent reality, but rather its author's view of reality. Hence, the structure of a model is a choice dictated by the phenomena at hand and the scientific paradigm used by the analyst. Models such as the one used by the Club of Rome in its famous report have been criticized by economists for focusing too much on the technicalities of computation and the exhaustivity of the description of reality as opposed to the sensible choice of the important relationships to model.

All the models that we will examine are neoclassical models: they concentrate on economic factors and use the tools of equilibrium analysis to ensure the coherence of the actions of the agents. Because of this common methodological background, all the models can be usefully seen as implementation of an ideal model that we would like to build were it not for limitations of data, time, money, and computational power. It will be useful to first examine this ideal model, and then turn our attention to problems of implementation.

### 4.2.1. The 'ideal' model

The ideal model which we present here is not the most general that one could imagine. Even if the resources could be found to build it, it would be too complex to be useful. We have tried to identify a framework that encompasses all the models listed above, and believe that we have succeeded with a minor exception concerning uncertainty, which will be discussed more fully below. At points where economic theory does not provide totally satisfactory guidance, our discussion will be more sketchy.

As for any economic model, we must study consumers and suppliers before including them in a framework that characterizes the equilibrium of the market. In the next few paragraphs, we discuss consumption, by far the most straightforward of the two sides of the market. Although one reads all too often allusion to the power of the international oil companies, model builders ignore all monopsony power and consider the consumption sector as competitive. One would like to disaggregate demand at the national level, because it is at this level that most decisions, such as taxation, that affect consumption are taken. At the very least, the demands of three groups should be distinguished, that of developed, developing and oil exporting countries.

Some models link the demand for oil to the total demand for energy, which allows for the study of the substitution between different forms of energy. The elasticity of demand with respect to income is an important factor for the study of the consequences of the growth rate of the economy of the consuming countries, which is usually taken to be exogenous. Also, an explicit representation of the tradeoffs between investment in conservation and production of energy provides as general a picture as one would need. Ezzati (1978) and Kalymon (1975) present complete models of the consumption sector.

Oil is not an homogeneous product, and the consequence of this heterogeneity is a problem that still requires more work. Refineries optimized for a specific type of crude may increase the market power of the supplier. The trade-off between technical efficiency and strategic positioning can be at least partially modeled as Ezzati (1978) shows, and belongs in our ideal model.

The demand for energy, often a primary input far up the production stream, is subject to very important lags in its adaptation to change in prices, because changes in demand often require changes in the capital stock. Consumers of energy, whether residential or industrial, and producers, or potential producers, of alternative sources of energy do not react instantaneously to changes in price, whether to reduce their consumption or to switch to cheaper sources. Although this has not been attempted in the models that we consider, an explicit modeling of these lags would be useful.

Finally, the backstop technology, so popular among theoreticians, has not been used in this literature. The backstop technology, solar power, fusion, or liquefied coal, is assumed to come on line and totally displace oil when its price reaches a certain level. This is not a very realistic assumption, and simulation analysts prefer to use a demand that levels out progressively as the price increases (see however Nordhaus (1973) and Houthakker and Kennedy (1978)).

Contrary to the modeling of demand, the modeling of supply presents us with serious methodological problems. We need information about reserves, disaggregated at the level of groups of nations whose role in the market are similar. This information should include the amount of oil available at different costs. As in the case of demand, a disaggregation by type of oil could also be useful. Oil reserves comprise a portion of, and sometimes a substantial portion of, the wealth of its owners. Their problem is to use it as wisely as possible.

Producers can usefully be allocated to two different categories. The first includes competitive suppliers. They maximize their profits, taking prices as given. Because the extraction of oil is the result of an intertemporal maximization problem, and is very sensitive to future expected prices, we must model the way in which the producers predict them. The accepted methodology at this point in most areas of economics is to assume some form of rational expectations: the expectations of the agents are the future prices generated by the model. This can be interpreted as an hypothesis that the world is robust to the publication of the work of the researcher and that the agents will not modify their behavior after seeing the price path generated by the model. They also face perfectly competitive markets, and their behavior can be summarized by some version of Hotelling's well known formula (see Section 5). Some of the competitive suppliers can be governments who act either directly as owners of resources or indirectly through taxation or licensing. In both cases, we assume that they try to maximize their wealth.

We will group the second category of suppliers under the term 'countries', eschewing for the time being the categorization OPEC, non-OPEC, as it prejudges some of the issues that the models under consideration are trying to solve. Furthermore, some non-OPEC countries, such as Mexico, are often described as behaving similarly to OPEC countries.

The problems faced by countries are very similar to those faced by competitive suppliers, except for differences in their investment opportunities (see Section 3). This will induce differences in the way in which they discount future earnings, and hence in the timing of extraction (see Hnyilicza and Pindyck, 1976). The models that explicitly describe the behavior of countries focus on the limits of their absorptive capacity and of their access to foreign capital markets. Moreover, most models assume away the phenomena which we have just described, and hence can use Hotelling's insights when modeling the behavior of countries. This has the benefit of focussing attention on market structure.

As in theoretical models, the objective of the countries is to maximize the discounted value of their consumption, $\Sigma_{t=0}^{t=\infty}\delta^{t}U_{t}(C_{t})$— of course, all simulation models use a discrete time formulation. In this case, the discount factor $\delta$ reflects their rate of time preference. On the other hand, models that assume that the countries act as competitors use a discount rate that represents the investment opportunities available to the country.

Up to this point in our discussion of supply, we have trodden in relatively safe water. Few economists would have strong disagreement with the inclusion in our ideal model of any of the variables that we have mentioned, although there would be doubt about the empirical importance of some of them. On the other hand, the consequences of membership in OPEC present difficult challenges because there is no agreement, among oil economists or among economists at large, about the proper representation of intracartel bargaining. We will therefore postpone treatment of this issue until we look at the problem of implementation. At this point, let us however make the following two remarks. First, no model explicitly includes imperfectly enforced agreements, and the fact that countries belong to OPEC is always modeled as a process of aggregation of utility functions and reserves. Second, because so little is known about the internal bargaining in the organization, in order to facilitate sensitivity analysis models should be built in such a way that reallocation of countries among different strategic subgroups is easy.

Lags in production are at least as important for the behavior of the market as lags in consumption. The 1973–74 price increase would probably not have lasted long if non-OPEC production had adjusted faster. A good treatment would include an explicit description of exploration, development and extraction sectors. None of the models that we survey do this.

Once the main actors have been set up, there remains a problem of representing their behavior. The best solution is probably to set up optimization problems that explicitly describe the objectives of the agents and the constraints that they face. Given the essentially dynamic nature of this market, these problems will generally use as data expected prices, and we must face the problem of expectations to which we have just alluded and to which we will return in Section 5.

One of the dificulties faced by the model builders in this literature is the necessity of constructing models with very long horizons. Indeed, some of the theories that we use rely heavily on the user cost of the resource, which can only be computed endogenously if we explicitly include exhaustion of at least the cheaper reserves. Furthermore, one should use a starting date anterior to 1970, so that the 1973–74 events can be explicitly studied (see Ben-Shahar, 1976 and MacAvoy, 1982).

Having so set up the stage, the model builder must use the data he or she has gathered to compute the equilibrium. Given the essentially non-stationary nature of this market where there is potential exhaustion of the reserves, it is important to understand that equilibrium is not a state in which the variables lay at rest. Rather, as is the orthodox definition in neoclassical economics, equilibrium refers to a set of consistent plans made by the agents and to the associated prices, when each agent behaves optimally given its objectives and the constraints that bear on his/her actions. These constraints can be imposed by the physical environment, in which case they are exogenous to the model, or they can be imposed on each agent by the economic system and the behavior of the other agents, in which case they are in general endogenous to the model.

Although the model sketched above generalizes practically all the features of the models in the literature, it still is not as complete as one would like. Only one model, Salant (1982), explicitly considers uncertainty (see also Hansen *et al.* (1985) discussed at length in the next section).[9] Salant makes an important technical contribution, but it is limited to two types of random factors: First, uncertainty due to the possibility of expropriation, either of oil fields or of the financial assets in a foreign bank. Both of these risks are equivalent to changes in the discount rate. Secondly, uncertainty that will be resolved at some known future date. For instance, we know now that we will learn in 1995 the cost of the backstop technology.

However, the recent experience of the oil market suggests that there is a lot of day-to-day uncertainty, for instance about the possibility of disturbances that will cut off production in some countries. The 1979–80 episode has shown that a relatively small and abrupt change in production can have drastic consequences on the price. We need models that enable us to explore better the dynamics of these changes, for two reasons. First, as Pindyck (1982) has argued, a proper accounting of the imperfection in our knowledge of future prices may be important for policy makers. Second, the irreversible investment decisions made by producers of oil, of other sources of energy, or by

---

[9] Fisher *et al.* (1975) argue that their model illustrates the existence of large uncertainty, but they actually only show that, in their framework, rapid changes in prices, predicted in advance, may obtain.

consumers, are made in the face of uncertainty, and this affects their behavior.

Models could also usefully include an endogenous treatment of the behavior of the governments of consuming nations, as they do of the producing countries. For instance, an analysis of the imposition of a depletion allowance tax embedded in a game with OPEC could be of interest (see however the discussion of the breeder reactor in Houthakker and Kennedy (1978)).

### 4.2.2. *Problems of implementation of the ideal model*
The exercise of building an ideal model on which there is consensus breaks down for two reasons. First, on some aspects, such as intra-OPEC bargaining, it cannot be completely specified, because there is no consensus. Second, it is so large and complicated that it would be impossible to solve, and there is no agreement on the proper way to simplify it. We therefore turn our attention to the various compromises made by the authors of the models on our list.

We will review the components of actual models in the same order that we have studied the ideal model and begin by discussing consumers. Generally, the models do not disaggregate demand between many consumer groups or among many uses. Most of them simply represent demand by a world demand curve, although some authors, such as Kalymon (1975), differentiate between OPEC and non-OPEC demand to study price discrimination between foreign and domestic consumers, (see also Houthakker and Kennedy, 1978). For a study of the long-term prospects of the oil market, this is a reasonable choice as disaggregated data on demand behavior is very difficult and expensive to generate. Even though demand is better understood than supply, there is still some disagreement among experts on the order of magnitude of the long-run elasticity of the aggregate demand for oil.

Indeed, the very complicated history of the oil market in the last 20 years creates extreme difficulties for econometric studies. There are very sudden variations in prices and it is difficult to disentangle short-term and long-term responses. Furthermore, all good estimates of demand require a model of price expectations, but how should we determine the expectations in 1982, after the price had begun its rapid descent from its peak? As noted in Section 3, the identification of demand also requires proper specification of the supply curve.

Demand lags are not generally studied explicitly in the models under consideration, except for Houthakker and Kennedy (1978) whose interest lies heavily on the demand side as they study the substitute sources of energy. When other models use demand lags, it is through the use of lagged prices or quantities demanded in the demand function. The modeling of the dynamics of demand should go beyond lags, and a more forward looking approach would be preferable.

Turning to production, the first vexing problem which we must face is to settle on the proper definition of reserves. As we have seen in Section 3, there are many concepts of reserves. The two that are most widely used in simulation models are potential reserves (sometimes called ultimately recoverable reserves) and proved reserves. Proved reserves refers to the amount of oil which is known to exist through the use of preliminary drilling that has conclusively shown the limits of specific fields. Potential reserves refer to the best estimate, based on available geological information and experience, of the total amount of oil that will be extracted from a given territory. Of course, there is considerable uncertainty about the magnitude of this last number, but the conclusions of the models that use this concept are typically not very sensitive to the specific number chosen. The real problem is to decide which is the relevant measure of the scarcity of oil.

In reality, proved reserves play a different role in countries such as the United States or Algeria, where the discovery of new fields is difficult, than in countries such as Saudi Arabia, where it is known with close to absolute certitude that proved reserves could be increased at minimal cost. We believe that potential reserves are the appropriate measure of scarcity for members of this last group. For them, the concept of proved reserves is at most akin to some measure of short-term capacity which could be expanded at low cost. Some models err on this point. For instance, Daly *et al.* (1982) use a model of production for the competitive fringe in which there is a cap on the ratio of production to reserves, that is production is restricted to a certain percentage of reserves. The amount of reserves is given exogenously, and one fears that this is tantamount to fixing the production of the fringe exogenously, although the paper does not present enough detail to enable us to understand the formulation completely. A similar problem arises in Gately (1983) where OPEC's policy is determined by a target capacity utilization rule, and the capacity is determined exogenously.

It might also be worth noting that on the supply side authors do not explicitly distinguish between different grades of oil. (Ezzati (1978) does distinguish between different grades in the demand side of his model, but this does not affect the supply behavior.)

It is somewhat surprising that very few models (see Crémer and Weitzman, 1976, and Salant, 1982) explicitly model competitive producers as forward looking profit maximizers, although the theory is well developed on this point. Most models simply assume a supply curve for competitive producers without theoretical justification. This supply curve sometimes shifts over time depending on aggregate production (Pindyck, 1978, Hnyilicza and Pindyck, 1976), or exogenously with time (Gately *et al.*, 1977).

In contrast, the supply behavior of OPEC governments is nearly always modeled explicitly. MacAvoy (1982) is an exception, and for good reasons, as the purpose of his exercise is to study the possibility of considering OPEC countries as competitive suppliers. It would be a nice addition in future efforts to pay more attention to some of the important non-OPEC suppliers which face similar constraints, Mexico being a primary example.

Many analysts use shortcuts in their models of the countries. The most common is to assume straight wealth maximization, the countries maximizing their discounted profits, or, in an interesting variation introduced by Kalymon (1975), the sum of net oil revenues and consumer surplus from domestic energy use. Some authors on the other hand simply assume some specific behavior for at least part of OPEC countries, as in Daly *et al.*, (1982).

As noted in Section 3, there is now general agreement in the descriptive literature that different countries have different objectives. Some try to model this difference of behavior from scratch. The most noteworthy and interesting example is Ezzati (1978). He uses the same model structure for all the countries—the only difference among them comes from the value of the parameters in the optimization problems that generate their behavior. This represents a clean and coherent modeling strategy.

Given that the producing countries have different objectives, and given the high cost of describing each individually, the difficult choice of an aggregation scheme must be made. Most models divide the producers in two categories: OPEC and non-OPEC. Quite often, in these models OPEC stands for only a subset of the members of the organization, the so-called cartel core, usually including at least Saudi Arabia and the UAE, but sometimes extended as far as Libya and Iran.

A more sophisticated study of intra-OPEC conflict requires differentiating between its members. Hnyilicza and Pindyck (1976) distinguish between saver and spender countries, who in their model have different discount rates. Daly *et al.* (1982), on the other hand, directly assume different supply curves for the different countries. They distinguish between price maximizers, output maximizers, and members of the cartel core. The terminology is not very well chosen as all countries would like to maximize the price at which they sell, and no country aims for the highest possible level of production. The basic idea is that the output maximizers (e.g. Iraq, Nigeria) are for all practical purposes part of the competitive fringe whereas the price maximizers face strong absorptive capacity constraints. Directly assuming a specific shape for the supply curve creates some difficulties as the underlying economic assumptions are not very transparent.

It is important to ensure some homogeneity between the functional forms used for different countries, and for different market structures. Pindyck (1978) provides an example of the pitfalls to avoid. In his model of a competitive structure, both the potential cartel and the competitive producers take the price as given and choose output in order to maximize their discounted profits. In particular, the competitive suppliers choose an output path that satisfies the Hotelling formula: the difference between the price and the cost of extraction increases at the rate of interest (see Section 5). There are no adjustment lags in their cost functions. When he turns his attention to a model where OPEC uses its market power, Pindyck models the competitive suppliers in a fundamentally different manner. He determines their output with the help of a supply curve, where price, cumulative past production, and past production enter. The two supply behaviors chosen for the two models are not consistent. Faced with the same price path, the competitive fringe would choose different outputs depending on the formulation. As a consequence, the increase in the profits of the cartel, which Pindyck attributes to the use of market power, could actually be, at least in part, due to the change in the behavior of the competitive fringe. Because this change has no theoretical or empirical justification, the exercise loses some of its interest.

After the countries have been allocated to different categories, one must describe the constraints imposed by membership in OPEC or at least in the cartel core. This task is easy in models, such as MacAvoy (1982), where for all practical purposes the organization does not exist.

Most of the other models assume that the relevant countries come to an agreement to maximize aggregate profit, and neglect bargaining and coordination problems. The most interesting attempt to model in some detail the bargaining process between countries is due to Hnyilicza and Pindyck (1976) who use Nash bargaining theory to study the agreement reached between saver and spender countries.

Whatever the model of OPEC, the production lags in the competitive sector play an important role in the solution that obtains. For instance, Crémer and Weitzman find hardly any monopoly power if competitive production can expand instantaneously, and they provide the most explicit, although still very rudimentary, description of these lags. Blitzer *et al.* (1975) assume that there are exogenously given bounds on OPEC production, and this assumption seems to be critical for understanding their results. Others generate lags by assuming that the discovery of proved reserves takes time and that only a certain proportion of these proved reserves can be extracted in any period (see MacAvoy, 1982). Finally, numerous authors introduce lags directly in the supply function (Hnyilicza and Pindyck, 1976, Gately *et al.*, 1977, Gately, 1983). As is the case for demand, more attention could usefully be given in future research to a better description of forward looking capacity expansion.

We have argued that the time frame of the ideal model would extend from before 1970 up to exhaustion. None of the implementations satisfy this requirement, although it would be easy to modify the model in Salant (1982) in this direction. Two models, MacAvoy (1982) and Ben-Shahar (1976, chapter 6), begin before 1973, and try to generate the first oil crisis as an endogenous phenomenon, but they have rather short horizons. The choice of this horizon is very important. The models that try to follow the post-1973 evolution of the price, usually extend over a fifty-year or so period, up to exhaustion of oil. Those who choose a shorter time frame face a difficult problem of evaluation of the oil left in the ground in the last year of their model. Some solutions to this difficulty, such as that used by Blitzer *et al.* (1975), seem to overemphasize the role of the price in the last period.

Having at last set up the stage, we can study the computation of equilibrium. As the following section will make clear, the theoretical literature finds it difficult to pinpoint the relevant equilibrium concept, even in the simplest case. And the computational problems are at least as difficult as the methodological problems. It is only if the market is assumed to be competitive that the problem does not arise, and this allows MacAvoy (1982) to easily ensure that demand equals supply in each period. Some other authors, interested in cartel models, simplify the problem by not even trying to endogenize OPEC's production. They take it as exogenous and compute the equilibrium by finding the prices that equalize residual demand and competitive supply (Gately *et al.*, 1977, Gately, 1983). The other semi-competitive technique, used for instance by Kalymon (1975), is to take as given an OPEC tax, that is, a surcharge above the cost of extraction imposed by the producing governments, and to compute the equilibrium by once again equating supply and demand.

Moving to a more explicit discussion of the interrelationships between the agents in the market, we turn to the important work of Salant (1982). He builds a model that generalizes on his theoretical work, which we will discuss in Section 5, by allowing for the presence of several competitive sectors and several Cournot players. This provides a very flexible framework, as we can, for instance, redefine some of the Cournot players to be different sub-groups within OPEC, but within each of these subgroups there must be a strong agreement to maximize aggregate profit. In particular, the case of a monolithic OPEC, used by much of the literature, is a special case of Salant's approach.

The treatment of models with a monolithic OPEC is very diverse (again, 'OPEC' is often modeled to be only a subset of the actual countries of OPEC). The most rudimentary use different rules of thumb for OPEC behavior (for instance, increase production by 2% per year or keep a constant ratio of reserves to production) and compare the discounted profits obtained by the use of the different rules (Gately *et al.*, 1977, Blitzer *et al.*, 1975). Although one can learn from this type of exercise when it is carried out carefully, it should only be employed with great caution when simulating the past. For instance, Gately (1983) uses a 'target-capacity-utilization' pricing rule to determine OPEC's production, with the capacity given exogenously at historical value. Not surprisingly, the model is found to track the 1974–81 period very closely. It should be noted that in this case we are nearly fixing the most difficult variable to predict, OPEC's production, at historical value, and the rest of the data falls in place by a very simple supply and demand adjustment.

Some models assume a more active role for OPEC. For instance,

Crémer and Weitzman (1976) assume that the cartel core commits itself to the maintenance of a price path in the future, and supplies the market with whatever amount is needed to fill the gap between demand and competitive supply. The cartel core chooses the price path to maximize its discounted profits. This type of computation seems in some sense to represent the asymmetry in power between producers better than models based on the Nash–Cournot assumption but, as we will see when discussing theoretical models, it suffers more from a strong lack of time consistency.

Some analysts use a more cautious strategy: they do not try to model OPEC's behavior at all. They fix some rule for its production and compute the associated equilibrium path, using the competitive model discussed above. If they have fixed production they obtain a price path (Ezzati, 1978), if they have fixed prices they obtain a production path (Daly *et al.*, 1982). Then they study at some intuitive level the resulting equilibrium to determine if it is 'sensible'. For instance, Ezzati computes how much OPEC countries would like to produce given the price that obtains, and assumes that the cartel is stable if that amount is smaller than the demand for their oil. (Even though in chapters 6 and 7, he seems to be maximizing an aggregate profit for OPEC taken as a whole, an examination of the model shows that this is equivalent to maximizing profits of countries one by one.) There is some wisdom to this strategy: even though we might not be able *ex ante* to fully describe the rule that determines whether a proposed outcome is a reasonable candidate as an equilibrium, we might be able *ex post* to come to an agreement on the acceptability of a specific solution. On the other hand, this approach gives very indeterminate results. Several price paths could look reasonable, and we would not know how to choose between them. Furthermore, we might focus on the first path that we find, whereas many others, some with quite different properties, would also be reasonable candidates. At the minimum, analysts who use this method should make an effort to ensure the exhaustibility of their search for solutions.

Whatever the method of computation of an equilibrium, the monolithic OPEC assumption hides a number of difficulties. First, it implicitly assumes that bargaining is not costly and yields an efficient solution. Second, it only seems reasonable when the parties can conduct efficiently transfer payments, monetary or political, between themselves. How else would one convince a country to subordinate its production decisions to the whole group? Third, how stable are the agreements that bind countries, and what are the determinants of this stability? Pindyck (1978) has taken a first step in answering this last question by computing the size of the gains from cartelization. He argues that stability is linked to the size of these gains, but comparing them with some measure of the gains from defection in a model where the description of the cartel and the competitive fringe are symmetrical could be fruitful. The same questions arise for any model that places countries in groups and models each group as one single agent with one unified goal.

We know of only one model that tries to explicitly represent the bargaining between OPEC countries in the formulation of their policy, Hnyilicza and Pindyck (1976). They divide the members in two groups. The saver countries have a lower discount rate than the spenders, because they have less opportunities for domestic investment and the international capital markets are not perfect enough to equalize them. OPEC chooses among all the production paths that maximize $\alpha$-times the profits of the saver countries plus $(1 - \alpha)$-times the profits of the spender countries, and the objective of the bargaining is the determination of $\alpha$, which is resolved through the Nash bargaining solution. The exercise is marred by the fact that the competitive solution that is used as a threat point is not computed in a fashion that is consistent with the cooperative solution. In the competitive solution, the discount rates are the same for both groups, and the implicit assumption seems to be that if the oil market became competitive, the imperfections in the international capital markets would disappear.

Moran (1982) complains that the Nash bargaining solution leads to unrealistic behavior, as Hnyilicza and Pindyck find that for the first ten years or so only the spender countries would produce, and the savers afterwards. This property of the solution is actually driven by the difference in the discount rates between the two groups, and would also hold in a competitive market. We find the presence of a very strong time inconsistency more troubling. In 1985, only the spender countries are producing, and the price is $4.65 per barrel. In 1986, only the saver countries are producing, and the price is $13.62 per barrel. Remember that those are Hnyilicza and Pindyck's predictions in 1976, and they represent the result of a binding agreement signed at that date. It is clear that come 1985, a spender country would find it optimal to conserve some of its oil for one more year in order to take advantage of the much higher price. Doing so would violate the agreement. This is the type of problems that Salant's solution avoids.

Notwithstanding these difficulties, we do learn a lot from the exercise conducted by Hnyilicza and Pindyck: the bargaining between the countries may substantially influence the production paths and the inability to transfer income between countries across time periods could have large costs for OPEC, as it rules out some forms of profit sharing.

Before turning to a short discussion of the main results of the models, we should go back to the data. The quality of the data is bad for three reasons:

1. because the time frame on which we can do regressions is short compared to the lags involved,
2. because some data refer to future values of non-stationary variables, as for instance future cost of extraction in the US, and
3. because of the poor quality of statistical data sources in many of the large producing countries.

The data difficulty is compounded as soon as we try to represent explicitly the optimization problems of countries, as we need more primitive data on objective functions, absorptive capacity, and government budget needs. Ezzati uses regressions on past data to find lower bounds on government expenditures. This creates two types of difficulties. First, the regressions generate representations of average behavior in the past. There is no good reason to use them as representations of bounds on future behavior. Second, as the conditions change, so will the policy, and such use of the data is subject to what macroeconomists have come to call the 'Lucas critique'.

### 4.3. Results

In this subsection, we review the results that have been obtained through simulation models, concentrating on those that throw light on some of the debates discussed in other sections. We do not survey the short- and medium-run predictions of prices, as those have already been ably reviewed in the literature (see Gately, 1984, for instance).

Most of the simulation models assume the 1973 price increase, and take the situation in its aftermath as the starting point for their analyses. MacAvoy (1982) provides an interesting exception. As we have noted earlier, he tries to test the hypothesis that the price increase would have happened in the absence of the 1973 crisis. He builds a competitive model of the market based on pre-1973 data, and uses it to simulate the post-1973 history in the absence of a crisis. MacAvoy argues that his model without cartel elements tracks well the post-1973 history, and concludes that OPEC was not an important factor in the history of the oil market in the 1970's.

This result hinges on the sensitivity of the supply curve to the level of proved reserves: a 1% decrease in reserves gives a short-run drop in supply of 1% and a long-run drop of 2% (page 37, table 2.10). During the beginning of the 1970s the level of proved reserves in OPEC countries increased rather slowly, and in the model this shifted the supply curve to the left, hence the price increase. We have some doubts that the reduction of the ratio of proved reserves to output for OPEC from 17.4 in 1970 to 15.1 in 1973 could by itself have such a strong effect, given the ease with which reserves can be expanded. But MacAvoy's hypothesis clearly deserves attention.

Ben-Shahar (1976) tries another exercise. He shows that, in his model, the optimal policy for a unified cartel would be to increase the price brutally at some point. This result seems to hinge on three factors: the presence of substantial lags in non-OPEC supply; the absence of lags in demand; and the fact that at prices of $4.00 per barrel, before the increase, the rate of growth of energy demand (4%) is higher than the rate of increase in non-OPEC oil supply (3.5%). In any case, the interpretation of the increase is very different from any found in the rest of the literature: it is the optimal policy of the cartel to keep prices low for some time before jacking them up suddenly.

The other models take the 1973 price increase as given, and compare the price evolution that they predict with the competitive solution. Pindyck (1978) obtains representative results: in percentage terms, the difference between prices with and without cartel is larger in the short run than in the long run, and depletion occurs earlier under competition.

*Ex post*, the predictions made by economists in 1974–75 look rather good. They predicted a long period of relatively small price increases, and some even forecasted a decrease in the first few years. The 1979–81 episode can probably be attributed to random elements, which are not incorporated in the models. The price as of 1989 is lower than was predicted, but the economists' record is vastly superior to that of the popular press and of futurologists who were seeing prices rising very steeply for a long period.

Because random factors are not included, none of the models warned of the sensitivity of the market to relatively small changes in the environment. Fisher *et al.* (1975) predicted sudden changes in prices, but this seems to be linked to the rather strange nature of the lags in their model. When this structure is corrected, the jumps disappear (Gately 1983).

Typically, the models for which it makes sense to compare the equilibrium of a static version of the model with that of a dynamic version do not find much difference between the two; exhaustibility is not important. In Crémer and Weitzman (1976), the prices are in both cases determined in great part by the constraints on capacity expansion in the competitive fringe. Kalymon (1975) computes an optimal price of around $8.68 for exports and $2.43 domestically, while the static optimization prices are $7.56 and $0.19 respectively (our computations).

Pindyck (1978) predicts that OPEC's share of world production will slowly increase over the long run. This conclusion is similar to that of other models. This increase in OPEC's share might shift market power over time and, from a methodological point of view, should make us even more weary of the time inconsistency problem. Within OPEC, production will slowly shift to the countries with the lower discount rate, as others extract their oil faster (see Hnyilicza and Pindyck, and Ben-Shahar who predicts a higher share for Saudi Arabia if the price is high enough). This issue should be studied in greater depth with the help of long-term disaggregated models.

### 4.4. Conclusion

The literature that we have surveyed in this section was very active between 1973 and 1981. Building on the seminal work of Nordhaus (1973), who studied the worldwide optimal allocation of energy resources, it identified in some detail the consequences of changes in the market structure.

From a practical point of view, the most important contribution of the simulation literature has been to pinpoint the importance of lags in non-OPEC supply for the market. Although few specialists would deny their potential importance, lags are not discussed in any length in other parts of the oil literature, and they deserve more attention both from informal modelers and theoreticians.

In recent years, interest in simple simulation models has fallen dramatically, and model builders have turned their attention to much larger energy balance models, focused on the demand side. Part of this decrease in activity can be attributed to lowered funding and reduced sense of urgency. The models were also facing very difficult technical problems: as the next section will discuss, we have great difficulties solving fully time consistent models.

We find the decline in the use of this methodology surprising, as it provides a useful way to approach certain phenomena. Simulation models are best considered as scratchpads to study certain insights: they enable us to study relatively rapidly and relatively easily the practical relevance of our theories. For instance, without such a model, it is nearly impossible to get a handle on the order of magnitude of the scarcity rent, and thereby on the importance of exhaustibility. Basically, simulation models impose only part of the discipline that formal theoretical treatment provides, but, because closed form solutions need not be found and because the results can be specialized to specific functional forms, they impose less restrictions on the phenomena that can be approached. On the other hand, we believe that their usefulness would be enhanced if, in presenting their conclusions, the authors put less emphasis on their quantitative predictions, which would only be valid if the models were a nearly complete representation of reality. They should rather emphasize the lessons for the study of the structure of the market, while paying close attention to the formulation of the model and to its theoretical consistency.

To end this section let us mention two important issues that still await deeper treatment by simulation models. First, lags are usually integrated in the model through arbitrary delays in the reaction of the agents. The decision problems of non-OPEC suppliers should be studied in more detail, so that the determinants of delays can be identified with precision. Second, uncertainty should be modeled explicitly, instead of being ignored. The techniques of Hansen *et al.*, discussed in detail in the next section, provide a potentially useful computational technique for this endeavor.

## 5. THEORETICAL MODELS

### 5.1. Introduction

A casual look at the index of the *Journal of Economic Literature* or the table of contents of the major economic journals will give a preliminary impression that much theory has been written on the oil market. However, this impression is misleading. The majority of these articles deal with issues of optimal use of limited stocks of natural resources, not, except incidentally, with problems of market imperfection. Although this literature is very interesting, we will not review it, except for some articles needed as background for our study. We will concentrate on the papers that discuss market structure.

In retrospect, and oversimplifying somewhat, the most striking aspect of the reflexes of theorists is that they cast the issue as a problem in the theory of natural resources rather than a problem in industrial organization. For instance, no mention of the oil market or of OPEC can be found in Professor Tirole's recent advanced industrial organization textbook (Tirole, 1988). As a consequence, theorists asked resource management questions—will a monopolist conserve more oil in the future?—rather than market structure questions—what type of quotas will improve the stability of the cartel? Some of Professor Adelman's writings that stress the low value of conservation for oil producers can be understood as a dissent from this approach. It is of course impossible to predict the consequences of the use of an alternative paradigm, but as he reads our survey, the reader might want to ask himself whether he thinks that the literature has tackled the essential questions.

The lack of a widely accepted neoclassical theory of government behavior will also be painfully clear in what follows. All models treat the members of the cartel as profit maximizers. There is no exploration of the consequences of differences of opinions or of political power within the countries, whereas many of the informal descriptions of the market stress this aspect. Furthermore, there is little awareness of the feedbacks between the oil extraction decisions and the development strategy of the countries, except for the choice of the discount rate. Can we really understand Algeria's oil policy without some description of its internal economic problems? A further remark on this issue serves as a useful guide for the rest of the section. The computation of optimal policy for OPEC countries provides predictions of their future actions. In contrast, the optimal policy for consuming countries is presented as a recommendation to their governments. For instance, in a very nice paper, Bergstrom (1982) computes the optimal excise tax for consuming countries. He then compares these figures with the actual excise tax, and finds some significant differences. But he does not test his prediction of oil production against actual data. Should we take it that most economists think of OPEC governments as more rational than the governments of OECD countries, or does distance blur the irrational?

## 5.2. Modeling production

There is much interesting literature on exploration for oil fields, and on the consequences of uncertainty about the size of reserves for the optimal extraction of a resource pool, or for the behavior of a competitive industry. However, these elements are not typically embedded in theoretical models of the oil market. Existing models have a much simpler structure: a certain number of countries own pools of resources, of diverse sizes, that can be extracted at some cost. The most basic models try to understand how the owners of larger stocks would exploit their market power. In the next subsection, we will examine the use of countervailing measures by large consuming nations.

This subsection will first present the basic models of competition, monopoly and oligopoly that we can find in the literature. Then, we will turn to some extensions of this basic model.

Because the literature focuses on the limited amount of resources and the intertemporal trade-offs faced by producers, it uses a dynamic framework with time extending from 0 to infinity. For some purposes it is more convenient to use a continuous time model, and for others it is more convenient to use a discrete time model. We will shift from one to the other as needed. There are $n$ producers, indexed by $i = 1, \ldots, n$, and producer $i$ owns $\bar{S}_i$ units of the resource. With positive discount rates producers will always choose to extract the cheapest oil first, and the cost can therefore be represented by the following reduced form. After $S_i$ units have been extracted, the cost of extracting a small extra amount $\epsilon$ is $c_i(S_i)\epsilon$ (more general functional forms are possible, for instance, we could add technical progress by making $c_i$ dependent on time). It is important to note that the functions $c_i$ must represent the cost net of any scarcity rent. The rent, equal to price minus cost, is endogenous to such a dynamic model (for an example of confusion on this issue see Reza (1981)). If we let $q_i(t)$ be the quantity of oil extracted by country $i$ in period $t$, all the models impose the constraint:

$$\int_0^\infty q_i(t)dt \leqslant \bar{S}_i, \tag{1}$$

or the equivalent in discrete time models.

The demand function used in all the models discussed below is separable in time and of the form $D(p, t)$ where $p$ is the price and $t$ is the date. This demand is often assumed to change suddenly at some date $T$ in the future when a 'backstop technology' becomes available. Typically, the backstop technology provides unlimited supplies of energy at constant marginal cost.

The demand function facing an individual country depends on the market structure, and its determination is the basic topic of the sequel.

As a basic benchmark, we consider first the case of a competitive market where suppliers and consumers alike take the prices as given. Then, if we let $\delta_i$ be the discount rate of country $i$, it solves the following problem:

$$\max_{q_i(\cdot)} \int_{t=0}^{t=\infty} (p(t) - c_i(S_i(t)))q_i(t)\delta_i(t)dt$$

$$\text{subject to } \begin{cases} dS_i(t)/dt = -q_i(t) \\ \int_{t=0}^{t=\infty} q_i(t)dt \leq \bar{S}_i \end{cases} \qquad (\mathscr{PC}_i)$$

The first equation expresses the fact that the stock is decreased at the rate of extraction and the second is the stock constraint (1). The Lagrangian of this problem can be written immediately, and we get the well known formula that Hotelling derived in his classic 1931 paper

$$\frac{d}{dt}[(p(t) - c_i(S_i(t)))\delta_i(t)] = c_i'(S_i(t)), \tag{2}$$

for any $t$ such that $q_i(t)$ is strictly positive.

This gives us a generalized supply curve, where the supply of country $i$ in any period depends on the whole path of prices. Note that for any two countries $i$ and $j$ facing the same price path, the costs of extraction $c_i(S_i(t))$ and $c_j(S_j(t))$ are equal in any period $t$ when their productions are both strictly positive. From these generalized individual supply curves it is easy to compute an industry supply curve, and the equilibrium is computed by setting demand equal to supply in each of the infinite number of periods. In the special case, where for all $i$ the cost function takes the special form $c_i(S_i) = c$, where $c$ is a constant, and the producers all have the same discount factor $e^{-rt}$, equation (2) becomes:

$$\frac{dp/dt}{(p - c)} = r. \tag{3}$$

This equation states that $p - c$ increases at the rate of interest $r$. With this formulation, given the price at time zero it is possible to compute the whole path of prices knowing only the discount rate. For any $p(0)$, the total aggregate demand over the entire infinite horizon can be computed. The equilibrium $p(0)$ makes this aggregate demand equal to the aggregate stock of resources which is available. This special case is used very often in the literature.

Hotelling proved that this competitive solution is efficient, by showing that it generates the output path that a social planner trying to maximize discounted social surplus would choose. It may be worth noting that the literature typically avoids some rather difficult technical problems associated with this continuous time/infinite horizon set-up. First, the integrability of the extraction and price paths is not explicitly studied, and second the transversality conditions that describe the behavior of the producers at infinity are typically ignored. An exception to this rule is the important but very difficult paper by Hansen, Epple and Roberds (1985), which uses linear-quadratic methods, common in macroeconomics, to solve the problem when there are two firms acting as competitors. The simplicity of the quadratic formulation allows them to deal with these problems even when uncertainty, both in the cost and demand functions, is present.

The competitive solution is used as a benchmark for two reasons. First, because it is efficient, it allows the computations of the distortions introduced by market power. Second, modelers implicitly identify the pre-1973 situation with a competitive market, and interpret the results as comparison with a world in which the cartel did not exist.

After the 1973 price increase, theorists became interested in the study of the consequence of monopolization in the market for a natural resource. The easiest strategy was to begin by studying a model in which the natural resource is completely monopolized by a single producer. Let us set $n$ equal to 1, then the problem $\mathscr{PM}$ of the monopolist is obtained by two changes to the problem $\mathscr{PC}_i$ of the competitor. First, now both price and quantity are decision variables, second a constraint is added to ensure that in every period demand is equal to production:

$$\max_{q_1(\cdot),\, p(\cdot)} \int_{t=0}^{t=\infty} (p(t) - c_1(S_1(t)))q_1(t)\delta_1(t)dt$$

$$\text{subject to } \begin{cases} dS_1(t)/dt = -q_1(t) \\ \int_{t=0}^{t=\infty} q_1(t)dt \le \bar{S}_1 \\ q_1(t) = D(p(t),t) \text{ for all } t \end{cases} \qquad (\mathscr{PM})$$

We expect a monopolist to limit production and increase price. But note that in the case of a natural resource, the situation is slightly more complicated. If the monopolist produces less in 1974, it will have more oil left in the ground, and the price must be lower some time in the future, maybe because the life of the resource is extended. Hotelling proved this to be true if the price remains finite and the marginal revenue becomes infinite as the quantity sold approaches zero, a case that he argued is quite common. Hansen et al. extend this result to their linear-quadratic framework. Note however that if the monopolist is going to face lower prices at some point, we might wonder whether in some circumstances it would not choose to do so earlier rather than later. And, actually, in a very influential paper, Stiglitz (1976) shows that for isoelastic demand curves, and zero cost of production, the behavior of a competitive and a monopolistic industry will be identical. On the other hand, with the same isoelastic demand curves, the monopolist does take a more conservationist policy when elasticity increases over time. A similar result holds if the extraction cost is strictly positive, independent of production in any period, and declining or stationary over time. Sweeney (1977) defines a 'market imperfection function', which can be defined not only in monopolistic markets but also when other distortions such as externalities or price control are present, and shows how the study of this function can facilitate comparisons of price paths. (See also Lewis, Matthews, and Burness (1979) for further discussion of the issue, Hoel (1978) for a discussion of the consequences of the presence of a backstop technology, and Schmalensee (1976) for a study of more general objective functions for the monopolist.)

In this respect, Tullock (1979) makes the interesting observation that if the elasticity of demand is less than 1 a monopolist will want to produce an infinitesimally small amount in any period. Hence, with an isoelastic demand of elasticity less than 1, and a zero cost of production, Stiglitz's result, viz. that the competitive and monopolistic paths are identical, holds only if we require the monopolist to extract all its oil over time, that is if we write the stock constraint (1) with an equality. If we do not, the monopolist will find it optimal to extract an arbitrarily small amount in each period.

Finally, Hotelling (1931, p. 149) points out that the extraction path of a monopolist could be discontinuous, even if the demand curve is stationary and the discount rate constant. This phenomenon will arise whenever the marginal revenue is increasing with output over some range. Thus price jumps which are ruled out in a competitive market are possible under monopoly.

The next stage in the development of the literature was to take seriously the fact that the market was neither perfectly competitive nor dominated by a monopolist, and to study the hybrid form that is actually observed. Two paths were open. The first was to study the problems of cohesion of the cartel. This would be feasible in a market where the cartel owns all the available resource, but the members discuss the allocation of output shares among themselves. Although a number of authors of simulation models are interested in this issue, we know of no theoretical work that tackles it. The second path was to recognize the presence of other producers outside OPEC, and to study their relationship with the cartel. As we will see, this creates very serious technical difficulties when the problem is set, as it should be, in a 'closed-loop' framework. These problems are still very difficult in the late 1980s; they were nearly impossible to tackle in the 1970s before the concepts of game theory had been integrated in economics. The only satisfactory solution has been proposed by Hansen *et al.* in the special case of two countries with linear-quadratic cost functions.

Let us begin with the simplest extension of Hotelling's framework. Following Lewis and Schmalensee (1980) and Loury (1986), assume that the $n$ producers are playing a Nash–Cournot game. That is each takes as given the extraction paths of the others. Then, country $i$ solves the problem:

$$\max_{q_i(\cdot),\, p(\cdot)} \int_{t=0}^{t=\infty} (p(t) - c_i(S_i(t)))q_i(t)\delta_i(t)dt$$

$$\text{subject to} \begin{cases} dS_i(t)/dt = -q_i(t) \\ \int_{t=0}^{t=\infty} q_i(t)dt \leq \bar{S}_i \\ q_i(t) + \Sigma_{j \neq i} q_j(t) = D(p(t), t) \text{ for all } t \end{cases} \quad (\mathscr{PN}_i)$$

The only difference with the monopolist problem comes in the last constraint where the country must meet only residual demand. Lewis and Schmalensee assume that for each country the cost of production is constant $(c_i(S_i) = k_i)$ and show that an equilibrium exists for this game, under a number of conditions, the most important being that the demand is stationary and that its elasticity is strictly decreasing in aggregate output. Specializing to the case of equal costs and equal reserves, prices and profits will decrease when the number of producers increase. Loury also assumes that all producers have the same constant cost and that the demand is stationary. He adds the assumption that industry revenue tends to zero when aggregate production tends to zero and shows that the usual convergence properties of static Nash–Cournot equilibria hold: if the number of producers becomes infinite and each of them becomes small, the outcome converges to that of a competitive industry. He uses his framework to prove a number of interesting results about the equilibrium path:

1. For each producer $i$ there exists a constant $c_i$ such that the solution $q_i(t)$ at each period is the equilibrium of a static Cournot equilibrium where the costs would be $k + c_i e^{rt}$, where $k$ is the common extraction cost and $r$ the discount rate. The producers with the highest reserves have the lowest $c_i$s. This shows precisely that large reserves lower the opportunity cost of extraction for a producer. (Part of this result can also be found in Lewis and Schmalensee's paper.)
2. If the price elasticity of demand is non-increasing in the quantity sold, the price will decrease over time.
3. The market share of the producers with the largest reserves increases over time.

In the linear-quadratic set up of Hansen *et al.* with two countries and no uncertainty, at any point cumulative extraction in a Nash–Cournot equilibrium will be intermediate between those in the monopolist and competitive solutions.

Salant (1976) proposed a similar model to study the case in which there is one large producer, the dominant producer, and a competitive fringe composed of many small producers. He assumes that the dominant producer takes the production path of the competitors as given while they take the price path as given. He shows that an equilibrium exists, and in his subsequent book (Salant, 1982) extends the model to allow for several large producers and several competitive sectors. We would expect that if some of the producers become very small the Salant equilibrium would converge to a Loury equilibrium. Whether this is true or not is still an open question, which should be resolved as a positive answer would provide a natural defense of the asymmetry between producers in Salant's set-up.

OPEC can also be described as a Stackelberg leader. It announces a price path, which the other producers take as given when choosing their own production. OPEC meets the residual demand, that is the difference between the market demand and this competitive output. In this manner, to every price path is associated a profit for the cartel. Its problem is to find the path that maximizes this profit. Crémer and Weitzman (1976) used this framework in a simulation model while Gilbert (1978), Newbery (1981), Ulph and Folie (1981), and Hansen *et al.* (1985) developed its theory.

Gilbert studies the simplest case: he assumes that the cost of oil extraction is nil, that the backstop technology can produce at a price $\bar{P}$, and the elasticity of demand is less than 1 when the price is less than $\bar{P}$. As long as the fringe is producing, the price path must follow Hotelling's rule, equation 3 with $c = 0$, and the price increases exponentially at the rate of interest. Given the assumptions on the demand curve, as soon as the fringe has finished producing, OPEC sets the price at $\bar{P}$. While the dynamics of the price are very similar to that of a competitive market in the period where the competitive fringe is producing, the price level is higher. The discussions by Newbery and by Ulph and Folie deal with more general cases, and they compare in detail the competitive and Stackelberg solutions, showing that the intuition derived from static models can be contradicted in the dynamic case.

There are difficult conceptual problems associated with the use of the dominant producer (Stackelberg) model. We compute an equilibrium path for the productions of the competitive fringe and the monopolist. But now consider the problem at date $t' > 0$. The dominant producer has used $\int_0^{t'} q_1(t)dt$ barrels of oil and has $S_1(t') = \bar{S}_1 - \int_0^{t'} q_1(t)dt$ barrels left in the ground. Similarly, producer $i$ in the competitive fringe has $S_i(t') = \bar{S}_i - \int_0^{t'} q_i(t)dt$ barrels left. Now, if we recomputed the equilibrium of the model starting from time $t'$ and assuming that the initial stocks are the $S_i(t')$s, we would not get the same equilibrium for the dates posterior to $t'$. That is, after the world has evolved along the equilibrium path for a time, it will continue along this path only if the agents are committed to that path. Of course, this is a strong form of time inconsistency which throws some doubt on the use of this model.

Let us restate this conclusion. In the Stackelberg model, as long as all the agents take as given the path of the decision variables of the other agents, and believe that they are, so to speak, engraved in stone, they have no incentives to modify their own decisions at any point in time. However, if they are caught by surprise at some time $t'$, and the equilibrium is recomputed at this time for the remaining periods, this new equilibrium will be different from the continuation of the original equilibrium.

The Salant–Loury type models are robust to this form of time inconsistency, but are subject to another, more subtle, form of the same problem. Assume that a producer learns at some date $t_0$, anterior to $t'$, that the equilibrium will be recomputed at date $t'$. During the interval $[t_0, t']$ it will in general not be in its best interest to follow the original equilibrium path. We therefore have a milder form of time inconsistency than in the dominant producer model. Along the equilibrium path, there is no incentive to deviate from the equilibrium, as Salant (1982) notes, but if recomputation of the equilibrium is a possibility the producers will deviate.

Lewis and Schmalensee (1982) discuss another problem of time inconsistency. Even if the monopolist did announce a future sequence of production it may be impossible to observe whether it is indeed following this sequence. They show that the monopolist would have incentives to overproduce in the first years. The argument that the monopolist could hide its production is very dependent on the assumption that there is a constant cost of extraction (they assume zero cost).

The non-observability of output certainly plays a role in the incentives to cheat of OPEC members, but this may not be the proper model to study this issue.

It is not very difficult, at least in a discrete time framework, to write down the definition of a completely time consistent equilibrium, especially if we consider a finite time model. (Newbery and Maskin (1988) find a nice way to limit the horizon by assuming that at some date $T$ a backstop technology will become available that will produce energy at a cost smaller than the minimum of the $c_i$s.)

We use backward induction.

- If we know the stocks of oil at the beginning of the last period, the computation of the prices and quantities is a straightforward exercise in static analysis. We can do this for any possible combination of stocks held by the different producers, and generate a function that relates the profit of each producer in the last period to the stock that it holds and the stocks held by its competitors.
- Having computed these functions, we turn to the analysis of the penultimate period. We assume that we know the stocks at the beginning of this period. For any combination of outputs, the inverse demand curve will yield current prices and the computation of the stocks at the beginning of the final period is trivial. Using the functions computed above, we compute the discounted profits over the two last periods for all the producers as a function of their *outputs* (at this point we are working with given stocks). This defines a game, whose equilibrium we can identify. Because we can do this for any possible combination of stocks held by the different producers at the beginning of the period before the last, we can compute functions that relate the equilibrium discounted profits of any producer to the *stocks* held at the beginning of this period.
- The preceding reasoning can be repeated period by period, going backwards in time. When we reach the first period we know the stocks, and the equilibrium has been identified.

Although this definition is straightforward, the resulting equilibrium has not been adequately described in the literature.

Hansen *et al.* (1985) make a significant contribution as they develop techniques that allow computations of totally time consistent equilibria in a set-up with a competitive fringe and a dominant supplier. Using techniques imported from macroeconomics, they represent the monopolist as predicting its own behavior over the future, although it cannot commit itself to any output path. Using this insight, a very general linear-quadratic model, including uncertainty, can be studied in a fully time consistent fashion. In one set of computations, the imposition of time consistency severely limits the power of the dominant producer, and the price path is very similar to that obtained under competition, although the allocation of production between competitors and the dominant firm changes.

What is the relevance of these theoretical results to the work of applied oil economists? First, they point out the indispensable role of simulation models which can compute numerical examples with realistic data, given that the theoretical models seem too difficult to solve at the present time. A particularly fruitful direction would be to exploit more fully the techniques of Hansen *et al.* which could form the basis for interesting simulation models more detailed than the examples that they present, and also for some theoretical work. Secondly, the best theorists have great trouble solving the simplest coherent model. Understanding what is best for Saudi Arabia in the complex 'real world' is orders of magnitude more difficult. For the scholar or policy maker trying to make sense of the market this should be an humbling thought.

On some other issues of interest to applied economists, theorists have done remarkably little work. The stability of OPEC, considered as a cartel, and the internal discipline problem it faces form one striking example. Osborne (1976) discusses a rule for punishing members who produce more than their quotas, but the model is not completely closed from a game theoretical viewpoint because, as noted in section 3, once a member has deviated there are no incentives for the others to retaliate.

There has also been little work on the issue, important in simulation and informal models, of the relationship between the development strategy of OPEC countries and their oil extraction policy. However, in the framework used by Crémer and Salehi Isfahani (1980), Hoel (1980) studies a country that has a limited absorptive capacity, faces imperfect international capital markets, and uses a maximim criterion to choose among its extraction paths. Under these conditions extraction may be delayed as the price increases. This result provides some theoretical support for the competitive view of OPEC which relies on the backward bending supply curve to explain the price jump of 1973.

Surprisingly, the theoretical literature has neglected the demand side, and there is little work that tries to endogenize the property of the demand functions. An exception is Chichilnisky (1981) who builds a simple macroeconomic model of consuming countries in order to study the variations of the terms of trade as oil exports increase. On a related topic, Hoel (1981) studies the optimal strategy of a monopolist who has some influence on the rate of return in international capital markets.

### 5.3. Games between producers and consumers

Consuming countries have a certain number of strategic tools at their disposition. They can impose import taxes on oil, they can store some oil and resell it later, and they can speed up the discovery of alternative energy sources. There is an interesting literature that tries to explore the optimal use of these measures to counterbalance the power of OPEC.

There is a tradition in international economics, represented by the work of Prebisch (1950) and Singer (1950), that argues that the asymmetry between the endowments of the industrialized 'North' and the resource-rich 'South' enables the former to exploit the latter. The events of 1973 and 1974 threw some doubt on this proposition and prompted some analytical work on the relative strengths of these two groups. The seminal work in this area is the paper by Kemp and Ohyama (1978), which has been nicely exposed graphically by Findlay (1979).

As is customary in international economics, dynamic elements are ignored. North is the only producer of consumption and capital goods, whereas South produces a natural resource (say oil) using capital goods which it has to import. Both countries have some endowment of capital goods, and labor is irrelevant to the model. The governments of the two countries control import and export taxes, there is no direct control of the quantity imported or exported although it is not clear whether this would make a difference. Kemp and Ohyama show that in this world the North has much more power than the South: it can drive the amount of consumption goods that the South receives in exchange for its resources down to zero. (The same point is made in a partial equilibrium framework by Dasgupta *et al.* (1983)). Findlay provides the following economic interpretation: taxes on the export of consumption goods do not alter the incentives of Southern producers. Indeed, because there is only one consumption good they will always try to maximize their profits measured in Northern currency. Once the South holds Northern currency, its purchases of consumption goods can be taxed at confiscatory rates. The model does not give symmetrical power to the South, because any export tax on oil will lower Northern production and hence South's own access to consumption goods. Lawrence and Levy (1982) point out that this result is very dependent on the asymmetry built into the model.

The models described above assume an unrealistic level of coordination between countries of the North or of the South. On the other hand, they may provide a theory for the hypothesis put forward by Mabro (1975a) of OPEC as an export tax fixing cartel. Note, however, that if the oil is owned by governments, they can manipulate the domestic price, and the meaning of an independently determined export tax is not clear. We doubt that such a model is a satisfactory representation of reality, but it is coherent.

Bergstrom (1982) uses a framework closer to the traditional resource based models to study the optimal tax response of consuming countries, while taking into account the absence of a central taxation authority. There are many countries, and each of them can be at the same time a producer and a consumer. Bergstrom studies the outcome of a tax setting game, in which the countries impose an excise tax on oil (not an import tax, this will make some differences for countries that are both importers and producers). Because he imposes the constraint that the tax must be constant over time, he can show that the model is isomorphic to a static model and can be easily solved. A single consuming country facing a monopolist producer would be able to capture the total rent by imposing a very high excise tax. In the more general model, the tax charged by a consuming country would depend on the domestic elasticity of demand for oil and would be larger for countries with a large share of world oil consumption.

Maskin and Newbery (1990) study the imposition of an import tax by a large buyer in a competitive market for a natural resource, when the buyer cannot commit itself to a tariff beyond the current period. Although they ask the question in an arbitrarily long infinite horizon set-up, they provide most of the answers in a two-period model. In each period, the importing country announces an import tax, the producer chooses an output and the market clears. In the first period, the producers base their production decisions not only on the current price of oil but also on their expectations of next period's price. Because this price will depend on the tariff in the second period, the model, as all time consistent models, must be solved backwards from the last period.

The most striking result is that the large importer may be better off if for some reason it is forbidden to set tariffs. This phenomenon can arise only when it places more weight than other consumers on second-period imports. Indeed, come the second period, it may have a strong incentive to set a high tariff in order to extract as much of the rent as possible. Because it cannot commit itself not to do so, the producers will be reluctant to wait for the second period to produce and the importer will end up importing more than it wants in the first period. It would be interesting to know whether this result becomes more or less likely in a model with more than two periods.

The importer will be worse off when it cannot commit itself to a future policy (it could always commit itself to the policy that it would follow in the no-commitment world, and can in general do better). Maskin and Newbery show that the availability of futures markets permits the importer to do as well without commitment as it could with commitment. They also show that with storage, it can obtain part of the benefits of futures markets.

From an applied point of view, these results show that the complexity of dynamic strategic interaction may create counterintuitive outcomes. They also show that the possibility to commit oneself not to use some policy instrument (tariffs in this case) can have positive value. Whether these phenomena are of practical importance is an important but extremely difficult question.

Dasgupta *et al.* (1983) study the optimal R&D program of an oil importing country. They build a model with one producer and one consumer country. At time zero, the importing country commits itself to a program of research and development for a backstop technology. Greater expenditures advance the date at which the technology will be available; they do not affect the probability of discovery which is one in any case. The exporting country chooses a path of extraction that maximizes its discounted profit given this date. They show that strategic considerations imply that the importing country will find it optimal to complete development of the backstop technology before the cartel plans to exhaust its reserves. The exercise is interesting and instructive. However, the recent drop in funding for alternative energy sources would lead us to believe that importing countries do not commit themselves to a long-run R&D program. It would be interesting, but very difficult, to rework the exercise without commitment. The same authors treat a related problem in Dasgupta *et al.* (1982) in a set-up less directly applicable to the oil market.

Many policy discussions have centered around the advisability for the consuming countries to build stockpiles of oil. Proposals to do so have in general been defended on the grounds that they would help resist future embargoes. Most theoretical work on stockpiling has been oriented towards agricultural markets where production is subject to recurring random events, which is not the case for the oil market.

In a two-country deterministic model where a producer has monopoly on the extraction of oil, Nichols and Zeckhauser (1977) study the incentives for the consuming country to shift its pattern of buying over time. They assume that the costs of production and storage are zero, that the demand curve is linear, and that there is no overall resource constraint. When there are only two periods, they derive closed form analytical solutions. Without stockpiling, the producer would charge the monopoly price in both periods. With stockpiling, the game goes as follows. In the first period, the producer announces a price. The consumers in the consuming country and its government decide how much oil to buy. At the beginning of the second period, the producer announces a new price, the government sells its stock at that price, and the consumers buy their demand in excess of this stock from the producing government. The authors compute the time consistent solution to this game.

They show that the price will be slightly higher than the monopoly price in the first period, and much lower in the second, in such a way that the welfare of both consumers and producers is increased. The stockpile bought in the first period shifts the second period demand curve to the left and induces a lower monopoly price in the second period. In effect, the stockpile enables the monopolist to charge a two-part tariff, with the cost of the stockpile being the entry fee, and the second period price the price per unit. The social gain from the presence of stockpiling is larger in models with a greater number of time periods, and decreases if there are many consuming countries which stockpile independently.

Much more work would be needed before a policy recommendation could be formulated on the basis of this model. The size of the stockpile would have to be very large, as would be the induced budget deficit (the consuming government buys dear and sells cheap). The gain in efficiency from stockpiling suggests that in a model without stockpiling but where the consuming country produces and imports oil, it should limit domestic extraction in the first period, exactly the opposite of the policy followed by the US government in the past.

It is also worth noting, as does Newbery (1984), that if, instead of stockpiling, the consuming government sets an *ad valorem* tariff *before* the producer sets its price in the second period, the consumer surplus is increased. However, this comes entirely at the expense of the producer; there is no gain in social surplus.

## 6. EMPIRICAL TESTS OF THE OIL MARKET

### 6.1. Introduction

This section reviews econometric studies of the oil market. In line with the emphasis of the other sections, this survey is limited to tests of hypotheses related to market structure and the functioning of the oil market. We therefore ignore the much larger econometric literature which estimates supply and demand functions for oil (Epple, 1985, Pesaran, 1988).

As we saw in previous sections, models of the oil market use a wide range of assumptions to come to vastly differing conclusions and policy implications. Only a handful of papers have tested this large variety of models. Compared to other applied fields, where the ratio of papers that propose models to those that test them is greater than 1, empirical tests of oil market behavior are quite rare. This is quite surprising given the importance of this sector in the world economy.

Econometric tests of market behavior are relatively new in economics. In the absence of the 'smoking gun,' proving collusive behavior has generally been thought very difficult (Porter, 1983). But in the 1980s a rapidly growing literature has devised tests that under certain circumstances can distinguish collusive and competitive behavior (for a sample see Appelbaum, 1979, Porter, 1983, Spiller and Favaro, 1984, and the papers in Bresnahan and Schmalensee, 1987). These tests are yet to be applied to the oil market where one faces the added difficulty of the intertemporal nature of the supply decision. Because supply is affected by expectations of future prices, we face the additional problem of econometric modeling of expectations.

Furthermore, many tests of collusive behavior are based on the occurrence and timing of price wars, of which the oil market has known at most one, in 1986. Periods of stable or rising prices, as observed until the beginning of the 1980s, do not provide much useful material for such tests.

Another reason for the scarcity of empirical work has been the unquestioned acceptance of the cartel model by most economists, supported by the widely publicized attempts of OPEC to fix price and later to ration output. The smoking gun—cartel meetings—was there for all to see, and there was no reason to go through complicated econometric procedures to uncover what seemed obvious to the naked eye.

Lack of econometric studies does not mean that oil economists have not spent a good deal of time looking at the facts. In the tradition of early industrial economics, several analysts have examined conduct in detail without running any regressions (Stocking, 1970, Adelman, 1972a, Jacoby, 1974, Blair, 1978). Because they dealt with the pre-1973 situation, they focused their attention on the major oil companies. This type of empirical work has continued since 1973, but the range of admissible variables enlarged enormously to include political motivations and specific national goals because the dominant agents are now governments, and it has become more difficult to draw conclusions from specific events.

The first few weeks of 1979 provide a good example of the limitations of unsystematic use of data. Professor Adelman has argued that monopoly action by Saudi Arabia caused the tripling of oil prices: on 'January 20, 1979—a day to remember — Saudi Arabia cut production from 10.4 to 8.0 mbd ... [and] drove the price up to $32 from $12' (Adelman, 1982, p. 55, see also Gately, 1986, p. 4, for a similar reasoning). *A priori*, the argument seems very persuasive because up until that date spot prices had not risen despite Iranian cutbacks that had begun three months earlier. However, others have disagreed. The trade press interpreted this action as the consequence of a decision to stop supplying all the residual demand at the official price. This is supported by the fact that over the previous quarter, Saudi output had increased by one-third to an all time high of 10 mbd to meet the Iranian shortfall. Furthermore, if the price increase was solely the result of the Saudi production cut, it would have been reversed, when a few months later, its output climbed back to 10 mbd, where it stayed until late 1981 (see also Crémer and Salehi-Isfahani, 1989). Skeet (1988) has yet a different view of the Saudi action, emphasizing the *increase* in their self-imposed production ceiling from 8.5 to 9.5 mbd in the same month. Moran (1982) has drawn attention to the political situation underlying the Saudi action. Saudi Arabia abandoned its policy of market stabilization in part because of dissatisfaction with the Camp David accords, and in part because of pressure from other oil producers. Our point is not to argue that one view or the other is preferable, but to show the reader that the historical evidence is subject to multiple interpretations, even when facts appear to speak for themselves.

## 6.2. Econometric tests

In this subsection we report on three econometric studies of the oil market which take three different approaches to testing for market behavior (Griffin, 1985, Matutes, 1988, Loderer, 1985). Griffin tries to infer market behavior from price and production data in a static framework, Matutes takes the dynamic issues resulting from exhaustibility into account and builds her test directly on the Hotelling model, and Loderer uses the 'event study' methodology popular in the finance literature to study the impact of OPEC annoucements on spot prices.

Griffin tests the cartel and the competitive models, but not the dominant firm model. For the cartel theory, he estimates the following equation with quarterly data for the years 1972–1983:

$$\ln Q_{it} = \alpha_i^1 + \gamma_i^1 \ln P_t + \beta_i^1 \ln Q_{it}^{00} \tag{1}$$

where $Q_{it}$ is output of country $i$ in time $t$, $P_t$ is the price of oil[10], and $Q_{it}^{00}$ is the output of other OPEC members. (The superscripts on $\alpha$, $\beta$, and $\gamma$ will enable us to differentiate between different models.) Following a suggestion of Adelman, he argues that the cartel theory implies constant output shares for OPEC members, and therefore bases his tests of cartel behavior on $\beta^1$. If OPEC engages in strict output sharing, $\beta^1$ will be equal to 1, and if there is only partial output sharing we will have $1 > \beta^1 > 0$. The results show a positive $\beta$ which is in most cases significantly different from unity. Thus, while the strict version of the

---

[10] This is the price index of imported crude oil to the US, which is a mixture of official and spot prices.

theory is rejected, the partial version is not. Griffin concludes that the cartel theory receives strong support from his data. However, a positive $\beta^1$ only implies that the outputs of OPEC members are positively correlated. It is difficult to imagine a coherent model, including the competitive model, that would not predict positive $\beta$'s, as all producers react similarly to changes in market fundamentals (Salehi-Isfahani, 1987).

Griffin tests separately three versions of the competitive model: the supply shock model (MacAvoy, 1982), the 'target revenue model' (Teece, 1982, and Crémer and Salehi-Isfahani, 1980),[11] and the property rights model (Johany, 1980). The estimated equations for these models are, respectively,

$$\ln Q_{it} = \alpha_i^2 + \gamma_i^2 \ln P_t, \tag{2}$$

$$\ln Q_{it} = \alpha_i^3 + \gamma_i^3 \ln P_t + \delta_i \ln I_{it}, \tag{3}$$

$$\ln Q_{it} = \alpha_i^4 + \theta_i G_{it}. \tag{4}$$

where $I_{it}$ is actual investment expenditures, interpreted as a fixed target investment standing for absorptive capacity, and $G_{it}$ is the percentage of government controlled production of oil.

Equation (2) is very close to the equations MacAvoy himself estimated. Griffin follows him in expecting a positive sign for $\gamma^2$, i.e., an upward sloping supply curve. For five of the eleven countries tested the model is rejected as $\gamma^2$ is significantly negative. Testing (2) as a nested case of (1) causes it to be rejected for an additional five.

For the target revenue model Griffin posits a 'strict variant', $\gamma^3 = -1$, $\delta = 1$, and a 'partial variant', $\gamma^3 < 0$, $\delta > 0$. The strict variant is rejected for all ten OPEC countries for which investment data was available, but the partial version is difficult to reject. However, Griffin dismisses this model because it shows a much poorer fit than the cartel model.

The property rights model predicts $\theta < 0$ in (4). It cannot be rejected for 6 of the 11 countries tested, but, again, noting a poor fit, Griffin concludes that the data provides little support for the property rights model.

As Griffin himself notes, these are simplistic tests of very complex models. Equations (2) and (3) describe supply curves which should be

---

[11] As authors of both this survey and of Crémer and Salehi-Isfahani (1980), we would like to stress that our model is not a target revenue model.

estimated jointly with demand. Moreover, treating oil as a non-exhaustible good makes the results less interesting.

Lack of dynamic considerations weakens particularly the test of competitive models based on a backward bending supply curve (see Section 3). In this model, countries respond differently to a price change depending on whether they interpret it as temporary or permanent. For a country with a binding absorptive capacity constraint, a long-term price increase calls for a decrease in production, whereas the same country would increase sales for a short-term price increase. Equation (3) assumes that all changes in the current price are perceived as permanent by suppliers, an assumption that is perhaps valid only for the price increase of 1973, but not for the price increases of 1979–80 which were generally perceived as short-term phenomena (see Section 2). The importance of dynamic considerations is reflected in the very low Durbin-Watson statistics for all estimates of (3); for many countries the statistic is smaller than 0.5 (Salehi-Isfahani, 1987). This is evidence of acute serial correlation.

For the sign of the estimate of $\gamma^3$ to more accurately reflect the shape of the supply curve, we must replace the current price $P_t$ in (3) by the long-term expected price. Salehi-Isfahani (1987) modified Griffin's specification in this direction by letting the 'long-term expected price', $P_t^*$, be adaptively formed by the following formula:

$$\ln P_t^* - \ln P_{t-4}^* = \lambda_i(\ln P_{t-4} - \ln P_{t-4}^*).\qquad(5)$$

After some transformations one obtains:

$$\ln Q_{it} = \alpha_i^3 + \gamma_i^3 \ln P_{t-4} + (1 - \lambda_i) \ln Q_{it-4} + \delta_i(1 - \lambda_i) \ln I_{it-4}\qquad(6)$$

This equation gives results that support the competitive model. All co-efficients have the expected signs, the acute serial correlation in Griffin's residuals disappear, and the fits are comparable to those he obtains for the cartel theory.

An ambitious and interesting attempt to derive a test for market behavior which takes account of exhaustibility is by Matutes (1988). She tests three different market structures:

1. competitive: all countries act as price takers;
2. cartel: all countries collude;
3. dominant firm: OPEC does not act as a single unit, some mem-

bers act competitively while one or more form a dominant supplier.

Matutes derives her testable hypotheses directly from the Hotelling formula. If country $i$ acts competitively, we have

$$P_t - M_{it}(q_{it}) = (1 + r_{it})[P_{t-1} - M_{it}(q_{it-1})], \tag{7}$$

where $M_{it}$ is the marginal cost of extraction, $r_{it}$ the rate of interest, and $q_{it}$ the output. If the country is part of a dominant supplier, price is replaced by marginal revenue, and we have

$$MR_{it}(q_{it}) - M_{it}(q_{it}) = (1 + r_{it})[MR_{it-1}(q_{it-1}) - M_{it}(q_{it-1})]$$

Assuming that demand has constant elasticity and marginal cost is a function of the output-capacity ratio allows her to derive the following testable equation:

$$y_{it} = \alpha_i x_{it}, \tag{8}$$

where

$$x_{it} = P_t - P_{t-1}(1 + r_{it})$$

$$y_{it} = h_{it} - h_{it-1}(1 + r_{it})$$

and $h$ is the ratio of oil output to excess capacity. The $\alpha_i$s depend on the cost of extraction and on the elasticity of demand facing the countries, that is on their strategic position in the market.

Simultaneous estimation of the system of equations (8) yields different $\alpha_i$s for different groups of countries, one composed of Saudi Arabia, Kuwait, Qatar, and the United Arab Emirates, and the other of other OPEC members. Matutes interprets this result to mean that the first group acts as a dominant firm while the other is part of the competitive fringe. Thus her results support the dominant firm hypothesis of the oil market. This result is strengthened when she takes into account differences in cost.

This conclusion rests solely on the differences between the $\alpha_i$s, that is the elasticity of demand facing the different countries, and on the assumption that countries in the second group act competitively. Theory does not tell us which $\alpha_i$ corresponds to which market structure, and factors other than strategic positioning could influence asymmetrically the elasticity of demand for the two groups. We find another difficulty in the assumption of perfect capital markets, implicit in her use of market interest rates. The relationship between price and output is affected by imperfections in this market and by domestic investment opportunities.

Loderer (1985) takes a different approach. If OPEC is a cartel, its policy decisions must have an impact on spot market prices. He compares the spot prices during the weeks following OPEC announcements with those forecast by a time series model which is estimated using past data. Statistically significant differences would show that the market finds OPEC's announcements of informational value, and this would be evidence in favor of the cartel hypothesis. Loderer finds that during 1974–1980 OPEC's announcements did not influence the market, but there is evidence of market impact for 1981–83.

The difference in regime identified by Loderer becomes more interesting when we note that the two periods differ in one important respect: before 1980, only prices were discussed at OPEC meetings, while in the second period some discussion of output quotas took place. The suggestion that the market started to take notice of OPEC only after it began acting as a classic cartel is reinforced by the following experiment. Loderer classifies the meetings for the second subperiod according to good news and bad news, the good-news meetings being those in which a quota system was adopted and bad-news meetings those with no decision. He finds that after good-news meetings spot prices increased whereas they decreased after bad-news meetings.

On the other hand, Loderer's conclusions run counter to the general belief that the 1970s were OPEC's powerful years and the 1980s saw the waning of its influence. Could OPEC really have had influence on the market when it was unable to stem the decline in price? One possible answer is that short-term market impact, the kind that Loderer's technique picks up, should not be confused with market power. Any group of producers that agreed on joint output cut could generate a blip in the spot price series as long as some traders believed that there would be a temporary decline in supply.

If participants in the market can predict the outcome of a particular meeting, there can be no 'announcement effect.' To see if market anticipation reduced forecast errors, Loderer compares two groups of meetings, those with 'large' price changes (defined as greater than 5%) and those with small price changes. He argues that the former were less well anticipated than the latter, but finds no evidence that forecast errors were any different for the two groups.

## 7. CONSENSUS AND OPEN ISSUES

The tasks that economists set for themselves are difficult. They want to understand the fundamental forces at work in markets and to predict, with some accuracy, the future course of prices and production. They also expect their analyses to be helpful to decision makers. In this section, we will review the contribution of our profession to the understanding of the oil market, and then turn our attention to the most important open questions for future research.

We have not, and will not, review in detail the record of prediction of future prices (see Gately (1984) and Manne (1986) for good surveys). In some respects, the record of economists looks dreadful. Quite a number predicted a rapid decrease of prices following an inevitable collapse of the cartel. Instead, came the 1979-1980 price increase. Then, as they were studying the possibility of a long-run real price staying close to $32, it slowly decreased back to its pre-1974 level, in real terms. Any economist who in 1980 would have predicted a decrease of this magnitude over the following decade would have had a difficult time getting into print! On the other hand, around 1973-74, economists were a minority when they refused to predict a continuous increase in price at a yearly rate of 3 to 10% over the long run. Their fast, and sometimes crude, computations of demand and competitive supply showed that even in the circumstances most favorable to OPEC, including a flawless performance as a unified certel, it had little incentive to increase the price. Digging further into the price setting mechanism rather than using straight extrapolation of time series clearly paid off.

Turning to the analysis of the structure of the market, the level of disagreement is unsettling. The literature gives the impression that there still are major disagreements over the basic tools of analysis to use. Since 1980, no new major hypothesis has been suggested to describe the basic forces at play, and the same arguments seem to be heard again and again. On the other hand, we feel that a consensus is emerging about the basic building blocks of the correct model of the market. The disagreements focus on relative orders of magnitude, but this is common in the study of most industries. In the next paragraphs, we turn to the terms of this consensus.

First, there is consensus about the fact that the oil extraction policies of the main producers are linked to their economic development.

Something like a backward bending supply curve plays some role. This is true of the competitive models of the market, while proponents of the cartel hypothesis link OPEC's capacity to increase prices to the fact that at high prices the incentives to cheat decrease. However, there has been very little work through simulation or theoretical models that has explored these insights in detail.

Second, there is consensus that OPEC is not a 'traditional' cartel. Its success in 1973–74 was achieved without any explicit rationing agreement and with none of the machinery that one would expect to find behind an engineered price increase of this magnitude.

Third, there is consensus that the traditional Hotelling scarcity rent explains little of the price. Nor does the marginal cost of production which is very low compared to the price, even if we include discovery and drilling.

Fourth, there is consensus that monopoly power exists in the short run. Through unilateral action, premeditated or not, some countries can have major impact on the price, because the short-run elasticity of demand is very low. A reduction in world production of 2 to 3% can upset the supply and demand balance.

On the other hand, there are important disagreements. Do the major OPEC producers have significant incentives to take advantage of their short-run market power? Do they have the power to maintain an artificially high price over the long run. At this point, these are empirical issues—how big is this or that effect?—as opposed to conceptual issues—how should we analyze this market? Oil economists face a more difficult task in the analysis of these issues than do economists studying other industries. First, the major producers are governments. Economists do not have a very good theory of governments, and certainly not a reduced form specification of their behavior which is easy to integrate into a more general model. Second, the data are unusually bad. Not because the numbers are especially untrustworthy, but because the market has been so far from any type of steady state that estimation becomes extremely difficult. For instance, as we have noted in Sections 3 and 6, the estimates of the long-run elasticity of demand are still very imperfect.

The arguments presented in the literature do not seem to induce many conversions from one school of thought to the other. The relationships between models is not presented very clearly, and not enough effort is spent criticizing both the logic and the applicability of competing interpretations.

There are a number of issues which we believe could be fruitfully researched in greater depth. The literature has paid much too little attention to uncertainty. The market is subject to large swings in price, and the way in which producers prepare for and adjust to the these swings deserves careful attention. The study of these phenomena requires vey different tools than the study of the effect of anticipated variations in price, or the adaptation to a sudden and permanent increase in price.

Uncertainty is intimately linked to the role of capacity. Fixed investments form a large component of the costs of extraction and refining, and increasing capacity requires a long lead time. Many producers have in the past carried excess capacity while others extract all they can (Mexico and the United Kingdom). Excess capacity has a cost, equal to the foregone earnings on the capital invested, and we need better explanations of its determinants. Two come immediately to mind. First, some producers carry excess capacity, when its cost is low enough, in order to take advantage of temporary upswings in the price. Second, excess capacity serves as a bargaining chip in intra-OPEC discussions. These hypotheses, and especially the first, should be amenable to theoretical analysis and could form the basis of interesting simulation models. Furthermore, econometric analyses of the determinants of excess capacity would be useful. Crémer (1979) provides some preliminary analysis of the role of fixed investment in an optimal resource extraction framework.

The role of strategic reserves and production in countries that are net importers also deserves more attention. Strategic reserves have been defended as a tool for price stabilization and as a weapon against OPEC. The Nichols and Zechauser (1977) work surveyed in Section 5 explores this role, and more could be done. It seems that modification of the rate of extraction in the United States would be a far cheaper instrument for putting pressure on a cartel. On the other hand, strategic reserves could play an important role in a world subject to strong variations in price.

On a related matter, the literature has paid too little attention to monopsony power in the oil market. The United States consumes about 25% of world production, and clearly this should give it some power. The EEC countries consume 15% of world oil, and have the political and administrative capacity to implement unified purchasing policies. The supply side is no more concentrated, and yet most authors think that the producers are much more powerful than the consumers. This is a question that theory in particular can illuminate.

To end this section on an humbling thought, it should be remembered that economic models cannot deal with some important issues. For instance, if political scientists are correct in their argument that the Saudi leadership is willing to forego profits in order to buy political stability in some of the OPEC countries and to obtain the goodwill of the United States, we will have a hard time integrating these facts in our models in anything but the crudest way.

## 8. CONCLUSION

The term 'cartel' is so automatically appended to OPEC by economists and lay people alike that the very wide range of disagreements among experts about the actual role of the organization is obscured. A minority believe that there is little market power, and, more importantly, the majority who believe otherwise put forth a wide variety of cartel hypotheses. Its functioning, its goals, and its reach are all subject to debate.

It took some time after the first oil crisis for the disagreements to surface. In 1973–74, when many economists turned their attention to this market, they were all content with the description of a monolithic cartel. Despite this consensus two very different types of analyses developed. Some policy oriented economists attempted to discover ways to speed up the inevitable collapse of the cartel, using the diversity of interests among its members. On the other hand, theorists and the builders of simulation models were predicting the long-run future as if OPEC's monopoly power were to last forever. The results obtained by the second approach took the urgency off the first: although prices were predicted to remain high there would not be much further increase. The 1973–74 shock was a one-time phenomenon caused by a change in the structure of the market, not the beginning of an upward, long-term trend.

During these first years after the crisis, economists simply applied the standard textbook definitions of cartels to OPEC. The frequent meetings of its oil ministers were proof enough of explicit collusion. Over time, however, doubts mounted as a careful comparison of reality and theory showed substantial differences. Explicit and rigid output rationing did not develop, nor could one identify mechanisms for punishing cheaters. The setting of a cartel price with no output targets did not fit the mold. New reflection was needed about the structure of the market.

Three approaches were taken. The first was to assume that the cartel was inoperative, and to explain recent history through changes in property rights and the unfolding of competitive forces. The second road, taken mostly by theoreticians and builders of simulation models, was to build models where imperfect competition was an important factor, but where there was no explicit agreement. Finally, a number of writers tried to explain OPEC as an explicit cartel of a special kind, a 'price setting' or a 'happy-go-lucky' cartel.

We believe that it is clear that the result of all these exercises has been to cast doubt on the amount of market power enjoyed by OPEC. To put it in different words, there are reasonable competitive scenarios that yield an outcome not too different from the actual observed outcome. We believe that the methodology for the study of the market should be changed. It now seems reasonable to begin by studying the competitive outcome, not as some kind of far-fetched benchmark, but as an approximation, however gross, that is at least useful as a building block for more realistic models.

Once the competitive scenario has been explored, it must be corrected by introducing the elements of market power that do certainly exist. A much more precise analysis is needed than what we find in the literature. An example among many: there has been no discussion of the difference between market power in the short and the long term. Clearly, Saudi Arabia has the ability to engineer substantial short-run price increases, and may be able in the long run to pull the price away from the competitive price. These are two different phenomena that need to be distinguished in any careful analysis. The previous section provides numerous other examples.

The tools necessary for this task are available. Since 1973, there has been a revolution in the field of Industrial Organization. It has sometimes been described as the introduction of game theoretical methods; we prefer to describe it as the careful and explicit analysis of strategic interactions. The theory, the econometrics and the policy recommendations of industrial organization economists have been overhauled. The literature on the oil market has benefited too little from these changes. The next task of oil economists should be to apply these new techniques. The same intellectual excitement that characterized the field in the 1970s will then return.

## BIBLIOGRAPHY

Adelman, Morris, A. (1972a), *The World Petroleum Market*, Baltimore: The Johns Hopkins University Press.

Adelman, Morris, A. (1972b), 'Is the oil shortage real: Oil companies as OPEC tax-collectors,' *Foreign Policy*, winter 1972–73, pp. 69–107.

Adelman, Morris, A. (1976), 'Oil import quota options,' *Challenge*, Vol. 18, No. 6, 17–22.

Adelman, Morris, A. (1979), 'International oil,' in W. J. Mead and A. E. Utton, eds., *US Energy Policy*, Cambridge Mass: Ballinger, pp. 23–28.

Adelman Morris, A. (1980), 'The clumsy cartel' *The Energy Journal*, Vol. 1, No. 1, 43–53.

Adelman, Morris, A. (1982), 'OPEC as a cartel,' in J. M. Griffin and D. Teece, eds., *OPEC Behavior and World Oil Prices*, London: Allen and Unwin, pp. 37–63.

Adelman, Morris, A. (1985), 'An unstable world market', *The Energy Journal*, Vol. 6, No. 1, 17–22.

Adelman, Morris, A. (1986), 'Scarcity and world oil prices,' *Review of Economics and Statistics*, August, pp. 387–397.

Applebaum, E. (1978), 'Testing price taking behavior,' *Journal of Econometrics*, Vol. 9, 283–294.

Bénard, André, (1980), 'World oil and cold reality,' *Harvard Business Review*, Nov–Dec. 1980, Vol. 58, No. 6: 91–101.

Ben-Shahar, Haim (1976), *Oil: Prices and Capital*, Lexington: Lexington Books.

Bergstrom, Theodore, C. (1982), 'On capturing oil rents with a national excise tax,' *American Economic Review* 72(1), March, 195–201.

Blair, John (1978), *The Control of Oil*, New York: Vintage Books.

Blitzer, Charles, Meeraus, Alex and Stoutjesdijk Ardy J. (1975), 'A Dynamic Model of OPEC Trade and Production,' *Journal of Development Economics*, 2(4) 319–335.

Bohi, Douglas, R. and Montgomery, W. David (1982), *Oil Prices, Energy Security, and Import Policy*, Washington, D.C: Resources for the Future.

Bohi, Douglas, R. and Russell, M. (1975), *U.S. Energy Policy: Alternatives for Security*, Baltimore: John Hopkins Press.

Bresnahan, Timothy, F. and Schmalensee, Richard (1987), *The Empirical Renaissance in Industrial Economics*, New York: Basil Blackwell.

Chichilnisky, Graciela (1981), 'Oil supplies, industrial output and prices: a simple general equilibrium macro analysis,' mimeo, University of Essex and Columbia University.

Choucri, Nazli (1976), *International Politics of Energy Independence*, Cambridge: MIT Press.

Crémer, Jacques (1979), 'On Hotelling's formula and the use of permanent equipment in the extraction of natural resources,' *International Economic Review* 20(2), June, 317–324.

Crémer, Jacques and Salehi-Isfahani, Djavad (1980), 'A Theory of Competitive Pricing in the Oil Market: What Does OPEC Really Do?' CARESS Working Paper #80-4, University of Pensylvania, Philadelphia.

Crémer, Jacques and Salehi-Isfahani, Djavad (1989), 'The Rise and Fall of Oil Prices: A Competitive Theory of the Oil Market,' Annales d'Economie et de Statistique.

Crémer, Jacques and Weitzman Martin, L. (1976), 'OPEC and the Monopoly Price of World Oil,' European Economic Review, 8(2), August, 55–64.

Daly, George, Griffin, James, M. and Steele Henry, B. (1982), 'Recent Oil Price Escalations: Implications for OPEC Stability,' in J. M. Griffin and David Teece, eds., OPEC Behavior and World Oil Prices, London: Allen and Unwin, pp. 145-174.

Danielsen, Albert, L. and Selby E. B. (1980), 'World oil price increases: sources and solutions,' The Energy Journal, Vol. 1, No. 4, October, 59–74.

Danielsen, Albert, L. (1982), The Evolution of OPEC, New York: Harcourt Brace Jovanovich.

Darmstadter, Joel, H. Landsberg, H. Morton, H. C. with Coda, M. J. (1983), Energy Today and Tomorrow: Living with Uncertainty, New Jersey: Resources for the Future, Prentice Hall.

Dasgupta, Partha, Gilbert, Richard, J. and Stiglitz, Joseph, E. (1982), 'Invention and innovation under alternative market structures: the case of natural resources,' Review of Economic Studies, October, XLIX(4), 567–582.

Dasgupta, Partha, Stiglitz, Joseph and Gilbert, Richard (1983), 'Strategic considerations in invention and innovation: The case of natural resources,' Econometrica, 51(5), September, 1439-1448.

Eckaus, Richard, S. (1973), 'Absorptive capacity as a constraint due to maturation processes,' in Jagdish N. Bhagwati and Richard S. Eckaus, eds., Development and Planning: Essays in Honor of Rosenstein-Rodan, Cambridge: M.I.T. Press, pp. 79-108.

Eckbo, Paul, L. (1976), The Future of World Oil, Cambridge, Mass: Ballinger.

Epple, Dennis (1985), 'The econometrics of exhaustible resource supply: a theory and an application,' In Energy, Foresight, and Strategy, Thomas J. Sargent, ed. Washington: Resources for the Future pp. 143-206.

Erickson, N. (1980), 'Developments in the world oil Market,' in R. K. Pachauri, ed., International Energy Studies, New York: John Wiley & Sons, pp. 9-16.

Ezzati, Ali (1976), 'Future OPEC price and production strategy as affected by its capacity to absorb oil revenues,' European Economic Review, 8(2), August, 107-38.

Ezzati, Ali (1978), World Energy Markets and OPEC Stability, Lexington: Lexington Books.

Fesharaki, Fereidun and Isaak Davis T. (1983), OPEC, the Gulf and the World Petroleum Market, Boulder, Colorado: Westview Press.

Findlay, Ronald (1979), 'Economic development and the theory of international trade,' American Economic Review Proceedings 69(2), May, 186-190.

Fisher, Dietrich, Gately, Dermot and Kyle, John F. (1975), 'The Prospects for OPEC: A Critical Survey of Models of the Oil Market,' Journal of Development Economics, Vol. 2, No. 4, 363-386.

Gately, Dermot (1979), 'The Prospects for OPEC Five Years after 1973/74,' European Economic Review, Vol. 12, 369-379.

Gately, Dermot (1983), 'OPEC: Retrospective and Prospects: 1973-1990,' European Economic Review, Vol. 21, 313-331.

Gately, Dermot (1984), 'A Ten-Year Retrospective: OPEC and the World Oil Market,' Journal of Economic Literature, Vol. 22, 1100-1114.

Gately, Dermot (1986), 'Prospects for Oil Prices, Revisited,' *Annual Review of Energy*, 1986.

Gately, Dermot, Kyle, John F. and Fisher, Dietrich (1977), 'Strategies for OPEC's Pricing Decisions,' *European Economic Review*, Vol. 10, 209–230.

Gilbert, Richard (1978), 'Dominant firm pricing policy in a market for an exhaustible resource,' *Bell Journal of Economics*, 9(2), Autumn, 385–395.

Green, D. J. (1988), 'The world oil market: an examination using small-scale models,' *The Energy Journal*, 9(3), 61–77.

Griffin, James M. and Teece D. (1982), eds., *OPEC Behavior and World Oil Prices*, London: Allen and Unwin.

Griffin, James M. (1985), 'OPEC Behavior: A Test of Alternative Hypotheses,' *American Economic Review*, 75(5), 954–963.

Griffin, James, M. and H. B. Steele (1980), *Energy Economics and Policy*, New York: Academic Press.

Hansen, Lars, Peter, Epple, Dennis and Roberds William (1985), 'Linear quadratic duopoly models of resource extraction,' in *Energy, Foresight, and Strategy*, Thomas J. Sargent, ed., Washington: Resources for the Future, 101–142.

Hartshorn, Jack, E. (1985), 'Government sellers in a resturctured oil market,' in *The Changing Structure of the World Oil Industry*, David Hawdon, ed., London: Croom Helm.

Hartwick, John, M. (1989), *Non-renewable Resources Extraction Programs and Markets*, volume 33 in *Fundamentals of Pure and Applied Economics*, Chur: Harwood Academic Publishers.

Hirshleifer, Jack (1988), *Price Theory and Applications*, 4th edition, Englewood Cliffs, N. Y. Prentice Hall.

Hnyilicza, Esteban, and Pindyck, Robert S. (1976), 'Pricing policies for a two-part exhaustible resource cartel,' *European Economic Review*, 8(2), August, 139–154.

Hoel, Michael (1978), 'Resource extraction, substitute production and monopoly,' *Journal of Economic Theory* 19(1), 28–37.

Hoel, Michael (1980), 'Optimal resource extraction with imperfect international capital markets and a limited absorptive capacity,' paper presented at a conference on Policy Issues in Energy Self-sufficient Strategies at Different Stages of Industrialization, Oaxaca, Mexico, 1–7 September, 1980.

Hoel, Michael (1981), 'Resource extraction by a monopolist with influence over the rate of return on non resource assets,' *International Economic Review*, 22(1), February, 147–157.

Hogan, William (1982), 'Policies for oil imports,' in J. M. Griffin and D. Teece, eds., *OPEC Behavior and World Oil Prices*, London: Allen and Unwin, 186–206.

Hogan, William (1989a), 'A dynamic putty-semi-putty model of aggregate energy demand,' *Energy Economics*, 11(1), 53–69.

Hogan, William (1989b), 'World oil price projections: a sensitivity analysis,' Discussion paper no. E-89-04 Energy and Environmental Policy Center, Harvard University.

Hotelling, H. (1931), 'The Economics of Exhaustible Resources,' *Journal of Political Economy*, April, 39, 137–75.

Houthakker, Hendrick, S. (1974), 'Policy issues in the international economy of 1970s,' *American Economic Review Proceedings*, LXIV(2), May, 138–140.

Houthakker, Hendrick, S. (1983), 'Whatever happened to the energy crisis?' *The Energy Journal*, 4(2), 1–8.

Houthakker, Hendrick, S. and Kennedy, Michael (1978), 'Long-range energy prospects,' *The Journal of Energy and Development*, IV(1), 1–28.

Jacoby, Neil, H. (1974), *Mutinational Oil: A Study in Industrial Dynamics*, Macmillan.

Jaidah, Ali, M. (1982), 'Downstream operations and the development of OPEC member countries,' in R. El Mallakh, ed. *OPEC: Twenty Years and Beyond*, Boulder: Westview Press pp. 17-32.

Johany, A. D. (1980), *The Myth of OPEC Cartel*, New York: Wiley & Sons.

Kalymon, Basil, A. (1975), 'Economic incentives in OPEC oil pricing policy,' *Journal of Development Economics*, **2(4)**.

Kemp, Murray, C. and Ohyama Michihiro (1978), 'On the sharing of trade gains by resource-poor and resource rich countries,' *Journal of International Economics*, **8(1)**, February, 93-115.

Kennedy, Michael (1973), 'An Econometric Model of the World Oil Market,' *Bell Journal of Economics and Management Science*, Vol. 5, No. 2, 540-577.

Lawrence, Colin and Levy Victor (1982), 'On sharing the gains from international trade: the political economy of oil consuming nations and oil producing nations,' *International Economic Review*, **23(3)**, October, 711-722.

Lewis, Tracy R., Matthews, Steven, A. and Burness H. Stuart (1979), 'Monopoly and the rate of extraction of natural resources,' *American Economic Review*, **69(1)**, March, 227-230.

Lewis, Tracy, R., and Schmalensee Richard L. (1980), 'On oligopolistic markets for nonrenewable natural resources,' *Quarterly Journal of Economics*, **95(4)**, November, 475-491.

Lewis, Tracy, R., and Schmalensee Richard L. (1982), 'Cartel deception in nonrenewable resource markets,' *The Bell Journal of Economics*, **13(1)**, Spring, 263-271.

Loderer, C. (1985), 'A test of OPEC cartel hypothesis: 1974-83,' *The Journal of Finance*, Vol. 40, No. 3, July, 991-1008.

Loury, Glenn, C. (1986), 'Theory of "oil" igopoly: Cournot equilibrium in exhaustible resources markets with fixed supplies,' *International Economic Review*, **27(2)**, June, 285-301.

Lowinger, T. C. and Ram R. (1984), 'Product Values as a Determinant of OPEC's Official Crude Oil Prices,' *Review of Economics and Statistics*, Vol. LXVI (November): 691-695.

Mabro, Robert (1975a), 'OPEC after the oil revolution', *Millennium: Journal of International Studies*, Vol. 4, No. 3, Winter 1975-76, 191-199. Reprinted in Mabro (1986).

Mabro, Robert (1975b), 'Can OPEC hold the line?,' *Middle East Economic Survey*, Supplement to Vol. XVIII, No. 19, 28 February 1975. Reprinted in Mabro (1986).

Mabro, Robert (1978), 'The Marker and the Market, the Heavy and the Light,' *Middle East Economic Survey*, Vol. 21, No. 48. Reprinted in Mabro (1986).

Mabro, Robert (1986), ed., *OPEC and the World Oil Market*, Oxford University Press.

MacAvoy, Paul, W. (1982), *Crude Oil Prices As Determined by OPEC and Market Fundamentals*, Cambridge: Ballinger.

MacAvoy, Paul, W. (1983), *Energy Policy: An Economic Analysis*, New York: Norton.

Mackie-Mason, J. K. and Pindyck R. S. (1987), 'Cartel Theory and Cartel Experience in International Minerals Markets,' in R. L. Gordon, H. D. Jacoby, and M. Zimmerman, eds., *Energy: Markets and Regulation, Essays in Honor of M. A. Adelman*, Cambridge: MIT Press, pp. 187-214.

Manne, A. S. and Schrattenholzer, Leo with Rowley Jennifer L. (1986), 'International Energy Workshop: price projections,' *The Energy Journal*, **7(3)**, 109-114.

Maskin, Eric and Newbery, David (1988), 'Disadvantageous oil tariffs and dynamic consistency', *American Economic Review* **80(1)**, 143-156.

Matutes, C. (1988), 'The center of OPEC: an econometric analysis,' mimeo. Department of Economics, University of Calif., Berkeley.

Mead, Walter (1979), 'The performance of government energy regulation,' *American Economic Review Proceedings*, May, **Vol. 69**, 352–56.

McKie, James, W. (1978), 'Oil imports: is any policy possible?' in W. J. Mead and A. E. Utton, eds., *U.S. Energy Policy: Errors of the Past, Proposals for the Future*, Cambridge Mass: Ballinger, pp. 29–44.

Mikdashi, Z. (1975), 'The OPEC process,' in R. Vernon, ed., *The Oil Crisis*, Norton.

Moran, Theodore (1978), *Oil Prices and the Future of OPEC*, Research paper R-8, Washington, D.C.: Resources for the Future.

Moran, Theodore (1982), 'Modelling OPEC Behavior: Economic and Political Alternatives,' in Griffin and Teece (1982), pp. 94–130.

Newbery, David (1984), 'Commodity price stabilization in imperfectly competitive markets,' in G. G. Storey, A. Schmitz, and A. H. Harris, eds., *International Agricultural Trade*, Boulder, Colorado: Westview Press.

Nichols, Albert L. and Zeckhauser, Richard J. (1977), 'Stockpiling strategies and cartel prices,' *The Bell Journal of Economics*, **8(1)**, Spring, 66–96.

Noreng, Oystein (1982), 'The relationship of non-OPEC exporters with OPEC,' in R. El Mallakh, ed., *OPEC: Twenty Years and Beyond*, Boulder: Westview Press.

Nordhaus, William D. (1973), 'The allocation of energy resources', *Brookings Papers on Economic Activity*, 3, 529–570.

*Oil and Gas Journal*, December 1988.

OPEC (1984), *OPEC Official Resolutions and Press Releases, 1960–1983*, Vienna.

Ortiz, R. (1982), 'The World Energy Outlook in the 1980s and the Role of OPEC,' in R. El Mallakh, ed. *OPEC: Twenty Years and Beyond*, Boulder: Westview Press, pp. 1–16.

Osborne, D. K. (1976), 'Cartel problems,' *American Economic Review*, **66(5)**, December, 835–844.

Penrose, Edith (1968), 'Government Partnership in the Major Concessions,' *Middle East Economic Survey*, August 30.

Penrose, Edith (1975), 'The Development of the Crisis,' in R. Vernon, ed., *The Oil Crisis*, Norton.

Pesaran, M. Hashem (1988), 'An econometric analysis of exploration and extraction of oil in the U.K. continental shelf,' UCLA Working paper No. 471.

*Petroleum Intelligence Weekly*, Special Supplement, October 21, 1985.

Pindyck, Robert, S. (1977), 'Cartel Pricing and the Structure of the World Oil Market,' *The Bell Journal of Economics*, Autumn, **Vol. 8**, No. 2, 343–60.

Pindyck, Robert, S. (1978), 'Gains to Producers from the Cartelization of Exhaustible Resources,' *Review of Economics and Statistics*, May, 238–51.

Pindyck, Robert, S. (1979a), 'The Cartelization of World Commodity Markets,' *American Economic Review Proceedings*, May, **Vol. 69**, No. 2, 154–58.

Pindyck, Robert, S. (1979b), *The Structure of World Energy Demand*, Cambridge: MIT Press.

Pindyck, Robert, S. (1982), 'OPEC Oil Pricing, and the Implications for Consumers and Producers,' in Griffin and Teece (1982).

Plaut, Steven, E. (1981), 'OPEC is not a cartel,' *Challenge*, November-December, 18–24.

Porter, R. H. (1983), 'A study of cartel stability: the Joint Executive Committee, 1880–1886,' *The Bell Journal of Economics*, **14(2)**, 415–426.

Prebisch, Raúl (1950), *The Economic Development of Latin America and its Principal Problems*, New York: United Nations.

Reza, M. (1981), 'An analysis of the supply of oil,' *The Energy Journal*, **Vol. 2**, No. 2, 77–94.

Rouhani, Fuad (1971), *A History of OPEC*, New York: Praeger.

Salant, Stephen, W. (1976), 'Exhaustible resources and industrial structure: a Nash-Cournot approach to the world oil market,' *Journal of Political Economy* **84(5)**, October, 1079-1093.
Salant, Stephen, W. (1982), *Imperfect Competition in the Oil Market*, Lexington: Lexington Books.
Salehi-Isfahani, Djavad (1986), 'Oil Supply and Economic Development Strategy: A Dynamic Planning Approach,' *Journal of Development Economics*, April, **Vol. 21**, 1-23.
Salehi-Isfahani, Djavad (1987), 'Testing OPEC Behavior: Further Results,' Department of Economics, VPI & SU, Working Paper #87-01-02.
Salehi-Isfahani, Djavad (1989), 'The political economy of credit subsidy in Iran: 1973-1978,' *International Journal of Middle East Studies*, August, **21(3)**, 359-79.
Schmalensee, Richard (1976), 'Resource exploitation theory and the behavior of the oil cartel,' *European Economic Review*, **7(3)**, September, 257-279.
Schneider, Steven, A. (1983), *The Oil Price Revolution*, Baltimore: Johns Hopkins University Press.
Scott, Bruce, R. (1981), 'OPEC, the American Scapegoat,' *Harvard Business Review*, Jan.-Feb., **59(1)**, 6-30.
Singer, Fred, S. (1983), 'The price of world oil,' *Annual Review of Energy*, **Vol. 8**, Annual Review Inc., Palo Alto.
Singer, Fred, S. (1985), 'Prospects for the world oil market' *The Energy Journal*, January 1985, **6(1)**, 13-16.
Singer, Hans, W. (1950), 'The distribution of gains between borrowing and investing countries,' *American Economic Review Proceedings*, May, **40**, 473-85.
Skeet, Ian (1988), *OPEC: Twenty-Five Years of Prices and Politics*, Cambridge: Cambridge University Press.
Spiller, Pablo, T. and Favaro E. (1984), 'The effects of entry regulation on oligopolistic interaction: the Uruguayan banking sector,' **15(2)**, 244-254.
Stiglitz, Joseph (1976), 'Monopoly and the rate of extraction of exhaustible resources,' *American Economic Review*, **66(4)**, September, 655-661.
Stobaugh, Robert, B. (1975), 'The Oil Companies in Crisis,' in R. Vernon, ed., *The Oil Crisis*, Norton.
Stocking, George, W. (1970), *Middle East Oil*, Nashville: Vanderbilt University Press.
Sweeney, James, L. (1977), 'Economics of depletable resources: Market forces and intertemporal bias,' *Review of Economic Studies*, **XLIV(1)**, February, 125-141.
Teece, David (1982), 'OPEC Behavior: An Alternative View,' in J. M. Griffin and D. Teece, eds., *OPEC Behavior and World Oil Prices*, London: Allen and Unwin pp. 64-93.
Tirole, Jean (1988) *The Theory of Industrial Organization*, Cambridge, Mass: MIT Press.
Tullock, Gordon (1979), 'Monopoly and the rate of extraction of exhaustible resources: note,' *American Economic Review*, **69(1)**, March, 231-233.
Verleger, Phillip, K. Jr. (1982a), *Oil Markets in Turmoil*, Cambridge: Ballinger.
Verleger, Phillip, K. Jr. (1982b), 'The determinants of official OPEC crude prices,' *Review of Economics and Statistics*, **Vol. 64**, May, 177-183.
Ulph, A. M. and Folie G. M. (1981), 'Dominant firm models of resource extraction,' in D. Currie, C. Peel, and W. Peters, eds., *Microeconomic Analysis: Essays in Microeconomics and Economic Development*, London: Croom Helm, pp. 77-99.
*Wall Street Journal*, January 10, 1989.

## EPILOGUE

While this monograph was in print, the Iraqi army invaded Kuwait and the 'third oil crisis' hit the world. A supply shock of about 7% of world production, compounded with fears of even larger cuts in the future, more than doubled petroleum prices. These events throw light on some of the issues that we have discussed in this monograph.

1. The crisis illuminates some aspects of the history of the market.
   - Iraq first justified the invasion by the fact that Kuwait was cheating on its quota. Later events, such as the annexation of Kuwait have cast doubt on this justification. However, Iraq could only use the cheating as an excuse because OPEC was unable to create consensus between its members and to police production agreements.
   - On the other hand, one could argue that threats of military or political retaliation were implicit in past agreements, and that we only observe the rare case where they had to be carried out. We find this story rather unlikely, but it does provide a coherent theory to argue in favor of a unified cartel.
2. The 1990 crisis might change the future behavior of the oil market.
   - Even if military threats were not important in the past, they might play a role in the future. It will be impossible to ignore the invasion of one OPEC member by another in any future analysis. Despite the apparent very high cost to Iraq of the invasion, the use of military threats to enforce cartel agreements does raise the likelihood of 'cooperative outcomes' where they may not have existed.
   - The political and military responses by the United States (and to a lesser extent the United Nations and the other countries) have so far been explained in part by the fear of monopoly control of the oil market. If we want to assess the wisdom of this rather extreme form of antitrust policy, it is very important to assess the cutoff point at which market power enables producers to "dictate" the price of oil.

# Index

# LONG-TERM CONTROL OF
# EXHAUSTIBLE RESOURCES

PIERRE LASSERRE

# Long-Term Control of Exhaustible Resources

*by*

Pierre Lasserre

*Département des sciences économiques,*
*Université du Québec à Montréal*

A volume in the Natural Resources and Environmental
Economics section

edited by

C. Henry
*Ecole Polytechnique*
*Paris*

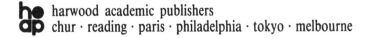

harwood academic publishers
chur · reading · paris · philadelphia · tokyo · melbourne

Harwood Academic Publishers

Post Office Box 90
Reading, Berkshire RG1 8JL
United Kingdom

3-14-9, Okubo
Shinjuku-ku, Tokyo 169
Japan

58, rue Lhomond
75005 Paris
France

Private Bag 8
Camberwell, Victoria 3124
Australia

5301 Tacony Street, Drawer 330
Philadelphia, Pennsylvania 19137
United States of America

**Library of Congress Cataloging-in-Publication Data**

Lasserre, Pierre.
    Long-term control of exhaustible resources / Pierre Lasserre.
        p. cm. — (Fundamentals of pure and applied economics, ISSN 0191-1708; v.
    49. Natural resources and environmental economics section)
    Includes bibliographical references and index.
    ISBN 3-7186-5134-3
    1. Natural resources. I. Title. II. Series: Fundamentals of
    pure and applied economics; v. 49. III. Series: Fundamentals of
    pure and applied economics. Natural resources and environmental
    economics section.
    HC59.L348   1991
    333.7—dc20                                                    91-763
                                                                     CIP

# Contents

# Introduction to the Series

Drawing on a personal network, an economist can still relatively easily stay well informed in the narrow field in which he works, but to keep up with the development of economics as a whole is a much more formidable challenge. Economists are confronted with difficulties associated with the rapid development of their discipline. There is a risk of 'balkanization' in economics, which may not be favorable to its development.

*Fundamentals of Pure and Applied Economics* has been created to meet this problem. The discipline of economics has been subdivided into sections (listed at the back of this volume). These sections comprise short books, each surveying the state of the art in a given area.

Each book starts with the basic elements and goes as far as the most advanced results. Each should be useful to professors needing material for lectures, to graduate students looking for a global view of a particular subject, to professional economists wishing to keep up with the development of their science, and to researchers seeking convenient information on questions that incidentally appear in their work.

Each book is thus a presentation of the state of the art in a particular field rather than a step-by-step analysis of the development of the literature. Each is a high-level presentation but accessible to anyone with a solid background in economics, whether engaged in business, government, international organizations, teaching, or research in related fields.

Three aspects of *Fundamentals of Pure and Applied Economics* should be emphasized:

— First, the project covers the whole field of economics, not only theoretical or mathematical economics.
— Second, the project is open-ended and the number of books is not predetermined. If new and interesting areas appear, they will generate additional books.

— Last, all the books making up each section will later be grouped to constitute one or several volumes of an Encyclopedia of Economics.

The editors of the sections are outstanding economists who have selected as authors for the series some of the finest specialists in the world.

*J. Lesourne*                                         *H. Sonnenschein*

# Long-Term Control of Exhaustible Resources

PIERRE LASSERRE

*Département des sciences économiques,*
*Université du Québec à Montréal*

## INTRODUCTION

Natural resources, especially exhaustible and non-renewable ones, have understandably always been a matter of concern to economists, politicians and even philosophers. Over time, this attention has taken various forms and experienced spurs of intense controversy alternating with periods of relative calm.

Resources have been important dimensions of economic development and the shaping of history. Major population movements have often been explained by economic considerations, in particular the availability of certain resources. Key steps in the development of modern economies have usually taken place in conjunction with the exploitation of some crucial natural resource while the realization of such dependency prompted the intellectual developments which shaped the discipline now known as natural-resource economics.

While early economists such as the mercantilists were keenly aware of the importance of adequate supplies, natural resources, in fact basically the issue of food supply, were first given a truly specific treatment with the work of Malthus, Ricardo, and Mill. Non-renewable resources only became the focus of much attention when Jevons raised The Coal Question (1865). If the British industrial revolution was made possible by the availability of coal as a source of energy, what was to be expected when coal reserves were to run out? Similar issues were to be raised recurrently during the following decades, the most recent version dating back to the recent oil crisis.

This monograph is concerned with the modern theory of non-renewable resource exploitation and its empirical implications. This is

1

a very broad and rich area; it is impossible to do it justice within sensible space constraints. The necessary compromise between completeness and depth of coverage is reflected in the organization of the monograph. Two basic sections, one theoretical, one empirical, provide a broad coverage of most important issues. The approach is analytical and formalized, but technical details are left out whenever they do not contribute to the understanding of a question. Then there are three additional sections, which cover specific areas in more detail. The choice of these areas was motivated by various considerations. In the case of Section 3, on joint products and the environment, it is the desire to put more emphasis on a subject and on methodologies that have not received enough attention in the literature. In the case of Section 4, on trade and the macroeconomy, I want to underline both the extensive work done to deal with natural-resource considerations, and the limits of current knowledge and approaches in that respect. Finally, in the case of Section 5, on resource taxation, the idea is to provide a unified and organized treatment of an area which is both very rich and difficult to approach without guidance.

Exhaustibility was one dimension of Jevons' concern. This dimension constitutes a major facet of modern resource economics, one often associated with the name of Hotelling. However growing scarcity is also manifest in the substitution of lower quality, or more costly, supply sources for the disappearing ones. This notion of Ricardian scarcity is also fundamental in the discipline. Section 1 starts by presenting the Hotelling and the Ricardian view and goes on contrasting their implications for the individual mine. The notion of economic reserves, the concept and desirability of exhaustion are then examined, and various complications are introduced: aggregation, exploration, as well as sectoral extraction and price. This may give the impression that exhaustible resource economics is a very specific area, one very remote from standard microeconomics. Quite the contrary, it is solidly rooted into the standard apparatus, as indicated by a discussion of welfare, competition, stability, and the issue of growth and survival. However, while standard economic theorems usually survive their transposition to a resource context, exhaustibility often affects the results in surprising ways. At first competition looks like monopoly; then it is found that monopoly does not differ from competition in the same way as in the standard analysis. In all cases, the analysis has to be dynamic and this is perhaps the main specificity of resource economics.

This emphasis on dynamic properties carries through to the empirical implications and tests of the theory, presented in Section 2. They fall into two broad categories, each corresponding to specific questions. First, is resource scarcity an issue? How can scarcity be measured? Are scarcity rents observable and what is their importance? Second, if scarcity is indeed an issue, do the dynamics of prices and rents conform to the predictions of the theory? The answer to this question should be easy to check. It is not, because it turns out that the predictions of the theory are clear-cut only under highly restrictive assumptions. As a result, many tests can be interpreted as tests of these assumptions rather than the fundamentals of the theory; the evidence is very ambiguous.

The three sections on special topics are very different from each other. Section 3, on joint products, starts with an analysis of joint production from composite reserves. This is not only empirically relevant: copper is most frequently associated with gold, and oil with gas. But joint production is also a natural way to approach environmental issues: smoke is produced as a by-product of many activities. Furthermore, the economics of non-renewable resources apply well to environmental issues. As argued later in the section, the environment can be viewed as finite, and its management as the mirror image of a mining problem: that of filling up a mine of finite capacity instead of removing material from it. While this brings up the dynamic aspects of external effects, the standard static approach may also be enlightening, as illustrated by the analysis of transnational pollution which closes the section.

Section 4, on trade and macroeconomic issues, starts with a clarification on the implications of trade for survival. Then it surveys the extensions of trade theory to resource contexts; despite considerable efforts trade theory remains unable to handle the most interesting issues raised by exhaustible resources. The literature on the Dutch desease, the major incursion of macroeconomics into natural resources, is also surveyed in the section. Here one finds that there was no attempt to incorporate the dynamics of resource constraints into the analysis, which remains basically static. The natural resource is treated as any other sector experiencing a real shock and motivates the comparative static analysis of that shock.

Section 5 deals with resource taxation. Taxation has been recognized as a very important aspect of resource exploitation, in part because the tax function doubles with that of collecting resource rents. An abundant literature studies the effects of numerous taxes; unlike the previous topic, it emanates from the resource literature directly. However, because it is technically involving and lacks uniformity in both methodology and areas of relevance, it is of difficult access to the non-specialist. While not devoid of technical difficulties, the treatment presented in Section 5 is progressive and uniform, starting with the effect of a royalty on a simple Hotelling mine and finishing, before turning to general equilibrium considerations, with a firm which holds heterogeneous reserves, is involved in exploration activities, and uses capital. This should leave the reader with a good understanding of both results and methodology.

*Acknowledgement* The author gratefully acknowledges financial support by the Université de Montréal, the Fonds FCAR pour l'aide et le soutien à la recherche, and the Social Sciences and Humanities Research Council of Canada. Part of the work was done while the author was on sabbatical leave at the Sloan School, which provided a stimulating environment as well as material support. Thanks are extended to Ernie Berndt, Robert Cairns, Gérard Gaudet, Tracy Lewis, John Livernois, Michel Moreaux, Robert Pindyck, Steve Salant, Anthony Scott, Margaret Slade, Ngo Van Long, who helped shape my understanding of resource economics over the years. I owe a special debt to Robert Cairns who made highly valuable comments on this monograph.

## 1. MAJOR THEORETICAL RESULTS

### 1.1. Hotelling rule and the views of Ricardo

Although Hotelling and Ricardo are probably the most widely quoted economists when it comes to resource economics, their perceptions of important realities are widely opposed. To Hotelling (1931), exhaustibility and non-renewability are the important characteristics to emphasize. In the Ricardian view, the resource sector is heterogeneous; supply sources differ in quality and their mix in equilibrium adjusts to demand. Exhaustibility is not really an issue, although depletion may be manifest in a drop in the quality of supply sources. It should also be recognized that Hotelling and Ricardo share with other authors the paternity of the ideas attributed to them. In particular, Gray (1914) studied the case of the individual competitive nine years before Hotelling (Crabbé, 1983).

*Hotelling*

In the world of Hotelling, the economy, just like the extractive firms which compose its resource sector, is endowed at time $t$ with a finite resource stock $S(t)$ whose consumption provides utility directly or, equivalently, which can be used to produce some consumption good. At what rate should this stock be depleted and when should exhaustion occur? Should the familiar rules governing supply decisions, such as the equality of price and marginal cost, be applied? Hotelling's model produced strong results which were in sharp contrast with conventional economic wisdom. They also emphasized time and dynamic aspects. In particular, it is socially desirable that price be set above marginal cost[1] by an amount identified as the scarcity rent. This rent represents the value conferred to the resource, over and above extraction and processing costs, by the fact that it will be exhausted some day. Its reflection in the price is desirable because it slows down extraction, thus postponing exhaustion.

The finite resource stock available to society is homogeneous, which means not only that it is of uniform quality, but that it is concentrated in a single location and that any unit of it is accessible at the same constant cost. Once these assumptions are made, there is no loss in further assuming extraction costs to be zero, which produces the most extreme version of the so-called 'Hotelling rule' to be explained below.

Although Hotelling studied both the behaviour of individual extractive firms and the point of view of society as a whole, I shall consider the latter case here, and present a most simple version of the model. Society attempts to maximize a rising and concave social welfare function defined on aggregate consumption $c$, over a possibly infinite period $[0, T]$:

$$\int_O^T e^{-rt} U(c(t)) \, dt.$$

---

[1] Hotelling actually assumes marginal cost to be zero.

$r$ is the constant discount rate. $U$ is defined as the consumer surplus arising from consumption in any period; consequently, as is well known, its first derivative $U'$ is equal to the price $p(t)$. The assumption that social welfare is additively separable over time is analytically convenient but not crucial to the results. As a second convenient simplification, it is assumed that consumption is drawn from the resource stock directly and at no cost

$$c(t) = -dS/dt \text{ with } S(0) = S_o,$$

the given initial reserve stock. The current value Hamiltonian associated with this constrained maximization is

$$h(c) = U(c) - \mu c$$

where $\mu$ is the costate variable associated with $S$, expressed in current value.[2] Commonly referred to as the *Hotelling rent*, or *scarcity rent*, it measures the opportunity cost of foregoing future consumption by extracting one marginal unit of the reserve stock at the current date. As a necessary condition we have[3]

$$U'(c) = \mu \qquad \text{or} \qquad p = \mu.$$

Although the resource is free in the sense that it can be extracted at zero cost, it is not freely available in all future time periods but is scarce. As a result, $\mu$ is strictly positive for finite values of $S$, so that consumption does not occur at an infinite rate. Price is optimally set strictly above marginal cost (zero). A gap between price and extraction cost need not be interpreted as a sign that market power is being exercised. It is socially optimal, from a global point of view, for Saudi Arabia to sell oil for more than its extraction cost. By how much should price exceed marginal cost? This is another issue to be discussed further below.

A second necessary condition is

$$d\mu/dt = r\mu(t)$$

or, since $p = \mu$

$$(dp/dt)/p = r. \tag{1.1}$$

---

[2] The conventionally defined Hamiltonian is $H(c,t) = e^{-rt}U(c) - Mc$, being the costate variable associated with $S$; thus $\mu = M e^{rt}$.

[3] Time arguments are omitted where no ambiguity arises.

Price should rise at the rate of discount. This result is known as *Hotelling rule* and has raised much interest and controversy. As we shall see, it usually fails to be verified empirically. On the other hand, it has such an obvious interpretation and stems so directly from basic capital theory that economists have attempted to improve upon the model rather than discard the basic methodology which underlies Hotelling's approach.

The interpretation of Hotelling rule is indeed straightforward. In the model mineral reserves represent an asset which is costlessly stored underground. If they are to be held willfully, their return must be comparable to the return on other assets. Being otherwise unproductive, reserves must produce capital gains at the rate of interest.

Hotelling's model also clarifies the issue of exhaustion. Suppose exhaustion is to occur at a finite date $T$. Then the condition $U' = \mu = p$ must hold at $T$ in particular.

$$U'(c(T)) = p(T)$$

Suppose $c(T) = c^+$ was strictly positive. Then, by splitting $c^+$ and consuming, say $c^+/2$ at $T$ and $c^+/2$ the instant after, at $T + \epsilon$, one could achieve a higher level of total discounted utility. This is so because $U'(c^+/2) > U'(c^+)$ for any downward-sloping demand curve. Consequently, in the socially optimum program, consumption must decrease toward zero when exhaustion is near; simultaneously, price must rise toward $p(T) = U'(0)$. If $U'(0) = \infty$, with price rising at the discount rate by (1.1), this cannot occur in a finite period; but if $U'(0)$ is finite, exhaustion will occur at a finite date $T$. In other words, if a resource is so important that its demand does not vanish when its price looms very high, society will spread its consumption very thinly over time so as not to exhaust it. It is optimal to exhaust oil reserves some day (as we have already lived without oil); but if no substitute form of energy was available, it might well be desirable to avoid such an outcome. As we shall see, this idea that some resources may be more crucial than others, and the issue of survival, were addressed in more detail by several authors. Presently however let us contrast Hotelling's view with that of Ricardo.

*Ricardo*

Ricardo (1817) was not interested in exhaustible resources explicitly, although he was concerned with the finiteness of good agricultural land. In his view, food supply adjusts to growing population and wealth through the cultivation of new land areas. The best quality lands, in terms of fertility, ease of cultivation, and market proximity, are put into production first. As demand increases, lower quality lands are cultivated, so that, at any one time, lands of varying fertility and characteristics are observed to contribute to food supply. Since the best lands produce the same food as the worst ones, but at a lower cost, and since food commands a uniform price, price exceeds marginal cost on all but the least productive units. The marginal land is that unit which barely covers its costs at the going price. All other units earn *Ricardian rents* on the excess of price over cost.

Exhaustibility is clearly not an issue here, as land, in a first approximation, is renewable in the sense that it remains available for future production. Ricardo's conceptualization does translate to exhaustible non-renewable resources though. Minerals are distributed into the earth crust non-uniformly. A deposit is the combined occurrence of a high enough grade, in sufficient volume, at a depth and location which permit extraction at reasonable costs. These conditions leave room for a tremendous variety among the mineral occurrences which qualify as deposits at any one time. For some deposits, price barely meets extraction costs while some others, as the best Ricardian agricultural lands, command a substantial rent.

Thus it is clear that some resource rents are Ricardian rents, not scarcity rents in the sense of Hotelling. On the other hand, mineral deposits do get exhausted, unlike land, and this implies that any deposit may command a scarcity rent. Consequently, prices and rents must satisfy some dynamic rule, in the spirit of Hotelling rule, which reflects the capital theoretic nature of extraction decisions. The real world probably stands somewhere between the Hotelling and the Ricardian representations.

In the next sub sections, I present some of the important theoretical results which have been obtained on various issues, by studying models which will be recognized to have a Ricardian bent or a Hotelling flavour alternatively or simultaneously. The choice of issues has been dictated by empirical relevance and also the traditional preoccupations of the economic profession. Thus the social optimality of perfect competition and the validity of the first and second theorems of welfare economics, have been investigated in a world involving non-renewable resources. Competitive and monopolistic behaviour have been contrasted, both between each other and from the point of view of standard monopoly theory. The point of view of growth theorists has also been adapted to a world with non-renewable resources, with the study of such issues as survival, growth in *per capita* consumption, and the importance of technological change.

## 1.2. The individual mine

The microeconomic problem of the individual mine was formally investigated by Gray (1914) much before Hotelling published his famous paper, which can be viewed as an aggregate, sectoral, treatment of the extraction problem. Gray had actually anticipated many of the refinements introduced later in order to provide a treatment which was more in conformity with the technological and geological reality and the textbook treatment of the conventional firm. In particular, marginal cost was made a rising function of the extraction flow $R(t)$ and the resource stock was allowed to be heterogeneous.

This heterogeneity has several dimensions: mineral deposits and oil fields differ in grade, viscosity, depth, volume, shape, location, site, the types of minerals found above and inside them, etc ... While it may be physical or economic, heterogeneity implies that extraction costs vary over the extraction program for reasons other than extraction rates. One fruitful way to model this property has been to let extraction costs depend, besides output rate, on the remaining reserve stock. In its simple version the idea is that extraction becomes more costly as the deposit becomes depleted; in a more sophisticated rationalization, it is argued that the order of extraction for the various parts of a deposit is selected optimally, and optimality requires that low-cost resources be extracted first. The validity of this postulate, which is further discussed in section 1.6, should be demonstrated as part of the solution.

This approach implies a cost function of the form $C(R, S)$, with $C_s \leq 0$. Such a function was introduced by Levhari and Liviatan (1977). Thus the competitive firm maximizes the present value of revenues minus costs with cumulative extraction required to remain lower than initial reserves

$$Max \int_0^T e^{-rt} [p(t) R(t) - C(R(t), S(t))] dt$$

subject to

$$- dS/dt = R(t) \text{ with } S(0) = S_o \text{ and } S(t) \geq 0 \text{ at all dates.}$$
$$(1.2)$$

Here, $p(t)$ is treated as exogenous to the firm, and $T$ must be interpreted as the endogenous date at which the firm shuts down its operations, whether or not reserves have been exhausted. In order to rule out such complications as temporary interruptions in production, it is assumed that $p(t)$ always is high enough to cover costs and does not rise faster than at the discount rate. A sufficient condition for existence of a solution is joint convexity of $C(\cdot)$ in $R$ and $S$; however, a solution also exists if average cost is convex in $R$ and has a minimum at $\underline{R(S)}$ (Lewis, 1979). Under these assumptions, the solution must satisfy the Maximum principle, so that price equals marginal cost plus rent, a sum often called full marginal cost

$$p = \partial C(R, S)/\partial R + \mu. \qquad (1.3)$$

The rule according to which the rent rises at the interest rate is now mitigated by a correction for changes in reserve quality, as measured by the correlation between $S$ and $C$

$$d\mu/dt = r\mu + \partial C(R, S)/\partial S, \text{ or}$$

$$\mu(t) = \mu(T) e^{-r(T-t)} - \int_t^T e^{-r(s-t)} (\partial C(R, S)/\partial S) ds \qquad (1.4)$$

The rent at $t$ is the discounted rent at $T$ plus the cumulated present value of all future effects on extraction cost of extracting the marginal unit at $t$. Because it reflects quality differences in the resource, the second term is interpreted as the Ricardian component of the rent while the first one is interpreted as the scarcity component (or Hotelling rent)[4] and may vanish under some configurations.

### 1.3. Economic reserves and exhaustion

The desirability of exhausting a deposit completely is closely linked to the presence of a Hotelling rent. At $T$, by the transversality condition on $S$, either $\mu > 0$ and $S = 0$ (complete exhaustion), or $\mu = 0$

---

[4] This interpretation is more meaningful when the model is used as a sectoral model, as in Levhari and Liviatan (1977).

and $S \geq 0$ (some resource is left in the ground). In both cases, the Hamiltonian must also vanish which, combined with (1.3), implies that extraction is carried out at a terminal rate which minimizes average cost. The Hotelling component of the rent is positive and exhaustion is optimal if price exceeds minimum average cost when reserves are down to zero; in fact, at any time, the Hotelling component of the rent is the present value of that gap. This is null if, as in the alternative possibility, there exists a positive level of reserves $S(T)$ below which minimum average cost exceeds price. This criterion may be used to define economic reserves; as one expects, non-economic reserves are left in the ground at $T$, and the definition is conditional on price at $T$[5].

## 1.4. Aggregation

These results are valid in the aggregate when the Hicksian aggregation criterion applies. But according to that criterion, in order to be considered identical, firms must have identical deposits. When this is true, rents are identical in all firms $i$, so that, by (1.3), marginal costs are equalized. In general, however, $\mu^i \neq \mu^j$ and marginal costs differ across firms.

Aggregation problems are now known to be acute in the presence of non-renewable resources. Blackorby and Schworm (1984) have shown that both the model with costs that rise as aggregate reserves diminish, and the Hotelling model in which aggregate revenues depend only on aggregate extraction rate, are inconsistent with the micro-economic reality which they aim to reflect. However, the modelling approach just described has routinely been applied at the sectoral level and has shaped what is now conventional wisdom on resource extraction in the aggregate. While some authors have explicitly attempted to treat a resource industry as a set of individual mines or deposits (see Section 1.6), several major sectoral results are based on the assumption of a single reserve stock and are vulnerable to the same kind of critiques which had occupied capital theorists *ad nauseam* for two decades when some of them turned to resource economics in the early

---

[5] If price rises after $T$, the competitive mine will stay in production in such a way as to maintain economic reserves at zero; in other words, it will ensure that, for $t \geq T$, $C[\underline{R}(S), S]/R(S) = p$.

seventies. For example Schultze (1974), who first explicitely modelled the entry and exit of mines characterized by U-shaped cost curves, and worked out the resulting sector price equilibrium trajectory, assumed all firms to extract from a common reserve stock rented out to them by some central planner.

## 1.5. Exploration[6]

In the extraction model described so far, it is assumed that ultimate reserves are limited to the known existing stock. Of course this is an oversimplification, which was criticized by many, including Benzoni (1988). Discoveries keep replenishing reserves; it is not uncommon for an extractive sector to experience a rise in reserves despite extraction.

In order to give the simple extraction model some realism, one may treat reserves as inclusive of future discoveries, which are uncertain. This has given rise to a literature on 'how to eat a cake or uncertain size' (Kemp, 1976; Loury, 1978; Robson, 1979).

As a more ambitious alternative, the exploration process may be introduced explicitely. Exploration may perform a combination of three basic functions. The first, perhaps the least crucial one, is to help reduce current and future extraction costs. In the Ricardian model presented above, higher reserves mean lower costs, which would be one explanation why firms do explore and hold reserves (Pindyck, 1978b, 1980). This view has been challenged on the ground that newly discovered reserves are often more costly to extract (Cairns, 1991).

The second, and most obvious, function of exploration is to generate discoveries, so that reserves are sufficient to permit extraction at a rate compatible with demand. As it is desirable to postpone exploration expenditures for as long as possible, reserves are allowed to go down to the lowest level compatible with an acceptable risk of supply disruption before they are replenished (Arrow and Chang, 1982). The rent rises as reserves diminish, and falls upon new discoveries. Ultimate scarcity depends on the availability of exploration prospects, and Hotelling rule is modified accordingly. If exploration prospects are infinite, as in Deshmuck and Pliska (1980), long-run resource prices are not expected to rise on average. If exploration prospects are limited, an attenuated version of Hotelling rule governs resource prices

---

[6] A simple model of exploration is also presented in the chapter on taxation.

(Lasserre, 1984). They rise on average, but at a rate lower than the interest rate.

However, as a third function, exploration also provides new information about undiscovered reserves; by updating estimates of remaining reserves in the light of exploration results, the planner may improve the use of the cake of unknown size over time (Gilbert, 1979). The first and the second functions have been combined into a single model by Quyen (1989). Bayesian up-dating enriches the model substantially. At any date of exploration, the higher the amount of resource discovered, the lower the resource price after discovery, which reflects the normal reaction to lucky outcomes, but also the higher the threshold reserve level at which exploration will resume, which reflects more optimism about future prospects. A major difference with the results of Lasserre is that the realized time path of the resource price may then exhibit a diminishing trend as a result of such revisions.

### 1.6. Sectoral extraction and the behaviour of price

Treating (1.3) and (1.4) as sectoral relationships and letting $p(t) = P(R(t))$ so that aggregate demand determines the equilibrium price for any output level, one has, by differentiating (1.3) and substituting for $\mu$ and $d\mu/dt$

$$dp/dt = (\partial P/\partial R)dR/dt =$$
$$(\partial^2 C/\partial R^2)dR/dt + (\partial^2 C/\partial R\partial S)dS/dt$$
$$+ r(p - \partial C/\partial R) + \partial C/\partial S \tag{1.5}$$

or

$$(\partial P/\partial R - \partial^2 C/\partial R^2)dR/dt = (\partial^2 C/\partial R\partial S)dS/dt$$
$$+ r(p - \partial C/\partial R) + \partial C/\partial S. \tag{1.6}$$

Since $\partial P/\partial R < 0$, it is clear from (1.5) that a sufficient condition for a rising price is for extraction to decrease over time. (1.6) clarifies under which circumstances this turns out to be the case. Assuming non-diminishing marginal costs ($\partial^2 C/\partial R^2 \geq 0$), the coefficient of $dR/dt$ is negative; consequently $dR/dt$ is negative if the right-hand side of (1.6) is positive. Although marginal extraction costs are probably non-increasing in reserves ($\partial^2 C/\partial R\partial S \leq 0$) so that the first term on the right-hand side is non-negative, the term $\partial C/\partial S$, which accounts for

the heterogeneity of reserves may dominate the first two terms, implying a decreasing price trajectory in equilibrium.

Thus the presence of Ricardian characteristics mitigates Hotelling's
prediction of a net price rising at the rate of interest. If the Hotelling
component of the rent (second term on the right-hand side of (1.6) )
is small and reserves are very heterogeneous (strong third term on the
right-hand-side of (1.6) ), the price may even diminish. However, as
Slade (1982b) pointed out, if the Hotelling component is present at all,
since it rises exponentially, it is likely to start dominating the other
terms over a long enough period.

## 1.7. Multiple deposits, capital, and other complications

At the microeconomic level, the Ricardian view implies that some
deposits may be in production while some may not. But while, in the
conventional agricultural interpretation, only demand conditions
determine whether land will be in production or out of production,
supply conditions keep changing in extractive sectors. In fact, unlike
agricultural land, deposits become exhausted and supply sources must
be replaced.

Herfindahl (1967) argued that the resource should be depleted in
strict sequence, beginning with the lowest cost deposit and progressing
to the highest cost. This view is in contrast with empirical evidence;
in a partial equilibrium framework, it relies on the assumption of
constant marginal cost; in a general equilibrium framework, other
issues come under consideration. Hartwick (1978) was the first to
attempt a general treatment. Several authors have also contributed to
clarify the analysis. Generalizing the earlier work of Solow and Wan
(1977), Lewis (1982) showed that sequential order is optimal if the
resource can be converted into consumable or storable capital, while
Kemp and Long (1980c) discussed the meaning of the constant
marginal cost assumption underlying the result, in a general equilibrium growth context. Salant, Eswaran, and Lewis (1983) studied the
length of the optimal extraction path, showing in particular that
infinite time might be optimal even if the price at which demand chokes
off is finite.

There is intuitive appeal to a behaviour consisting in postponing
expenditures for as long as possible; but since full marginal cost not
only varies with output, but also includes rent, which is itself affected

by deposit size, the notion of least cost deposit must be treated cautiously. In most reasonably general cost configurations, social optimality requires simultaneous exploitation of several deposits (Cairns and Lasserre, 1986; Hung, 1986). Furthermore, Slade (1988) argues that none of the non-stochastic, theoretically-derived, order-of-extraction rules is consistent with empirical regularities in mineral-industry extraction profiles. Those regularities—a secular decline in both present-value price and average grade of ores mined, combined with a negative correlation between grade and price over the business cycle—are compatible with the predictions of Slade's model where prices are driven by a martingale process and firms hold rational expectations.

It is not clear that this literature provides much more information on theoretical resource price paths than the aggregate model of Levhari and Liviatan presented above; however, most models (see, e.g. Hanson, 1980; Hung, 1986) predict price to rise, at a rate lower than the discount rate, and conclude that situations of declining resource prices are either impossible or exceptional. One such exception occurs when firms have to build up capacity in order to produce (Puu, 1977; Campbell, 1980; Kemp and Long, 1984a; Gaudet, 1983; Lasserre, 1985a); in such circumstances, Cairns and Lasserre (1986) show that young resource sectors may be characterized by decreasing prices, although prices sooner or later will be on a rising trend. They also show that rigid capacities may cause short-run swings around a rising long-run trend, a widely empirically observed phenomenon which was studied by Slade (1982a; 1988). Another benefit of keeping track of individual firms within a sector has been to point to the variety of individual behaviours and circumstances which may coexist in a resource sector. Firms may be out of production because they have exhausted their reserves or because they delay production; when they produce, their output may be increasing or decreasing irrespective of what happens to sectoral output[7]. Finally, oligopoly situations may result in simultaneous extraction even when social optimality requires a strict sequence. Although they do not address that issue explicitly, several of the oligopoly models presented in Section 1.12 illustrate this phenomenon.

---

[7] In fact this Ricardian analysis of sectoral production has led some authors to modify the conventional treatment of the individual mine to take account of quality variations within individual deposits (Krautkraemer, 1989; Cairns, 1986).

Closely related to the Ricardian view is the treatment of resource substitutes. Nordhaus (1973) first coined the term of 'backstop' technology to refer to a technology which can be introduced as a substitute for a less expensive one. The existence of that technology puts a ceiling on the price which can be asked for the less expensive source. For example, in Figure 1.3, if $p$ is the price of oil, $p^{max}$ may be the price of nuclear energy. The backstop technology is usually considered to be reproducible; however, it can be an alternative exhaustible resource, as when coal is considered an alternative to oil. In fact, Nordhaus provided a world model of energy supply with an estimation of the order, dates, and prices of introduction of alternative supply sources into the third millennia. While Nordhaus' model was more empirical and heuristic than analytical, his basic idea stimulated much theoretical work. In all those papers, a single natural resource is available in finite amount and must eventually be replaced by a reproducible alternative. In the early versions (e.g. Hoel, 1978), the reserve stock is known, the cost of the alternative source is known and constant, and competitive or monopolistic behaviours are envisaged. In more recent contributions, the authors have relaxed one or several of those assumptions. Alternative market structures and strategic behaviours were considered by Salant (1979), Stiglitz and Dasgupta (1982), Hoel (1983), and Hung *et al.* (1984); the size of reserves, the cost of producing the substitute, or the date of the discovery which is to make it available, were treated as uncertain or endogenous (Kemp and Long, 1982a). Reinganum and Stockey (1985) treated the research for the substitute as a racing game while Swierzbinski and Mendelsohn (1989) focused on the implications of the fact that firms measure such relevant data as the cost of a substitute with endogeneous precision.

## 1.8. Welfare, competition, and stability

From a welfare point of view, exploiting a non-renewable resource is a problem of allocating a finite stock of a commodity between competing uses at different dates. As is well known, the competitive equilibrium in such an intertemporal set-up yields an efficient allocation provided, among other conditions, a complete set of forward markets exists. If agents can trade the resource now for all future dates, they have the necessary information to compute the value of using one unit of the resource at one particular date relative to some other date. But this is precisely the information required to compute $\mu$ in a formula such as (1.3). Although the presence of a wedge between price and marginal cost does not fit the usual description of an efficient equilibrium, (1.3) is clearly a necessary condition for efficiency since it has been obtained as a first-order condition for competitive profit maximization. In fact the apparent contradiction is easily reconciled when the rent is recognized to be part of the marginal cost, as it measures the cost, in terms of lost future revenues, of using one marginal unit of reserves.

While the detailed implications of adapting the intertemporal Walrasian framework to a world involving non-renewable resources have been investigated and described well (see, e.g. Dasgupta and Heal, 1979, chapters 4 and 8; de La Grandville, 1980), the real question is whether 'the absence of futures and risk markets is any more serious for the intertemporal allocation of natural resources than it is, say, for the allocation of investment' (Stiglitz, 1974b). One major difference which comes to one's mind is the fact that, while errors in the capital accumulation programme can be corrected at some cost, extraction decisions are irreversible and may have very costly consequences if mistakes are discovered too late. The issues of long-run stability and short-run adjustment become crucial from that point of view.

In the absence of a complete set of forward markets, firms will make extraction decisions according to a modified version of (1.5) where the price $p$ and the inverse demand function $P$ must be interpreted as expectations[8]. Similarly, $\mu$ must be interpreted as the expected value of the rent. The issue of stability can be illustrated as follows. Consider the dynamic system [(1.2); (1.3); (1.4)]; as discussed earlier, this system may alternatively imply ultimate exhaustion (presence of a positive Hotelling's component in the rent) or a strictly positive stock of reserves may be left in the ground at $T$ (the strictly Ricardian case); let us focus on the second possibility. A momentary equilibrium is a situation where expectations are fulfilled; assume that such is the case in (1.2)–(1.4) so that $\mu$ represents both the actual and the expected rent which will be treated as a price. It is easily shown that the dynamic system has a steady-state, long-run, equilibrium ($S^* = S(T); \mu^* = 0$) where extraction has stopped. This steady state reflects the transversality

---

[8] This assumes that the modified, stochastic, problem admits (1.5) as a certainty equivalent form. Although this is not the case in general, more generality in this context would only obscure the treatment of the problem.

conditions discussed earlier (Section 1.3). Indeed $S^*$ is the reserve level below which the minimum unit extraction cost exceeds the price; it is optimal to leave the remaining reserves in the ground forever and, accordingly, to assign a value of $\mu^* = 0$ to the marginal reserve unit. Let us characterize the behaviour of the dynamic system in a neighbourhood of the steady state equilibrium, that is to say in situations which may be considered delicate, as the resource is about to become too costly to extract, hence unavailable.

In the tradition initiated by Hahn (1966), it has been argued by Stiglitz (1974a) and Dasgupta and Heal (1974, 1979) that the sequences of momentary equilibria which satisfy (1.2), (1.3), and (1.4) may have catastrophic outcomes: only one such sequence is socially optimal, but they all satisfy short-run efficiency conditions; as a result, competition with incomplete futures markets may allow society to pick a sequence of momentary equilibria which involves excessive resource consumption with no warning being given by the price system. As we shall see, the pessimism of those authors may be exaggerated.

With competition insuring that (1.3) holds, the supply of resource is $R = R(\mu, S)$, with

$$\partial R/\partial \mu = 1/(P' - \partial^2 C/\partial R^2) < 0;$$

$$\partial R/\partial S = (\partial^2 C/\partial R \partial S)/(P' - \partial^2 C/\partial R^2) > 0\,[9].$$

The isoclines in Figure 1.1, noted $\Delta S = 0$ and $\Delta \mu = 0$, are derived from (1.2) and (1.4) with $R$ given by (1.3). Their slope is obtained by totally differentiating (1.1.) and (1.4) to get

$$d\mu/dS|_{\Delta S = 0} = -\partial^2 C/\partial R \partial S > 0. \tag{1.7}$$

$$d\mu/dS|_{\Delta \mu = 0} = \tag{1.8}$$

$$- [\partial^2 C/\partial S^2 + (\partial^2 C/\partial R \partial S)\partial R/\partial S]/[r + (\partial^2 C/\partial R \partial S)\partial R/\partial \mu)]$$

$$= A(d\mu/dS|_{\Delta S = 0}) \quad \text{where}$$

$$A = [(P' - \partial^2 C/\partial R^2)\,(\partial^2 C/\partial S^2)/(\partial^2 C/\partial R \partial S)^2 + 1]/$$

$$[r(P' - \partial^2 C/\partial R^2)/(\partial^2 C/\partial R \partial S) + 1].$$

---

[9] Since $\partial^2 C/\partial R \partial S$ is negative under the assumption that marginal cost is lower, the higher are the reserves.

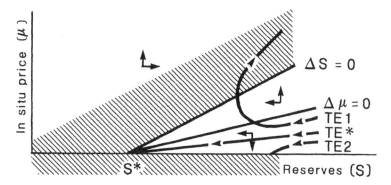

FIGURE 1.1 The dynamics of reserve stock and price in temporary equilibrium.

It is easily verified that $A < 1$; as a result, $d\mu/dS|_{\Delta\mu=0} < d\mu/dS|_{\Delta S = 0}$ as represented in Figure 1.1[10].

In Figure 1.1, the direction of changes in $S$ and $\mu$ on either sides of the isoclines are represented by horizontal and vertical arrows, respectively. Those are determined by checking the sign of the partial derivative of the right-hand side of (1.2) and (1.4) with respect to $\mu$, still with $R$ given by (1.3).

$$\partial(dS/dt)/\partial\mu = -\partial R/\partial\mu > 0$$

$$\partial(d\mu/dt)/\partial\mu = r + (\partial^2 C/\partial R\partial S)(\partial R/\partial\mu) > 0.$$

On any temporary equilibrium sequence, such as $TE1$ or $TE2$, $S$ and $\mu$ move in the direction indicated by those arrows. It can be seen that only one such sequence leads to the steady state equilibrium. Since this equilibrium is also a necessary condition for optimality, it follows that all temporary equilibrium sequences other than $TE*$ are suboptimal.

Stiglitz, Dasgupta, and Heal have argued on those grounds that perfect competition without future markets, although it implies efficiency in the short run, is not likely to lead to efficiency in the long run. Quite the contrary, catastrophic mistakes are to be expected. A closer look at Figure 1.1 does not corroborate such an alarmist view.

---

[10] The case where $\Delta\mu$ has a negative slope is easily ruled out; it implies that it is optimal to leave valuable resources in the ground for ever, or that valuable resources are given a negative price.

First note that even in the most hopelessly myopic world, the hatched regions in Figure 1.1 are ruled out: the region above $\Delta S = 0$ because, there, $S$ is increasing as if oil were pumped back into the ground; all other hatched regions because they involve negative values for either $S$ or $\mu$. This leaves only two types of erroneous temporary equilibrium sequences: that illustrated by $TE1$ and that illustrated by $TE2$. Suppose the myopic economy is on $TE1$. It follows that path until it gets some unambiguous indication to do otherwise. This message arrives when $TE1$ is about to cross the $\Delta S = 0$ isocline: continuing on along $TE1$ would involve negative extraction. Since $S$ is higher than $S^*$ at that point, the remaining reserves are still worth extracting, minimum average cost being below price, and people realize that $\mu$ had been too high. A downward revision puts the economy on a path closer to $TE^*$; no catastrophe has occurred and the cost of the mistake is simply to have been too conservative over a period. Suppose now that the myopic economy operates along $TE2$ instead. Here, a warning occurs when the path reaches the horizontal axis, so that $\mu$ is about to become negative. Again, at that point, $S$ is higher than $S^*$; anybody realizes that it is inadequate to observe a price of zero for reserves that can be extracted at a cost which is below price. Somehow $\mu$ is revised upward and the economy continues on along some new path above $TE2$. No catastrophe has occurred in the sense that the warning was given before reserves were depleted; the cost of the mistake was to use the resource too thriftlessly over some period.

   Why does this analysis lead to far less pessimistic an interpretation than earlier ones? This is yet another aspect of the Ricardian–Hotelling dichotomy. The case which was just examined is the Ricardian version of the general model. A similar analysis for Hotelling's polar case shows that the myopic economy does not receive any unambiguous warning until reserves are exhausted[11]. This holds true for simple one-factor models such as the one used here; it remains true in models involving substitution of capital for the resource as the later becomes more scarce (Dasgupta and Heal, 1979, chapter 8). To conclude, the absence of a complete set of future markets may be more damaging in the case of exhaustible resources than when the allocation of other

---

[11] The analysis is slightly different as exhaustion does not occur as a steady state equilibrium in the Hotelling case.

durable goods is concerned. This is more likely to be the case when the resource is highly homogeneous (Hotelling type) than when it occurs in a variety of qualities (Ricardian type) because suboptimal sequences of temporary equilibria may go undetected in the former case until the resource has been exhausted. Even then, as Solow (1974a) has pointed out, the type of myopia which causes this result is so extreme that it needs to be qualified. In reality economic agents do observe other indicators than prices; excessive rates of depletion are likely to be detected, and $\mu$ to be adjusted accordingly, before their consequences become too serious. Solow used the very instability of resource markets as another argument in favour of his moderate interpretation. He pointed out to the instability of the market for resource flows, the market which was assumed to be in (temporary) equilibrium in the above analysis. Indeed suppose that $p$ does not rise fast enough so that (1.5) and, equivalently, (1.2) are out of equilibrium. Holders of reserves want to get rid of an asset which produces insufficient capital gains; by selling more of the resource, they deplete the price, further aggravating the temporary disequilibrium. Such a runaway from resources is enough of a signal for not-so-myopic agents to realize that $\mu$ had been overvalued in the previous temporary equilibrium sequence and to write off part of their reserves as capital losses: the revision that was called for in the extraction programme thus occurs before such a signal as extraction stoppage is observed.

In fact such adjustments, which break the sequence of temporary equilibria, may be one of the reasons why empirical verifications of Hotelling's price rule and its variants have not been very conclusive (Chapter 2). While central to the operation of any market involving valuable durable and storable goods, they are largely determined by market anticipations. Indeed as Salant and Henderson (1978), and Salant (1983), have shown, this is why attempts to control prices on such markets are vulnerable to speculative attacks.

### 1.9. Other imperfections

With the above qualifications, the absence of perfect futures markets has been shown to cause problems in resource sectors. This market incompleteness should not lead one to ignore other types of market imperfections encountered in the exploitation of non-renewable resources. Some occur because property rights are imperfectly defined.

For example some oil deposits are jointly owned by many agents. This has caused problems of too rapid extraction in Texas and California, and required public regulation. Property rights problems are not limited to known reserves. The allocation of exploration rights, and the extent to which subsequent reserves belong to their discoverers, raise complex issues with both allocative and distributive implications. Since the solution of those problems usually involves public intervention, they are exacerbated in areas where jurisdictional rights are poorly or incompletely defined, such as the oceans and space, and when particular information difficulties arise, as when extraction is accompanied by pollution, or when costly exploration information cannot be appropriated readily.[12]

## 1.10. Growth and survival

If scarcity types, i.e. the mix of Ricardian and Hotelling characteristics, affect the consequences of mistakes in resource management, it should not come as a surprise that the future of our economies depends on both their type of resource endowment and the way they utilize them. This has led some authors to investigate such notions as the importance of resources, and their role in the growth and survival of an economy. Some resources such as energy are clearly essential; the disappearance of some others may go almost unnoticed. While oil is a very important commodity it is clearly not indispensable as humanity has lived without it for most of its existence. Let aggregate output $Y$ be defined by the production function $G(L, K, R, X)$, where $L$ and $K$ represent the services of capital and labour, respectively, while, as before, $R$ represents the flow of resource used as input in aggregate production. $X$ is a variable which accounts for Ricardian characteristics of the resource: as cumulated extraction increases, extraction costs rise so that net aggregate output is reduced. Here, for analytical convenience, $X$ is defined as the inverse of cumulated extraction

$$X(t) = 1 / \int_o^t R(s)ds, \qquad (1.9)$$

---

[12] For general, but more detailed, treatments of those issues, see Eswaran and Lewis (1984a), the appropriate chapters in Fisher (1981), or Hartwick and Oleweiler (1986); for an emphasis on risk and uncertainty, see Dasgupta (1982); for an emphasis on environmental issues, see Tietenberg (1985), Kneese (1984), Johanson (1987). On the role of information in exploration, see Dodds and Bishop (1983).

so it can be interpreted as a stock input whose level tends to zero if cumulated extraction tends to infinity; $\partial G/\partial X \geq 0$, with equality in the pure Hotelling case.

If $G(L, K, O, X) > 0$, the resource may be useful, but it is not necessary for production. This may represent the case of copper and oil, but probably not that of energy in general, nor that of water. So assume $G(L, K, O, X) = 0$ in order to focus on the most important and difficult cases. Since this is an aggregate technology, zero production actually means death; so it is reasonable to assume that society will be willing to pay a very high price for the marginal unit of resource when $R$ is close to zero: the value of $\partial G(L, K, O, X)/\partial R$ is infinite. For the Ricardian model of resources, this implies that price will always meet extraction costs. If the resource is available in infinite supply, an important issue becomes whether extraction costs rise at a low enough rate that the economy is able to substitute capital for the resource in such a way as to maintain a non-vanishing level of consumption when $X$ tends to zero. If the resource stock is finite, it is not optimal to leave any amount of it in the ground (the economy has Hotelling's characteristics). But since the resource is necessary for production, it is not optimal to exhaust it in any finite period. Again the question is whether it is possible for the economy to substitute capital for the resource in such a way that consumption of the finite stock can be spread over an infinite period while maintaining a non-trivial consumption level forever.

As Dasgupta and Heal (1979, p. 199) have argued, the simplest laboratory in which to explore such questions is the CES production function[13]

$$G(L, K, R, X) = \{\beta_1 f(L, K, R)^\pi + \beta_2 X^\pi\}^{1/\pi}$$

where $\pi = (\sigma_x - 1)/\sigma_x$, $\sigma_x$ being the elasticity of substitution between the input aggregator $f(L, K, R)$ and $X$, while $\beta_1$ and $\beta_2$ must be non-negative and sum to one. This formulation can be interpreted as follows. Net output $Y = G(\cdot)$ is obtained by allocating some of $L$, $K$ and $R$ to aggregate production and the rest to the production of $R$; given a target level of R the quantity of inputs devoted to its production

---

[13] Kemp, Long, and Shimomura (1984) approach the issue of survival without parameterizing the technology, and with several resources, non-nul extraction costs, and technological change. Kemp and Long (1984b) extend the analysis to account for situations where a country does not have control of the finite resource stock.

depends on the level of $X$: the lower $X$ (i.e. the higher cumulated extraction), the more inputs are necessary for resource production, and the higher the cost. In that sense, a drop in $X$ can be interpreted as degradation at the Ricardian margin; the easiness with which this degradation can be offset by increases in the use of other inputs is measured by $\sigma_x$. It is reasonable to assume that $\sigma_x$ is smaller than unity because, otherwise, it is possible to produce a strictly positive output without using any amount of $L$, $K$, or $R$, provided $X$ is strictly positive[14]. Besides substitution at the Ricardian margin, which may help maintain the level of $R$, inputs can be substituted for $R$ and $R$ can be allowed to diminish. Because the cost or quality of $R$ are irrelevant to this second type of adjustment, it can be recognized to represent a substitution at the Hotelling margin. Its easiness depends on substitution elasticities within $f(\cdot)$.

As a particular case, if $\beta_2 = 0$, then $G(\cdot) \equiv f(\cdot)$; if furthermore $S$ is finite so that $X$ must always exceed a strictly positive level $\underline{X}$, we have the pure Hotelling case which has been analyzed by Dasgupta and Heal (1979), following Solow (1974b) and Stiglitz (1974b). They take $f(\cdot)$ to be a linearly homogeneous C.E.S. function

$$f(L, K, R) = \{\alpha_1 K^\eta + \alpha_2 R^\eta + \alpha_3 L^\eta\}^{1/\eta}$$

where $\eta = (\sigma_R - 1)/\sigma_R$, $\sigma_R$ being the elasticity of substitution between $K$ and $R$; $\alpha_i > 0$, $\Sigma \alpha_i = 1$. Normalizing $L$ to one, one has

$$F(K, R) = \{\alpha_1 K^\eta + \alpha_2 R^\eta + \alpha_3\}^{1/\eta}. \tag{1.10}$$

If $\sigma_R > 1$, $F(K, 0) > 0$: the resource is not necessary for production. If $\sigma_R < 1$, the Hotelling economy is doomed[15]. It is not surprising that the ease with which capital can be substituted for resource flows determines the fate of the economy and the importance of the resource to its survival. What is more striking is the fact that the limiting case arises when the elasticity is one, when the technology is Cobb-Douglas[16]. Here again we have clear-cut results due to Solow: If $\alpha_1$, the share of

---

[14] In fact if $\sigma_x \geq 1$, $f(\cdot)^\pi = 0$ when $f(\cdot) = 0$, so that $Y = \beta_2 X \geq 0$. This could represent the case of an amenity resource such as the environment in general, which can be depleted to help produce manufacturing goods, but also produces amenity services if left untouched.

[15] Indeed it can be shown in that case that productivity tends to a finite value as $R$ tends toward zero; as a result production, hence consumption, must eventually decline to zero.

[16] For a defence of the Cobb-Douglas function in this context, see Kemp and Long (1980a)

capital in aggregate income, exceeds $\alpha_2$, the share of the resource, the resource, although *necessary* for production, is not *essential* for survival of the economy. Capital can be substituted fast enough for production eventually to require only minute amounts of $R$ in such a way as never to exhaust reserves. If instead $\alpha_2 > \alpha_1$, the economy is doomed. In fact casual empiricism suggests that the first alternative prevails: data on factor shares indicate that $\alpha_2$ is about 5% while the share of capital is around 20%.

These optimistic results apply to Hotelling-type economies. However, aggregate resource economies have definite Ricardian characteristics and the use of lower quality resources constitute yet another way to alleviate resource constraints on production. Let us assume $\beta_2 > 0$ in order to consider this possibility. First, remember that if $S$ is finite, we have a mixed Hotelling/Ricardian economy: although non-homogeneous, $S$ will be exhausted completely. The problem turns out to be entirely similar to that of a pure Hotelling economy: survival is a matter of being able to produce a non-trivial amount of $F(\cdot)$ when $R$ tends to zero. All the above results remain valid.

Consider the pure Ricardian case now, where $S$ is infinite so that $X$ tends to zero. By assumption, $\sigma_x \leq 1$. If $x < 1$, increases in $F(\cdot)$ will not be able to offset the fact that $X$ tends to zero[17]. So the fact that the economy is Ricardian will not release it from the necessity to substitute $K$ for $R$ as in the Hotelling economy. This leaves $\sigma_x = 1$ as limiting case, which is investigated by Lasserre (1989) under the assumption that substitution of capital for resource flows at the Hotelling margin would not be sufficient to avoid disappearance of the economy. Through adjustment at the Ricardian margin, it turns out that the catastrophic outcome predicated under that assumption for the Hotelling economy can be avoided. A necessary and sufficient condition for survival in that case is

$$\beta_2 \leq \alpha_1 \beta_1. \tag{1.11}$$

This means that the share of resource stock services in aggregate income must not exceed the combined share of all other inputs, $K$, $L$, and $R$, times the proportion of capital in the expenditures on those inputs.

---

[17] In order to see this, write $G(\cdot)$ as $Y^\pi = \{\beta_1 F(K, R)^\pi + \beta_2 X^\pi\}$ and divide by $X^\pi$ to get $(Y/X)^\pi = \beta_1 (X/F(K, R))^{-\pi} + \beta_2$, with $-\pi > 0$. It follows that, when $X$ tends to zero, $\lim Y = \lim \beta_2^{1/\pi} X = 0$.

TABLE 1.1    Survival with Exhaustible Resources

| Substitution of K for R | Share of K relative to R | Pure Hotelling Case S finite, $\beta_2 = 0$ | Mixed Case S finite, $\beta_2 > 0$ | | Pure Ricardian Case S infinite, $\beta_2 > 0$ | |
|---|---|---|---|---|---|---|
| | | | Substitution of other inputs for reserves | | | |
| | | | easy ($\sigma_X > 1$) | difficult ($\sigma_X < 1$) | $\sigma_X = 1$ | easy ($\sigma_X > 1$) |
| Easy ($\sigma_R > 1$) | Irrelevant | RESOURCE NOT NECESSARY | | | | |
| $\sigma_R = 1$ | $\alpha_2 < \alpha_1$ | Resource necessary but inessential | Resource necessary but inessential | | | |
| | $\alpha_2 \geqslant \alpha_1$ | economy is doomed | economy is doomed | | | Res. inessent. if $\beta_2 < \alpha_1 \beta_1$ |
| Difficult ($\sigma_R < 1$) | Irrelevant | | | | | |

Table 1.1 provides a recapitulation of survival conditions for a resource economy. Even if one abstracts from the cases where the resource is trivially non-necessary, it does not appear likely that resource constraints will cause our economies to disappear. Capital can be substituted for resource flows in aggregate production; capital can also be used to offset the rise in extraction costs in a Ricardian economy. Survival is certain if the elasticity of substitution exceeds unity on either of those two margins; the economy is doomed if elasticities are lower than unity on both margins; in the limiting Cobb-Douglas cases, survival is possible if either the share of expenditures on $R$, or the share of the rental cost of $X$, is not too high relative to the appropriate shares of capital[18]. This analysis has been carried out while abstracting from several important considerations. Among those are population growth and technological change. Here again intuition has been aided by Stiglitz (1974b)'s simplified analysis of the Cobb-Douglas, pure Hotelling, case: the rate of resource augmenting technological change at least must be equal to the rate of population growth times the share of natural resources.

## 1.11. Monopoly

Because nature restricts the number of supply sources of several non-renewable resources, and because it also imposes their location, thus making the entry game less sophisticated, market power is perhaps more likely to be observed in resource sectors than in other areas of economic activity. On the other hand, while no other source of oil is as cheaply accessible as Middle Eastern oil, several alternative deposits are available at higher costs, as in the Ricardian version of the theoretical model developed above. To this limitation to market power, one must add the stock nature of extractive resources: when a monopoly restricts supply in any given period, it raises the reserve stock it will hold during subsequent periods, which amounts to increasing its own supply over those periods. In that sense, a resource monopoly competes with itself over time.

---

[18] Data on aggregate shares suggest that those conditions are met. For the more complex Ricardian model introduced here, the presence of two margins makes the calculation of shares more difficult. In particular, since $X$ is the inverse of cumulated extraction, it reflects the stock of existing and potential reserves. The calculation of its rental cost requires data on the value of that stock; for an attempt at evaluating it, see Boskin *et al.* (1985).

The detection of monopolistic behaviour is also more difficult in resource sectors: as shown above (1.3), competitive profit maximizing requires that price be higher than marginal cost by the amount of the resource rent. As a result (Pindyck, 1987; Cairns, 1990b), standard measures of market power such as the Lerner index have to be modified.

Attitudes toward monopolistic behaviour have also been somewhat different in the case of non-renewable resources. First monopolistic behaviour has often been adopted by nations rather than private companies. This is often considered socially more acceptable, especially when those nations belong to the Third World. Second, and more important, as a monopoly restricts supply, it may be perceived as an objective ally by conservationists. Finally, and somewhat in contradiction with the last argument, resource monopolists to some extent have been described as powerless because, as mentioned above, they have to compete with themselves over time. As will be shown now, some of those attitudes are based on misunderstandings.

The Ricardian/Hotelling dichotomy can be usefully carried over to the analysis of the resource monopoly. For simplicity however, I will follow the lead of Hotelling, choosing to assume nul or constant marginal extraction costs and further assuming that reserves are homogeneous and finite. Let the inverse demand be $p = P(R, t)$ and marginal revenue be $m = \partial[P(R, t)R]/\partial R = \gamma p$, where $\gamma = (1 - 1/\epsilon)$, $\epsilon$ being the elasticity of demand. For a monopoly which maximizes the present value of its net revenue stream $\int_0^T e^{-rt} P(R, t) R dt$ subject to $\int_0^T R(t) dt \le S(0)$

$$m = \mu^m \qquad (1.12a)$$

and

$$(dm/dt)/m = r \qquad (1.12b)$$

where $\mu^m$ is the resource rent, as determined by the monopoly. If, instead, the sector was competitive, the following special versions of (1.3) and (1.4) would have to hold

$$p = \mu^c \qquad (1.13a)$$

and

$$(dp/dt)/p = r. \qquad (1.13b)$$

Thus, for a monopoly, marginal revenue, rather than price, is set equal to the rent (plus marginal cost if the latter is non-nul); under both monopoly and competition rent rises at the rate of interest, but the monopoly rent is not equal to the competitive rent in general.

Combining (1.12b) with the definition of $m$

$$(dm/dt)/m = (dp/dt)/p + ((d\gamma/dt)/\gamma = r \qquad (1.14)$$

it follows that price rises at the same rate under monopoly and competition if $d\gamma/dt = 0$, i.e. if the elasticity of demand is constant. If it is constant over the whole demand schedule, then price and output are identical under both market structures because, of all possible price trajectories which follow an exponential path, only one will imply an extraction path which exactly uses up the resource stock when taken over an infinite period[19].

This paradoxical result – that, under some circumstances, a resource monopoly behaves like a competitive firm – is due to Stiglitz (1976). It has been widely accepted and often interpreted to mean that monopoly was perhaps less of a nuisance in resource sectors than in conventional activities. Recently, Gaudet and Lasserre (1988) have argued that this interpretation was in fact a misunderstanding and that the essence of monopoly behaviour, in extractive sectors like in others, was indeed to restrict supply, in a socially damaging fashion. They first point out that a conventional monopolistic firm also behaves like a competitive one if it faces an isoelastic demand curve and produces at zero cost up to the capacity limit imposed by the presence of a fixed input: this is the textbook case of a firm facing a vertical marginal cost curve. Then they argue that Stiglitz's monopoly is the dynamic analogue of this textbook case: the monopoly faces a fixed reserve stock which works as a capacity constraint over the whole extraction period. In comparison with the textbook case, the paradox is not that the monopoly behaves like a competitive sector when demand is isoelastic; the paradox is that this seems to occur as a very special case while it is very easy to find alternative demand configurations that produce the same result in the static

---

[19] Under both market structures the extraction programme lasts forever. Suppose to the contrary that reserves are exhausted after a finite period $T$. Because demand is isoelastic, price shoots up from a finite level to infinity at $T$, and so does marginal revenue. Thus, whether it is competitive or monopolistic, the firm could have achieved higher profits by keeping some reserves at $T$ in order to take advantage of the higher price. This proves that there is no finite date at which it is optimal to exhaust.

analysis[20]. The explanation is simple: unlike its static textbook counterpart, the resource monopoly has the possibility to reallocate output over time within the limits of the overall reserve constraint. Facing an isoelastic demand, it cannot profit from doing so; but other demand configurations leave more opportunities. If anything, the resource monopoly has more possibilities to exercise market power than the conventional firm.

It is when marginal cost rises with output that monopoly and competition differ in a rich fashion. Gaudet and Lasserre go on to argue that, for Stiglitz's model, rising marginal cost may be interpreted to mean that it is more expensive to acquire large amounts of reserves than small amounts. Once endowed with the possibility to choose an initial reserve stock, the resource monopoly turns out to pick a lower quantity than a competitive firm facing identical constraints. This is true whether $S(0)$ is the result of previous exploration activities or otherwise acquired. The resource monopoly has the restrictive behaviour that can be expected from any monopoly.

Solow (1977) gives additional insights into the reasons for a monopoly to explore less. One of them is that the monopoly can be viewed as having a sort of monopsony power on the exploration side: while both exploration by a monopoly and competitive exploration will reduce the rent, the monopoly, unlike the competitive firm, is aware of that effect and acts accordingly. Another reason arises when extraction costs are affected by the level of reserves, as in Pindyck (1978a, 1980). As a monopoly produces less, this cost effect will assume less importance.

### 1.12. Duopoly and oligopoly

The problems that have made dynamic industrial organization so challenging during the past 15 years were also at the core of theoretical research in resource economics. They include the adaptation to a dynamic context of concepts which were developed in a static framework, the Cournot–Nash duopoly and the Stackelberg duopoly in particular; they include efforts to tackle such issues as commitment

---

[20] The static monopoly with a vertical marginal cost curve may elect to produce less than a competitive firm under some demand configurations. Such is the case whenever the marginal revenue curve cuts the horizontal axis at a level which does not exceed the quantity at which the marginal cost curve becomes vertical.

and dynamic consistency; they also include the synthesis of work from various origins: the link between rational expectations and dynamic consistency, the link between sub-game perfectness in game theory, and closed-loop solution concepts in dynamic programming.

A landmark contribution in resource industrial organization is Salant's (1976) paper on duopoly. In an attempt to model the world oil market, Salant assumes that supply originates from two sources: a cartelized group of identical firms or countries on one hand and a fringe of identical competitive firms or countries on the other hand. All firms operate on a common market where demand chokes off when price exceeds $p^{max}$. The focus is not on technological or geophysical differences but on behavioural differences. Thus both sectors are assumed to hold homogeneous reserves of identical accessibility: marginal extraction cost will be taken to be zero in the version presented here.

The innovative part of the paper consists in treating the two sectors as a dynamic Cournot duopoly. Unlike the static counterpart, however, the two firms are not treated symmetrically: the competitive fringe takes the price as given and adjusts production accordingly; the cartelized sector sets the price and supplies whatever quantity is requested to meet demand, given the quantity supplied by the fringe. Both actors play simultaneously, while taking the decisions of their counterpart as given; thus the equilibrium is a Nash equilibrium. However, they do so while maximizing the present value of their profits, given their reserve constraint. As explained above for the competitive firm and for the monopoly, this imposes some constraints on the price trajectory over time. In fact if the competitive fringe is currently producing

$$(dp/dt)/p = r \qquad (1.13)b$$

and similarly for the cartel

$$(dm/dt)/m = r. \qquad (1.12)b$$

While those two dynamic constraints were developed and presented above as mutually exclusive alternatives, they must hold simultaneously in the duopoly case, as long as both sectors are in production. Another crucial difference with the monopoly case has to do with the definition of m. For the cartel, marginal revenue is defined on the residual demand, as opposed to the entire demand schedule. Indexing

by 'c' (competitive) and 'm' (monopoly) the variables which are specific
to the competitive fringe and the cartel, respectively, and assuming
demand to be time autonomous, price is $P(R^c + R^m)$, residual
revenue to the cartel is $R^m P(R^c + R^m)$, so that $m$ is now defined as

$$m = P(R^c + R^m)[1 - 1/\epsilon^m]. \tag{1.15}$$

In equilibrium, three alternative patterns of production may be
envisaged: both types of firms produce simultaneously; the cartel
produces alone, or the competitive fringe produces alone. Under all
circumstances, the decision to produce, or not to produce, must be
considered optimal by each type of firm. Thus when both types
produce simultaneously, (1.12b) and (1.13b) must hold. When the
competitive fringe is not producing but holds reserves, price must be
rising at a faster rate than the discount rate: this makes it more
profitable to hold on to reserves than to produce. This case is in fact
ruled out because, if price was expected to rise at such a rate,
speculative purchases would occur, causing the price to shoot up to
a level where it could no longer be expected to rise that fast. When
the competitive fringe is not producing because it has exhausted its
resource, it must not be in a position to wish it had kept reserves
instead: the price must not rise faster than the discount rate. Similarly,
when the cartel is not in production, $m$, which is equal to price since
$R^m = 0$, must not rise faster than the discount rate. Imposing those
constraints on the alternative production configurations that can be
envisaged, it can be shown that the sole possible pattern is one where
the cartel and the fringe produce simultaneously in an initial phase,
and the cartel produces alone in a final phase. As can be seen on Figure
1.2, the cartel's marginal revenue rises smoothly at the rate $r$ over the
whole period, as would be the case if a monopoly was alone on that
market. However, $m$ is defined on the residual demand, which differs
from total demand over the first period. So there is a definite
difference, which in fact is evident in the price trajectory: price rises
at the rate $r$ as long as the competitive fringe is in production, but rises
at a lower rate once the cartel is alone on the market[21].

---

[21] If demand was isoelastic, $p$ and $m$ would rise at the same rate but exhaustion would
not occur in a finite time for either the cartel or the fringe. In fact the first phase would
last forever with the cartel and the fringe sharing a constant proportion of the market
and behaving as a truly competive industry, i.e., for that matter, as a true monopoly.

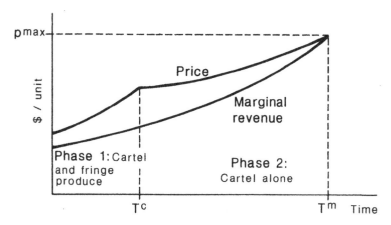

FIGURE 1.2 Price and marginal revenue in Salant's duopoly model.

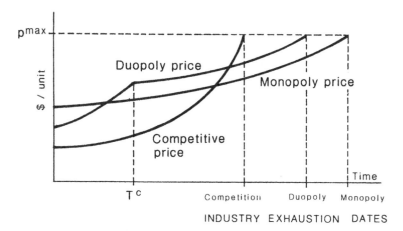

FIGURE 1.3 Price trajectories under competition, duopoly and monopoly.

In that equilibrium, the cartel, without purposely attempting to affect the quantities produced by the fringe, announces a price trajectory which induces the competitive fringe to produce, while leaving some of the demand for it to satisfy residually. At $T^c$, the cartel's market share has increased to one, so that there is no jump in $m$ when it takes over completely in the second phase. As compared with the competitive, and the monopoly, equilibrium, Salant's duopoly lies inbetween (Figure 1.3).

Industry reserves last longer than under competitive exploitation, but exhaustion occurs earlier than under monopoly. The value of the firms in the cartel is raised by the exercise of market power, but not as much as under full monopoly; furthermore, as in many static oligopoly models, firms in the fringe benefit more from the cartelization than cartel members. This leaves industry structure unexplained theoretically, although, on heuristic grounds, it is thought that cartelization is more likely to occur when it yields high private benefits than otherwise. Pindyck (1978b) compared the gains from cartelization of several exhaustible resources and found empirical justification for this belief.

Salant's model can be generalized to firms with rising, although identical, marginal costs. It retains the empirically disturbing prediction that the cartel's market share increases over time until, in a final phase, it controls the totality of the market. Although it is clear that those results might not hold in a model with exploration and entry, one may wonder whether they are not produced by the assumption that all firms have identical costs. After all Middle Eastern oil is much cheaper than North Sea oil and the latter might have been in production before the creation of OPEC, had it been less expensive to extract. Another questionable feature of Salant's model is the use of a Nash concept of equilibrium. Is it realistic to assume that a cartel will take the quantity decisions of the competitive fringe as given?

Ulph (1982) studies a similar cartel model as Salant, but adds the assumption that firms have constant marginal costs, which differ in the fringe $(C^c)$ and in the cartel $(C^m)$. When extraction costs are sufficiently lower in the cartel and initial cartel reserves are sufficiently abundant, the following pattern arises. In an initial phase, the cartel is alone on the market and sets price and quantity in such a way that $m - C^m$ rises at the rate of interest[22]; $p - C^c$ rises at a lower rate and accordingly, the fringe is not producing. When the price reaches a certain level, it becomes optimal for the fringe to enter the market and this requires $p - C^c$ to start rising at the rate of discount, which is compatible with $m - C^m$ rising at the same rate if the share of the cartel diminishes over time. So in that second phase, both the cartel and the fringe produce simultaneously, with the fringe increasing its

---

[22] With constant marginal costs, $p$ and $m$ must be replaced by $p - C^c$ and $m - C^m$ respectively in (1.12b) and (2.13b).

market share. This goes on until the cartel exhausts its reserves and the fringe produces alone, at a competitive rate, in a last phase.

While this pattern is much more compatible with empirical evidence, there is another advantage to retaining the Nash concept of equilibrium in this context. If at each and any date, the programme is interrupted and the agents are allowed to reconsider their announced trajectories, they will stick to their initial decisions, and choose to continue the programme which was selected in the first place. In control language, the open loop (no revision) and the closed loop (perpetual revision) solution concepts give the same result for this problem. The equilibrium trajectories are dynamically consistent. In the language of game theory, the Nash equilibrium just described is also sub-game perfect: the two players are not committed to their announced strategies nor to the actions (price for the cartel or quantity for the fringe) that result from the implementation of those strategies. But given the opportunity to change their minds at any date, they maintain their earlier decisions. One reason for this intertemporal consistency is that their expectations are being fulfilled: if we think now of the relevant price and quantity trajectories as of expectations held by the parties, the values taken by those variables in equilibrium as time goes by are exactly the values which were expected in the first place; this is a rational expectations equilibrium.

In contrast, when Ulph examines the Stackelberg alternative as a behavioural assumption, he finds dynamic inconsistency in some configurations. In the Stackelberg model, the leader knows that the fringe reacts to his price decisions so that, instead of taking the fringe's output as given, he takes its determination into account when choosing a price trajectory. The result is not an equilibrium in price and quantity trajectories as in the case of the Cournot–Nash duopoly[23], but the solution of the following constrained optimization problem

$$\underset{R^m(t)}{Max} \quad \int_o^T e^{-rt}[P(R^{c^*}(t) + R^m(t)) - C^m]R^m(t)\,dt$$

---

[23] A Nash equilibrium is defined as a price trajectory selected by the cartel, and a quantity trajectory selected by the fringe, such that each of those trajectories is profit-maximizing for the group which selects it, given the other side's choice.

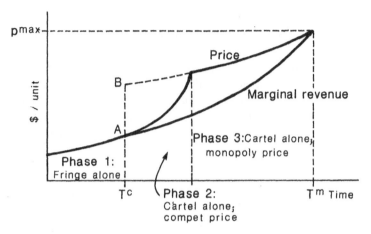

FIGURE 1.4 Price and marginal revenue of the cartel: Ulph's Stackelberg model.

subject to

$$\int_o^T R^m(t)\,dt \le S_o^m$$

$$R^{c*}(t) \text{ solves } \{Max \int_o^T e^{-rt}[p(t) - C^c]R^c(t)dt \mid \int_o^T R^c(t)dt \le S_o^c\}$$

$$p(t) = P(R^{c*}(t) + R^m(t))$$

When $C^c$ is sufficiently small relative to $C^m$ and $S_o^c$ sufficiently abundant, Ulph finds the solution to involve three phases (Figure 1.4). In the first one, the fringe produces alone and $p - C^c$ rises at the discount rate. In the second phase, the fringe has exhausted its reserves and the cartel takes over while maintaining a price policy which is a continuation of the trajectory followed in the first phase. Finally, in the last phase, the cartel adopts the pricing policy that his monopoly position on the market justifies: $m - C^m$ rises at the discount rate. Why does not the cartel adopt monopoly pricing as soon as the fringe has exhausted its reserves, at the beginning of phase 2? Because that would involve an upward jump in price, from A to B. Knowing that the price was going to jump, the firms in the fringe would not produce as described in phase 1 because they had rather keep some reserves in order to take advantage of the price rise at $T^c$. In order to induce them into exhausting early, the cartel must announce that the price trajectory of phase 2 will indeed be followed. But is this credible? Once the fringe has exhausted its reserves, nothing prevents the cartel from acting in its best interest, which is to adopt the monopoly price immediately. The solution devised at time zero is dynamically inconsistent, in the sense that it will not be continued if it is allowed to be revised during its application. Since it is not in his interest to stick to it once it has eliminated the competitive fringe, the price trajectory announced by the cartel is not credible. This is how the issue of commitment, common in game theory, also arises in the non-game-theoretic framework of the Stackelberg resource duopoly.

Resource cartels were also studied, in particular, by Ulph and Folie (1980), and Lewis and Schmallensee (1980). Newberry (1981) addressed the problem of dynamic inconsistency more specifically, while Eswaran and Lewis (1984b) provided a good discussion on alternative behavioural assumptions in resource oligopolies. Reinganum and Stockey (1981) widened the strategy space by allowing threats and punishments to defectors while Loury (1986), under the assumption of precommitment (open loop strategies) generalized the analysis to $n$ players. Understandably, his analysis has all participants play in quantities since it is no longer clear what could distinguish a cartel from the fringe when the number of non-cooperative players is high. Some interesting additional problems arise when a substitute to the resource can be introduced (Hoel, 1983; Dasgupta and Stiglitz, 1981) or when exploration and discoveries enter the picture (Hartwick and Sadorsky, 1989).

## 2. EMPIRICAL TESTS AND PRICE STUDIES

### 2.1. Reminder

At the basis of natural resource economics is the treatment of exhaustible reserves as assets. Resource prices and flows must be selected in such a way as to simultaneously equilibrate the market for resource flows and the (possibly implicit) market for reserves. As is too obvious from the previous section, that principle underlies a multiplicity of models, which in turn generate a multiplicity of predictions. This makes it extremely difficult unambiguously to test the underlying principle, as opposed to alternative features of the models built around it.

As most tests involve resource prices, a reminder of the major theoretical predictions in that respect is appropriate. Hotelling's simplest model calls for a steady rise in the net price of non-renewable resources, with interest rate being the central determinant of the growth rate. While this result holds with only slight modifications under alternative market structures, it is seriously affected when a number of important and empirically relevant complicating factors are taken into account. The price does not rise as fast when the resource is heterogeneous; U-shaped price trajectories and other patterns may arise in presence of exploration, technological change, or delays in capacity build-up, as well as changes in demand over time. In a world involving uncertainty, various forms of Hotelling rule arise, depending on the stochastic processes and the variables affected by them. While the stochastic rule is sometimes simply a version of its non-stochastic counterpart written in terms of expected values (Deshmukh and Pliska, 1980; Slade, 1988), the presence of uncertainty usually introduces complications of a much larger magnitude[24] (Pindyck, 1980; Arrow and Chiang, 1982; Lasserre, 1984a; Quyen, 1988). For those reasons, while most empirical studies in that area present themselves as tests of the Hotelling principle, they are rightly interpreted as attempts to identify the relevant empirical variables and specification for the purpose of resource price modelling, within the capital theoretic framework of Hotelling, rather than being interpreted as tests of that theory.

Besides the relevance of the capital theoretic approach to natural resource economics, Hotelling rule has been interpreted as a statement about resource scarcity. The rise in rent is indicative of rising scarcity, which is the empirical fact needing to be tested. Indeed, one of the best known early empirical studies of resources (Barnett and Morse, 1963) focuses on scarcity rather than prices *per se*. Moreover, it is based on a purely Ricardian view, implying that scarcity arises from increases in extraction costs rather than exhaustibility. The authors use two alternative measures of Ricardian scarcity: absolute productivity of

---

[24] Several empirical studies (for example Heal and Barrow, 1980; Smith, 1979; Slade, 1982; Hall and Hall, 1984) assume either implicitly or explicitly that under uncertainty the expected rate of increase of net resource price must equal the expected rate of interest.

either labour or labour and capital; and productivity in extractive sectors relative to productivity in manufacturing sectors. Within the long-run focus of their study which was based on US data for 1870–1957, they do not find any statistical support for the hypothesis of rising scarcity. In some instances, Americans have transmitted increased (lower cost) resources to subsequent generations, and productivity of extractive sectors has kept pace with productivity in manufacturing industries. If one focuses on the most recent years in their first study period, this conclusion is perhaps less solidly founded. So the study was updated (Barnett, 1979) to include the 1958–1973 period and the data base was enlarged to cover several OECD countries besides the United States. For several sectors, a change in the long-run trend seems to be occurring in the most recent years of the data base, although the new trend remains statistically insignificant.

While Barnett and Morse's study was interpreted by many as a dismissal of Hotelling's theory, other resource economists were quick to point out that it bore little relationship with that theory. Indeed, in the pure version of Hotelling's model, costs (and productivity) are constant but a scarcity rent drives a wedge between price and marginal cost. What ought to be tested is the presence of scarcity rents, as well as the behaviour of rents and prices over time.

## 2.2. Evidence on scarcity rents

The existence of rents is fairly well documented for the oil and gas industry over the last two decades. While extraction costs in the Persian Gulf region often do not exceed a few dollars for oil which is never sold below 12 dollars and has often reaped a price in the 30 dollar range, rents are also identified in other oil producing areas of the world. Even if, as argued by Devarajan and Fisher (1982), some of those rents simply remunerate previous exploration activities, rents have been shown by Lasserre (1985b) to exist on unexplored land. However, it is not clear at all that those rents are indeed scarcity rents; as argued, among others, by Pindyck (1987), much heuristic evidence suggests that they probably include a substantial monopoly component.

The evidence is even more controversial in non-oil sectors. Stollery (1983) tested the existence of resource rents in the Canadian nickel industry, after correcting for the non-competitive structure of that sector. While he found significant resource rents, his model was too crude[25] not to be open to alternative interpretations. Cairns (1986), whose own early estimations had led him to conclude that rents were negligible (Cairns, 1981) convincingly argued that Stollery's results were also consistent with a myopic model of mark-up pricing by nickel firms. In order to limit the scope for alternative interpretations, it became clear that more sophisticated models of the technology had to be tested. Besides the mere presence of rents, those models also investigated the compatibility of price and rent paths with the theory of natural resources.

### 2.3. Evidence on the behaviour of rents and prices over time

Smith (1979) studies a wide range of resource prices while controlling for such important factors as extraction costs, new discoveries, changes in market structure, and changes in the institutional environment. He finds little evidence to back Hotelling-type models and concludes that simple time series models have the best predictive power. Slade (1982), however, argues that declining price-path can be explained by technological change. Her model implies that the scarcity component in the equation describing the price path will eventually become dominant and cause the price to rise. Under sensible assumptions, this implies convex, rather than linear price trajectories. She successfully tested this property for several metals. More recently, Slade (1988) reverted to a position which is closer to that of Smith. Although the focus of her paper is grade selection rather than prices *per se*, she provides evidence that long-run copper prices appear to be generated by a martingale rather than by a process involving a rising component due to Hotelling scarcity.

Smith also devotes considerable attention to another aspect of resource price formation, which was first studied by Heal and Barrow (1980). Those authors argue that resource pricing is affected by arbitrage in asset markets, and that those markets may not exhibit the full information equilibrium assumed by simple models. In their empirical work, they find confirmation that changes in interest rates, more than their level, are important in determining metal price

---

[25] For example, Stollery used heroic assumptions to measure marginal extraction costs in a very secretive industry.

movements. This can be rationalized if there is uncertainty about future prices of resources relative to other assets. Although the supply side of their model is remote from Hotelling's — it does not take account of the depletable nature of resources — they interpret their results to confirm the importance of capital theoretic considerations in the formation of resource prices. Capital theoretic aspects, they argue, extend to other assets and, for that reason, resource prices may be expected to exhibit movements that are more complicated than the partial equilibrium model of Hotelling predicts. In a later paper, Heal and Barrow (1981) include proxies for resource depletion and cost changes, so that they claim that the simple version of the Hotelling model is nested within their model, and is rejected.

A better theoretical foundation for their model is perhaps to be found in the recent work of Gaudet and Khadr (1991) and Gaudet and Howitt (1989) who present a two-good capital-asset-pricing model of resource extraction and capital investment involving an explicit allocation of assets between resources and other types of capital, with production uncertainty in both the extractive and the non-extractive sectors. In both models, there exists a third asset with the characteristics of a risk-free bond, which yields the risk-free return $r$, and the solution is derived in general equilibrium. It is shown that the rate of increase of the net resource price must be more or less than the rate of interest, depending upon whether it is negatively or positively correlated with the marginal utility of consumption. These models have not been tested, however, although the authors provide clues on the way to go about it.

Another group of economists have taken a diametrically different approach to the objective of testing time consistency in resource prices or rents. Their emphasis is on the supply side, and they use a partial equilibrium framework, without any consideration for the pool of alternative assets which may affect demand. Farrow (1985), Halvorsen and Smith (1987), and Dea et al. (1988) adapt modern factor demand estimation methods to resource firms. From cost, production, factor utilization, and reserve data, it is possible to estimate a restricted cost function, from which the shadow price of in situ resources (the rent) can be computed, using the fact that the latter is related to the effect of reserves, or cumulated extraction, on marginal extraction cost. The appropriate version of equation (1.4)

$$d\mu/dt = r\mu + \partial C(R, S)/\partial S, \tag{1.4}$$

provides a test of the theory of natural resources. In fact, if $\mu$ is computed from (1.3) using the estimated value of $\partial C/\partial R$

$$p = \partial C(R, S)/\partial R + \mu \tag{1.3}$$

and $d\mu/dt$ is approximated as the variation in $\mu$ from one observation to the next one, (1.4) can be expressed entirely in terms of estimated parameters and observed variables, so that it can be tested as an additional constraint to the estimation of the cost function. While each paper uses a different variant of that procedure, and applies it to different data set (aggregate nonferrous metal mines in Canada in the case of Halvorsen and Smith; Canadian asbestos in the case of Dea *et al.*; confidential single mining company data in the case of Farrow), they all reject the hypothesis that the firms behave according to (1.4), as implied by the non-stochastic theory of natural resources. In this vein of empirical investigation too, it seems that the next step is to connect the resource asset with the rest of the portfolio in the economy and to test the corresponding more sophisticated, and stochastic, pricing rule.

Miller and Upton (1985) also test the theory of exhaustible resources using estimates of the *in situ* prices of a resource. However, instead of using time-series data on resource prices, they use panel data on asset prices to test what they refer to as the Hotelling Valuation principle. They exploit the fact, noted above, that both the asset market for reserves, and the market for resource flows, must be in equilibrium. Indeed, if resource price are expected to rise according to Hotelling rule, then the value of current reserves will be proportional to current resource prices, net of extraction costs, times reserve size. According to Tobin's q theory, this value will be reflected in the prices of firm stocks, which provides the basis of Miller and Upton's test equation.

$$V^i(t)/S^i(t) = \alpha + \beta[p^i(t) - \partial C^i/\partial R^i]$$

where $V^i(t)$ is the total market value of firm $i$ at $t$ and $C^i$ is evaluated at $t$. From the fact that this equation is a better predictor of share prices for oil and gas firms in the US than alternative share valuation methods, the authors find a confirmation of Hotelling's theory. The difference in methodology with previously described tests is also revealing. The authors of those tests attempted to check whether resource price paths conformed to a certainty version, or a certainty analogue, of Hotelling rule. They do not appear to do so. This may imply that the theory of natural resource does not have any role in the determination of resource price behaviour; it may also imply that the appropriate stochastic version of that theory is not to be formulated in terms of expected prices and that, if it can be formulated in terms of expected prices, the formation of expectations must be given proper attention. Indeed, using a simple model of lagged expectations formation, Agbeyegbe (1989) rationalizes Barrow and Heal's finding that metal prices appear to be determined by changes in the interest rate rather than its level.

Despite the existence of a substantial body of empirical literature on the theory of natural resources, as it has evolved from the basic contribution of Hotelling, its empirical validity still remains an open question, which will not be resolved overnight. Apparently conflicting results probably reflect the use of highly simplified formulations of the theory, and the resulting focus of most authors on very partial explanations of the evidence. Cairns (1990a) offers a careful discussion which aims at reconciling several apparent contradictions in that literature . . . before providing his own additional, and mixed, evidence on Canadian gold mines.

## 3. JOINT PRODUCTS AND THE ENVIRONMENT

### 3.1. Introduction

Joint production is a frequent occurrence in natural resource industries. In one type of instance, pollution is produced jointly with the desirable product. For example, mine concentrators are often heavy water polluters while smelters are responsible for various emissions into the atmosphere. In another type of instance, several metals coexist in the same ore, each facing a specific demand. In fact many Canadian copper mines would not be in operation if it were not for the gold which is recuperated from the same ore. But the associated product may also face a weak demand and be simply discarded. This is what happens to some of the helium associated with American natural gas. Helium may become a highly valuable product in the future; should something be done about it? The physical nature of the products must also be taken into account when studying joint products. Some, such as noise, are pure flows. Some, such as gold, are perfect durable goods. Some, such as helium, can be released into the atmosphere at no cost, but can also be stored for future demand. Finally, several pollutants are stocks which build up in the atmosphere, on land, or in the water. Here it is worthwhile noticing that the problem of optimally accumulating an undesirable stock is very similar to the problem of the mine, which is optimally to deplete a valuable stock. Principles of public finance, basic capital theory, and the theory of the mine can be applied, together or alternatively, in order to highlight the issues and study the answers. One set of issues is purely positive: how should the conventional model of the mine be adapted for joint production? What is the rent on an individual resource in composite ore? Should the net price of individual resources rise at the interest rate? To what extent may a high demand for one resource cause another one to be wasted and is there any link between the prices of the resources being produced from the same ore? The other issue is normative. Should goverment intervene in some instances of joint production and how? Should clean-up activities or pollution abatement efforts be promoted and how? Does the fact that pollution is often a transnational externality affect the analysis?

## 3.2. Joint production from composite reserves

Pindyck (1982) provides a treatment of the joint production from composite ores problem. He uses the example of helium, jointly produced with natural gas, to motivate his paper. Markets are assumed competitive everywhere. There are two production stages. First, the composite ore is extracted at an average and marginal cost $MC(S)$ which depends on existing reserves only. Second, the individual resources are separated out from the ore at a cost $C^i(y^i, R)$ which depends, for each individual component $i$, on the rate of production $y^i$ and on current extraction $R$ of composite ore. The following reasonable assumptions are made: $\partial C^i/\partial y > 0$, $\partial^2 C^i/\partial y^{i2} > 0$, $\partial C^i/\partial R < 0$, $\partial^2 C^i/\partial R^2 > 0$, $\partial^2 C^i/\partial y^i \partial R < 0$, $\partial(C^i/R)/\partial R > 0$, $C^i(0, R) = 0$, and $C^i(y^i, 0) = \infty$.

With $a^i$ and $b^i$ respectively designating the unit cost of storage and the quantity stored for good $i$, and with $p^i$ and $q^i$ designating price and quantity of good $i$ sold, the problem of the competitive firm is to choose $R, y^1, \ldots, y^n, q^1, \ldots, q^n$ in such a way as to

$$Max \int_0^\infty e^{-rt} \left[ \sum_i p^i q^i - MC(S)R - \sum_i C^i(y^i, R) - \sum_i a^i b^i \right] dt \tag{3.1}$$

subject to

$$dS/dt = -R, \ S(0) = S_0$$

$$db^i/dt = y^i - q^i, \ b^i(0) = 0, \ i = 1, \ldots, n$$

$$S, R, y^i, q^i, b^i \geq 0, \ i = 1, \ldots, n$$

Since the industry is assumed competitive, all prices are treated as given in the maximization but in the industry equilibrium $p^i = p^i (q^i)$, $i = 1, \ldots, n$. This problem is only slightly more complicated than the problem of the single resource mine treated earlier. The major difference is not so much the summations over $n$ resources in the objective function as the presence of a two-stage production process. What was considered the output of the firm in our earlier treatment is only a composite ore which still needs to be separated out in Pindyck's problem. As will become clear presently, the analog of the market price in the earlier problem is in fact here the transfer price for extracted ore. The Hamilton–Lagrange function is

$$H = e^{-rt} \left[ \sum_i p^i q^i - MC(S)R - \sum_i C^i(y^i, R) - \sum_i a^i b^i \right. \tag{3.2}$$

$$\left. - \mu R + \sum_i \lambda^i (y^i - q^i) + \sum_i \Theta^i b^i \right]$$

with $\Theta^i = 0$ if $b^i < 0$, $\Theta^i \geq 0$ if $b^i = 0$. As before the Lagrange multipliers $\Theta^i$ and costate variables $m$ and $\lambda^i$ are expressed in current value.

Maximizing the Hamiltonian with respect to R gives

$$\mu = - \left[ \sum_i \partial C^i / \partial R + MC(S) \right]$$

$$\mu = [p - MC(S)] \tag{3.3}$$

where $p \equiv - \Sigma_i \partial C^i / \partial R$ is the transfer price for extracted ore. Thus the rent can still be viewed as the difference between price and marginal cost of extraction, provided the appropriate transfer price is used. Why can $p$ be interpreted as a transfer price? It represents the joint value to the separation departments, in terms of cost savings, of the marginal unit of extracted ore. Differentiating (3.3) with respect to time

$$d\mu/dt = dp/dt - (\partial MC/\partial S)(dS/dt).$$

Combined with the necessary condition $d\mu/dt = r\mu - e''(\partial H/\partial S)$, this gives

$$dp/dt = r(p - MC(S)) \qquad (3.4)$$

which is the analog of (1.5) under the current assumptions on the extraction cost function. Looking now at the separation and storage phase, we have the following first-order conditions for a maximum with respect to $y^i$ and $q^i$

$$- \partial C^i / \partial y^i + \lambda^i = 0, \, i = 1, \ldots, n \qquad (3.5)$$

$$p^i - \lambda^i = 0, \, i = 1, \ldots, n \qquad (3.6)$$

so that

$$p^i = \partial C^i(y^i, R)/\partial y^i. \qquad (3.7)$$

The price of each resource is equal to its marginal production cost, given the optimal input of ore. This may appear in contrast with the previous result on the single-resource mine, (1.3), according to which price was equal to marginal cost plus rent. But again, this is now the second phase of the extraction-separation process. A fictive transfer price $p$ has been paid for the extracted ore, and $C^i(y^i, R)$ is the variable cost function of product $i$, conditional on the fixed factor $R$. In (1.3), $\mu$ drives a wedge between price and marginal cost because $R$ is the rate of output in the relevant cost function. There is no such wedge in (3.7) because $R$ is fixed and marginal cost is defined on variations in $y^i$ instead. The minimization by choice of $R$ of the total cost of producing $i$, which is the sum of variable cost $C^i(y^i, R)$ and fixed cost $\mu^i R$, requires

$$\mu^i = - \partial C^i / \partial R. \qquad (3.8)$$

This provides an evaluation of $\mu^i$ An alternative evaluation of $\mu^i$ is obtained by starting from the total cost of producing all $n$ resources

$$TC = \sum_j C^j(y^j, R) + MC(S)R. \tag{3.9}$$

The marginal cost of producing resource $i$ is

$$\partial TC/\partial y^i = \partial C^i/\partial y^i + \left\{ \sum_j (\partial C^j/\partial R)\partial R/\partial y^i \right\} + MS(S)\partial R/\partial y^i$$

$$= p^i + (\partial R/\partial y^i)\left[ \left\{ \sum_j (\partial C^j/\partial R) \right\} + MC(S) \right]$$

$$= p^i - (\partial R/\partial y^i)[p - MC(S)] \tag{3.10}$$

which yields the analog of (1.3)

$$p^i = MC^i + \mu^i \tag{3.11}$$

where $MC^i \equiv \partial TC/\partial y^i$ and $\mu^i = (\partial R/\partial y^i)[p - MC(S)]$.

We now have the answer to some of the positive issues raised above. The rent on the composite ore is given by (3.3); the rent on any individual resource buried in composite ore is given in (3.11) or, alternatively, by (3.8). As far as the price paths, there is an analog to Hotelling rule, but it governs the transfer price of the extracted ore only. Indeed if the reserves are homogeneous, so that MC(S) is constant at MC, (3.6) implies that the net transfer price $p$ - MC is rising at the rate of interest. But there is no general prediction concerning the time paths of individual resource prices.

For each i, differentiating (3.6) with respect to time and combining with the necessary condition giving the time path of $\lambda^i$, $d\lambda^i/dt = r\lambda^i - e^{rt}\partial H/\partial b^i$, one has the usual condition on the price of a storable good

$$dp^i/dt \leq rp^i + a^i \tag{3.12}$$

which holds with equality if $b^i > 0$[26]. This shows that the resource in low current demand will be stored only if its storage cost is low: if $a^i$ is high, (3.12) cannot hold with equality with $p^i$ remaining low.

---

[26] One notes the similarity between this expression and (3.4), the condition which must be satisfied by the price of a natural resource in equilibrium. A natural resource is a commodity stored underground at no cost, but which is costly to recover.

The description of the solution is completed by a set of transversality conditions which will not be repeated here. Pindyck also examines the extent to which the demand for one resource will affect the price behaviour of the other resources. He argues that this depends strongly on the availability and cost of storage. 'Consider a composite containing one resource in high demand (e.g. natural gas) and a second resource whose demand today is small but very inelastic, or is expected to be much larger in the future (e.g. helium). Suppose storage of the second resource is costly. Then, relative to what would prevail if they could be produced independently, jointness of production will reduce the current price of the second resource and speed up its exhaustion, and at the same time will raise the current price of the first resource and delay its exhaustion. The cheaper the cost of storage, the more this effect is reduced'.

The answer to the normative question of government intervention is also contained in the analysis just presented since, with minor changes, the latter can be interpreted as the search of a social optimum. Although some helium may be released in the atmosphere in the competitive equilibrium, this release will be optimal. Of course this conclusion does not apply if there is an externality attached to any of the jointly produced components as happens when one output, whether good or bad, does not have any market. In that case, there is a competitive, and a social, version of problem (3.1). Suppose that the instantaneous social welfare function is the sum of consumer surpluses on individual goods i

$$W(q^1, \ldots, q^n) = V^1(q^1) + \ldots + V^n(q^n), \text{ where}$$

$$V^i(q^i) = \int_0^{q^i} P_i(q^i) \, dq^i. \tag{3.13}$$

Substituting $V^i(q^i)$ for $p^i q^i$ in (3.1) gives the social version of the problem. In the absence of externalities, its solution is identical to the solution of the competitive extraction problem just outlined.

Suppose now that there is no market for good $n + 1$; the solution to the social problem is now different from the solution to the competitive problem. In fact, indexing variables by 's' for social and 'c' for competitive.

$$\mu^c = [p^c - MC(S^c)] \tag{3.3c}$$

where $p^c \equiv -\sum_{i=1}^{n} \partial C^i/\partial R$ is the transfer price for extracted ore in a competitive firm.

$$\mu^s = \left[ p^s - MC(S^s) \right] \qquad (3.3s)$$

where $p^s \equiv -\sum_{i=1}^{n+1} \partial C^i/\partial R$ is the transfer price for extracted ore in a social optimization context. If good $n + 1$ is a non-appropriable good no cost is incurred in the private competitive set-up in order to produce it; thus $p^c$ is defined over $n$ goods. In a social welfare maximization context, society prefers to make it available and $\partial C^{n+1}/\partial R$ is the reduction in its production cost associated with a marginal increase in $R$. For any given level of $S$ and $R$, $p^s > p^c$, so that $\mu^s > \mu^c$; but then the implied time trajectory of the transfer price, as given by the analog of (3.4), is also affected; the gap between $p^c$ and $p^s$ keeps rising, and if equalities (3.3c) and (3.3s) are to be maintained over time, $R^c$ and $R^s$ must follow different paths. This in turn affects the marginal production costs of all private goods. Despite the assumption that the production technologies are separable for all $n + 1$ goods ($\partial^2 C^i/\partial y^i \partial y^j = 0$), and that the analysis has been carried out in a partial equilibrium framework, all real variables are different in the socially optimal solution than in the private one. In this particular case it may be conjectured that, in the socially optimal solution, the higher transfer price is spread over a higher number of separation departments, so that the contribution of each one is lower than in the private setup. As a result the production of all private goods is increased. The opposite may be expected if the non-private product is a 'bad'. In order to implement the socially optimum solution, a government would need all the information required to set the right subsidized price trajectory for good $n + 1$. This includes all the $n + 1$ transformation technologies, the extraction technology, the $n$ demand schedules for private goods, and the social welfare function attached to good $n + 1$.

### 3.3. Optimum pollution stocks and clean-up

Pindyck's model is adequate for the study of jointly produced goods which affect private or social welfare as flows. It has two weaknesses. First, in several instances of pollution, it is the stock of a particular component which matters. Think of the greenhouse effect or think of the saturation of ocean or inland dumping sites. Undesirable stocks build up as economic activity proceeds. They may be associated with activities unrelated to the exploitation of exhaustible resources, as happens with the production of domestic waste; or they may be associated with the use of exhaustible resources, as is to a wide extent the case when the consumption of energy adds to the greenhouse effect. Second, there are ways—pollution abatement and clean-up efforts—to reduce undesirable emissions or to control the growth of the undesirable stock. The model presented now clarifies those aspects of the problem and can easily be adapted to various special cases.

Society extracts a resource whose transformation or consumption releases a certain pollutant. A typical example is energy and air pollution. The pollution is cumulative; the damage stock D grows in proportion to the resource extraction rate, but can also be affected by various pollution control efforts $e$ whose unit cost is $w$[27].

$$dD/dt = nR - e, \ e \geq 0; \ D(0) = D_o \text{ small.} \tag{3.14}$$

The instantaneous social welfare function is $V(R) + U(-D)$ with $V$ defined by (3.13) and $U$ rising and concave, so that $V'$ is the price of the resource and $U'$ can be interpreted as the value to society of reducing the damage stock by one unit. For society, assuming zero extraction cost, the problem to solve by choice of $R$ and $e$ is

$$Max \int_0^T e^{-rt}[V(R) + U(-D) - we]dt \tag{3.15}$$

subject to (3.14) and the usual exhaustibility and non-negativity constraints (1.2). The Hamiltonian is

$$H = e^{-rt}[V(R) + U(-D) - (w - \eta - \lambda)e - (\lambda n + \mu)R]$$

where $\eta$ is the Lagrangian multiplier associated with the non-negativity constraint on $e$ and $H(\cdot)$ has been written in such a way that $\lambda$, the costate variable associated with $D$, is non-negative and represents the social gain from a drop in $D$.

For a maximum the following necessary conditions must be satisfied

$$V'(R) = P(R) = \lambda n + \mu \tag{3.16}$$

$$w = \eta + \lambda \tag{3.17}$$

$$d\mu/dt = r\mu \tag{3.18}$$

---

[27] It is not difficult to introduce nature's absorption capacity to the analysis; this can take the form of a constant, or a term proportional to D, being subtracted from (3.14).

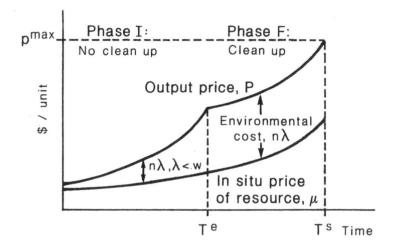

FIGURE 3.1 Socially optimal price and rent.

$$dλ/dt = rλ - U'. \tag{3.19}$$

Two situations may arise (See Figure 3.1). If $η = 0$, so that $e \geq 0$, (3.17) implies that $λ = w$, which is assumed constant; (3.19) reduces to

$$U'(-D) = rw. \tag{3.20}$$

which defines a constant level of damage $D^{s*}$. $e$ is actually chosen so as to offset the polluting effect of resource extraction and consumption, in order to maintain the level of $D$ at $D^{s*}$. Clearly this characterizes a situation where $D$ has reached the level at which society is willing to devote control efforts to the prevention of further increases. This final phase (phase $F$) may be preceded by a situation where society does not find it necessary to check the growth of $D$; such initial phase (phase $I$) is observed if, as postulated above, $D_o < D^{s*}$. Thus $n$ is positive, so that, by (3.17), $λ < w$, and $e = 0$; since $e = 0$, $D$ is rising. This phase leads into phase $F$ which begins when $D$ reaches $D^{s*}$ from below.

Under the assumption that demand chokes off at $p = p^{max}$, the socially optimal price of energy rises in such a way that (3.16) is maintained, while $μ$ grows at the rate of interest. In the final (mature) phase, $λ$ is constant at $λ = w$ (Phase $F$); but in the initial phase $I$, $λ$ grows according to a modified Hotelling rule, (3.19). For example,

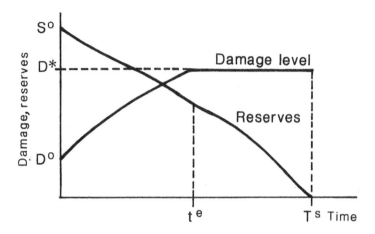

FIGURE 3.2 Socially optimal reserves and damage level.

such a rule should be expected to govern the price at dumping sites until treatment facilities are built and process domestic waste at unit cost $w$. Thus in phase $F$, $p^s$ maintains a constant gap $nw$ above the exponential curve $\mu^s$, while in phase $I$ this gap is smaller than $nw$ and increases over time. $T^s$ is the exhaustion date, and $t^e$ signals the transition from phase $I$ to phase $F$, when $e$ becomes positive. These dates must be such that reserves are exactly exhausted over $[0, T^s]$; this is achieved by appropriate choice of $\mu^s(0)$. Figure 3.2 describes what happens to reserves and damage. During phase $I$, reserves diminish while damage increases, with $e = 0$; during phase $F$, reserves still diminish, but damage is maintained at $D^s*$ by appropriate cleanup efforts. In the special case where there is no exhaustibility constraint as, perhaps, when the production of domestic waste is associated with general economic activity, the solution just described applies with $\mu = 0$ and $S$ vanishing from the analysis; in the final phase, the price is constant.

Although highly simplified[28], this model confirms the general intuition that, while some pollution may be acceptable, society is willing to devote resources to clean up or prevent further damage when

---

[28] Plourde and Yeoung (1989) analyse a slightly more sophisticated model of industrial pollution in a stochastic environment.

pollution levels become high enough. It is interesting to compare the competitive outcome with the socially optimal solution just described. Under perfect competition, if pollution costs are not internalized, firms will solve the following problem

$$Max_R \int_o^T e^{-rt} pRdt \text{ subject to (1.2)} \qquad (3.21)$$

The solution must satisfy $p = \mu^c$ and $d\mu^c/dt = r\mu^c$, with $\mu^c(0)$ chosen so as to exactly exhaust reserves at $T^c$. Of course, in the competitive solution, $D$ increases over the whole period $[0, T^c]$. It can also be shown that exhaustion occurs faster than is socially optimum as shown in Figure 3.3 where the competitive and socially optimal price and rent paths have been drawn on the same time scale[29]. Implementation of the social optimum not only requires an appropriate clean-up or abatement effort to be extended; it also requires the price of energy to be raised in order to slow its consumption.

The current period provides many instances of attempts to move toward social outcomes of the type just described, either through direct public intervention, or by creating institutions to implement those outcomes. Among the instruments that have been advocated or introduced are output and input taxes, regulations requiring certain pollution abatement equipment, tradable and non-tradable emission taxes and quotas, etc. (Buchanan and Tullock, 1975; Baumol and Oates, 1975; Tietenberg, 1985; Kneese, 1984; Johanson, 1987). Given the tremendous amount of information required to characterize the social

---

[29] In both cases, optimality requires that $p = p^{max}$ when exhaustion occurs. Suppose $p^c$ was everywhere above $p^s$; at all dates prior to $T^c$ $R^s$ would be higher than $R^c$; then if at $T^c$ reserves are exactly exhausted under the competitive price path, they must be more than exhausted under the socially optimum path. Hence the latter is not feasible, a contradiction. A similar contradiction can be obtained if it is assumed that $p^c$ is everywhere below $p^s$. This proves that the $p^c$ and the $p^s$ paths must cross at least once. In order to prove that $T^c < T^s$ it is sufficient to further prove that $p^c$ cuts $p^s$ only once, and from below. Whether $p^c$ cuts $p^s$ in phase $I$ or $F$

$$(dp^s/dt)/p^s = (r\mu^s + nr\lambda - nU')/p^s$$
$$= (r(\mu^s + n\lambda) - nU')/(\mu^s + \lambda n)$$
$$< r = (dp^c/dt)/p^c$$

Since no intersection can occur at later dates as $p^c$ continues growing at a faster rate than $p^s$, this completes the proof.

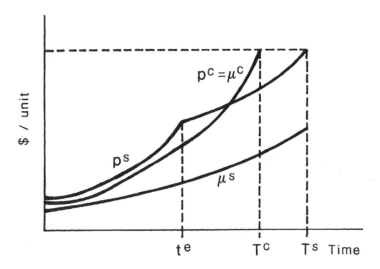

FIGURE 3.3 Competitive, and socially optimal, prices.

optimum and the monitoring costs involved in its implementation, any
movement in the right direction can be considered an achievement, and
it is a reasonably ambitious objective to aim at accomplishing such
improvements in the most efficient way. An abundant economic literature discusses the ways and means of doing so and several practical
applications are now in process.

### 3.4. Transnational pollution in general equilibrium

The fact that the control of pollution is a second-best proposition
stresses the need for a general equilibrium analysis. Another complicating factor is the fact that pollution is very often a transnational or
transjurisdictional problem. Acid rain across European or the Canada-
USA borders, the control of pollution in the Mediterranean Sea, the
Rhine River or the St-Laurence Seaway, or the problem of the ozone
layer are just some important illustrations of this reality which is also
a complicating factor at the regional and municipal levels. Merrifield
(1988) analyses alternative policy options, from a positive, and from
a welfare, point of view, within a general equilibrium model of bilateral
trade with transnational pollution. He uses the North American acid
deposition issue as an example. The essence of his analysis, which is

static, is the impact of abatement on prices, the movement of goods and productive resources between the countries, and hence their welfare. As key features of the model, pollution is treated as an input $D^i$ to the production function of each sector, $i = 1, 2$, in each country $A$ and $B$. Although it is productivity enhancing at the sectoral level, pollution has an international social cost because the aggregate transnational pollution which results from individual sources in both countries, $D = D(D^{1A}, D^{2A}, D^{1B}, D^{2B})$, $\partial D/\partial D^{ij} > 0$, determines the efficiency $g(D)$, $g' < 0$, of capital in each sector. Thus the production of sector $i$ in country $A$ is[30]

$$y^{iA} = F^{iA}(g(D)K^{iA}, L^{iA}, E^{iA}, Z^{iA})$$

where $Z^{iA}$, the regulatory level of pollution abatement equipment, is one of the policy instruments used by each country, independently or in a coordinated manner. A number of interesting real life features are reflected in this formulation. Not only is the transnational pollution level $D$ out of government control because each country regulates its own industries only, but national emission levels are also out of direct government control because the policy instruments which are feasible are also indirect. Indeed, for any regulated level of abatement equipment, firms are free to increase pollution until its marginal product value is zero. Nonetheless the choice of the $Z^{iA}$ by governments affect the equilibrium outcome.

Besides the use of equipment abatement regulation, the author considers the impact of product taxes. He finds that only the former have an unambiguous impact on pollution flows. Because of capital flows between countries, an attempt to reduce pollution by way of a new tax on the output of polluting industries could actually increase pollution. Two other interesting results or reminders are worth stressing. First, a coordinated action, which requires agreement on the choice of an instrument and agreement on the way this instrument is used, is shown to benefit the two countries in differing fashions. In fact, when the use of one instrument unambiguously increases the welfare of one country, there is the possibility of a welfare reduction for the other country. While the author does not discuss the strategic implications of this result, it is clear that they are far-reaching. Such

---

[30] In equilibrium the countries specialize.

a discussion is attempted in Mäller (1989) who finds a similar result in the framework of a parameterized non-cooperative game applied to the European acid rain issue. According to this author, some instruments such as the taxation of emission exports, must be preferred to more efficient ones because they generate enough tax surplus to compensate net losers and are more likely to be implementable on that ground. A second interesting result is that, perhaps unlike conventional trade theory wisdom, the small country is more likely to gain from unilateral action because its abatement efforts, besides reducing domestic pollution, may raise the relative scarcity of the small country products and improve its terms of trade, which attracts a flow of capital from the big country.

## 4: TRADE AND MACROECONOMIC ISSUES

### 4.1. Resource models with trade: survival revisited

Trade is frequently invoked as a way to alleviate national technological, or natural resource, constraints. In that tradition, several authors have re-examined the conclusions of the literature on survival, presented in Section 1. While they came up with interesting new theorems, the major contributors to this literature have often either failed to explain why they obtained different results or offered misleading explanations.

Mitra *et al.* (1982) have examined to what extent a small open economy, which depends on an imported resource for production, is under a similar threat of disappearance as the closed, resource-dependent, economy which was studied in Section 1. The basic philosophy is similar to that of Solow (1974b), Stiglitz (1974b) and Dasgupta and Heal (1979) in that trivial cases are ruled out by assumption: the technology is such that survival is impossible without at least some natural resource being used. Mitra *et al.* provide necessary and sufficient conditions on the technology and terms of trade, ensuring survival.

For the particular case of a Cobb-Douglas technology, while Solow had found that survival of the autarkic economy was possible if the elasticity of output with respect to reproducible capital exceeded that with respect to exhaustible resources, Mitra *et al.* establish the possibility of survival even if Solow's condition is violated. They interpret their result as "only a reflection of the familiar 'gains from trade' thesis" (p. 121). This interpretation is inappropriate. Their model of a two-sector economy that trades some of its production against a foreign resource which it needs as an input is not comparable with Solow's one-sector growth model under finite resource constraint. The terms of trade are given exogenously. Changes in the terms of trade affect the easiness with which capital can be substituted for the natural resource in production. If the resource price increases too rapidly relative to the price of exported goods, the open economy is unable to buy enough natural resource, while simultaneously creating enough new capital and maintaining a positive level of consumption. While such easiness of substitution is what is implicitly specified in Solow's share condition, it is unlikely that rising terms of trade are compatible with a constant aggregate share in Mitra *et al.* Indeed, in their model, each of the two sectors has a Cobb-Douglas technology, so that the aggregate technology is not of the Cobb-Douglas type.

So does trade enhance theoretical survival prospects? A closer examination suggests that the answer is negative. The model analysed in Section 1 may be interpreted as a world model. Introduce sub-sectors and countries in such a model: the feasible set can only shrink as more constraints must be satisfied. In particular, impose the condition that the natural-resource-importing part of the world economy must finance its imports by exporting some of its production; then there will be a real drain from the resource-importing part of the world toward the rest of the world. Under such circumstances it is unlikely that its chances of survival will be higher than if it owned some natural resources of its own. This is the essence of Kemp and Long (1984b)'s results. They consider a country with a Cobb-Douglas aggregate technology, while also allowing for non-constant returns to scale. The resource used as a necessary input in production must be acquired under exogenously specified trade terms. This is a major, and well-defined, departure from the world model of Section 1, where the sole constraint in that respect is that imposed by the fact that reserves affect production costs (the Ricardian case) or that reserves are available in finite quantity (the Hotelling case). In fact, in the world model of Section 1, output is divided into consumption and capital accumulation

$$dK/dt = Y - c.$$

In the open economy model of Kemp and Long

$$dK/dt = Y - c - \mu R,$$

where $\mu$ is the world price of the natural resource. Clearly, capital accumulation possibilities for the natural-resource-importing part of the world are more restricted in the open economy case. The two models can be made otherwise identical by postulating the same aggregate Cobb-Douglas production function of K and R, which implies a Hotelling world where reserves do not affect production costs, and by postulating that $\mu$ rises at the rate of interest, as it should in competitive equilibrium in the Hotelling case[31]. Then it is possible to compare the world model with the open economy model. Not surprisingly, Kemp and Long find that survival is impossible for the open economy, even when the Solow conditions hold, unless there is resource-saving technological change[32].

Our intuition that trade improves an economy's lot is based on comparisons in which trade releases some constraints relative to the no-trade situation, rather than imposing additional constraints. Once it is realized that the literature on survival with trade has imposed additional constraints relative to the literature on survival for the closed economy, its results are no longer ambiguous. All theorems where the trading economy appears to escape the survival conditions spelled out for the world model rely on an implicit release of the resource constraint, usually obtained by postulating a resource price trajectory which is less severe than the exponential path associated with the Hotelling case.

---

[31] In the analysis of Section 1, efficiency was not imposed, so that the time trajectory of $\mu$ remained unspecified. However, it is clear that if survival is feasible in general, it is feasible for the efficient solution in particular. While an exponential trajectory for $\mu$ is dual to a fixed homogeneous reserve contraint (Hotelling case), there is no simple duality relationship between the price trajectory and the natural resource constraint, including its impact on costs, in general (see equation (1.5) and the ensuing discussion). As a result our comparison between the world, and the open economy, models will be limited to the Hotelling case.

[32] Another survival possibility occurs if the open economy can buy a stock of natural reserves against some of its capital. Once this is done the autarkic option is open; since the latter is formally equivalent to the world model of Section 1, Solow's share condition applies.

## 4.2. Trade models with natural resources: the basic trade theorems

As is well known, among the four basic trade theorems, two have little to do with trade. They are statements about the structure of production as it relates to endowments (Rybczynski), and the impact of relative output prices on relative input prices (Stolper–Samuelson). The remaining two focus on the effects of trade: what will country A export given its factor endowment and the factor endowment of country B (Heckscher–Ohlin); what impact will trade have on domestic factor prices (Factor price equalization theorems).

This basic theory derives from the 2 × 2 Heckscher–Ohlin model of production. This model is basically static in the sense that production results from the combination of indestructible factors of production[33] within a time invariant technology. One of its major weaknesses is to abstract from the fact that a substantial proportion of world trade involves non-renewable resources and that such resources are important production inputs in most countries. Thanks to several authors, including, overwhelmingly, Kemp and Long (1980b, 1982b, 1984b, 1984d), the basic trade theory has partially been extended to include finite resources as endowments.

Kemp and Long (1984d) consider several alternative ways to introduce non-renewable resources in trade models. None of them involves Ricardian resources; for such non-homogeneous resources there is no trade theory to date. One alternative is the opposite polar case of the standard Heckscher–Ohlin model; Kemp and Long call it the anti-Heckscher–Ohlin model; it could also be called the pure resource trade model. In that model, two homogeneous non-renewable resources (Hotelling resources for short) are substituted for the usual non-produced and indestructible factors of production. However, many of the most interesting trade questions would involve countries endowed with a combination of indestructible factors of production such as capital and labour, and Hotelling resources such as oil. Kemp and Long consider two such models. One is called generalized Heckscher–Ohlin model because it differs from the standard Heckscher–Ohlin model only by the addition of one Hotelling

---

[33] These factors are usually called Ricardian factors in the trade literature, because they are not produced. In order to avoid any confusion with the notion of a Ricardian resource (a non-renewable, non-homogeneous, resource available in unlimited quantity) emphasized throughout this book, they will be called indestructible factors here.

resource to the indestructible factors of production; it is a three-factor model. In the second one, called hybrid, one factor of production is a Hotelling resource while the other factor is of the indestructible type; the hybrid model is a compromise between the Heckscher–Ohlin, and the anti-Heckscher–Ohlin, models.

In the rest of this section, I shall present those resource trade models in a summarized fashion, and sketch the existing results in each case. Obtaining those results was not a trivial endeavour, as it implied recasting traditional formulations in such a way as to allow for the intertemporal dimension imposed by the presence of non-renewable resources on production decisions and the resulting equilibria. The authors also had to reconsider the relevance of such notions as factor endowments, factor intensity, terms of trade, and specialization. They had to innovate in their solution techniques, so that, besides the new trade theorems, their contribution has a methodological interest. I shall try to give a flavour of it while also pointing to the limitations of the endeavour. This is summarized in Table 4.1. Let us start with the anti-Heckscher–Ohlin model.

*Anti-Heckscher–Ohlin model*
The production of good $i$ is

$$Y^i = f^i(R_1^i, R_2^i), \; i = 1, 2 \qquad (4.1)$$

where $f^i(\cdot)$ is assumed to be homogeneous of degree one, strictly quasi-concave and such that each input is essential. $R_j^i$ is the flow of resource $j$ used in sector $i$. If $p$ is the price of good one relative to the price of good two, i.e. the terms of trade, gross national product is

$$Y = Y^1 + pY^2. \qquad (4.2)$$

For any given levels of $p$ and aggregate extraction $R_1$ and $R_2$, $Y$ is maximized by optimally allocating $R_1$ and $R_2$ between the two sectors,

$$Y = Y(p, R_1, R_2)$$

and the linear homogeneity of the sectoral production functions carries over to the aggregate level so that

$$Y = R_1 Y(p, 1, R_2/R_1) \equiv R_1 y(p, \rho) \qquad (4.3)$$

TABLE 4.1

Trade with Resources: Summary of Existing Results

| Models Characteristics | Conventional Heckscher–Ohlin | Anti-Heckscher–Ohlin | Generalized Heckscher–Ohlin | Hybrid |
|---|---|---|---|---|
| Factor endowments | 2 indestructible factors, K and L | 2 stocks of Hotelling resources, $S_1$ and $S_2$ | 1 Hotelling resource S; 2 indestructible factors, K and L | 1 Hotelling resource S; 1 indestructible factor, K |
| Technology | For each good, a lin. homog. function of K and L | For each good, a lin. homog. function of the $R_1$ and $R_2$ flows | For each good, a lin. homog. function of R, K, L; R separable | For each good, a lin. homog. function of R and K |
| Concept of factor intensity | Ex.: ind. 1 intensive in K relative to L | Ex.: ind. 1 intensive in $R_1$ relative to $R_2$ | Ex.: ind. 1 intensive in K relative to L; both ind. have same intens. in R | Ex.: ind. 1 intensive in R relative to K |
| Trade equilibrium | Static; characterized by terms of trade p | Dynamic; there exists conditions under which p is constant over time | Dynamic; there exists conditions under which p is constant over time | Not characterized or imposed in deriving theorems; p exogenous |
| Classic theorems 0; S-S; Ry; FPE)* | Yes | Recognizable version exists for the constant p equilibrium | Recognizable version exists for the constant p equilibrium | No theorem under the equilibrium p |

*H-O: Heckscher–Ohlin; S-S: Stolper–Samuelson; Ry: Rybczynski; FPE: Factor price equalization.

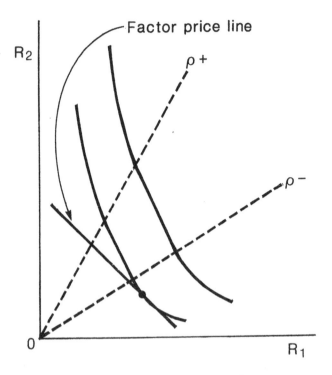

FIGURE 4.1 Isoquants and cone of diversification: anti-Heckscher-Ohlin economy.

where $\rho \equiv R_2/R_1$. One important property of $y(\cdot)$ affects patterns of specialization and trade: when the two industries differ in their factor intensities, for any given $p$, there exist two values of $\rho$, $\rho^-(p)$ and $\rho^+(p)$, such that, for $\rho \leq \rho^-(p)$, the economy is specialized in one good, for $\rho \geq \rho^+(p)$, the economy specializes in the other good; in-between both goods are being produced. Thus in Figure 4.1, which represents isoquants for $y(\cdot)$, the economy is diversified inside the cone of diversification delimited by the dashed lines $\rho^-$ and $\rho^+$.

So far nothing distinguishes the model from a conventional Heckscher–Ohlin trade model. The planning problem for each country, though, is very different from the static problem to be solved in the conventional trade model. Country A, asumed to behave competitively with respect to the rest of the world must jointly solve two extraction problems of a similar nature as the Hotelling problem of Section 1 (country indices are omitted unless otherwise indicated)

$$\underset{\{R_1, R_2\}}{\text{Max}} \int_0^\infty e^{-rt} W[Y(p, R_1(t), R_2(t)), p]dt \qquad (4.4)$$

subject to

$$dS_i/dt = -R_i(t); \quad R_i(t) \geq 0; \quad i = 1, 2$$

$$S_i(t) \geq 0; \quad S_i(0) = S_{io} > 0 \text{ given}; \quad i = 1, 2$$

where $W(\cdot)$ is an indirect utility function, assumed to be increasing and strictly concave in $Y$.

Here it is very important to note that $p$ is assumed to be constant. This crucial assumption is in general violated in the two-country equilibrium of a trade model involving non-renewable resources. A terms of trade equilibrium in such a model is in general a trajectory rather than a single number. One of the beauties of Kemp and Long's research programme in this area has been to specify models, and to spell out conditions, under which equilibria with constant terms of trade occur. In such models, the standard Heckscher–Ohlin trade theorems survive, in recognizable form, the substitution of non-renewable factors of production for the indestructible factors of the conventional model. The key ingredients for this result are the type of scarcity – since the shadow prices of a Hotelling resource rise at the interest rate, relative natural resource prices are constant – and the properties of the aggregate production function $Y(\cdot)$ – at constant relative factor prices, when the economy is diversified, the proportion of good 1 relative to good 2 in aggregate production is indeterminate; consequently it can be chosen to be constant. Under the assumption of constant terms of trade, those properties imply, for problem (4.4), the existence of a solution where aggregate output diminishes as factor prices rise according to Hotelling rule, while the composition of output remains constant. If, furthermore, preferences are such that relative marginal utilities are not affected by the level of output, and if those properties are characteristic of both countries, relative output prices (the terms of trade) remain constant in trading equilibrium, validating the initial assumption. The results can be presented in the form of one existence theorem and four (clones of the standard) trade theorems

*Theorem 4.1 (existence)*
(i) If preferences are strictly convex, homothetic and the same in each of two free-frading countries, and

(ii) if the rate of time preference is everywhere the same and marginal utility is of constant elasticity,

then there exists a trading equilibrium with constant terms of trade.

*Theorem 4.2 (Rybczynski)*
Let the terms of trade be constant and let both goods be produced along an optimal trajectory; let the same be true after a small increase in $S_i(0)$ there is, at each point of time at which production takes place, an increase in the relative and absolute output of the commodity which is relatively intensive in its use of the $i$th resource.

*Theorem 4.3 (Stolper-Samuelson)*
Let the terms of trade be constant and let both goods be produced along an optimal trajectory; let the same be true after a small increase in $p_j$ the price of the $j$th good. As a result of the increase in $p_j$ there is, at each point of time at which production takes place, an increase in the marginal product (in each industry) of the resource used relatively intensively in the $j$th industry and a reduction in the marginal product (in each industry) of the other resource.

*Theorem 4.4 (Heckscher–Ohlin)*
Let there be a trading equilibrium with constant terms of trade and let preferences be strictly convex, homothetic and the same in each country. Then the country which initially is relatively well endowed with the $i$th Hotelling factor will export the commodity which is relatively intensive in its use of that factor.

*Theorem 4.5 (factor price equalization)*
If and only if there be a trading equilibrium with both goods being produced along an optimal trajectory in each country, then the marginal product of each resource is the same in both countries.

*Remarks*
i) The assumption of a constant terms of trade equilibrium is central to most of these results.

ii) In theorem 4.5 the trading equilibrium does not necessarily involve constant terms of trade.

iii) In the constant terms of trade equilibrium the notion of endowment is simplified: the extraction rates in both countries diminish at the same rate, so that the initially better endowed country remains so over the whole programme. Similarly, comparative dynamics are simplified; if production increases at one point in time as a result of an exogenous change in a variable, production will be higher at all dates. Also, the concept of a change in the terms of trade is as trivial as in the static case: the terms of trade cannot improve at one date and worsen at some other time.

### Generalized Heckscher–Ohlin model

The anti-Heckscher–Ohlin model is just as extreme as the Heckscher–Ohlin model. The countries in that model do not exhibit the combination of Hotelling endowments and indestructible factor endowments which seems to be the natural ground for interesting new issues to come into focus. The generalized Heckscher–Ohlin model has the necessary ingredient. Unfortunately, as explained below, it is constructed in a way that prevents it from answering any question having to do with differences in industry resource intensities and countries' relative resource endowments.

In each country two final goods can be produced with three internationally immobile factors of production: two conventional, indestructible factors, say $K$ and $L$, and one Hotelling resource $S$. $K^i$ ($L^i$, $R^i$) represent the portion of $K$ ($L$, $R$) used by the $i$th sector, whose production is

$$Y^i = R_i^a f^i(L^i, K^i) \tag{4.4}$$

where $f^i(\cdot)$ is homogeneous of degree $1 - a$, $0 < a < 1$. Consequently, the technology in each sector is linearly homogeneous in the three factors. What is more important, each sector is equally intensive in its use of the Hotelling resource: since the exponent $a$ is common to both sectors, if $Y^i = Y^j$, $L^i = L^j$ and $K^i = K^j$, then $R^i = R^j$. This assumption is crucial both to the derivation of the trade theorems for this model, and to depriving them of much potential interest.

In fact, from (4.2) and (4.4), gross national product is

$$Y = R^a \lfloor (1 + p)(f^1(\cdot) + pf^2(\cdot)) \rfloor. \tag{4.5}$$

Since $R$ enters this expression multiplicatively, the maximization of $Y$ by choice of $L^i$ and $K^i$ depends on $K$, $L$ and $p$ only, and not on $R$

$$Y = R^a Y^*(p, K, L). \tag{4.6}$$

In both countries, $Y$ is affected by the level of $R$, which diminishes as the unit rent on $S$ rises exponentially. But this does not affect the allocation of $K$ and $L$ between sectors. As a result, if tastes are identical in each country, and if, in each country, the relative valuations of each good are independent of income, $p$ may remain constant in equilibrium over the whole extraction period. As with the anti-Heckscher–Ohlin model this permits using the highly simplifying constant-terms-of-trade assumption in the formulation of each country's planning problem

$$\underset{\{R\}}{\text{Max}} \int_0^\infty \exp\left( \int_0^t -r(s)ds \right) W\{ [R(t)]^a Y^*(p, L, K) \}dt \tag{4.7}$$

subject to

$$dS/dt = -R(t); \; R(t) \geq 0$$

$$S(t) \geq 0; \; S(0) = S_o > 0 \text{ given}$$

where $W(\cdot)$ is an indirect utility function, assumed to be increasing and strictly concave[34].

*Theorem 4.6 (existence)*[35]

(i) If preferences are strictly convex, homothetic and the same in each of two free-trading countries, and

(ii) if the rate of time preference is everywhere the same and marginal utility is of constant elasticity,

then there exists a trading equilibrium with constant terms of trade.

---

[34] If the country is allowed to borrow and lend at the going interest rate $r(t)$, the intermediate function in (4.7) is $Y(\cdot)$ instead of $W[Y(\cdot)]$; the results are only slightly different.

[35] Slightly weaker conditions apply in the case where the free-trading nations are able to borrow and lend at the given, not necessarily constant, rate of interest.

### Theorem 4.7 (Rybczynski)[36]

Let the terms of trade be constant and let both goods be produced along an optimal trajectory; let the same be true after a small increase in $L$ $(K)$. As a result of the increase in $L$ $(K)$ there is, at each point of time at which production takes place, an increase in the relative output of the commodity which is relatively intensive in its use of $L$ $(K)$.

### Theorem 4.8 (Stolper-Samuelson)[37]

Let the terms of trade be constant and let both goods be produced along an optimal trajectory; let the same be true after a small increase in $p_j$, the price of the $j$th good. As a result of the increase in $p_j$ there is, at each point of time at which production takes place, in each industry, an increase in the ratio of the marginal product of the indestructible factor used relatively intensively in the $j$th industry over the marginal product of the other indestructible factor.

### Theorem 4.9 (Heckscher-Ohlin)

Let there be a trading equilibrium with constant terms of trade. Then the country which initially is relatively well endowed with $L$ $(K)$ will export the commodity which is relatively intensive in its use of $L$ $(K)$.

### Theorem 4.10 (factor price equalization)

If, and only if, there is a trading equilibrium and both goods are produced along an optimal trajectory, then the ratios of the marginal products of $K$ and $L$ are the same in both countries.

### Remarks

i) Again the equilibrium in theorem 4.10 need not involve constant terms of trade.

ii) The restrictions which ensure the existence of an equilibrium with constant terms of trade, especially the assumption of identical resource intensities in both sectors, restrict the model to conventional predictions

---

[36] Some additional, relatively minor, properties can be established when the countries can borrow and lend at a given rate of interest $r(t)$.

[37] The theorem is slightly reinforced when the countries can borrow and lend at the rate $r(t)$.

on the indestructible factors. Nothing can be said about the pattern
of trade between a well resource-endowed country and another
country; in particular, if resource processing is a resource intensive
activity, none of the above theorems tells us that a well resource-
endowed country will export the processed resource in a world where
unprocessed resource is an immobile factor!

*Hybrid theory*
The trade model called hybrid by Kemp and Long is geared toward
the questions left unanswered by the generalized Heckscher–Ohlin
model. It is a $2 \times 2 \times 2$ model where one factor of production, say
$K$, is indestructible while the other is a Hotelling resource $S$. Given the
rate of extraction $R$ and the terms of trade, maximized gross national
product is

$$Y = Y_1 + pY_2$$

$$= Y(p, R, K).$$

This function has the property displayed in Figure 4.1 where $K$ (instead
of $R_2$) must be read on the vertical axis, and $R$ (instead of $R_1$) must
be read on the horizontal axis, while $\rho^+$ and $\rho^-$ are redefined accordingly and represent upper and lower bounds of capital relative to the
extraction rate within which the economy is diversified. Suppose the
economy is specialized in the Hotelling-resource intensive industry. If
the relative price of $R$ relative to $K$ monotonically increases as a result
of the exponential rise in the rent, the switch from that specialization
to a specialization in the $K$ intensive industry will occur instantaneously.
Suppose the other country was already specialized in the $K$ intensive
industry; then only one good would be produced. Suppose the resource
intensive product was indispensable; then its price would shoot to
infinity as a result of the switch in specialization. More probably, in
such a setup, the price of the resource intensive good would start rising
before its production was interrupted. One may speculate that, at least
over a phase, the equilibrium $p$ would gradually change so as to alter
the slope of the linear part of the isoquant in Figure 4.1 in such a way
that it coincided with the slope of the factor price line for an extended
period. The resource intensive industry could thus stay in production.
For these intuitive, but compelling, reasons, it is very unlikely that the
terms of trade would remain constant in an equilibrium of this model.

However, this is the assumption under which the theorems are derived, with the caveat that, here, the authors do not provide any sufficient condition under which an equilibrium with constant terms of trade would exist. In view of the foregoing argument, this is hardly surprising. The hybrid theory of international trade is thus incomplete to date. The theorems owed to Kemp and Long depart from the general equilibrium tradition of trade models; they can be viewed only as partial equilibrium properties of two-sector open economies. Furthermore, the prediction of a sudden switch from a resource intensive specialization to a capital intensive specialization is very much a product of the constant terms of trade assumption and is likely to give a highly misleading view of what actually happens in general equilibrium[38]. The extension of trade theory to setups involving Hotelling resources will be complete only when the general equilibrium solution to Kemp and Long's hybrid model is characterized and the corresponding trade theorems are spelled out. Because relative prices and the shares of each sector in gross national product are likely to vary over time in the solution, as well as relative factor endowments, those trade theorems may be far more remote from the classical ones than was the case with the anti-Heckscher–Ohlin and the generalized Heckscher–Ohlin models.

## 4.3. The Dutch Disease and the Macroeconomy

*Introduction*

For any individual country, what is the impact on the manufacturing sector of a resource bonanza such as a major discovery or, if the country already is endowed with natural resources, a shift in world demand? What happens to its exchange rate, its unemployment level and its inflation? Among those questions, the first two are central to the pure theory of international trade. As explained in the previous section, however, extensions of that theory to include Hotelling resources did not provide satisfactory answers: the theorems available rule out terms of trade variations and cannot handle situations involving, say, a capital and/or labour intensive manufacturing

---

[38] The authors discuss this issue to some extent (pp. 394–5). In an earlier paper, they have shown that a theorem of Rybczynski type holds when the terms of trade rise exponentially in favour of the resource intensive good.

sector coexisting with another, resource intensive, sector.

This leaves the analyst with the tools of partial equilibrium analysis. One important example of this approach is the partial general equilibrium analysis which has been associated with Dutch Disease economics. Dutch disease is a phenomenon that affects an open macroeconomy after some sudden, exogenous, improvement in its material situation. The name, coined by *The Economist* (1977), is meant to evoke the tough awakening which follows excessive libations. Although normally associated with the adverse effects of resource booms, it has matured to designate most of the evils associated with any favourable, temporary, macro shock: a shrinkage in the manufacturing sector, possibly accompanied by irreversible losses in human capabilities, an appreciation in the real exchange rate, unemployment, inflation, etc . . .

There is an abundant literature on the Dutch Disease; there are also excellent syntheses of that literature. In fact Corden (1984), and Neary and van Wijnbergen (1986a) provide the necessary background and references. The theoretical subsection which follows relies on their contributions heavily; it focuses on real aspects and leaves monetary questions out. The Dutch Disease is also very much a practical problem, so that its analysis is geared toward policy implications; those will be discussed in a special subsection together with some individual country experiences.

*Theoretical framework*
Most of the well-established theoretical basis underlying the Dutch Disease is static and can be brought to light using the Core Model of Corden and Neary, also adopted by Neary and van Wijnbergen (1986a). A boom is caused by some major technological improvement specific to some sector, or by a windfall discovery of some resource, or still by an exogenous rise in the demand for an exported good. There are three sectors; the booming sector $B$ produces a commodity which is traded on the world market and not locally consumed; the manufacturing sector $M$ produces for both local consumption and for the international market, where its price is exogenously determined; the non-tradeable sector $N$ is oriented toward domestic markets exclusively. The boom has two basic effects on the economy: the spending effect and the factor movement effect[39].

---

[39] This effect is often referred to as the resource movement effect; the resource involved is not the natural resource but some conventional factor of production.

The *spending effect* is the direct income effect of the boom. The additional income injected into the economy raises the demand for both $M$ and $N$ which are assumed to be normal[40]. Since the former is traded on the international market, its price cannot move; the price of $N$ rises, which implies a real exchange rate appreciation.

If there is inter-sector factor mobility this price rise also causes a factor reallocation from sector $M$ to sector $N$: the manufacturing sector shrinks. This is one form of the *factor movement* effect. This effect may take several other forms which depend on the productive structure of the economy and the specific properties of the factors of production involved. Sector $B$ may use its own internationally hired factors of production; then it it completely isolated from the domestic economy. Alternatively, as will be assumed in the sequel, it may compete with $N$ and $M$ for one or several factors. Capital may be internationally mobile or immobile and, irrespective of this property, it may be sector specific (no competition with other domestic types of capital) or intersectorally mobile. Assume that capital is internationally immobile, sector specific, and fixed in the context of the current static analysis, while labour is internationally immobile but intersectorally mobile. Assume also that labour supply is fixed at $L$ in the aggregate and that demand determines its intersectoral allocation. In obvious notation and remembering that output prices in $B$ and $M$ are exogenously given

$$L_M + L_B + L_N =$$
$$L^M(w) + L^B(w) + L^N(w/q) = L \qquad (4.8)$$

where $w$ is the real wage, expressed in terms of $M$, while $q$ is the real price of $N$, also in terms of $M$. (4.8) defines the labour market equilibrium line $LL$ in Figure 4.2.

The sole product market which must clear domestically is the market for $N$. Since $B$ is not consumed domestically and since the price for $M$ is given, the demand for $N$ is a function of $q$ and real income $y$. Equilibrium on the $N$ market must satisfy

$$S(q/w) = D(q, y)$$

which defines the $NN$ locus in Figure 4.2.

---

[40] $M$, $N$, and $B$ will be used to designate the goods, as well as the sectors, alternatively.

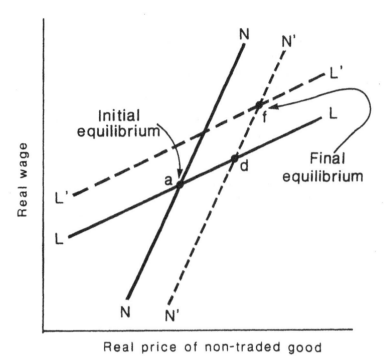

Real price of non-traded good

FIGURE 4.2 Spending and factor-movement effects of a boom.

The factor movement effect has several components. First, the boom directly raises $L^B(\,\cdot\,)$, shifting the $LL$ locus up. The additional demand is met by labour movements away from $N$ and $M$. Second, since the spending effect, shifting $NN$ to the right, has raised $q$, labour demand has increased (without shifting) in that sector. The net effect is ambiguous in $N$. On the contrary, in $M$, there is no change in labour demand; $M$ loses workers to both $B$ and $N$. So the final equilibrium, besides higher $w$ and $q$, involves a labour reallocation away from $M$, toward $B$ and, possibly, toward $N$. The rise in $q$ (a real exchange rate appreciation) and the shrinking of the manufacturing sector, are the agreed-upon symptoms of the Dutch Disease[41].

---

[41] The exogenous rise in $y$ has often been labelled inflationary and the rise in $q$ and $w$ assimilated to inflation; of course they are just a once-and-for-all shock, and once-and-for-all relative price adjustments in this static model of the real side of the economy.

Before turning to more controversial symptoms, a few remarks are appropriate. First, the fact that the existing traded good sector has been labelled $M$ should not obscure the fact that it may just as well be an open agricultural sector. The so-called deindustrialization effect is in fact a reduction in the size of the existing world trading sector, whatever its activity. Indeed, in several developing countries, the sectors which suffered from a resource boom were agricultural sectors. Second, the scenario just described must only be viewed as a consensus approximation of the real effects of a resource boom. Other equilibrium models may yield quite different outcomes; those are considered unlikely. For example, nobody seriously questions the assumption that all goods are normal in the analysis. Similarly, the 'paradox' model of Corden and Neary (Corden, 1984) is not considered empirically relevant. In that model, the factors are still assumed internationally immobile, but the assumption of intersectoral capital immobility is relaxed; capital can move freely between $M$ and $N$, while labour can move between $M$, $N$, and $B$. Taken in isolation from the B sector, $M$ and $N$ constitute a Heckscher–Ohlin economy, whose endowment in labour is reduced when the factor movement effect has labour move toward the $B$ sector. By Rybczynski theorem, this reduces the output of the labour intensive sector and raises, at least in relative terms, the output of the capital intensive sector. If $M$ is the capital intensive sector, the Rybczynski effect may cause an expansion of $M$, which may offset the spending effect and reverse the conventional deindustrialization prediction.

Deindustrialization and real exchange rate appreciation remain also the likely outcomes when the assumption of international capital immobility is relaxed, with capital remaining sector specific. In the plausible case where, in each sector, capital rents move in the same direction as output when capital is immobile, international mobility will cause international capital flows toward the sectors where rents have increased –B and, possibly, $N$– and away from $M$. This will moderate the price and rent effects of the boom while adding to the quantity adjustments. Deindustrialization will be more pronounced. In the extreme case of perfect international capital mobility and constant returns to scale in all sectors, the $M$ sector can be in production only if its input prices are identical to those in the rest of the world. Since the spending effect of the boom raises $w$, effectively allowing $B$ to pay workers a rent over and above world wage,

$M$ disappears entirely while $q$ adjusts so as to ensure zero profits.

The nature of the shock is not always irrelevant as assumed so far. While maintaining the assumption that $B$ is not domestically consumed, consider the difference between a boom caused by a local discovery, at given world demand conditions, and a boom caused by a shift in world demand given existing reserves. In the former instance the relative price of $B$ is unchanged while in the latter it is increased, as well as the rent on the resource in the ground. Suppose that $B$ involves some processing which may be carried out at the point of origin (domestically) or at the point of destination (abroad), with transportation costs per dollar unit being lower for the processed than for the unprocessed commodity. If capital is more expensive domestically than in the rest of the world, it is easy to construct examples where domestic processing is optimal before a rise in the resource rent while, after the boom, processing is more profitable abroad. In that case, besides the usual spending and factor movement effects, a price shock will cause processing to migrate abroad, while a discovery will cause the domestic processing industry to expand[42].

The full-employment equilibrium framework used so far has not permitted the question of unemployment to be raised. Taking account of the spillovers between markets arising from wage and price rigidities, Figure 4.2 can be partitioned à la Malinvaud (1977) into a region of classical unemployment $C$, a region of Keynesian unemployment $K$, and a region of repressed inflation $R$[43]. The boom shifts the equilibrium and the region limits in the way indicated in Figure 4.3. The new equilibrium, identical to point $d$ in Figure 4.2, is drawn on the assumption that there is no factor movement effect, implying that sector $B$ is completely isolated from $M$ and $N$. Price and wage rigidities

---

[42] For example, suppose that the cost of making one unit of the processed resource available on the world market is

$$C_D = \mu^{1/2} V_D^{1/2} + T_p \qquad \text{with domestic processing and}$$
$$C_W = \mu^{1/2} V_W^{1/2} + T_r \qquad \text{with processing abroad}$$

where $\mu$ is the resource rental, $V_D$ ($V_W$) is the domestic (foreign) rental price of capital, and $T_p$ ($T_r$) is the unit transportation cost of the processed (raw) commodity. With $V_D = 4$; $V_W = 1$; $T_p = 1$; $T_r = 3$, one can check that domestic processing is preferable when $\mu = 1$ while processing abroad is preferable when $\mu = 4$.

[43] For a more detailed exposition, see Neary and Wijnbergen (1986b, pp. 19–23); for a complete textbook treatment with a numerical example, see Campan and Grimaud (1988).

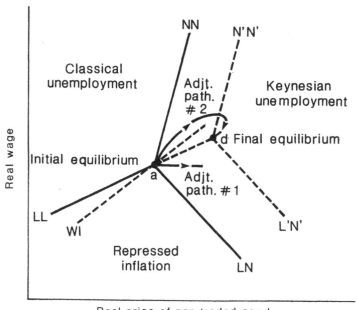

FIGURE 4.3 Effects of a boom with wage and price rigidities (no factor-movement effect).

prevent any instantaneous adjustment from *a* to *d*. The question becomes: assuming the economy will eventually reach the new equilibrium *d*, what situations will emerge during the transition, i.e. which regions will the path between *a* and *d* cross? *a* is the initial point on that path. Not surprisingly, since the initial shock amounts to a Keynesian income stimulus which would be administered in a full employment situation, it moves the region of Keynesian unemployment away from the initial equilibrium, leaving it at the limit between regions *C* and *R*: right after the shock, the labour market is in equilibrium but there is excess demand for *N* which calls, somehow, for a rise in *q*. What will happen to *w* while *q* rises? If *w* stays constant, as in path 1, the economy enters a phase of repressed inflation, involving both excess demand for *L* and for *N*. If, on the contrary, the increase in *q* is foreseen and taken into account in wage settlements, an adjustment path such as 2 may occur, causing the emergence of classical unemployment combined with excess demand for $N$. Whether one or the other is more likely to occur crucially depends on economic institutions, in particular the prevalent type of wage indexation. Van Wijnbergen (1984b) assumes that real consumption wage can be reduced only by temporary unemployment. If only $N$ was consumed, the constant real consumption wage would be on a straight line through the origin and $a$; if only $M$ was consumed it would be on an horizontal line through $a$. In general the consumption wage is constant along a line such as $WI$. For a country like Saudi Arabia where much of the consumption basket is imported, $WI$ is almost horizontal, and likely to lie below point $d$. $d$ can be reached from $a$ without going below $WI$ (reducing the consumption wage). For such countries the adjustment is less likely to involve unemployment. For countries such as Mexico and Venezuela where a substantial part of the consumption is local, non-traded, production, the $WI$ curve is probably above $d$ and the adjustment to a lower consumption wage at $d$ must involve a period of unemployment; an adjustment path such as 2 is perhaps to be expected. According to Neary and van Wijnbergen these results accord well with the stylized facts of the adjustment of several countries to natural resource discoveries and increases in the prices of resources.

Wage and price rigidities often coexist with factor rigidities, such as the reluctance of labour to move to another sector. If the labour force in the $M$ sector cannot be reduced as much as required by the new equilibrium, unemployment can be avoided in that sector only if its wage is set lower than in the $B$ and $N$ sectors. Attempts to maintain wage parity with other sectors will cause unemployment in $M$.

*Policy implications and individual country experiences*
The symptoms of the Dutch Disease are basically negative aspects of a good event. Does the Dutch Disease call for a cure? Clearly such a cure should not jeopardize the underlying benefits. Preventing the economy from adjusting to its new equilibrium in order to keep $M$ from shrinking would also prevent society from reaping some of the benefits of the boom. Intervention, even temporary, may be damaging. For example, despite the negative connotation of the term, overshooting of the exchange rate during the adjustment period, which Neary and Purvis (1983) have shown may occur, is not a bad thing in itself; preventing such overshooting may involve a slower adjustment and a postponement of the period when maximum benefits can be realized.

The arguments in favour of a cure to the Dutch Disease are the usual arguments in favour of government intervention: correction of market imperfections and externalities on efficiency grounds, and for distributional purposes. Protection of the $M$ sector by tariffs or exchange rate policy on distributional grounds should be avoided, as the same aim can be achieved in a less distortive fashion by taxing $B$ and subsidizing the workers in $M$ and/or compensating those who move. The case for specific government intervention on efficiency grounds is weak: if imperfections are present, they are likely to be present whether or not the economy enjoys a resource boom; existing corrective features may have to be adjusted, but this does not call for new measures. However, some externalities, which are latent in the economy but do not require intervention in normal circumstances, may have to be corrected during the adjustment period.

A version of the infant industry argument is sometimes invoked when it is expected that the $M$ sector will have to recover once the boom is over. Its decline during the boom, it is argued, may involve irreversible physical and human capital losses which will preclude a later recovery. This argument requires some externality in order to be valid. Lack of information and foresight, and, especially, imperfect capital markets, may affect private decisions among small firms, especially in developing countries. In all countries, the learning-by-doing argument, which claims that technology is to some extent a public good that firms can assimilate only progressively by practicing their trade, may also justify intervention.

Whether explicitly on those grounds or for other reasons, governments have been deeply involved in the management of resource booms. This is true of very diverse countries and is documented in an abundant literature (see several of the contributions in Neary and van Wijnbergen, 1986b, and for a focus on developing countries, many of the references in Decaluwé and Martens, 1988). Most resource rich countries seem to have experienced the major symptoms of Dutch Disease, and to have adopted a mixture of purely macroeconomic policies (monetary and exchange rate policies), together with policies concerning the use of the resource bonanza. The following paragraphs are devoted to the latter type only. It is appropriate to distinguish between developed countries, poor developing countries, and capital-surplus developing countries.

In the last, population was small relative to the magnitude of the boom. The prospect of running out of resource was considered remote enough to preclude a transitory adjustment to a temporary period of prosperity; a permanent adjustment to a higher growth trajectory was requested. In most instances governments considered two basic options: investment in the local economy and investment in the rest of the world. Since the local economy was close to non-existent, the first option often took the form of mega-projects, while the non-traded sector also grew substantially. Both requested substantial imports of labour. In that respect, the experience of capital surplus countries was different from the standard model (*The Economist*, 1988). The conditions under which such projects were carried were not otherwise very different in capital surplus countries, than in developing countries. If one can judge from the evidence on big projects in such countries (Gelb, 1986), foreign and portfolio investment is likely to have been a better way to carry wealth into the future than direct domestic investment. While investments in local projects often failed to pass standard viability criteria, their justification may have run along standard infant industry and learning-by-doing arguments. It must be noted here that, since they enjoyed a capital surplus, these countries, unlike other developing countries, did not face imperfect capital markets.

The experience of developed countries broadly appears to conform with the theoretical model. In those countries, however, it is often difficult to separate out the impact of the resource boom from other influences. In particular the depressing effect of higher energy prices on the world economy may have affected the traded sectors in those countries as much as the Dutch Disease. Also, the decline in the share of manufacturing and the growth in the share of the service sector, which characterize mature economies, may mistakenly be interpreted as a symptom of Dutch Disease. Resource rents varied in magnitude, high on oil and gas during the Opec golden area, lower on other resources, but a substantial part accrued to the public sector (see Forsyth, 1986, on Great Britain and Australia; Kremers, 1986, on the Netherlands; Helliwell, 1981, on Canada). Nevertheless, most authors find that resource rents have been spent mostly on consumption. This is true of those rents which did accrue to the public sector as taxes and levies. This is also true of the substantial part which was distributed directly in the form of higher wages or lower energy prices. Of course some public investments resulted from resource rents; those are difficult to evaluate, though, because resource revenues were not earmarked for particular purposes, with such exceptions as some energy infrastructure investments which were financed out of oil revenues, and investments into the Alberta Heritage Savings Trust Fund.

In developing countries, a high proportion, about four-fifths, of the windfalls were also received by governments. They used them with three central objectives: growth of the non-oil economy, the extension of national control, and reduced oil dependance (Gelb, 1986). About half of the windfall was invested into the local economy, with a disappointing impact on growth. On average, the non-oil economies of Algeria, Ecuador, Indonesia, Nigeria, Trinidad and Tobago, and Venezuela, were 4.1 per cent smaller during 1979–81 than they would have been had they maintained their 1967–72 growth trajectories (p. 78). Even correcting for specific country circumstances that might have explained a slowdown in growth, actual performance for 1972–81 appears to have fallen well short of potential, a likely sign of Dutch Disease. It must be pointed out that several investments, notably in transportation and education, with their long gestation lags, may not have produced much of their return over Gelb's study period. However, even if this could be adjusted for, it is clear that the yield on domestic investment has fallen well short of that available abroad. While they have increased the sphere of domestic control, governments have not succeeded in reducing the dependance on oil and gas exports as a source of foreign revenues. Indonesia appears to have been the most successful in strenthening its agriculture and industry. One apparent explanation for this relative success is less reliance on big capital intensive industrial projects. As Warr (1986) points out, Indonesia was also to a certain extent lucky, for internal political reasons, to abstain from borrowing heavily on international markets in the late 1970s, thus avoiding the debt crisis which was to plague many other LDCs in the 1980s.

## 4.4 Other issues

Many other fascinating issues have been raised in the area of international relations involving natural resources. It is impossible to do justice here to the imagination and cleverness of the authors who have tried to throw some light on those issues. The interested reader is invited to refer to the original papers.

Given the relative inability of extended standard trade theory to deal with natural resources, some authors have used computable international general equilibrium models to address certain questions. Chichilnisky (1986) constructs a two-region model of the world, with an industrial North producing consumption and industrial goods using labour capital and oil, and a monopolistic oil exporting South purchasing some of those goods. What the author shows is that, depending on the technology and the initial level of prices, a rise in the price of oil may benefit both the North and the South in general equilibrium. This points to the possibility of international cooperation. However, configurations exist where the interests of both regions diverge, as is more frequently assumed within the North-South debate. Chichilniski *et al.* (1986) use a similar approach but focus on international indebtness. In their North-South model, the trade surplus of the South is used to finance the development of the oil sector, so that there is an explicit link between the financial and the production sectors. The paper studies the impact of changes in the values of the debt on both the borrowing and lending regions. Who benefits and who loses from the accumulation of debt? Is cooperation a possibility or do the regions necessarily have conflicting interests? A loan may have a beneficial effect on the equilibrium of the lending country, because it leads to more abundant oil exports and lower oil prices. This externality may in some circumstances justify the compensation of private banks for extending privately unprofitable loans to the South, or to help them reschedule debts.

The same issue is examined from a different point of view in the literature on the recycling of oil revenues. Raucher (1987), Hillman and Long (1985), and Hoel (1981), among others, consider alternative forms of the joint capital-investment/extraction decisions of countries with influence on the rate of return on non-resource assets. In all cases the optimal extraction rate is affected by the necessity to take account of its impact on the capital market. In some circumstances, it may be optimal for an oil exporting monopoly to subsidize oil importers' borrowing.

The influence of resource producers on financial markets has also recently been examined under a new light by Phlips and Harstad (1988). In their paper, two duopolists extract their given reserves while having access to a futures market for their output, whose demand is stochastic. The problem is formulated as a two-stage game; the existence of futures markets is found to be profit enhancing and profitable speculation transforms the temporal evolution of extraction rates and the spot price.

The desirability to process non-renewable resource exports domestically is a constant scheme in the development literature. Although more sporadically, it has also been addressed in the resource literature, which is reviewed by Kumar (1988). Kumar introduces his own, versatile and pedagogical, framework. Three major elements play a crucial role in the results.

If the first element, the necessity to acquire processing capital services on the international market under balance of payment constraint, is the sole consideration, the bang-bang solution to the planning problem of the country involves a final phase of domestic processing, which may or may not follow a finite period over which the economy is diversified and a finite period over which no processing takes place. This works as follows. As the resource rent rises exponentially, processing, possibly as a hypothetical alternative, uses the ore more and more parsimoniously; as a result, the marginal product of one unit of ore in processing rises and, at some stage, its value overtakes the (constant) marginal product value of ore in the form of unprocessed exports. At this point, domestic processing starts. This result relies on the absence of a general equilibrium mechanism whereby the absolute and relative prices of both the unprocessed resource and the processed resource would rise over time to reflect increased ore scarcity.

The second element is transportation costs; if they are lower for the processed resource than for the bulkier, unprocessed, resource, the opposite result, illustrated in footnote 42, is likely to arise. At low resource rent, processing may be highly resource intensive and justify domestic processing to save on transportation costs. As the rent rises over time, processing becomes more intensive in other factors, so that the transportation cost advantage of domestic processing is reduced, and the whole activity may be displaced.

The third element is market power. Kumar shows that domestic processing may be optimal for a resource monopoly while foreign processing would be adequate if the same resource was exploited competitively. This result is obtained in the absence of transportation cost differences.

## 5. TAXATION

### 5.1. Introduction

Taxation is a very important aspect of non-renewable resource exploitation. The *in situ* resource being most often under public ownership, the tax system is used as a device by which the public collects the rent owed to it by the user of the resource. This role is unique to resource taxation, although it is played with instruments that are not necessarily particular to extractive sectors. In fact the major instruments of resource taxation are the royalty, the severance tax, various leases for the right to explore or exploit, but also the rate of return tax, import and export tariffs, and, not least of all, the corporate income tax, usually with special provisions.

Besides rent appropriation, the taxing institutions are naturally concerned with efficiency. Resource taxes usually alter taxpayer behaviour. While this is true in any economic activity, the particular effects to be considered are often unusual and highly specific in resource industries. Firms may alter their plans with respect to rates of extraction, cut-off grades, and mine or oil-field lives, as well as their choice of inputs and their exploration activities[44]. As they occur in economies which are likely to be subject to various other distortions, those effects should ideally be analysed in a second-best framework.

Resource tax revenues are merged with other tax incomes; they are used to serve the same purposes as regular taxes, such as income redistribution and stabilization. However their share of general tax revenues is in some instances so high that the authorities are led to design their resource taxes with those purposes in mind. For example, during the 1970s, Canadian oil taxes were discussed in redistributive terms (Heaps and Helliwell, 1985) as well as rent collecting devices; similarly, the proceeds of North Sea oil and gas were considered an important macroeconomic matter.

To complicate matters, the taxing authorities are subject to various constraints which may lead them to behave strategically: import tariffs on resource products may be set so as to extract a rent which would

---

[44]For good introductions to resource tax systems and taxation issues see Harberger (1955), Conrad and Hool (1980), Heaps and Helliwell (1985), and, for a more theoretical approach, Dasgupta, Heal, and Stiglitz (1980).

otherwise be collected by the exporting country; resource extracting regions may be under different jurisdictions which compete for activity and revenues.

Obviously, the field is rich in fascinating issues, some of which are almost untouched, some others more thoroughly explored. In the next subsections, I shall deal with the distortive effects of various taxes, first in a simple Hotelling world, then in a simple Ricardian world, and, finally, in more complex situations involving capital decisions, exploration, and stochastic events. I will also briefly go over second-best situations and general equilibrium, risk sharing, and strategic behaviour on the part of the taxing authorities.

## 5.2. Resource taxation in a simple Hotelling world

The simple Hotelling world of this subsection is a particular case of the model described in 1.2. The firm extracts a homogeneous resource from a given initial stock of reserves $S_0$. Its extraction cost $C(R)$ is independent of $S$, and the fact that input prices do not appear in $C(\cdot)$ implies that those prices are assumed constant over time. In reality some taxes, such as the corporate income tax, affect factor prices so that the after-tax cost function is different from the before-tax cost function. For this reason, the corporate income tax will be given a separate treatment; at this stage all taxes are of a kind which does not affect the input mix. It is also assumed that the firm does not incur any particular cost and does not realize any particular benefit at closure time $T$, whether tax induced or of a technological nature. In particular, all inputs are leased and perfectly malleable, so that the firm has no residual value at $T$. Finally, aggregation issues are avoided by making the assumption that all firms are identical; this rules out entry and exit, a possibility discussed in Burness (1976), to whom we owe much of the analysis presented now and whose methodology has set the standards for this vein of literature.

The effect of alternative taxes will be described by comparing the extraction programmes of a firm or industry under taxation, and without tax. The no-tax solution, which is also the social optimum under competition, will be denoted by attaching the superscript '*' to the relevant variables; thus, for example, $T^*$ and $S^*(t)$, respectively, denote the optimal terminal date, and the stock of remaining reserves at $t$, in a no-tax situation. $T$ and $S(t)$ now refer to tax situations and, as before, it will be made clear whether they should be understood as optimized or not. Unless otherwise mentioned the focus is on the competitive case, so that, in the tradition of partial analysis, any departure from the '*' solution can be interpreted as a distortion away from the first-best situation.

The competitive firm selects an extraction path $R(\cdot)$ and a closure date $T$ is such a way as to solve

$$\text{Maximize} \int_{\theta}^{T} e^{-rt} [p(t) R(t) - C(R(t)) - Z(S(t), R(t), p(t), t)] dt$$

$$(5.1)$$

subject to

$$- dS/dt = R(t) \geq 0, \text{ with } S(0) = S_0 \text{ given} \qquad (5.2)$$

where $Z(S, R, p, t)$, the tax function, takes up various specific forms depending on the tax under study. As before, it is assumed that $p$ does not rise at more than the discount rate and is high enough at all dates to cover extraction costs and the tax. $C(\cdot) + Z(\cdot)$ is jointly convex in $(S, R)$ for $\underline{R} \geq R \geq 0$, where $\underline{R}$ is the extraction rate at which average cost-plus-tax is minimum.

As a first approximation, an oil company or a mine may be subject to the following taxes during its extraction phase[45]:

$Z(\cdot) = f(t)$: franchise tax or license fee or fixed property tax;
$Z(\cdot) = s(t)R(t)$: severance tax or royalty;
$Z(\cdot) = s(t)p(t)R(t)$: ad valorem severance tax or royalty;
$Z(\cdot) = g(t)S(t)$: ad valorem property tax[46];
$Z(\cdot) = u(\cdot)[p(t)R(t) - C(R)]$: profit, rate of return, or resource rent tax.

The Hamiltonian for problem (5.1) is (omitting time arguments)

$$H(\cdot) = e^{-rt} [(p - \mu)R - C(R) - Z(S, R, p, t)]. \qquad (5.3)$$

---

[45]The corporate income tax is treated in a separate section.

[46]Property taxes are often defined according to land area; then, since this is invariant as $S$ gets depleted, the franchise tax is a good representation, especially if $f(t)$ is periodically adjusted to reflect changes in land value. In a resource extraction context, the property derives its value from its reserve content; the property tax should be based on the value of remaining reserves. While there are several ways to evaluate the value of $S(t)$, an important special case is $g(t)S(t) = ge^{rt}S(t)$ which applies a fixed rate to the true value of remaining reserves.

By the maximum principle

$$p = \mu + dC/dR + \partial Z/\partial R. \qquad (5.4)$$

This condition differs from the no-tax case not only because of the tax term, but because $\mu$ is likely to differ from $\mu^*$. Although the discount rate is unaffected by the tax under the current assumptions, Hotelling rule may take a different form than in the no-tax case because of the possibility that the tax depends on remaining reserves

$$d\mu/dt = r\mu + \partial Z/\partial S. \qquad (5.5)$$

At $T$, the Hamiltonian must vanish. If $T$ is finite, this implies

$$p = \mu + C(\cdot)/R - Z(\cdot)/R.$$

Combining this with (5.4) one has at $T$

$$dC/dR + \partial Z/\partial R = C(\cdot)/R + Z(\cdot)/R. \qquad (5.6)$$

In order to focus on industry effects, and keeping in mind the aggregation issues already mentioned, assume that (5.4)-(5.6) are sectoral relationships and that sector demand is $p(t) = P(R(t))$, with $P(\cdot)$ decreasing in $R$[47]. In the perfect information equilibrium price must equalize the supply and demand of $R$, a condition which is imposed by substituting $P(\cdot)$ for $p(t)$ in (5.4). Totally differentiating the resulting expression with respect to $t$, and eliminating $\mu$ and $d\mu/dt$ using (5.4) and (5.5), one has

$$(dR/dt)[dP/dR - d^2C/dR^2 - \partial^2Z/\partial R^2 - (\partial^2Z/\partial R\partial p)(dP/dR)]$$
$$= r[p - dC/dR - \partial Z/\partial R] + \partial Z/\partial S + \partial^2Z/\partial R\partial t$$
$$- (\partial^2Z/\partial R\partial S)R. \qquad (5.7)$$

Together with the terminal condition (5.6), this differential equation defines the optimal extraction path $R(\cdot)$ implicitly. In particular, in the absence of a tax, it reduces to

$$(dR^*/dt)[dP/dR - d^2C/dR^2] = r[p - dC/dR] \qquad (5.7^*)$$

which is a particular case of (1.6) and is immediately seen to imply that $R^*$ decreases over time.

---

[47] It is easily verified that this meets the earlier assumption on the rate of growth of $p(t)$.

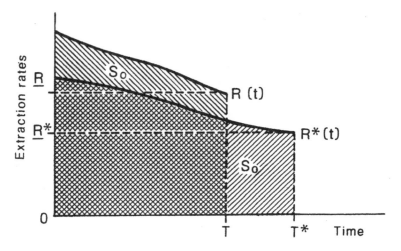

FIGURE 5.1 Hotelling model: effect of a franchise tax.

It is now possible to analyze the effect of alternative taxes on the optimum extraction path, on its duration, and on the rent. In order to do this Burness (1976) used a technique which lends itself to a graphical analysis in $(R, t)$ space.

Figure 5.1 depicts the case of a *franchise tax* $(Z(\cdot) = f(t))$. Since the same stock $S_0$ is extracted with, and without, a tax, the areas under the curves $R(t)$ and $R^*(t)$ must be identical, so that the reserve constraint (5.2) can be readily checked on the diagram. Furthermore, by (5.6), marginal cost exceeds average cost at $T$ while, in the no-tax case, (5.6) requires marginal cost to be equal to average cost at $T^*$. It follows that $R(T)$ exceeds $R^*(T^*)$ as depicted. Finally (5.7) reduces to (5.7*). This means that if, at some date $t$, extraction rates were identical with and without a tax, then $R(t)$ and $R^*(t)$ would have the same slope; but then $R(t + \epsilon) = R^*(t + \epsilon)$ and, as a result, the slopes are also identical at $t + \epsilon$. Repeating this argument, it follows that, if $R(t) = R^*(t)$ at some $t$, then $R(t) = R^*(t)$ at all dates. Since at closure time $R(T) > R^*(T^*)$ and the curves are downward sloping, this requires $T < T^*$. However two curves which differ only in that one, $R(t)$, covers a shorter period than the other one, $R^*(t)$, cannot generate identical areas. This violation of the reserve constraint implies that there does not exist any date $t$ at which

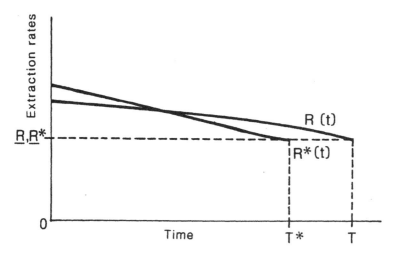

FIGURE 5.2 Hotelling model: effect of a constant severance or royalty.

$R(t) = R^*(t)$. This leaves only two possibilities: either $R(t)$ is every-where above $R^*(t)$, or the opposite. It is immediate to check that, with $\underline{R} > \underline{R}^*$, the areas under the curve can be identical only in the former case, as depicted in Figure 5.1. The franchise tax thus causes existing reserves to be depleted faster than in the absence of tax. The intuitive explanation is that this shortening of the extraction period allows the firms to pay a lower cumulative tax bill than if they did not adjust their extraction trajectory.

Now consider a *severance tax or royalty*. The same approach is followed as with the franchise tax. By (5.6), $R(T) = R^*(T^*)$. (5.7) reduces to

$$(dR/dt)[dP/dR - d^2C/dR^2] = r[p - dC/dR - s(t)] + ds/dt. \tag{5.7s}$$

Assume that the tax rate is constant $(ds/dt = 0)$; if at some date $t\,R(t) = R^*(t)$, then $dR/dt > dR^*/dt$. In other words, if the $R$ and $R^*$ paths cross each other, $R$ must cut $R^*$ from below; furthermore, this can happen only once. It is also easily seen that both paths cannot meet the area-under-the-curve condition while terminating at identical extraction rates $R^*(T^*) = R(T)$, unless they do cross each other and the steeper one spans a shorter period. The solution must be as depicted in Figure 5.2.

At any given initial reserve level ($t = 0$), imposing a constant severance tax causes $R$ to be reduced relative to the no-tax case; furthermore, the extraction period is lengthened. Unlike the franchise, the firm cannot avoid the tax by shortening the extraction period. Instead, the tax has the effect of an increase in marginal cost, whose static output reducing effect carries out to the dynamic context of resource extraction; however, since the tax cannot affect total cumulative extraction in the Hotelling model, the reduced extraction rate translates into a longer extraction period. When the tax rate is not constant, anything can happen. In particular, it is possible to select $s(t)$ in such a way that $rs(t) = ds/dt$ at all dates; in that case, (5.7) reduces to (5.7*) and the tax does not affect the extraction path. What is the yield of such a neutral tax? It is easily determined. The transversality condition (5.6) reduces to

$$P(R) = \mu + C(R)/R + s. \tag{5.6s}$$

This compares with the tax free case

$$P(R^*) = \mu^* + C(R^*)/R^*. \tag{5.6*}$$

Since $R^* = R$, it follows that $\mu + s = \mu^*$ at $T = T^*$. Also, since both $s$ and $\mu$ grow at the rate $r$, they represent the same proportion of each other and of $\mu^*$ at all dates. Thus this particular severance tax is collecting a constant proportion of the tax-free rent, which is also the before-tax rent. It is in fact equivalent to a rent tax, which also leaves the extraction path unaffected, as shown further below.

The *ad valorem severance tax or royalty* turn out to have identical properties as their output based counterparts. Let us now investigate the effect of a *property tax based on the value of the resource property*. Since $Z(S, R, p, t) = g(t)S(t)$, (5.7) reduces to

$$(dR/dt)[dP/dR - \partial^2 C/\partial R^2] = r[p - \partial C/\partial R] + g(t). \tag{5.7g}$$

As a result, if the tax-free and the property tax extraction rates cross each other, $dR/dt < dR^*/dt$. Since (5.6) requires $R(T) = R^*(T^*)$ for this tax, the extraction paths indeed must cross if the surfaces they generate are also to be identical. The sole possible configuration is depicted in Figure 5.3. It requires a faster extraction than in the tax-free situation, which is selected by the firm as a way to shorten the period over which

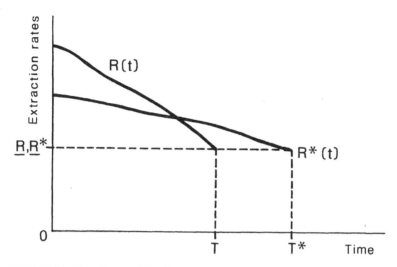

FIGURE 5.3 Hotelling model: effect of a property tax based on the value of the resource property.

it is liable to pay the property tax; this result applies whether or not the resource unit is properly evaluated.

A *pure profit tax*, such as the rate-of-return tax was advocated by Garnaut and Ross (1975, 1979) and further discussed by, among others, Heaps and Helliwell (1985), and Heaps (1985). Naturally, being based on pure profits, the interest for this type of taxation has arisen from its potential neutrality. As shown now, if a neutral tax is defined as a tax which leaves the competitive extraction path unchanged, the rate of return tax is not neutral in the progressive rate versions which have usually been implemented. With $Z(\cdot) = u(\pi)\pi$, $\pi = pR - C(R)$ being pure profits, (5.7) reduces to

$$(dR/dt)\{(dP/dR - d^2C/dR^2)[1 - (u + \pi du/d\pi)] \qquad (5.7\pi)$$
$$- (2du/d\pi + \pi d^2u/d\pi^2)(p - dC/dR)[(p - dC/dR)$$
$$+ RdP/dR]\} = r[(p - dC/dR)[1 - (u + \pi du/d\pi)]$$

or after some manipulations

$$dR/dt = (dR*/dt)[(dP/dR - d^2C/dR^2)[1 - (u + \pi du/d\pi)]$$

$$/\{(dP/dR - d^2C/dR^2)[1 - (u + \pi du/d\pi)] - (2du/d\pi$$

$$+ \pi d^2u/d\pi^2)(p - dC/dR)[(p - dC/dR) + RdP/dR]\}].$$

Since (5.6) requires $R(T) = R*(T*)$, the tax is neutral if and only if (5.7$\pi$) reduces to (5.7*). It can be verified that this is the case if and only if the tax rate $u(\pi)$ is chosen in such a way that

$$2du/d\pi + \pi d^2u/d\pi^2 = 0 \text{ for all } \pi^{[48]}. \tag{5.8}$$

Besides the flat rate tax, this condition is satisfied by

$$u(\pi) = A - B\pi^{-1}, 0 < A \leq 1, B > 0.$$

It can be seen that this gives a progressive tax, with $u(\cdot)$ rising in $\pi$ and tending toward $A$ as $\pi$ tends to $\infty$. However, for low values of $\pi$, $u(\pi)$ is negative. In fact $Z$ is simply a negative profit tax $u(\pi)\pi = -B + A\pi$.

Tax authorities can implement a progressive rate of return taxes while preserving neutrality only if they accept to subsidize low profits. In cyclical industries such as resource extraction, this implies sharing a higher proportion of the risk than under a flat-rate tax. Governments have avoided this route and, instead, those progressive rate of return taxes that have been implemented are distortive. However their exact effect depends on the elasticity of demand and the value of the resource. A tax whose yield is positive, rising, and convex, in $\pi$ must satisfy $u + \pi du/d\pi < 0$ and $2u + \pi d^2u/d\pi^2 \geq 0$. It can be shown that such a tax slows down the extraction of highly valuable Hotelling resources ($\mu$ high) whose demand elasticity is relatively high ($dP/dR$ small) and, conversely, speeds up the extraction of widely available Hotelling resources ($\mu$ small) whose demand elasticity is high ($dP/dR$ high in absolute value).

### 5.3 Resource taxation in a simple Ricardian world

It will be remembered that, in a Ricardian model of resource extraction, ultimate cumulative extraction depends on economic conditions. This happens because geological conditions are not homogeneous, so that extraction costs vary as extraction proceeds. Closure occurs when price

---

[48]If we write the tax as $G(\pi(R,p)) \equiv Z(R,p)$, it can be seen that (5.8) is in fact $d^2G/d\pi^2 = 0$, meaning that the tax is linear in $\pi$.

no longer covers marginal extraction cost and this condition determines the amount of reserves left in the ground and deemed uneconomical. Obviously, taxation may affect it. Analysis is harder than in the Hotelling case because one has to identify both effects on the extraction rate and effects on ultimate cumulative extraction; those effects in turn affect the extraction period. While the extra complexity may justify the use of numerical methods[49] (Gamponia and Mendelsohn, 1985), Heaps (1985) provides general analytical methods for the study of alternative taxes in such a context; Conrad and Hool (1981) deal with the issue of grade selection on a daily basis; Slade (1984) stresses the practical limits of theoretical results at the current level of generality.

The methodology must be altered so as to monitor both $R$ and $S$ simultaneously over time and at closure date. The extraction cost function is now $C(R, S)$ instead of $C(R)$, as in the general model of Section 1.2. By choice of $R(\cdot)$ and $T$, the competitive firm solves

$$Max \int_0^T e^{-rt}[p(t) R(t) - C(S(t), R(t))$$

$$- Z(S(t), R(t), p(t), t)]dt \qquad (5.9)$$

subject to

$$- dS/dt = R(t) \geq 0, \text{ with } S(0) = S_0 \text{ given.} \qquad (5.2)$$

In order to focus on Ricardian characteristics, $C(\cdot)$ and $C(\cdot) + Z(\cdot)$ are assumed to be such that complete exhaustion is uneconomic. Formally, whatever $p(t)$, there is a strictly positive level of $S$ below which $pR - C(S, R) - Z(S, R, p, t) \leq 0$ for all $R$, including $\underline{R}(S)$ the extraction rate at which average cost, gross of tax, is minimum. The same regularity conditions apply as in the Hotelling case: $p$ does not rise faster than at the discount rate; $C(\cdot) + Z(\cdot)$ is jointly concave in $S$, $R$ for $R \geq R(s)$. The Hamiltonian is

$$H(\cdot) = e^{-rt}[(p - \mu)R - C(S, R) - Z(S, R, p, t)] \qquad (5.10)$$

Almost as in the Hotelling case, necessary conditions are

$$p = \mu + \partial C/\partial R + \partial Z/\partial R. \qquad (5.11)$$

---

[49]Numerical methods have also been used for the study of non-linear taxation, and tend to prevail in stochastic models (Mackie-Mason, 1987; Virmani, 1986).

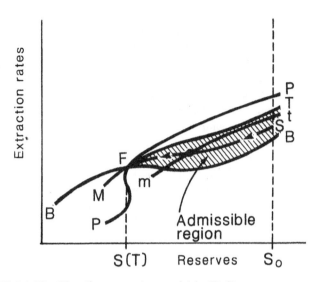

FIGURE 5.4 The Ricardian extraction model in (R, S) space.

$$d\mu/dt = r\mu + \partial C/\partial S + \partial Z/\partial S. \qquad (5.12)$$

One transversality condition at $T$ requires the Hamiltonian to vanish which, combined with (5.11), in turn implies

$$(\partial/\partial R)[C(S,R)] + (\partial/\partial R)[Z(S,R,P(R),t)] \qquad (5.13)$$
$$= C(S,R)/R + Z(S,R,P(R),t)/R.$$

The second transversality condition is specific to the Ricardian model with incomplete exhaustion. Since $S(T) > 0$, $\mu(T) = 0$; combined with the condition that the Hamiltonian vanishes at $T$, it implies

$$P(R) = C(S,R)/R + Z(S,R,P(R),t)/R \text{ at } t = T. \qquad (5.14)$$

The analysis of this problem is more difficult than its Hotelling counterpart because $S(T)$ is now endogenous and $S(t)$ does not vanish from the relevant expressions as readily as before. Heaps (1985) provided a beautiful first treatment of a more general version of the problem. The methodology used now is slightly different from Heaps'.

Because the transversality conditions now specify both $S$ and $R$ it is necessary to characterize the solution in a $(S, R)$ space rather than the convenient time space used above. In Figure 5.4, the *BB* locus represents the $(S, R)$ pairs that satisfy (5.13). Thus on $BB$, for all relevant levels of $S$, $R$ is such that average cost, inclusive of the tax, is minimized; its slope depends on the technology, the geology, and the tax system. The terminal point of the extraction program must be on $BB$. It must also satisfy (5.14), the condition that profits vanish at closure date. This condition is represented by locus $PP$, whose general shape and curvature is easily inferred from the assumptions on $C(\cdot) + Z(\cdot)$ and $P(\cdot)$: starting from $BB$, a change in $R$ is a movement away from the (gross) cost minimizing rate; in order to maintain zero profits, $S$ must increase accordingly. If $p$ was unaffected by $R$ in equilibrium, the $PP$ locus would be vertical as it crosses $BB$; but since in general $p$ diminishes as $R$ rises, thus reducing profits, $PP$ must have a finite positive slope at its intersection with $BB$, at $F$. As it satisfies both (5.13) and (5.14), $F$ is the terminal point for the extraction programme. At $T$, the programme must also satisfy (5.11), represented by the $MT$ locus, whose slope at $F$ is lower than that of $PP$ because $MT$ has the same relationship with $PP$ as marginal cost with average cost, $F$ being the point of minimum average cost. At other dates (5.11) must also be satisfied, but with $\mu > 0$; mt is one of the corresponding loci, which must cut $BB$ further to the right of $F$, the higher $\mu$. Now the solution can be characterized. The extraction path, represented by the arrowed line, must lie above $BB$ (output above gross-cost minimizing rate), on the right of MT ($\mu$ is non-negative), start on the vertical through $S_0$ (initial reserves equal $S_0$), and end up at $F$. The higher the path, the higher the extraction rate, and the shorter the period necessary to use a given quantity of $S$. Note that the various loci in Figure 5.4 may shift over time if the problem is not time autonomous, that is if the tax function may shift over time.

Let us characterize the dynamics of the extraction path. Substituting the equilibrium condition $P(R) = p$ into (5.11), differentiating the resulting expression with respect to time, and using (5.11) and (5.12) to substitute for $\mu$ and $d\mu/dt$, one has

$$(dR/dt)\left[dP/dR - \partial^2 C/\partial R^2 - \partial^2 Z/\partial R^2 - (\partial^2 Z/\partial R\partial p)(dP/dR)\right]$$
$$= r\left[p - \partial C/\partial R - \partial Z/\partial R\right] + \partial C/\partial S + \partial Z/\partial S$$
$$+ \partial^2 Z/\partial R\partial t - (\partial^2 C/\partial R\partial S + \partial^2 Z/\partial R\partial S)R. \qquad (5.15)$$

Since this differential equation is non-autonomous, its trajectories may cross in $(R, S)$ space, making a qualitative analysis impossible in general in that space. Heaps provides conditions under which such crossing is impossible in his model. As in most tax models, the price is taken as exogenously given, and Heaps' conditions involve restrictions on its trajectory combined with restrictions on the technology and the tax environment. In the foregoing model, the assumption of a time autonomous demand schedule, combined with the market equilibrium requirement, suppress that source of time dependency. The sole source of time dependency is the tax; it disappears when the tax parameters are constant or time autonomous, as is the case in most practical applications and as is assumed in the sequel unless otherwise mentioned.

Consider now alternative taxes, using, as before '*' subscripts to designate variables, functions, or expressions in the tax-free situation. The tax-free situation is characterized by

$$(\partial/\partial R)\big[C(S^*, R^*)\big] = C(S^*, R^*)/R^* \text{ at } t = T^*, \quad (5.13^*)$$

$$P(R^*) = C(S^*, R^*)/R^* \text{ at } t = T^*, \quad (5.14^*)$$

$$(dR^*/dt)\big[dP/dR - \partial^2 C/\partial R^2\big] = r\big[p - \partial C/\partial R\big]$$
$$+ \partial C/\partial S - (\partial^2 C/\partial R \partial S)R. \quad (5.15^*)$$

A *franchise tax*, $Z = f$, leaves $(5.15^*)$ unaffected; thus the family of possible trajectories from which the solution is selected is unchanged by the tax and those trajectories do not cross in $(R, S)$ space. However, both terminal conditions are altered:

$$(\partial/\partial R)\big[C(S, R)\big] = C(S, R)/R + f/R. \quad (5.13f)$$

$$P(R) = C(S, R)/R + f/R \text{ at } t = T. \quad (5.14f)$$

It appears readily that the *BB* locus shifts up from $B^*B^*$, while the *PP* locus shifts to the right from $P^*P^*$, as drawn in Figure 5.5. So the franchise tax reduces the total amount of resource extracted ($S(T) > S^*(T^*)$). Does it also speed up extraction as in the Hotelling case? The answer depends on whether the *SF* curve lies above or below the $S^*F^*$ curve. Suppose the taxed curve *SF* lies below the tax free curve $S^*F^*$. For the taxed programme, when reserves are down to $S(T)$, from $(5.11)$, $P(R) = \partial C(S(T), R)/\partial R + \partial Z/\partial R = \partial C(S(T), R)/\partial R$; this is smaller than $\partial C(S(T), R^*)/\partial R$ by the assumption that $R^* > R$. But, from $(5.11^*)$, $\partial C(S(T), R^*)/\partial R = P(R^*) - \mu^*$. Combining these properties, $P(R) < P(R^*) - \mu^*$; but since $R^* > R$, $P(R^*) < P(R)$ which contradicts $\mu^* > 0$. Consequently, the *SF* trajectory must lie above the $S^*F^*$ trajectory, as drawn, a result conforming with the intuition that

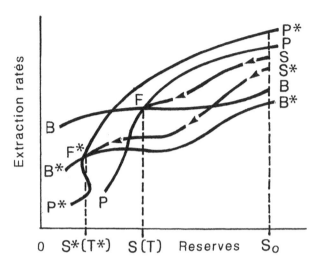

FIGURE 5.5 Ricardian model: effect of a franchise tax.

a given quantity of reserves will be extracted faster with a franchise tax because this reduces the period over which the tax is being paid and the total tax bill. This time inefficiency which was also observed in the Hotelling case comes in addition to the reduction in ultimate reserve extraction induced by the franchise tax in the Ricardian model.

With a *constant severance tax*, $Z(\cdot) = sR(t)$, terminal conditions (5.13) and (5.14) become

$$(\partial/\partial R)[C(S, R)] = C(S, R)/R. \qquad (5.13s)$$

$$P(R) = C(S, R)/R + s \text{ at } t = T. \qquad (5.14s)$$

Thus the $BB$ locus is unchanged from $B^*B^*$ and the $PP$ locus shifts to the right. As far as the dynamics of the solution path are concerned, (5.15) becomes

$$(dR/dt)[dP/dR - \partial^2 C/\partial R^2] = r[P - \partial C/\partial R - s] + \partial C/\partial S. \qquad (5.15s)$$

Suppose that the $SF$ and the $S^*F^*$ paths did cross, unlike in Figure 5.6. At their intersection $dR/dt > dR^*/dt$, which means that, in the $(S, R)$ plan of Figure 5.6, $SF$ would cut $S^*F^*$ from below. But, since $S^*F^*$ must

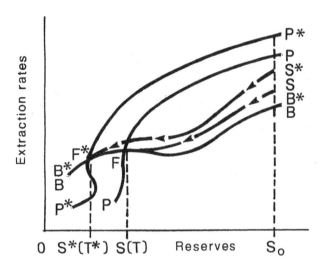

FIGURE 5.6 Ricardian model: effect of a constant severance or royalty.

lie everywhere above $B*B*$ if extraction is to proceed at a rate higher than the average-cost-minimizing rate $R(S)$, and since $B*B*$ is identical to $BB$, $SF$ would have to cut $S*F*$ again, this time from above, in order to reach its terminal point $F$ on $BB$. This would contradict $dR/dt > dR*/dt$[50]. Hence the $SF$ path must not cut the $S*F*$ path in Figure 5.6. The effects of the tax are now clear. There is a reduction in ultimate extraction. Since $SF$ is below $S*F*$, it takes longer in the taxed case to extract any given amount of reserves; however, since the ultimate amount is reduced, $T$ may be higher or lower than $T*$. Similar results arise in the case of *ad valorem* severance taxes or royalties.

A property tax based on $S(t)$, $Z = gS(t)$, will shift $BB$ up and $PP$ to the right, since (5.13)* and (5.14)*, respectively, become

$$(\partial/\partial R)[C(S, R)] = C(S, R)/R + gS/R. \qquad (5.13g)$$

$$P(R) = C(S, R)/R + gs/R \text{ at } t = T. \qquad (5.14g)$$

Consequently, more reserves are left in the ground at closure. Instead of (5.15)*

---

[50]Heaps finds this to be a possibility in the case of a variable tax.

$$(dR/dt)[dP/dR - \partial^2C/\partial R^2] = r[P - \partial C/\partial R] + \partial C/\partial S + g.$$

$$(5.15g)$$

Thus, if they cross, the paths must be such that $dR/dt < dR*/dt$ at their intersection; $SF$ must cut $S*F*$ from above. But is this admissible? If it is, there may exist instances where a property tax slows down the extraction of a given amount of reserves. For example, in Figure 5.8, suppose that the tax is imposed when reserves are $S_0'$ instead of $S_0$. Then, by the principle of optimality, the portion of the figure on the left of the vertical through $S_0'$ still represents the solution to the new problem. For that new problem, the relevant part of $S*F*$ is everywhere above the relevant part of $SF$ which implies that the tax reduces the extraction rate relative to the tax free situation at any $S < S_0'$. This is counterintuitive as accelerated extraction is a way to avoid part of the tax burden. Let us show that this counterintuitive outcome is in fact ruled out. Suppose that the configuration of Figure 5.8 is possible. Then when $S = S(T)$ (and $\mu(T) = 0$), by (5.11), $\partial C(S(T), R)/\partial R = P(R)$ and, by (5.11)*, $P(R*) = \partial CS(T), R*)/\partial R + \mu*$; since by assumption $R* > R$, so that $P(R) > P(R*)$, it follows that $\mu* < \partial C(S(T), R)/\partial R - \partial C(S(T), R*)/\partial R$, a difference which is itself negative by the assumption of rising marginal cost. But this implies $\mu* < 0$, an impossibility. Thus the property tax reduces the ultimate amount of reserves extracted, and accelerates the rate at which those reserves are exploited, as represented in Figure 5.7; the counterintuitive configuration of Figure 5.8 is ruled out.

In the case of a *profit tax, possibly progressive*, $Z(\cdot) = u(\pi)\pi$, where $\pi = pR - C(S, R)$ and $u(\cdot)$ is non-decreasing, it is immediately apparent that the transversality conditions are not affected by the tax, so that the $BB$ and $PP$ loci stay at their tax free positions. Concerning the dynamics of the solution, (5.15) becomes

$$(dR/dt)[(dP/dR - \partial^2C/\partial R^2)(1 - (\pi du/d\pi + u))$$

$$\qquad (5.15)\pi$$

$$- (\pi d^2u/\partial d\pi^2 + 2du/d\pi)((\partial\pi/\partial R)^2 + R(dP/dR)(\partial\pi/\partial R))]$$

$$= [r(p - \partial C/\partial R) + \partial C/\partial S - R\partial^2C/\partial R\partial S](1 - (\pi du/d\pi + u))$$

$$+ (\pi d^2u/d\pi^2 + 2du/d\pi)[R(\partial\pi/\partial R)(\partial C/\partial S)].$$

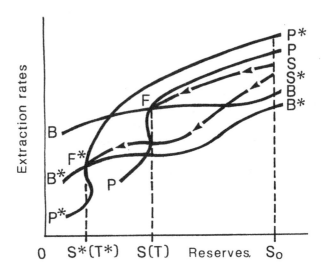

FIGURE 5.7 : Ricardian model: effect of an *ad valorem* property tax based on resource property value.

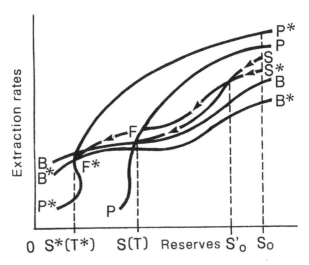

FIGURE 5.8 Ricardian model: an impossible configuration with *ad valorem* property tax.

This simplifies to (5.15)* if and only if $\pi d^2 u/d\pi^2 + 2du/d\pi = 0$, which is the same neutrality condition (5.8) as in the Hotelling case. Again a progressive rate of return tax is not neutral unless it takes the form of a negative profit tax, linear in $\pi$ and negative at low values of $\pi$. The effect of existing progressive rate of return taxes is not without ambiguity and depends on the particulars of the industries that are subject to it: technology, geology and demand conditions. With inefficient general taxation it is not surprising either that efficiency inducing resource taxation, as described by Hung and Long (1982), remains a theoretical proposition.

### 5.4 The corporate income tax

The corporate income tax is particular in two major respects. First it is actually a tax on capital income; its analysis requires the explicit introduction of capital in the model. Second, it is not specific to extractive sectors; on the contrary, as it affects most industries, its pressure is supposed to be spread evenly over an economy. The corporate income tax is a major element in most computations of effective tax rates; while these rates differ across countries and over time, one often expects them, according to the Schanz–Haig–Simons rule, to be identical for identical types of capital across sectors. But the corporate income tax contains special provisions for extractive firms. The most important and widespread of those provisions, the depletion allowance, is normally meant to reduce taxable income by the cost of the resource used over the period. Does it conform with the Schanz–Haig–Simons rule or with any alternative taxation principle? As will be argued below, neither its interpretation nor its rationale are very clear and its effect of reducing the effective tax rate in resource industries has been questioned repeatedly since Harberger (1955) criticized it.

Let us start with a partial efficiency analysis of the same type as in the previous subsection. In order to keep the model simple while endowing it with capital explicitly, assume that capital is the sole input and is fully malleable. If $V$ is its asset price, its pre-tax rental price is

$$v = (r + \delta)V - dV/dt \qquad (5.16)$$

where $\delta$ is the physical depreciation rate. Reality can be further simplified by assuming that all investment is financed by retained earnings. Under this assumption, the discount rate is the same before, and after, tax and can be assumed to equal the exogenously given after-personal-income-tax interest rate.

Ignoring such features as the investment tax credit[51], the fundamental characteristics of the tax, besides its rate $u$, are the deductions involved in the definition of the tax base: the depreciation allowance, a proportion $\theta$ of the value of undepreciated capital $C$, aims at reflecting capital expenditures in the current period; the depletion allowance, a proportion $\beta$ of the value of current extraction $pR$, aims at reflecting current non-renewable resource consumption. The tax is $u(pR - \beta pR - \theta C)$ and the firm chooses an investment programme $I(\cdot)$, thus also an extraction programme, to maximize the present value of its cumulative after-tax income flows. Omitting time arguments when no ambiguity arises the problem is

$$Max \int_0^T e^{-rt}[pR - VI - u(pR - \beta pR - \theta C)]\,dt$$

$$+ J(C(T), K(T), V(T)) \qquad (5.16)$$

subject to

$$dS/dt = -R; \; S(0) = S_0 \text{ given} \qquad (5.2)$$

$$dC/dt = VI - \theta C; \; C(0) = C_0 = V(0)K_0 \text{ given} \qquad (5.17)$$

$$dK/dt = I - \delta K; \; K(0) = K_0 \text{ given} \qquad (5.18)$$

$$R = F(S, K). \qquad (5.19)$$

(5.17) is the rule which specifies the book value of undepreciated capital for tax purposes. $J(\cdot)$ is the residual value of the firm at closure. It is the net result of selling any remaining capital at $T$ and clearing with the tax authorities any discrepancy between $K(T)$ and $C(T)$; typically, since tax depreciation is usually faster than physical depreciation, the firm must reimburse the excess of tax depreciation over economic depreciation at $T$. $F(\cdot)$ is the production function, in a Ricardian model.

With malleable capital, if the tax provisions at closure amount to a continuation of previous provisions with respect to depreciation (see Gaudet and Lasserre, 1984), then problem (5.16) is equivalent, as in

---

[51]The investment tax credit can easily be incorporated into the analysis; I choose here not to complicate the notation.

the literature based on Jorgenson (1963), to a problem involving the direct choice of $K(\cdot)$, where the services of $K$ are paid at their before-tax rental rate $v$

$$Max \int_0^T e^{-rt}[pR - C(S, R) - u(pR - zC(S, R) - \beta pR)]dt$$

(5.20)

subject to (5.2)

where $C(S, R) \equiv vK(S, R)$, $K(S, R)$ being the input requirement function associated with the production function (5.19); and $z = \theta/(r + \theta)$ is the present value of a dollar of undepreciated capital which can be depreciated indefinitely at rate $\theta$.

(5.20) is a particular case of (5.9), so that the corporate income tax can now undergo a similar analysis as the taxes studied in the previous subsection. The comparison between the tax-free situation and the programme under corporate income tax is further facilitated if one divides through by $(1 - uz)$, assumed constant, to get the equivalent problem

$$Max \int_0^T e^{-rt}[\alpha pR - C(S, R)]dt$$

(5.21)

subject to (5.2)

where $\alpha \equiv [1 - (1 - \beta)u]/(1 - uz)$. Since (5.21) differs from the tax-free problem by the output price only, its solution is described by (5.13)*, (5.14)* and (5.15)* where $p$ or $P(R)$, and $dP/dR$, are respectively replaced by $\alpha p$, $\alpha P(R)$, and $\alpha dP/dR$. Locus $BB$, which will be remembered to represent pairs $(S, R)$ such that $R$ minimizes gross average cost, is unaffected by the tax and remains identical to $B^*B^*$. Locus $PP$, representing the zero profit condition which must also be satisfied at $T$, lies to the right (left) of $P^*P^*$ if $\alpha > 1 (< 1)$. Finally, comparing (5.15)* with its taxed version, if the trajectories for $(S^*, R^*)$ and $(S, R)$ pairs were to cross they would be such that, at their intersection,

$$dR/dt = dR^*/dt - (\alpha - 1)(dP/dR)/[(dP/dR) - \partial^2 C/\partial R^2].$$

(5.22)

This makes an intersection of $SF$ and $S^*F^*$ in Figure 5.9 impossible. Indeed, suppose that $\alpha < 1$ so that $F$ lies on the right of $F^*$. (5.22)

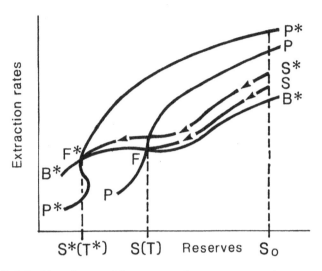

FIGURE 5.9   Ricardian model: corporate income tax, $\alpha < 1$

implies $dR/dt > dR^*/dt$, which means that $SF$ cuts $S^*F^*$ from below. But this is an impossible configuration if $SF$ is to terminate at $F$, below $S^*F^*$. It follows that $SF$ is everywhere below $S^*F^*$, as drawn, if $\alpha < 1$, which means that the tax causes less reserve to be extracted, and at a slower rate. Conversely, $SF$ lies everywhere above $S^*F^*$, with $F$ on the left of $F^*$, if $\alpha > 1$. Neutrality arises if $\alpha = 1$. Inspecting the formula for $\alpha$, it is clear that $\alpha$ reflects the tax treatment of $K$, as measured by $z$, the value of 1\$ of investment in future tax depreciations, relative to the tax treatment of the resouce, as measured by $\beta$. The depletion allowance may be used to adjust the tax treatment of the resource so as to balance the tax treatment of capital in such a way as to eliminate the distortions resulting from the corporate income tax. This requires setting $\beta = 1 - z$; the more favourable the treatment of capital, the less favourable the depletion allowance should be. One type of capital has to be taxed more heavily when the other type is taxed lightly, in order to leave the overall production incentive unaffected. This result, derived here for the Ricardian case, also applies to a Hotelling resource (Gaudet and Lasserre, 1984).

The focus on neutrality in a partial equilibrium set-up represents a narrow point of view as resource sectors are just some among many others in the economy and as several taxes, the corporate income tax in particular, affect both resource industries and other industries. In a second-best world, when other sectors are subject to distorting taxation, it is more meaningful to compare the tax treatments of various sectors and inputs than to wonder about tax neutrality in resource industries alone. Gaudet and Lasserre (1986) have discussed the corporate income tax and the depletion allowance from that point of view for a Hotelling resource. They define a hypothetical tax which collects a proportion $\tau$ of true capital income in non-extractive sectors and a proportion $\tau^e$ in extractive sectors. True capital income is defined as $pR - \delta VK$ in a non-extractive sector, where $R$ is interpreted as output not subject to any resource constraint; in extractive sectors, true capital income is $pR - \delta VK - \eta R$, where $\eta$ is the value of the *in situ* resource. Then they compute the values of $\tau$ and $\tau^e$ at which the hypothetical taxes have the same real effects as the corporate income tax on non-extractive sectors and extractive sectors, respectively. Those values of $\tau$ and $\tau^e$ represent both marginal and average effective rates of the corporate income tax. Gaudet and Lasserre find that, given the other parameters of the corporate income tax, the depletion allowance can be selected in a way which equalizes effective tax rates on capital income in extractive and non-extractive sectors. This result is achieved when the depletion allowance is precisely set at the value of *in situ* resource consumption, i.e. for $\beta = \mu/p$. The common effective tax rate is then

$$\tau = \tau^e = (u - uz)/[1 - uz - (1 - u)\delta V/v]. \qquad (5.23)$$

The same result is valid for the Ricardian model, as is shown now.

Let the hypothetical tax on true capital income apply the same effective rate $\tau$, given by (5.23), in all extractive and non-extractive sectors. The corporate income tax is equivalent to the hypothetical tax if extraction rates are identical under both regimes. Those programmes must satisfy (5.11)c and (5.11)$\tau$, where 'c' and '$\tau$' refer to corporate-income-tax and pure-capital-income-tax situations, respectively. The former is obtained in solving problem (5.20) the usual way

$$p(1 - u)/(1 - uz) - \mu^c\{[1 - u(\beta p/\mu^c)]/(1 - uz)\} = \partial C/\partial R$$
$$(5.11c)$$

where $\mu^c$ is the *in situ* value of the resource under the corporate income tax.

Similarly, in order to obtain (5.11)$\tau$, one must solve the problem of the firm under the hypothetical tax on true capital income $\tau(pR - \delta VK - \eta R)$ where $\eta$ is the true value of the *in situ* resource under the tax. As with (5.20), that problem is equivalent to

$$Max \int_0^T e^{-rt}[pR - vK(S, R) - \tau(pR - \delta VK(S, R) - \eta R)]\, dt$$

$$(5.24)$$

subject to (5.2)

As a necessary condition one has

$$p(1 - \tau)/(1 - \tau\delta V/v) - \mu^r[1 - \tau/(1 - \tau\delta V/v)] = \partial C/\partial R$$

where the fact that $\eta$ represents the true value of the *in situ* resource has been used to set it equal to the shadow price $\mu^r$. With $\tau$ given by (5.23), this gives

$$p(1 - u)/(1 - uz) - \mu^r(1 - u)/(1 - uz) = \partial C/\partial R$$

$$(5.11\tau)$$

(5.11)$\tau$ and (5.11)c will be identical at all dates if $\beta p/\mu^c = 1$ and $\mu^c = \mu^r$ at all dates. If the first condition is imposed by setting $\beta = \mu^c/p$ at all dates, it can be verified by further characterizing the solutions of both problems (5.20) and (5.24) that the second condition indeed also will be satisfied. This completes the proof that a depletion allowance equal to the true value of current reserve consumption ensures the equality of effective tax rates in extractive and non-extractive corporate sectors. While existing versions of the depletion allowance involve a constant rate $\beta$, so that they can only approach such an outcome, effective tax rate uniformity across sectors is apparently the rationale for this special provision of the corporate income tax. As argued below, it is hard to find any such rationale for the provisions of the corporate income tax with respect to exploration.

## 5.5 Exploration

The issue of exploration has been deliberately ignored so far. Initial reserves were treated as exogenously given and the focus was on decisions having to do with the best exploitation of existing reserves, the so-called intensive margin (Livernois and Uhler, 1987). In reality, reserves are the result of prior exploration efforts and are largely endogenous. Their determination is governed by decisions at what is known as the extensive margin. Although widely recognized, the effect of taxation at the extensive margin has not received the same thorough treatment as its effect at the intensive margin. As a simplified, but enlightening, way to look at this process, assume that the extraction phase studied so far is preceded by an exploration period of endogenous duration over which the firm extends exploration efforts to progressively accumulate the stock $S_0$. Extraction starts up when exploration is over, which can be viewed as a simplification of reality. The start-up date is endogenous; however, since the durations of both the extraction and the exploration periods are themselves endogenous, there is no loss of generality in using the convention that the start-up date is $t = 0$[52].

In this extended problem, the firm must select in a first phase its flows of exploration inputs and, in a second phase, its flows of extraction inputs, in such a way as to maximize net cumulative discounted revenues from extraction, minus cumulative compounded exploration expenditures, net of taxes

$$Max \int_0^T e^{-rt}[pR - C(S, R) - Z(\cdot)]dt - EX(S_0) \qquad (5.25)$$

subject to

$$- dS/dt = R(t) \text{ with } S_0 \text{ endogenous} \qquad (5.2)$$

and

$$EX(S_0) \text{ defined by } (5.26)$$

$EX(S_0)$ is the optimized value of cumulative net of tax exploration expenditures, obtained by selecting exploration inputs so as to

$$Min \int_{-T_x}^0 e^{-rt} ex(s, S)dt \qquad (5.26)$$

subject to

---

[52]This would not be so if the problem was not time-autonomous.

$$dS/dt = s(-t) \text{ with } S(-T_x) = 0 \text{ and } S(0) = S_0 \qquad (5.27)$$

$s$ is the rate of discoveries; $ex(\cdot)$ is the after-tax cost of discoveries, rising and convex in $s$, non-decreasing in $S$ (Lasserre, 1985a; Devarajan and Fisher, 1982); $-T_x$ is the endogenous date at which exploration activities begin. Problem (5.26) is formally similar to a Ricardian mining problem with this difference that, instead of optimally depleting a reserve stock, the firm optimally builds such a stock up to the target level $S_0$. As was done in the analysis of the extraction problem, it is possible to make a distinction between a Hotelling view of exploration, where cumulative discoveries do not cause any shift in discovery costs $(\partial ex(\cdot)/\partial S = 0)$, and a Ricardian view, where discoveries become more costly as $S$ increases $(\partial ex(\cdot)/\partial S > 0)$[53]. The corresponding value function $EX(S_0)$ is convex and rising in either case.

When $S_0$ is given, problem (5.25) reduces to the tax problem studied earlier, since $EX(S_0)$ is a constant in that case. When $S_0$ is endogenous, the transversality condition which must be satisfied at $t = 0$ is

$$\mu(0) = dEX(\cdot)/dS. \qquad (5.28)$$

It says that the shadow value, for extraction purposes, of the marginal unit of *in situ* reserves, must equal the marginal cost of producing it at the end of the exploration phase. As pointed out by Lasserre (1985a) this marginal cost is inclusive of the rent that unexplored land might command.

It is now possible to study the effect of taxation on exploration by examining the impact of alternative taxes on (5.28). With the exception of the corporate income tax, the taxes examined above do not affect exploration costs; they leave the right-hand side of (5.28) unaffected. But to the extent that they do tax extraction, they reduce $\mu$ on average and, in most instances, it can be shown that $\mu(0)$ is reduced. As a result the optimal level of $S_0$ is reduced; mining taxes cause a contraction at the extensive margin.

---

[53]For a stochastic formulation of the Hotelling view, see Arrow and Chiang (1982), and Lasserre (1984a); for a stochastic formulation of the Ricardian view, see Lasserre (1985b).

The case of the corporate income tax is more complex. In most countries, the corporate income tax includes special provisions for exploration expenditures. Often those are immediately deductible against income from other resource operations so that, in most instances, the after-tax cost of one dollar of exploration expenditures is $(1 − u)$. Assuming this to be the case in the foregoing model, the relation between net compounded cumulative exploration expenditures under corporate income tax and in the absence of tax is $EX(S) = (1 − u)EX^*(S)$. As a result

$$dEX/dS = (1 − u)dE^*/dS.$$

Having determined the effect of the tax on the right-hand side of (5.28), it remains to verify whether, for any given $S_0$, the tax reduces $\mu$ in a smaller or in a greater proportion. While it is difficult in general to compute $\mu$ and $\mu^*$ explicitly to find out, it can be shown that a pure rent tax at a rate $\phi$ is neutral and reduces the resource rent to a proportion[54] $(1 − \phi)$ of its original value. As shown above, when $\beta$ is set equal to $1 − z$, the corporate income tax is such a tax. Indeed when $\beta = 1 − z$ the objective functional in (5.20) reduces to

$$Max \int_o^T e^{-rt}(1 − uz)[pR − C(S, R)]dt$$

so that the rate of the pure rent tax in that case is $uz$ and

$$\mu = (1 − uz)\mu^*.$$

This shows that, in the benchmark case of a neutral corporate income tax, the left-hand side of (5.28) is reduced in a smaller proportion than the right-hand side. The tax induces a higher level of exploration in that case. In tax regimes that depart from the neutral case, this expansion at the extensive margin is likely to be less acute, the more favourable the treatment of extraction activities relative to exploration activities.

Of course, given the uncertainty associated with exploration, results obtained within a non-stochastic framework must be considered only indicative. Campbell and Lindner (1983, 1985a, 1985b) have attempted a stochastic treatment of the resource rent tax. They focus on

---

[54]The neutral royalty presented above in a Hotelling model is an example of this property.

exploration, with full or partial loss offset and with risk-neutral or risk-averse firms. Exploration is modelled as a costly process which yields information on the value of incompletely known deposits. Once the optimum level of information has been acquired, the deposit is exploited or abandoned. Here tax provisions with respect to loss offset turn out to matter. The authors find that the resource rent tax with full loss offset is neutral with respect to exploration effort, as in the non-stochastic set-up, if firms are risk neutral. With risk-averse firms, an increase in the rate of resource rent tax with full loss offset results in the taxing authority bearing a greater share of project risk. Because this amounts to a reduction in the firm's degree of risk aversion, promising deposits are explored less and unpromising ones are explored more. With partial loss offset neutrality is lost even when the firms are risk neutral.

Leland (1978), and Hyde and Markusen (1985), apply an optimal-taxation approach to the same problem, also cast into a two-period static mould. There are two levels of uncertainty. First, the firm must determine whether or not there is a deposit in a given track of land; if there is one, the probability of finding it depends on exploration expenditures. Second, once the result of exploration activities is known, there remains uncertainty about the size of reserves, and the firm must select production expenditures in that context. The government is completely informed about the firms, although it may differ from them in its *ex-ante* and *ex-post* assessments of uncertainty[55]. It selects a set of tax instruments in order to achieve three targets: optimal level of exploration activity; optimal level of extraction activity; some pre-specified distribution of expected resource rents. The first two tax instruments can easily be related to the above analysis of the corporate income tax: they specify in what proportions the government and firms share exploration costs, as well as production costs and revenues. The third instrument specifies the state dependent bonus bid that firms will agree to submit, if they behave competitively, in order to secure the right to exploit the parcel[56]. Since the government shares equally in production expenditures and revenues, this amounts to a pure *ex-post*

---

[55]In that sense there may be disagreement. However, the differences being public knowledge, there is no information asymmetry.

[56]Note that in practice, bonus bids are not state dependent. For an extended empirical and theoretical discussion and bibliography on the subject, see Ramsey (1980).

rent tax. However, unlike the certainty case, optimality is not generally compatible with the absence of a bonus bid. The latter has the role of redistributing wealth across states in such a way that a firm's expected marginal utility is constant across states. Such redistribution is not needed if the firms are risk-neutral; in that case, the pure rent tax is optimal, and neutral, in the absence of any state dependent bonus bid, as in Campbell and Lindner and as in the non-stochastic model analysed earlier. With respect to the *ex-ante* exploration decision, Hyde and Markusen point out that both the government and firms benefit from exploration activities, since they are going to share in the proceeds; as a result, the marginal condition for optimal exploration is similar to a Lindahl pricing rule, involving the sum of government and firm expected marginal utilities, as with any public good. In a non-stochastic framework, this explains why, according to (5.28), neutrality arises when the tax system affects exploration expenditures in the same proportion as the resource rent. However, because government and firm incomes move in opposite directions, this simple result no longer holds in a stochastic environment with risk aversion, unless agents have identical constant risk aversions and hold identical subjective probability distributions.

## 5.6 Optimal taxation and tax incidence in general equilibrium

Optimal taxation issues have crept repeatedly into the previous sections, although I tried to confine the analysis to more descriptive aspects and criteria, using concepts such as neutrality and distorting effects, or effective tax rates, rather than optimality. Indeed, as Simons (1977) and Long and Sinn (1984) have reasserted, the problem of optimal natural resource taxation is a second-best problem. As such it must be studied within the proper general equilibrium framework.

As was shown above, a depletion allowance is the resource analogue of true economic depreciation; for the particular form of corporate income tax studied earlier, it ensures the equalization of effective tax rates across all corporate sectors in the economy. Because it corresponds to the Haig–Simons rule and ensures the equality of marginal products across sectors, this particular system has been advocated, among others, by Dasgupta, Heal and Stiglitz (1980). However Long and Sinn give an example where it is suboptimal to extend this rule to extractive sectors when it is already applied to the rest of the economy.

In their three-sector example, consumers are taxed on their interest income and equate the marginal rate of time preference to the net-of-tax rate of interest while, for firms, the depletion allowance equates the return from holding the resource with the gross rate of interest. In equilibrium, this results in too rapid an extraction rate. In the model of Long and Sinn, an efficient second-best tax on the extractive firm is a tax on real cash flow where the tax rate equals that on interest income and interest is tax-deductible. Clearly, this result is dependent on the treatment of consumers relative to firms in the given tax set-up. For example, if firms are financed by retained earnings and dividends are taxed at the same rate as other sources of income, the consumer rate of time preference is equal to the after-tax discount rate of firms; in that case it is probably optimal to extend the Schanz–Haig–Simons rule to extractive sectors.

Tax incidence also belongs to the realm of general equilibrium analysis. Resources have generally been ignored in theoretical incidence analyses à la Harberger (1962), although taxes and subsidies are generally key features of resource sectors. Recently, however, the use of computable general equilibrium models has brought new results in this important area; an extensive bibliography is to be found in Decaluwé and Martens (1988) and Hertel (1988) discusses the theoretical issues involved and their empirical relevance. Those contributions share a major deficiency: neither of them incorporates the dynamics of resource depletion.

Competitive equilibrium is not always the appropriate equilibrium framework for the analysis of resource taxation. Strategic behaviour on the part of countries or jurisdictions may play an important role, as resource finiteness, in quantity and number of locations, reduces the number of actors. With the obvious analogy of the Opec cartel in mind, Brander and Spencer (1984), and Bergstrom (1982), have shown how non-cooperative international policy equilibrium could be characterized by export cartels and rent-extracting tariffs set by importing countries. In other circumstances, two producer areas under different jurisdictions may compete for sales on a common market. Using the example of coal in Wyoming and Montana, Kolstad and Wolak (1983) study a duopoly model where the duopolists are the governments of each coal state, competing with tax instruments. As is often the case in duopoly models of resource extraction, exhaustibility is not treated as an explicit factor, the model is static. Nonetheless, the authors derive the appropriate tax reaction functions and the resulting equilibrium, under the assumption of Cournot-Nash competition. They also investigate Stackelberg behaviour. The model is then used to compute numerically the tax rates that would prevail under alternative assumptions in each state.

## BIBLIOGRAPHY

Agbeyegbe, T. D. (1989), 'Interest Rates and Metal Price Movements: Further Evidence', *Journal of Environmental Economics and Management* **16(2)**, 184–92.

Arrow, K. and S. Chang (1982), 'Optimal Pricing Use and Exploration of Uncertain Natural Resource Stocks', *Journal of Environmental Economics and Management* **9(1)**, 1–10.

Barnett, H. J. (1979), 'Scarcity and Growth Revisited', in Smith, V. K. (ed.), *Scarcity and Growth Reconsidered*, Johns Hopkins University Press (for *Resources for the Future*), Baltimore.

Barnett, H. J. and C. Morse (1963), *Scarcity and Growth: The Economics of Natural Resource Availability*, Johns Hopkins University Press, Baltimore.

Baumol, W. J. and W. E. Oates (1975), *The Theory of Environmental Policy*, Prentice-Hall, Englewood Cliffs, New Jersey.

Benzoni, L. (1988) 'Sur la portée de la théorie hotellinienne des ressources épuisables', *Revue d'économie politique* **98(1)**, 159–73.

Bergstrom, T. C. (1982), 'On Capturing Oil Rents with a National Excise Tax', *American Economic Review* **72(1)**, 194–201.

Blackorby, C. and W. Schworm (1984), 'The Structure of Economics with Aggregate Measures of Capital: a Complete Characterization', *Review of Economic Studies* **51(4)**, 633–50.

Boskin, M. J., M. S. Robinson, T. O'Reilly and P. Kumar (1985), 'New Estimates of the Value of Federal Mineral Rights and Land', *American Economic Review* **75(5)**, 923–936.

Brander, J. A. and B. J. Spencer (1984), 'Trade Warfare: Tariffs and Cartels', *Journal of International Economics* **16(3/4)**, 227–242.

Buchanan, J. M. and G. Tullock (1975), 'Polluters' Profits and Political Response: Direct Controls versus Taxes', *American Economic Review* **65**, 139–147.

Burness, H. S. (1976), 'The Taxation of Non-renewable Natural Resources', *Journal of Environmental Economics and Management* **3**, 289–311.

Cairns, R. D. (1981), 'An Application of Depletion Theory to a Base Metal: Canadian Nickel', *Canadian Journal of Economics* **14(4)**, 635–648.

Cairns, R. D. (1986), 'A Model of Exhaustible Resource Exploitation with Ricardian Rent', *Journal of Environmental Economics and Management* **13**, 313–24.

Cairns, R. D. (1991), 'The Economics of Exploration for Non-Renewable Resources: an Interpretive Survey', *Journal of Economic Surveys*, forthcoming.

Cairns, R. D. (1990a), 'Geological Influences, Metal Prices and Rationality', *Resources and Energy*, **12**, 143–71.

Cairns, R. D. (1990b), 'A Contribution to the Theory of Depletable Resource Scarcity and its Measures', *Economic Enquiry*, **28(4)**, 744–55.

Cairns, R. D. and P. Lasserre (1986), 'Sectoral Supply of Minerals of Varying Grade', *Scandinavian Journal of Economics* **88(4)**, 605–626.

Campan, E. and A. Grimaud (1988), 'Le syndrome Hollandais', rapport technique no 8810, GREMAQ, Université de Toulouse I, France.

Campbell, H. F. (1980), 'The Effect of Capital Intensity on the Optimal Rate of Extraction of a Mineral Deposit' *Çanadian Journal of Economics* **13(2)**, 349–55.

Campbell, H.F. and R.K. Lindner (1983), 'On the Optimal Resource Rent Tax', *Economic Letters* **13**, 263–268.

Campbell, H. F. and R. K. Lindner (1985a), 'Mineral Exploration and the Neutrality of Real Royalties', *Economic Record* (March), 445–449.

Campbell, H.F. and R.K. Lindner (1985b), 'A Model of Mineral Exploration and Resource Taxation', *Economic Journal* **95(3)**, 146–160.

Chichilnisky, G. (1986), 'Prix du pétrole, prix industriels et production: une analyse macroéconomique d'équilibre général', in Gaudet, G. and P. Lasserre, eds.

Chichilnisky, G., G. Heal and D. McLeod (1986), 'Ressources naturelles, commerce et endettement', in Gaudet, G. and P. Lasserre, eds.

Conrad, R. F. and B. Hool (1980), *Taxation of Mineral Resources*, Lexington Books, Lexington.

Conrad, R. F. and B. Hool (1981), 'Resource Taxation with Heterogeneous Quality and Endogenous Reserves', *Journal of Public Economics* **16**, 17–33.

Corden, M. W. (1984), 'Booming Sector and Dutch Disease Economics: Survey and Consolidation', *Oxford Economic Papers* **36**, 359–380.

Crabbé, P. J. (1983), 'The Contribution of L. C. Gray to Economic Theory of Exhaustible Natural Resources and its Roots in the History of Economic Thought', *Journal of Environmental Economics and Management* **10**, 195–220.

Dasgupta, P. S. (1982), *The Control of Resources*, Basil Blackwell Publications Ltd., Oxford.

Dasgupta, P. S. and G. M. Heal (1974), 'The Optimal Depletion of Exhaustible Resources', *Review of Economic Studies*, Symposium on the Economics of Exhaustible Resources, 3–28.

Dasgupta, P.S. and G.M. Heal (1979), *Economic Theory and Exhaustible Resources*, James Nisbet and Co. Ltd., Digswell Place and Cambridge University Press.

Dasgupta, P.S. and J.E. Stiglitz (1981), 'Resource Depletion under Technological Uncertainty, *Econometrica* **49**, 85–104.

Dasgupta, P.S., G.M. Heal and J.E. Stiglitz (1980), 'The Taxation of Exhaustible Resources', in Hughes, G. A. and G. M. Heal, eds., *Public Policy and the Tax System*, George Allen and Unwin, London.

Dasgupta, P.S., R. Gilbert and J. Stiglitz (1983), 'Strategic Considerations in Invention and Innovation: The Case of Natural Resources', *Econometrica* **51(5)**, 1439–1448.

Dea, C., P. Lasserre and P. Ouellette (1988), 'Prix des ressources et règle d'Hotelling', 25th International Conference of the Applied Econometrics Association, Washington, D.C.

Decaluwé, B. and A. Martens (1988), 'Bibliographie relative aux modèles calculables d'équilibre général appliqués aux économies en développement', Cahier no 1188, Centre de recherche et développement en économique, Université de Montréal.

Deshmukh, S. D. and S. R. Pliska (1980), 'Optimal Consumption and Exploration of Non-renewable Resources under Uncertainty', *Econometrica* **48(1)**, 177–200.

Deshmukh, S. D. and S. R. Pliska (1983), 'Optimal Consumption of a Nonrenewable Resource with Stochastic Discoveries and a Random Environment', *Review of Economic Studies* **50(3)**, 543–554.

Devarajan, S. and A. C. Fisher (1982), 'Exploration and Scarcity', *Journal of Political Economy* **90(6)**, 1279–1290.

Dodds, D. and R. C. Bishop (1983), 'On the Role of Information in Mineral Exploration', *Land Economics* **59(4)**, 411–417.

Eswaran, M. and T. R. Lewis (1984a), 'Appropriability and the Extraction of a Common property Resource' *Economica* **51(204)**, 393–400.

Eswaran, M. and T. R. Lewis (1984b), 'Ultimate Recovery of an Exhaustible Resource Under Different Market Structures', *Journal of Environmental Economics and Management* 11(1), 55-69.

Eswaran, M., T. R. Lewis and T. Heaps (1983), 'On the Non-existence of Market Equilibria in Exhaustible Resource Markets with Decreasing Costs', *Journal of Political Economy* 91(1), 155-167.

Farrow, S. (1985), 'Testing the Efficiency of Extraction from a Stock Resource', *Journal of Political Economy* 93(3), 452-487.

Fisher, A. (1981), *Resources and Environmental Economics*, Cambridge University Press.

Forsyth, P. J. (1986), 'Booming Sectors and Structural Change in Australia and Britain: A Comparison', in Neary, J. P. and S. Van Wijnbergen, eds.

Gaffney, M. (1967), *Extractive Resources and Taxation*, University of Wisconsin Press, Madison.

Gamponia, V. and R. Mendelsohn (1985), 'The Taxation of Exhaustible Resources', *Quarterly Journal of Economics*, 165-181.

Garnaut, R. and A. C. Ross (1975), 'Uncertainty, Risk Aversion, and the Taxing of Natural Resources', *Economic Journal* 85, 272-287.

Garnaut, R. and A. C. Ross (1979), 'The Neutrality of the Resource Rent Tax', *Economic Record* 55(150), 193-201.

Gaudet, G. (1983), 'Investissement optimal et Coûts d'adjustement dans la théorie économique de la mine', *Revue canadienne d'économique* 16(1), 39-51.

Gaudet, G. and P. Howitt (1989), 'A Note on Uncertainty and Hotelling Rule', *Journal of Environmental Economics and Management*, 16(1), 80-86.

Gaudet, G. and A. M. Khadr (1991) 'The Evolution of Natural Resource Prices under Stochastic Investment Opportunities: An Intertemporal Asset-Pricing Approach', *International Economic Review*, forthcoming.

Gaudet, G. and P. Lasserre (1984), 'L'impôt sur le revenu des sociétés et le coût du capital pour l'entreprise minière', *Revue canadienne d'économique* 17(4), 778-787.

Gaudet, G. and P. Lasserre (1986), 'Capital Income Taxation, Depletion Allowances, and Non-renewable Resource Extraction', *Journal of Public Economics* 29, 241-253.

Gaudet, G. and P. Lasserre (1988), 'On Comparing Monopoly and Competition in Exhaustible Resource Exploitation', *Journal of Environmental Economics and Management* 15(4), 412-418.

Gelb, A. H. (1986), 'Adjustment to Windfall Gains: A Comparative Analysis of Oil-exporting Countries', in Neary, J. P. and S. Van Wijnbergen, eds.

Gilbert, R. J. (1979), 'Optimal Depletion of an Uncertain Stock' *Review of Economic Studies* 46, 45-57.

Gray, L. C. (1914), 'Rent Under the Assumption of Exhaustibility', *Quarterly Journal of Economics* 28, 466-489.

Hahn, F. H. (1966), 'Equilibrium Dynamics with Heterogeneous Capital Goods', *Quarterly Journal of Economics* 88, 65-94.

Hall, D. C. and J. V. Hall (1984), 'Concepts and Measures of Natural Resource Scarcity with a Summary of Recent Trends', *Journal of Environmental Economics and Management* 11, 363-379.

Halvorsen, R. and T. R. Smith (1984), 'On Measuring Natural Resource Scarcity', *Journal of Political Economy* 92(5), 954-964.

Halvorsen, R. and T. R. Smith (1987), 'A Test of the Theory of Exhaustible Resources', mimeo, University of Washington, Seattle.

Hanson, D. A. (1980), 'Increasing Extraction Costs and Resource Prices: Some Further Results', *The Bell Journal of Economics* 11(1), 335-342.

Harberger, A. C. (1955), 'Taxation of Mineral Industries', reprinted in Harberger, A. C. (1974), *Taxation and Welfare*, Little, Brown and Company, Boston.

Harberger, A. C. (1962), 'The Incidence of the Corporate Income Tax', *Journal of Political Economy* **70**, 215-240.

Hartwick, J. M. (1978), 'Exploitation of Many Deposit of an Exhaustible Resource', *Econometrica* **46(1)**, 201-217.

Hartwick, J. M. and N. Oleweiler (1986), *The Economics of Natural Resource Use*, Harper and Row Publishers, New York.

Hartwick, J. M. and P. Sadorsky (1990) 'Duopoly in Exhaustible Resource Exploration and Extraction', *Canadian Journal of Economics* **23(2)**, 276-93.

Heal, G. and M. Barrow (1980), 'Relationship Between Interest Rates and Metal Price Movements', *Review of Economic Studies* **47**, 161-181.

Heaps, T. (1985), 'The Taxation of Nonreplenishable Natural Resources Revisited', *Journal of Environmental Economics and Management* **12(1)**, 14-27.

Heaps, T. and J. F. Helliwell (1985), 'The Taxation of Natural Resources', in Auerbach, A. and M. Feldstein, eds., *Handbook of Public Economics*, North Holland, Amsterdam.

Helliwell, J. F. (1981), 'Using Canadian Oil and Gas Revenues in the 1980's: Provincial and Federal Perspectives' in T. Barber and V. Brailovsky, eds., *Oil or Industry?*, Academic Press, London.

Herfindahl, O. C. (1967), 'Depletion and Economic Theory', in Gaffney, M., ed.

Hertel, T. W. (1988), 'General Equilibrium Incidence of Natural Resource Subsidies: The Three Factor Case', *Journal of Environmental Economics and Management* **15(2)**, 206-223.

Hillman, A. L. and N. V. Long (1985), 'Monopolistic Recycling of Oil Revenue and Intertemporal Bias in Depletion and Trade', *Quarterly Journal of Economy* **99**, 598-624.

Hoel, M. (1978a), 'Resource Extraction, Substitute Production, and Resource Monopoly', *Journal of Economic Theory* **19(1)**, 28-37.

Hoel, M. (1978b), 'Resource Extraction and Recycling with Environmental Costs', *Journal of Environmental Economics and Management* **5**, 220-235.

Hoel, M. (1981), 'Resource Extraction by a Monopolist with Influence Over the Rate of Return on Non-resource Assets', *International Economic Review* **22(1)**, 147-157.

Hoel, M. (1983), 'Monopoly Resource Extractions Under the Presence of Predetermined Substitute Production', *Journal of Economic Theory* **30(1)**, 201-212.

Hoel, M. (1984), 'Extraction of a Resource with a Substitute for Some of its Uses', *Canadian Journal of Economics* **17(3)**, 593-602.

Hotelling, H. (1931), 'The Economics of Exhaustible Resources', *Journal of Political Economy* **39(2)**, 137-175.

Hung, N. M. (1986), 'On Simultaneous Extraction from Several Resource Deposits', Cahier no 8619, Départment d'économique, Université Laval.

Hung, N. M., M. C. Kemp, and N. V. Long (1984), 'On the Transition from an Exhaustible-resource Stock to an Inexhaustible Substitute', in Kemp, M. C. and N. V. Long, eds.

Hung, N. M. and N. V. Long (1982), 'Efficiency-inducing Taxation for a Monopolistically-supplied Depletable Resource: The Case of Stock-dependent Extraction Cost', in Kemp, M. C. and N. V. Long, eds.

Hyde, R. and J. R. Markusen (1982), 'Exploration Versus Extraction Costs as Determinants of Optimal Mineral Rights Leases', *Economic Record* **58(162)**, 224-234.

Jevons, W. S. (1865), *The Coal Question*, 3rd edition (1906), MacMillan and Co., London.

Johanson, P.O. (1987), *The Economic Theory and Measurement of Environment Benefits*, Cambridge University Press.

Jones, R.W. and P.R. Kenen (1984), *Handbook of International Economics*, Vol. I, Elsevier Science Publishers, Amsterdam.

Jorgenson, D.W. (1963), 'Capital Theory and Investment Behavior', *American Economic Review* **53**, 247-259.

Kemp, M.C. (1976), 'How to Eat a Cake of Unknown Size' in *Three Topics in the Theory of International Trade: Distribution, Welfare, and Uncertainty*, North Holland, Amsterdam.

Kemp, M.C. and N.V. Long (1980a), 'A Modest Defense of the Use of Cobb-Douglas Production Functions in the Analysis of Exhaustible Resources', in Kemp, M.C. and N.V. Long, eds.

Kemp, M.C. and N.V. Long, eds. (1980b), *Exhaustible Resources, Optimality and Trade*, North Holland Publishing Company, Amsterdam.

Kemp, M.C. and N.V. Long (1980c), 'On the Optimal Order of Exploitation of Deposits of an Exhaustible Resource', in Kemp and Long, eds.

Kemp, M.C. and Long, N.V. (1982b), 'Rybczynski's Theorem in a Context of Exhaustible Resources: The Case of Time-contingent Prices', *International Economic Review* **23(3)**, 699-710.

Kemp, M.C. and N.V. Long (1984a), 'Toward a More General Theory of the Order of Exploitation of Non-renewable Resource-deposits' in Kemp, M.C. and N.V. Long, eds.

Kemp, M.C. and N.V. Long (1984b), 'The Problem of Survival: An Open Economy' in Kemp, M.C. and N.V. Long, eds.

Kemp, M.C. and N.V. Long, eds. (1984c), *Essays in the Economics of Exhaustible Resources*, Elsevier Science Publishers, Amsterdam.

Kemp, M.C. and N.V. Long (1984d), 'The Role of Natural Resources in Trade Models', in Jones, R.W. and P.S. Kenen, eds., *Handbook of International Economics*, Vol. I, Elsevier Science Publishers, Amsterdam.

Kneese, A.V. (1984), 'Measuring the Benefits of Clean Air and Water', *Resources for the Future*, Washington.

Kolstad, C.D. and F.A. Wolak (1983), 'Competition in Interregional Taxation: The Case of Western Coal', *Journal of Political Economy* **91(3)**, 443-460.

Krautkraemer, J.A. (1987), 'The Cut-off Grade and the Theory of Extraction', *Canadian Journal of Economics* **2(1)**, 146-160.

Krautkraemer, J.A. (1989), 'Price Expectations, Ore Quality Selection, and the Supply of a Nonrenewable Resource', *Journal of Environmental Economics and Management* **16(3)**, 253-67.

Krautkraemer, J.A. (1988), 'Ore Quality Selection and the Supply Response to Nonrenewable Resource Taxation', *Mathematical and Computer Modelling* **11**, 894-898.

Kremers, J.J.M. (1986), 'The Dutch Disease in the Netherlands', in Neary, J.P. and S. Van Wijnbergen, eds.

Kumar, (1988), 'On Optimal Domestic Processing of Exhaustible Natural Resource Exports', *Journal of Environmental Economics and Management* **15(3)**, 341-54.

La Grandville, O. de (1980), 'Capital Theory, Optimal Growth, and Efficiency Conditions with Exhaustible Resources', *Econometrica* **48(7)**, 1763-1776.

Lasserre, P. (1984), 'Reserves and Land Prices with Exploration Under Uncertainty', *Journal of Environmental Economics and Management* **11**, 191-201.

Lasserre, P. (1985a), 'Discovery Costs as a Measure of Rent', *Canadian Journal of Economics* **18(3)**, 474-484.

Lasserre, P. (1985b), 'Exhaustible-Resource Extraction with Capital', in Scott A.D., ed., *Progress in Natural Resource Economics*, Oxford Economic Papers, Oxford.

Lasserre, P. (1989), 'Survival with a Ricardian Resource', mimeo, Université de Montréal.

Lasserre, P. and P. Ouellette (1991), 'The Measurement of Productivity and Scarcity Rents: the Case of Asbestos in Canada', *Journal of Econometrics*, forthcoming.

Lee, D.R. (1984), 'The Economics of Enforcing Pollution Taxation', *Journal of Environmental Economics and Management* **11(2)**, 147–160.

Leland, H. (1978), 'Optimal Risk Sharing and the Leasing of Natural Resources with Application to Oil and Gas on the OCS', *Quarterly Journal of Economics* **92**, 413–438.

Levhari D. and N. Liviatan (1977), 'Notes on Hotelling's Economics of Exhaustible Resources', *Canadian Journal of Economics* **10**, 177–192.

Lewis, T.R. (1979), 'The Exhaustion and Depletion of Natural Resources', *Econometrica* **47(6)**, 1569–1572.

Lewis, T.R. (1982), 'Sufficient Conditions for Extracting Least Cost Resources First', *Econometrica* **50(4)**, 1081–1083.

Lewis, T.R. and R. Schmallensee (1980), 'Oligopolistic Markets for Nonrenewable Natural Resources', *Quarterly Journal of Economics* **95**, 475–491.

Livernois, J.R. and R.S. Uhler (1987), 'Extraction Costs and the Economics of Nonrenewable Resources', *Journal of Political Economy* **95(1)**, 195–203.

Long, N.V. and H.W. Sinn (1984), 'Optimal Taxation and Economic Depreciation: A General Equilibrium Model with Capital and an Exhaustible Resource', in Kemp, M.C. and N.V. Long, eds.

Loury, G.C. (1978), 'The Optimal Exploitation of an Unknown Reserve' *Review of Economic Studies* **45**, 621–36.

Loury, G.C. (1986), 'A Theory of Oil'igoploy: Cournot Equilibrium in Exhaustible Resource Markets with Fixed Supplies', *International Economic Review* **27(2)**, 285–311.

Mackie-Mason (1987), 'Nonlinear Taxation of Risky Assets and Investment, with Application to Mining', Working Paper no 87-1, Department of Economics, University of Michigan, Ann Arbor, Michigan.

Mäler, K.-G. (1989), 'The Acid-Rain Game', mimeo, Dept. of Economics, University of Stockholm.

Malinvaud, E. (1977), *The Theory of Unemployment Reconsidered*, Oxford, Basil Blackwell.

Merrifield, J.D. (1988), 'The Impact of Selected Abatement Strategies on Transnational Pollution, the Terms of Trade, and Factor Rewards: a General Equilibrium Approach', *Journal of Environmental Economics and Management* **15(3)**, 259–284.

Miller, M.H. and C.W. Upton (1985), 'A Test of the Hotelling Valuation Principle', *Journal of Political Economy* **93(1)**, 1–25.

Mitra, T., M. Majumdar and D. Roy (1982), 'Feasible Alternatives Under Deteriorating Terms of Trade', *Journal of International Economics* **13**, 105–134.

Neary, J.P. and D.D. Purvis (1983), 'Real Adjustment and Exchange Rate Dynamics', in Frenkel, J., ed., *Exchange Rates and International Macroeconomics*, Chicago University Press, Chicago.

Neary, J.P. and S. Van Winjnbergen (1986a), *Natural Resources and the Macroeconomy: a Theoretical Framework*, in Neary J.P. and S. Van Winjnbergen, eds.

Neary, J.P. and S. Van Winjnbergen, eds. (1986b), *Natural Resources and the Macroeconomy*, MIT Press, Cambridge, Massachusetts.

Newberry, D.M.G. (1981), 'Oil Price Cartels and the Problem of Dynamic Inconsistency', *Economic Journal* **21**, 617–46.

Nordhaus, W.D. (1973), 'The allocation of Energy Resources', *Brookings Papers on Economics Activity* **3**, 529–576.

Philips, L. and R.M. Harstad (1988), 'Interaction between Resource Extraction and Future Markets: A Game-theoretic Analysis', 25th Conference of the Applied Econometrics Association, Washington, D.C.

Pindyck, R.S. (1978a), 'Gains to Producers from the Cartelization of Exhaustible Resources', *Review of Economics and Statistics* **60(2)**, 238-251.

Pindyck, R.S. (1978b), 'The Optimal Exploration and Production of Nonrenewable Resources', *Journal of Political Economy* **86(5)**, 841-861.

Pindyck, R.S. (1980), 'Uncertainty and Exhaustible Resource Markets', *Journal of Political Economy* **88(6)**, 1203-1225.

Pindyck, R.S. (1982), 'Jointly Produced Exhaustible Resources', *Journal of Environmental Economics and Management* **9(4)1**, 291-303.

Pindyck, R.S. (1987), 'On Monopoly Power in Extractive Resource Markets', *Journal of Environmental Economics and Management* **14(2)**, 128-142.

Plourde, C. and D. Yeoung (1989) 'A Model of Industrial Pollution in a Stochastic Environment' *Journal of Environmental Economics and Management* **16(2)**, 97-105.

Puu, T. (1977), 'On the Profitability of Exhausting Natural Resources', *Journal of Environmental Economics and Management* **14**, 185-199.

Quyen, N.V. (1988), 'The Optimal Depletion and Exploration of a Nonrenewable Resource', *Econometrica* **56(6)**, 1467-1471.

Quyen, N.V. (1989), 'Exhaustible Resources: A Theory of Exploration', Cahier 8905, Groupe de recherche en économie de l'énergie et des ressources naturelles, Université Laval, Québec.

Ramsey, J.B. (1980), *Bidding and Oil Leases*, JAI Press, Greenwich, Connecticut.

Raucher, M. (1987), 'Trade with Exhaustible Resource when Demand Reactions are Lagged', *European Economic Review* **31(8)**, 597-604.

Reinganum, J. and N. Stockey (1985), 'Oligopoly Extraction of a Nonrenewable Common Property Resource: The Importance of the Period of Commitment in Dynamic Games', *International Economic Review* **26(1)**, 161-73.

Ricardo, D. (1817), 'Principles of Political Economy and Taxation', in P. Sraffa and M.H. Dobbs, eds. (1951), *The Works of David Ricardo*, Cambridge University Press, Cambridge.

Robson, A.J. (1979), 'Sequential Exploitation of Uncertain Deposits of a Depletable Natural Resource', *Journal of Economic Theory* **21**, 88-110.

Salant, S. (1976), 'Exhaustible Resources and Industrial Structure: A Nash-Cournot Approach to the World Oil Market', *Journal of Political Economy* **84(5)**, 1079-1093.

Salant, S. (1979), 'Staving off the Backstop: Dynamic Limit-Pricing with a Kinked Demand Curve', in *Advances in the Economics of Energy and Resources*, Vol. 2, 187-204, JAI Press, Inc.

Salant, S. (1983), 'The Vulnerability of Price Stabilization Schemes to Speculative Attack', *Journal of Political Economy* **91(1)**, 1-38.

Salant, S., M. Eswaran, and T. Lewis (1983), 'The Length of Optimal Extraction Programs When Depletion Affects Extraction Costs', *Journal of Economic Theory* **31(2)**, 264-74.

Salant, S. and D.W. Henderson (1978), 'Market Anticipations of Government Policies and the Price of Gold' *Journal of Political Economy* **86(4)**, 627-48.

Schultze, W.D. (1974), 'The Optimal Use of Nonrenewable Resources: The Theory of Extraction', *Journal of Environmental Economics and Management* **1(1)**, 53-73.

Scott, A.D. (1976), 'Who Should Get Natural Resource Revenues', in Scott, A.D., ed., *Natural Resource Economics: A Test of Federalism*, University of British Columbia Press, Vancouver.

Simons, P. (1977), 'Optimum Taxation and Natural Resources', *Recherches Economiques de Louvain* **43(2)**.

Slade, M.E. (1982a), 'Cycles in Natural Resource Commodity Prices: An Analysis of the Frequency Domain', *Journal of Environmental Economics and Management* **9**, 138–148.

Slade, M.E. (1982b), 'Cycles in Natural-resource Commodity Prices: An Analysis of the Time Domain', *Journal of Environmental Economics Management* **9(2)**, 122–137.

Slade, M.E. (1984), 'Tax Policy and the Supply of Exhaustible Resources: Theory and Practice', *Land Economics* **60(2)**, 133–147.

Slade, M.E. (1988), 'Grade Selection under Uncertainty: Least Cost Last and Other Anomalies', *Journal of Environmental Economics and Management* **15(2)**, 189–205.

Smith, V.K. (1979), 'Natural Resource Scarcity: A Statistical Analysis', *Review of Economics and Statistics* **61(3)**, 423–427.

Smith, V.K. (1979), *Scarcity and Growth Reconsidered*, Johns Hopkins University Press (for *Resources for the Future*), Baltimore.

Solow, R.M. (1974a), 'The Economics of Resources and the Resources of Economics', *American Economic Review*, Papers and Proceedings.

Solow, R.M. (1974b), 'Intergenerational Equity and Exhaustible Resources', *Review of Economic Studies*, Symposium.

Solow, R.M. (1977), 'Monopoly, Uncertainty, and Exploration' in A. Blinder and P. Friedman, eds., *Natural Resources, Uncertainty, and General Equilibrium Systems*, New York.

Solow, R.M. and F.Y. Wan (1977), 'Extraction Costs in the Theory of Exhaustible Resources', *Bell Journal of Economics* **7(2)**, 359–370.

Stiglitz, J.E. (1974a), 'Growth with Exhaustible Natural Resources: The Competitive Economy', *Review of Economic Studies*, Symposium, 123–138.

Stiglitz, J.E. (1974b), 'Growth with Exhaustible Resources: Efficient and Optimal Growth Paths', *Review of Economic Studies*, Symposium, 139–152.

Stiglitz, J.E. (1976), 'Monopoly and the Rate of Extraction of Exhaustible Resources', *American Economic Review* **66(4)**, 655–661.

Stiglitz, J.E. and P. Dasgupta (1982), 'Market Structure and Resource Depletion: A Contribution to the Theory of Intertemporal Monopolistic Competition', *Journal of Economic Theory* **28(1)**, 128–164.

Stollery, K.R. (1983), 'Mineral Depletion with Cost as the Extraction Limit: A Model Applied to the Behavior of Prices in the Nickel Industry', *Journal of Environmental Economics and Management* **10(2)**, 151–165.

Swierzbinski, J.E. and R. Mendelsohn (1989) 'Information and Exhaustible Resources: A Bayesian Analysis' *Journal of Environmental Economics Management* **16(3)**, 193–208.

*The Economist* (1977), 'The Dutch Disease', nov. 26–dec. 2, 82–83.

*The Economist* (1988), 'Asia's Migrant Workers', sept. 10–16, 21–24.

Tietenberg, T.H. (1985), 'Emissions Trading: An Exercise in Reforming Pollution Policy', *Resources for the Future*, Washington.

Ulph, A.M. (1982), 'Modelling Partially Cartelized Markets for Exhaustible Resources', in Eichhorn, H., R. Henn, U. Newmann and R.W. Shephard, eds., *Economic Theory of Natural Resources*, Physica-Verlag, Würburg-Wien, 269–291.

Ulph A.M. and G.M. Folie (1980), 'Exhaustible Resources and Cartels: an Intertemporal Nash-Cournot Model', *Canadian Journal of Economics* **13(4)**, 645–658.

Virmani, A. (1986), 'Efficiency of Practical Resource Rent Tax System: Threshold Rates and Income Taxes', Report no DRD164, World Bank, Washington, D.C.

Warr, P.G. (1986), 'Indonesia's Other Dutch Disease: Economic Effects of the Petroleum Boom', in Neary, J.P. and S. Van Wijnbergen, eds.

Wijnbergen, S.V. (1984), 'The Dutch Disease: A Disease After All?', *The Economic Journal* **24**, 41–55.

Withagen, C. (1985), *Economic Theory and International Trade in Natural Exhaustible Resources*, Springer-Verlag, Berlin.

# Index

For Product Safety Concerns and Information please contact our EU
representative GPSR@taylorandfrancis.com Taylor & Francis Verlag GmbH,
Kaufingerstraße 24, 80331 München, Germany

Printed and bound by CPI Group (UK) Ltd, Croydon, CR0 4YY
08/05/2025
01864391-0002